Cognitive Development

Cognitive Development

Thomas Floyd Gross
University of Redlands

 Brooks/Cole Publishing Company
Monterey, California

With great appreciation for their contribution to my life, I dedicate this book to my parents, Robert C. Gross and Emelyn M. Gross.

Brooks/Cole Publishing Company
A Division of Wadsworth, Inc.

Printed in the United States of America

10 9 8 7 6 5 4 3 2 1

Library of Congress Cataloging in Publication Data

Gross, Thomas Floyd, [date]
  Cognitive development.

  Bibliography: p.
  Includes index.
  1. Cognition in children.   I. Title.
BF723.C5G75   1984   155.4'13   84-14982
ISBN 0-534-03363-6

Sponsoring Editor: *C. Deborah Laughton*
Production Editor: *Carol Rost*
Manuscript Editor: *Jonas Weisel*
Permissions Editor: *Carline Haga*
Interior and Cover Design: *Vernon T. Boes*
Cover Photo: *Bonnie Hawthorne*
Art Coordinator: *Judith L. Macdonald*
Interior Illustration: *John Foster*
Photo Researcher and Editor: *Judy Blamer*
Typesetting: *Graphic Typesetting Service, Los Angeles, California*
Cover Printing, Printing, and Binding: *Malloy Lithographing, Inc., Ann Arbor, Michigan*

Credits

Page 24, Figure 2.2, Table 2.1, and Table 9.1, adapted from "Information-Processing Models of Intellectual Development," by D. Klahr. In R. H. Kluwe and H. Spada (Eds.), *Developmental Models of Thinking*. Copyright 1980 by Academic Press, Inc. Reprinted by permission.

Page 40, Table 3.1, adapted from *Piaget's Theory of Intellectual Development: An Introduction*, by H. Ginsburg and S. Opper. Copyright © 1969 by Prentice-Hall, Inc. Reprinted by permission.

Page 42, Table 3.2, adapted from "Structures and Strictures: Some Functional Limitations on the Course of Cognitive Growth," by R. Case. In *Cognitive Psychology*, 1974, *6*, 544–573. Copyright 1974 by Academic Press, Inc. Reprinted by permission.

Page 53, Figure 4.3, from "A Facial Dimension in Visual Discrimination by Human Infants," by R. A. Haaf and R. Q. Bell. In *Child Psychology*, 1967, *38*, 893–899. Copyright 1967 by the Society for Research in Child Development, Inc. Reprinted by permission.

Page 56, Figure 4.4, adapted from "A Comparative and Analytical Study of Visual Depth Perception," by R. D. Walk and E. J. Gibson. In *Psychological Monographs*, 1961, *75*, No. 15. Copyright 1961 by the American Psychological Association. Reprinted by permission.

Page 58, Figure 4.5, from "Visual Shape Perception in Early Infancy," by M. Schwartz and R. H. Day. In *Monographs of the Society for Research in Child Development*, 1979, *44*, Serial No. 182. Copyright 1979 by the Society for Research in Child Development, Inc. Reprinted by permission.

Page 63, Figure 4.6, from "A Developmental Study of the Discrimination of Letter-Like Forms," by E. J. Gibson, J. J. Gibson, A. D. Pick, and H. A. Osser. In *Journal of Comparative and Physiological Psychology*, 1962, *55*, 897–906. Copyright 1962 by the American Psychological Association. Reprinted by permission.

Page 63, Figure 4.7, from "Effects of Distinctive Features on Recognition of Incomplete Pictures," by F. S. Murray and J. M. Szynczyk. In *Developmental Psychology*, 1978, *114*, 356–362. Copyright 1978 by the American Psychological Association. Reprinted by permission.

Page 77, Figures 5.1 and 5.2, from *Development of the Concept of Space in the Child*, by M. Laurendeau and A. Pinard. Copyright 1970 by International Universities Press, Inc. Reprinted by permission.

Page 94, Figure 6.3, from "Developmental Differences in Intake and Storage of Visual Information," by K. Sheingold. In *Journal of Experimental Child Psychology*, 1973, *16*, 1–11. Copyright 1973 by Academic Press, Inc. Reprinted by permission.

Page 96, Figure 6.4, from "A Developmental Comparison of the Processing of Two Types of Visual Information," by D. L. Finkel. In *Journal of Experimental Child Psychology*, 1973, *16*, 250–266. Copyright 1973 by Academic Press, Inc. Reprinted by permission.

Page 108, Figure 6.5, from "Retrieval Time from Semantic Memory," by A. M. Collins and M. R. Quillian. In *Journal of Verbal Learning and Verbal Behavior*, 1969, *8*, 240–247. Copyright 1969 by Academic Press, Inc. Reprinted by permission.

Page 108, Table 6.2, from "Semantic Retrieval in Children and Adults," by K. Nelson and S. M. Kosslyn. In *Developmental Psychology*, 1975, *11*, 807–813. Copyright 1975 by the American Psychological Association. Reprinted by permission.

Page 118, Figure 7.2, from "Encoding and Incidental Memory in Children," by M. F. Geis and D. M. Hall. In *Journal of Experimental Child Psychology*, 1976, *22*, 58–66. Copyright 1976 by Academic Press, Inc. Reprinted by permission.

Page 122, Figure 7.4, from "Thematic Elaboration and Proximity in Children's Recall, Organization, and Long-Term Retention of Pictorial Materials," by A. A. Baumeister and S. Smith. In *Journal of Experimental Child Psychology*, 1979, *28*, 132–148. Copyright 1979 by Academic Press, Inc. Reprinted by permission.

Page 123, Table 7.1, from "Interaction Between Encoding and Retrieval Operations in Cued Recall," by R. P. Fisher and F. I. M. Craik. In *Journal of Experimental Psychology: Human Learning and Memory*, 1977, *3*, 701–711. Copyright 1977 by the American Psychological Association. Reprinted by permission.

Chapter Opening Photographs

Preface

This book is concerned with what we currently know about children's knowledge and the controversy surrounding the intellectual basis of knowledge. There are a variety of opinions about what children know, why they act as they do, and how aware they are of their own and others' knowledge states. This variety of opinion and a proliferation of ideas and interests within the field of cognitive development can be a bit disconcerting to students becoming acquainted with the field. I trust this text will begin to allay some of that confusion.

In spite of a relatively short history, there is much public and scientific interest in cognitive development. Consequently, much research has been conducted and information gathered on the cognitive skills of infants and children. This book provides a summary of this research and a framework for organizing this vast body of information. In addition to summarizing and organizing what we currently know about children's cognitive development, this book also exposes students to differing views about what we believe our observations of children's behavior mean. This book will prompt readers to challenge popular notions about what children know, to become sensitive to the limitations of our methods for studying children, and to be critical of our theoretical accounts of development. Used in this fashion, this book will serve as a springboard to more advanced studies in the area of cognitive development.

For Whom Is this Text Written?

For most things of an academic nature, even introductory works such as this, we presume some background or prerequisite knowledge. Accordingly, this book is written for the upper division undergraduate or beginning graduate student of psychology, child development, or education. Students using this book should have taken an introductory course in psychology, and it would be helpful if they have also completed a course in child development. Because student backgrounds are so diverse, I've written Chapters 2 and 3 as introductions to the two major theories that organize material throughout the book (i.e., Piagetian and information-processing theories). These chapters should reacquaint the knowledgeable reader, or provide the new student, with basic concepts and terminology requisite for understanding material presented in later chapters.

The Basic Structure of the Text

I've organized the material in this book by contrasting two contemporary theories of cognitive development: Piagetian and information-processing theory. Piagetian theory stems from the work of the Genevan psychologist Jean Piaget and his colleagues. Information-processing theory is a conglomeration of ideas stemming largely from American psychology laboratories. Whereas both theories attempt to identify major components of the intellect and the manner in which information is acquired, remembered, and used, they differ markedly in what they believe children know, how the intellect should be characterized, and what are believed to be the important mechanisms responsible for the development of the intellect. This text examines, within this framework, the major cognitive processes (perception, memory, and problem solving) and issues in cognitive development (e.g., "What is the relationship between language and cognitive processes?" and "How can we use what we know about cognitive development?"). I decided to organize the text on the basis of theory because theories help us to clarify our thinking, to formulate interesting questions, and to specify important issues within our discipline.

Some limitations of this organization are that not all research fits easily into either of these two series (especially some research discussed in this text under the information-processing category) and that other viable explanations of cognitive development are possible. However, information processing and Piagetian theory are currently the most visible theories and the ones that generate the majority of research on cognitive development.

The Scope of the Text

This text covers the major dimensions of cognitive research. Chapter 1 defines cognition and presents an historical examination of the roots of cognitive psychology, both in America and Europe. Chapters 2 and 3 are basic introductions to information-processing and Piagetian theory. (Also included in Chapter 3 is an introduction to neo-Piagetian theory.)

Chapters 4 and 5 address major research in this area, focusing upon perceptual development during infancy. Chapters 6, 7, and 8 address issues in memory development. Because of current interest in information-processing models of memory, two models are considered: the multistore model (Chapter 6) and the levels-of-processing model (Chapter 7). Piaget's model of memory function is presented in Chapter 8.

Both information-processing and Piagetian approaches to problem solving are considered respectively in Chapters 9 and 10. Chapter 9 considers two contemporary ways that information-processing theorists conduct problem-solving research with children, the analysis and the synthesis approaches. The analysis approach attempts to discern components of the intellectual system and to examine how these components interact to produce performance. Another approach, the synthesis approach, attempts to generate rule systems that define performance on specific problems. Chapter 10 examines Piaget's belief that there are stage-related changes in children's knowledge states that produce changes in the way that children understand and attempt to solve problems.

Chapter 11 considers research from a relatively new area of interest in cognitive development, metacognition. Whereas early chapters (Chapters 4–10) consider what children are able to do, Chapter 11 addresses the question "When do children become aware of their own and other's cognitive states and the situational factors that influence cognitive ability?" Metacognitive knowledge about perception, memory, and problem solving are considered.

Next, in Chapter 12, follow language and cognition. Due to the vast amount of research in this area, I've only described the ways that psychologists and psycholinguists view the relationship between language and cognition. Two extreme positions are initially considered, i.e., "Is language a prerequisite of thought?" or "Is language only a manifestation of some basic intellectual system?" In addition to these positions, a third, intermediate position is considered: that language has a regulatory role incognitive activity and serves as an executive system to help the user organize appropriate behavior and solve problems.

The final chapter (Chapter 13) addresses the question of how knowledge of cognitive development might be applied to the practical problems confronting humankind. Specifically, three special uses of this knowledge are considered in its application to psychometry, education, and therapy. In all chapters, the skills and abilities of younger children are contrasted with those of older children and adults, to give the reader a developmental perspective.

Towards the goal of encouraging students to adopt a critical attitude toward research, I've peppered the chapters with discussions of the methodology used by both information-processing and Piagetian theorists. I've also included a critique section at the end of each chapter. This raises criticisms with respect to basic theory as well as the methodology peculiar to a particular line of research. It is my hope that after reading this text, students will gain an understanding of what we currently know about cognitive development and how we have attempted to explain it. I also hope that students will view this knowledge as a developing one rather than a final statement of facts.

Text Approach

I have written with the intention of emphasizing the empirical basis of our understanding of children's knowledge. It is my conviction that to present information in a matter-of-fact manner fails to stress an important tenet of science: that all "truths" are tentative. What constitutes our current understanding of cognitive development is based upon conclusions drawn by scientists who formulate questions and devise methodologies by which their questions can be answered. It is by understanding the truly humanistic nature of the process of science that we develop a sensitivity to the limitations of knowledge.

Acknowledgments

I am especially grateful to the following people who reviewed the book: Dr. Steve Ceci, Cornell University; Dorothea Halpert, City University, New York; Dr. Elaine Justice, Old Dominion University; Dr. Timothy Murphy, University of Pittsburgh; Dr. Marion Perlmutter, University of Minnesota; Dr. Frederick Schwantes, Northern Illinois University; and Dr. Michael Wapner, California State University, Los Angeles.

Thomas F. Gross

Contents

4 AN INFORMATION-PROCESSING ACCOUNT OF PERCEPTUAL DEVELOPMENT 45

5 A PIAGETIAN VIEW OF PERCEPTION 71

6 A MULTISTORE MODEL OF MEMORY   89

7 A LEVELS-OF-PROCESSING MODEL OF MEMORY   115

8 A PIAGETIAN MODEL OF MEMORY   129

9 AN INFORMATION-PROCESSING APPROACH TO PROBLEM SOLVING   145

13 APPLICATIONS 227

1

An Introduction to and History of Cognitive Psychology

Occasionally we're all prone to reminisce about the past. Doing so, we commonly find ourselves struggling to recall people, places, and events, and these lapses tend to be more likely as we push deeper into our memories. You may wish to test your own memory by trying to remember the name of your second-grade teacher, the names of ten of your second-grade classmates, and how you spent a typical day while in the second grade.

If you are like most, you probably can't recall much about your childhood. I know that I must have called my teacher by name many times, but with only a fair degree of confidence can I say that I think her name was Mrs. Kamm. Whereas I had closer personal relationships with my classmates, I confess that

I can remember but four of their names (there were probably 30 other students in that class). I would also guess that I attended about 180 classes that year, but I have little recollection of how I spent that time.

Although each of us experienced childhood, our recollections of those early years are quite poor. The memories are often fictions we have created for ourselves or stories others have told us about those times (Loftus & Loftus, 1980). Furthermore, the few memories we do have are often concrete and static images; we remember even less about how we behaved and what we thought, or what we believed and felt. Curiously, then, much of what we intuitively "know" to be true of children and childhood is based on beliefs that we as adults have either created or adopted.

Despite our ignorance about our own childhood, we readily acknowledge that children don't know as much about the world as we. With a little observation of children's behavior, we also realize that they don't think as we do either. We could cite many examples of the qualitative differences between the thought of children and adults. For instance, the other day the neighbor girl (about 4 years of age) was standing on the sidewalk looking into the street. As she stood there by herself, she repeated aloud, "Don't play in the street. If you play in the street you'll get spanked." As adults we give little thought to controlling impulses. We have little need for a conscious, self-regulatory system of the kind this young child uses. However, for this child and others her age, overt self-instruction may be useful for bridling impulsivity.

Yet another example of the qualitative difference between the thought of children and adults was recently related to me by a friend. This friend had received a telephone call from a 4-year-old named Kristen. Kristen had been given a colorful shirt as a birthday present and wanted to show it to my friend. To do this, she held the telephone receiver to her shirt so my friend could "see" what it looked like. Kristen's amused father asked his daughter if she could also see what my friend was wearing. Kristen thought for a moment and then looked into the receiver. "I don't know," she said, "but it must be black."

The child who reasons in this manner, though endearing in her naiveté, demonstrates something very remarkable about her understanding of the world and the way it operates. It is an understanding that is not entirely explained by a lack of information about things, but rather reflects a special way of perceiving, thinking about, and operating upon the world.

Within the past 20 years, child development specialists have become particularly interested in examining the qualitative changes that occur in children's thinking. This interest in cognitive development reflects the belief that development is more than a quantitative growth of knowledge. When children communicate ideas, attempt to discover information, or solve problems, we believe they also reveal something about their intellectual structure. This text presents two opinions about what this intellectual structure is like, how it operates, and how it changes with age. These views will be referred to as the *information-processing* and *Piagetian* positions.

COGNITION DEFINED

As the discerning reader has probably concluded, *cognition* refers to knowledge and thought. More specifically, it refers to processes associated with the acquisition, organization, retention, and use of knowledge. In keeping with this definition, we'll examine the development of cognitive skills associated with perception, memory, and conceptual processes (that is, things that we do with information—problem solving, concept discovery, rule use, and so on). In addition to considering how children perform in each of these areas, we will also consider issues related to children's awareness of variables affecting cognition (their own and others), an area of study known as *metacognition.*

COGNITIVE PSYCHOLOGY: A BRIEF HISTORY

The content of experimental psychology over the past century has shown a remarkable consistency. For instance, there has been a persistent interest in the study of perception, memory, learning, and thinking. Despite the uniformity that has characterized the subject matter of experimental psychology, fluctuations have occurred in the scope of this inquiry. These changes reflect general attitudes about the nature of the mind, human nature, and the place of humans in nature (Mueller, 1979). Such changes have ultimately affected how research is conducted and what issues are deemed appropriate to the domain of scientific inquiry.

Within the brief history of psychology, two paradigms have organized our attempts to understand behavior. One of these is the Lockean model (after the philosophy of John Locke—1632 to 1704) and the other is the Kantian model (after the philosophy of Immanuel Kant—1724 to 1804).

Lockean and Kantian Views of Humankind

Within the Lockean view of man, it is believed that the contents of the mind originate outside the body. Locke proposed that the mind is devoid of content at birth, being like a tabula rasa (blank slate). Simple ideas are essentially mirrorlike images of elements in the external world. Higher-order forms of reasoning occur as simple ideas are manipulated and recombined via some set of quasi-mathematical principles.

In contrast to the Lockean position is the model of thought proposed by Kant. In this philosophy it is argued that all experience is interpreted by the organism. Through innate capacities, experiences are given meaning. Both sensations and other mental activity are believed to be organized by innate organizational schemes and categories.

Truly creative and novel thought is impossible within the Lockean view of mental life, because all thought originates in past experience. What appear to be creative or new ideas can be explained away as the mere recombination of previously acquired simple ideas. Kant, however, argued that new and original thought is possible through the transcendental dialectical quality of the mind. A completely novel or unexpected idea could be conceived by imagining its inverse. By knowing gravity, for example, one might also be able to conceive of its opposite—the absence of gravity—although few have or ever will experience such.

In summary, a number of differences separate these two models. The Lockean view directs attention to the external world as the source of all ideas, whereas the Kantian view emphasizes the importance of the internal realm of human existence and places importance on innate organizational schemes and capacities. The two views also differ with respect to how understanding evolves. The Lockean view is basically a "bottom-to-top" approach. That is, higher forms of reasoning and understanding occur as simple ideas are combined. This approach to understanding the nature of knowledge is primarily reductionist—that is, if one is to appreciate what knowledge and thought are, one must first discover the basic elements or units of knowledge and thought. On the other hand, the Kantian view is better characterized as a "top-to-bottom" view. That is, through the application of some generalized scheme or pattern, we can understand or interpret experience. The whole rather than the parts gives meaning to experience. The Lockean view advances a mechanistic accounting of mental activity. People are reactive. If all understanding is a consequence of past experience, then we are in a sense victims of our experience; our behavior and thoughts are predetermined by our pasts. The concept of selfhood or free will cannot apply since there is no uniquely individual contribution to behavior. On the other hand, the Kantian view recognizes the individual's contribution to development. Man is endowed at birth to give some meaning and order to experience.

Lockean and Kantian Themes in American Psychology

These two philosophies have been important in the development of the science of psychology, emphasizing as they do two radically different ways of conceptualizing the nature and origin of thought. At least within the early half of the century, the Lockean model of man and mind predominated in scientific inquiry in Europe and America (Rychlak, 1979). For a variety of reasons much of American psychology became identified with this view. Only recently has its hold on American psychology been loosened and alternative models accepted as scientifically credible.

The mechanistic model.   Great pressure was put on the new discipline of psychology to adopt the Lockean perspective, and much of this influence came from the natural and physical sciences. With the discoveries and advances toward the end of the 1800s in chemistry, physics, and biology, the temptation to imitate the sciences preceding psychology must have been great. An inspection of the content and method advocated by these sciences also reveals their strong Lockean inclination. What are usually referred to as the hard sciences examined external, physical world phenomena. They were primarily concerned with questions that pertain to structure (that is, what are the elements of which things consist?) and efficient cause (that is, what are the physical forces at work within the universe or the organism that make other things happen?). In their attempt to answer these questions, scientists advocated a methodology that became synonymous with science itself. It was a method of systematic observation of concrete and measurable phenomena. Anything that was not observable and measurable could not be studied scientifically.

In medicine the Lockean influence could be found in the guise of the medical model. The model held that disease entities or biochemical imbalances cause illness. The attribution of thought and behavioral disorders to purely psychological causes was considered backward and was viewed as a return to the magical explanations that characterized reasoning in the Middle Ages. They were explanations that poorly suited science.

The medical model also encouraged the identification of the causes of pathology. In this pursuit causal agents were believed to be physical entities invading the body (viruses and bacteria) or physical trauma that occurred to the body. In any case the source of illness was localized in the external or physical world. Whereas the medical model prompted great advances in medical science, it also fostered the belief that the roots of psychological illness, and by extension mental activity, could be explained by forces external to people.

It should be noted that the socioeconomic climate at the turn of the century was also ripe for a Lockean interpretation of the human condition. A review of popular literature at this time suggests a society preoccupied with machinery (Brosseau & Andrist, 1970). Awesome mechanical devices were rapidly replacing the common laborer in fields and factories. As this technology grew, the parallel between man and machine was easily drawn—much as people of our age have been quick to draw comparisons between human intellect and the computer. The machines with their orderly structure and their perfunctory methodical operation, transforming substance and energy into product, provided the most Lockean of metaphors for humans.

These impressions likely influenced the early psychologists as they set out to answer questions about the mind. Like the questions asked by their counterparts in medicine and science, psychologists asked what the mind consisted of and how it operated. The machine metaphor was likely a reassurance to them; it fostered a belief that with persistence, they too might understand the workings of the mind, as a good mechanic understands the particulars of a machine.

Since machines are powered by energy forces, early psychologists reasoned that other physical and mental systems must have forces or energies that propel or motivate them. They believed that the forces responsible for behavior had two possible origins. One was within the individual in the form of a "will," and the other was external in the form of stimuli, which impinged upon the organism, pushing or pulling it in some particular direction. Under the influence of the Lockean model, at least in America, the forces responsible for behavior were ultimately localized in the external world.

Perhaps the most crucial factor in the Lockeanization of American psychology was the rejection of a methodology rather than a thoughtful commitment to any particular view of humankind (Rychlak, 1979). One of the most widely used methods for studying the mind or consciousness during the late 1800s was introspection. Early psychologists attempted to make it a rigorous scientific method. The procedure involved a trained observer (someone with over 10,000 introspections was considered to be reliable) who described in detail his or her sensations following some brief experience (for example, a 1.5-sec experiment may have required 20 minutes of introspective description) (Lieberman, 1979).

Introspection, however, had powerful opponents, and under critical examination, the method met its demise—and consequently a suspension of the study of mental activity itself. With the popularization of Freud's theory of psychosexuality, the idea was broached that at least some mental activity was below the individual's threshold of consciousness. Even among those who relied upon introspection as a method for studying mental activity, there was dissension about the availability of the phenomena being studied. One school of psychology, referred to as the Wurzburg School of Imageless Thought, proposed that in some cases thought occurs spontaneously, without any conscious activity that could be recounted. Introspection, depending as it did upon the assumption that all mental activity is open to individual examination, was severely undermined by the ideas advanced by Freud and by the Wurzburgers.

The *coup de grace* for introspection occurred as extraspective methodology became the method of choice of the natural and physical sciences. Closed as it was to public scrutiny, introspection was prone to subjective interpretations by its practitioners. Since thought could not be externalized, and thereby observed, it was dropped from that list of things that scientists could study. If thought could not be studied scientifically, then one might appropriately ask, what was left for the psychologist to study? The answer, which seemed obvious enough to some psychologists, was behavior.

The strongest advocate of this view was John B. Watson. Watson (1924) argued that because of the method that scientists were compelled to use, the scientific study of humans requires the study of behavior alone. In the interest of parsimony, it was subsequently proposed that no more of a theory of behavior (now equated with psychology) was required than one that predicts and consequently allows for the management of behavior. If we could understand behavior by examining the relationships that hold between antecedent and consequent events, then we need not postulate entities such as "minds" and "wills." (Psychologists didn't deny the presence of some form of mental life, but they believed discussions of consciousness offered nonsignificant insights to understanding human behavior.) Thus for a time, the internal processes associated with mental activity were conveniently dismissed on primarily methodological rather than theoretical grounds. The Lockean model, steeped as it was in a primarily extraspective, mechanistic, and deterministic view of man, became firmly implanted in the first half-century of American psychology.

The presence of this model is found in virtually all American experimental psychology of the time. The theories of Tolman, Hull, Spence, and Skinner, to name but a few, reflected concerns for the relationships that hold between stimuli and responses, and the role and nature of reinforcement (Greeno, 1980). Although some psychological theories of thinking were explicitly structured to explain mediating mechanisms (that is, systems that intervene between the presentation of a stimulus and the emission of a response), which accounted for more complex forms of reasoning, it was clear that these mechanisms also had their origin in experience (cf. Maltzman, 1955).

In other areas of early psychological research, we find little interest in speculation about mental processes. Until the 1950s, verbal learning research focused on largely nontheoretical questions, such as what factors strengthen or weaken associations between words or facilitate or inhibit the retention of information in memory (Postman & Keppel, 1969). During the 1950s, though, a number of research articles began to describe the special characteristics of information retention under short-term memory conditions. Miller (1956) reported on capacity limitations following short retention intervals. Others observed that information could be retained without rehearsal for only brief periods of time (Peterson & Peterson, 1959), that information is organized as it is acquired (Bousfield, 1953), and that information is recoded or stored in modalities other than those in which an experience occurs (Glanzer & Clark, 1963). Although these data weren't organized into any comprehensive theory of memory until the late 1960s (Atkinson & Shiffrin, 1968; Waugh & Norman, 1965), a subtle shift had occurred in the nature of psychology. Scientists were actually studying the characteristics of some internal mental structure. Furthermore, they were studying the processes involved in mental activity with little appeal to the stimulus-response explanations peculiar to learning theory.

Early developmental research. A history similar to that of the experimental learning research was also to be found, with a few exceptions, in developmental research. With the publication of Darwin's work on species evolution in 1856, the scientific and intellectual community began to consider developmental processes seriously. In both Europe and America, a number of scholars began to theorize not only about species development but about individual development as well. These developmental theories advanced the idea that some, if not a major portion of, development is predetermined by some genetic blueprint. Both G. Stanley Hall and James Baldwin proposed developmental theories advancing just such notions. Hall (1912) proposed that the stages of species evolution are relived during individual development. He argued the need for special types of instruction coinciding with each stage of development. Adolescence, for example, was seen as a period of heightened creativity and idealism—a perfect time for moral and aesthetic training.

Baldwin (1930) also believed that genetic heritage influences the course of development, but, unlike Hall, he emphasized the adaptive nature of the individual. Baldwin believed that we aren't necessarily held hostage by our biology. Rather, he believed that character is modified through the interaction of self and society. Through this reciprocal interaction, both the individual and society develop.

Like the other methods and theories of early psychology, neither Hall's nor Baldwin's ideas attracted substantial attention. Because of a lack of a rigorous methodology and the changing interests of these two men, their views on development were superseded by ideas coming from the more systematic research programs in child-study laboratories that explored behavioral phenomena. In these laboratories, questions were asked about such matters as when children are responsive to specific kinds of learning (as, for example, when children can be conditioned operantly or respondently) or what properties of stimuli facilitate the generalization of responses from one situation to another.

As was typical of explanations of adult learning, stimulus-response (S-R) learning models were proposed to account for developmental changes in learning and thinking. Both Spiker (1971) and the Kendlers (1970), for example, offered revised S-R theories of children's discrimination learning. Children, it was found, don't learn in the same way as adults. In both revisions, mediators had to be introduced to account for the differences between learning in children and adults; adults used mediators spontaneously—young children didn't. In time the mediator itself became the focus of developmental research (White, 1965).

The shift toward cognition.   It is ironic that from early research, so heavily endowed with Lockean ideas, a more Kantian position developed. There emerged within psychology a growing interest in understanding how responses are generated (as compared to studying the response *per se*). The shift was subtle but important, for it marked a transition from the study of events external to humans to those within. Above all, this research had the *de facto* blessing of the scientific community. The door had been opened, slight as it was, for the study of cognition.

In response to interest in the process by which individuals use or interpret information (and indeed the postulation of mediators implied that information is being interpreted), psychologists began to speak of learning less as an incremental acquisition of habit strength (that is, the increased probability of making a response as a function of reinforcement—the language of behaviorism) and began to speak more freely of hypotheses, rules, and strategies (the language of cognition). Researchers proposed that, as adults solve problems, they entertain and test hypotheses, or guesses about the solution to problems (Bruner, Goodnow, & Austin, 1956; Levine, 1966; Restle, 1962) and use logical, decision-making rules (Bower & Trabasso, 1963; Laughlin, 1966; Levine, 1966; Restle, 1962).

Other psychologists eagerly reconsidered the nature of human reasoning in light of advances in computer technology. Newell, Shaw, and Simon (1958) published a thesis on human problem-solving, patterning their discussion after the flow of information and decision-making that accompanies the activities specified by sophisticated computer programs. Influenced by this work, Miller, Galanter, and Pribram (1960) proposed that human behavior is characterized by plans, strategies, and tactics (hierarchically and sequentially arranged to guide the individual toward some goal).

Developmental assessment of cognitive ability was also conducted. Children were found to perform differently than adults (Bruner et al., 1956; Mosher & Hornsby, 1966), but, barring simple descriptions of these differences, little explanation was offered for why these developmental differences occur.

Related to the reorientation of psychology toward a study of cognition, other areas of developmental research were moving toward more Kantian positions. Prior to the 1950s, language studies were primarily normative. Research centered around atheoretical descriptions of language development (Rebelsky, Starr, & Luria, 1967). By the late 1950s through the 1960s, a view was advanced that, as children learn a language, they actively attempt to construct a theory of grammar (cf. Brown & Bellugi, 1964). Furthermore, the work of several psycholinguists (Chomsky, 1968; Lenneberg, 1967) advanced the notion that children are actually born with some innate structure that sensitizes them to oral communication, allowing them to understand specific properties of language intuitively (cf. Chomsky, 1968).

As can be seen from the preceding discussion, cognitive psychology, as it evolved in America, is an amalgamation of ideas stemming from experimental psychology, verbal learning, and psycholinguistic research. Common to this research is the attitude that the organism is an information user. Information-processing theory (the rubric for this collection of themes) focuses on discovering the structure of this system and how information flows through it. An attempt is made to understand how the individual acquires, evaluates, and adjusts to information, and how he or she persists in such a manner that some goal is reached.

Whereas this approach has become much more Kantian in its assumptions about human nature, there lingers within it the vestiges of its Lockean past. The clear focus of this theory is on the internal state of humans; however, some cognitive theorists remain at least tacitly committed to the notion that whatever these things are that mediate responses to the environment, they are ultimately linked to past experience (Rychlak, 1979, pp. 201–219). For others infused with the cognitive spirit, stimulus-response justifications are omitted from their discourse altogether; such discussion is viewed as trivial to larger, more interesting theoretical issues (Miller et al., 1960). This reasoning is a curious twist on the justifications advanced by the behaviorists nearly 60 years ago for excluding the study of cognitive activity from psychology.

By the mid-1960s, the study of cognition was well underway in America. The sense of euphoria in psychology's newfound freedom to theorize about the internal mechanisms and events that accompany mental life is found in Neisser's (1967) foreword to his text, *Cognitive Psychology*. He states, "A generation ago, a book like this would have needed at least a chapter of self-defense against the behaviorist position. Today, happily, the climate of opinion has changed, and little or no defense is needed." Palermo (1970) wrote with equal enthusiasm about the changes that had accompanied psychology's passage into the 1970s. He noted that "psychology is showing all of the signs of entering another scientific revolution." And in view of psychology's past, he observed about his participation in a conference on imagery and thought, "proposing a symposium on imagery at a psychological convention [in the fifties] might have been considered a joke." A new way of perceiving the individual in a uniquely cognitive fashion had evolved. It is a way of thinking about thought that, while Lockean in heritage, is Kantian in its treatment of the important dimensions of human knowledge. Each person is a thinker, a user of information, one who interacts with the world and as such interprets his or her experience.

Lockean and Kantian Themes in European Psychology

Whereas the flavor of American psychology during the first half of this century was unmistakably Lockean, European psychology evolved in a much different fashion, consequently producing its own unique brand of cognitive psychology. The history of European psychology reveals a greater latitude in its content and methods for studying psychology than is found in America. European psychologists were clearly less concerned with the extraspective, objective methodology advocated by the natural and physical sciences. Psychiatry and applied psychology, for instance, freely treated the mind as the content of psychological inquiry. In fact many European psychologists had little interest in the empirical validation of their theories. They believed there are other equally valid ways of testing a theory (for example, as with logical, rational evidence, Ricoeur, 1977).

Sigmund Freud.   Undoubtedly one of the most recognizable and influential figures in psychology's history is Sigmund Freud. Freud's psychology, articulated as the psychoanalytic theory, is a unique blend of Kantian and Lockean themes (Rychlak, 1979). Freud's contribution to psychology is important in that he broke step with the traditional interpretation of mental illness. Quite unlike the medical community of which he was a part, he reasoned that mental illness need not be explained by physical trauma or genetic condition. Indeed, he proposed that neurosis is an attempt by the individual to reach some state of balance or equilibrium in mental functioning. Mankind, Freud believed, is caught in a conflict between the demands of the *id* (an irrational, unconscious portion of the mind) and the restrictions of the *superego* (a system of the mind that houses social values). The superego and the id were seen as antagonistic. (We have, for instance, an instinct to express our sexuality; yet, our society places a number of restrictions on how we can express this impulse.) In explaining the resolution of this dilemma, Freud reasoned that another portion of the mind, the *ego*, effects compromises. By exercising the ego, we maximize instinctual gratification while minimizing guilt and shame arising within the superego. This tripartite theory of the mind is somewhat Kantian in its accounting of behavior (Rychlak, 1979). Through the operation of ego functioning, individuals fashion their own being while attempting to mediate an interminable conflict. In discussing development, however, Freud introduced theoretical concepts that also have Lockean flavor.

As Freud viewed it, development occurs as a consequence of some innate plan that inevitably unfolds. It is a plan marked by the individual's ability to obtain gratification of need states through compromise. Freud, however, could not escape the reductionist influences around him. As such he was compelled to discuss some energy source that powers psychic activity. Such theorizing was accomplished by introducing the notion of *libido* (a sexual, growth energy force) and *thanatos* (a death instinct that explained the degenerative process). Despite the Kantian notions of self-direction advanced by Freud, he was ultimately compelled in the true Lockean tradition to empower mental processes with energy forces. Furthermore, these energy forces are directly tied to the physical body itself. Instincts, Freud reasoned, are the psychological manifestations of biological, physical needs.

In reaction to Freud's emphasis on pathology and abnormality, other psychologists trained either by Freud or influenced by his theorizing, elaborated upon psychoanalytic theory, especially that aspect of it concerning the ego. These psychologists, known as ego-psychologists, elevated the individual to a more rational level, less in the grips of a constant and unrelenting set of pressures. A human being is viewed not as a victim of either instinct or morality, but rather a being who weighs alternatives, considers solutions and choices, and acts upon information in a reasonable and considerate fashion (Erikson, 1963, 1968). The position minimized the importance of those Lockean energy forces present in psychoanalytic theory.

Gestalt psychology.   In addition to this speculation about the nature and function of the mind which typified European psychoanalytical circles, there was also forming in Germany during the 1920s a group of psychologists devoted to the study of phenomena more closely related to the content of American experimental psychology. Led by Wertheimer, Kohler, and Kofka, this school of thought came to be known as *Gestalt psychology.*

Gestalt psychology was based on the notion that the whole experience is greater than the sum of its component parts. A painting, for example, is more than its hues and colors, brush strokes, texture of canvas, and patina of finish. To appreciate a painting out of the context of the whole is not to "see" the painting at all.

The perception of the whole was believed to occur as a consequence of organization that occurs at the level of the brain. The organism creates the summative experience—collating, synthesizing, and interpreting bits of sensory information. A number of organizational principles were proposed, one of these being that of *figure-ground.* In all perception there is some element in the stimulus field that is the focus of our attention. This central element is called the figure. Likewise, as we identify the figure, other sensory information recedes—that is, becomes the ground. The operation of figure-ground can be appreciated by viewing Figure 1-1. While attending to the black-and-white

Figure 1-1. A reversible figure that can be seen as a vase or as two faces.

figure, you may focus on the black, thus seeing two kissing faces. Or, your attention may shift to white at which time you see a white vase set against a dark background.

Typical of Kantian philosophy, Gestalt psychologists believed that these organizational principles are innate and to be found in all species. Furthermore, the Gestalt psychologists believed that all perception is organized and, hence, interpreted via these innate structures.

Similar themes could be found in Gestalt ideas about memory. Memory, they believed, is more than a simple one-to-one correspondence between some memory image and its counterpart in the real world. Quite the contrary, Gestalt psychologists believed that memories are stylized expectations or impressions about what one believes he or she has experienced (Bartlett, 1932).

The Gestalt approach to problem solving was also radically different from the American approach to learning and thinking. Gestalt psychologists believed, for example, that when solving problems, organisms test hypotheses—that is, formulate guesses about solutions to problems. The Gestalt psychologists, therefore, proposed the notion of one-trial learning. If individuals test hypotheses and discover the correct solution, they should be correct on every trial thereafter. It was a theory quite different from the Americans who argued that learning consists of the growth of habit strength (a tendency to respond to whatever had received the most reinforcement).

Unfortunately, a variety of factors (for example, the strength of behaviorism, the strength of extraspective methodology advocated by the natural sciences, the lack of a rigorous methodology of their own, and turmoil in Europe) contributed to the abandonment of Gestalt psychology as an organized school. Nevertheless, examining the topics and theories that constitute contemporary cognitive psychology shows a striking correspondence to those notions advanced by Gestalt psychologists. Though the school was disbanded, the work of Gestalt psychologists on mental activity had a powerful influence on the development of contemporary psychological theories.

Jean Piaget. Although Gestalt psychology faded from the psychological scene in Europe by the late 1930s, another European of that era had begun in relative obscurity to advance a theory of cognition that was to have profound implications for all psychology, especially the psychology of cognitive development. If one individual were to be credited with the upsurge of interest in cognitive development, this recognition would without doubt have to be given to the Swiss psychologist Jean Piaget. Piaget's contribution to child development is enormous, and as is typical of the European psychologies, his represents a mix of both Kantian and Lockean themes.

The seeds of Piaget's theory of development can be found in his early childhood interests in biology and epistomology (that is, the study of the nature, acquisition, and source of knowledge). Piaget's formal educational training was in biology; however, following completion of his doctoral work, he obtained employment under Theophile Simon in the laboratory of Alfred Binet in Paris. (Simon and Binet had developed the first practical standardized intelligence test in 1911.) As a research assistant to Simon, he helped in the standardization of the French language editions of English reasoning tests.

It was during his tenure with the Binet laboratory that he began to formulate his now famous theory of cognitive development (Piaget, 1952). In the process of administering standardized tests to children, Piaget became increasingly disenchanted with the product-oriented approach to intelligence testing which characterized the Simon-Binet testing program. According to this approach a mental test score reflects some amount of ability or capacity to reason. What was of interest to Piaget was the variety of answers children give to test items— something that was ignored in the traditional approach to testing. Younger children, for example, give answers to questions that are qualitatively different from those of older children. When asked, "What is an orange?" for example, an older child might say, "It's a fruit," or "It's something to eat." A younger child might give answers such as "It's something that is round," or "It's yellowish." Older children describe the object in terms of some superordinate class of objects, such as fruits or edibles. The younger child describes the object by its physical properties of shape and color. It was these apparent differences in the quality of children's thought that intrigued Piaget and initiated a lifelong study of child development.

Like many European psychologists who were his contemporaries, Piaget took as the content of psychology the internal realm of man's existence. Although he didn't formally study psychoanalysis, it is clear that he was acquainted with the major psychoanalytic writers of the day and well versed in their clinical method (which he adapted to suit his own research interests). Like Freud, Piaget proposed that development proceeds in a sequential, stagelike fashion. In Kantian form and similar to the ideas advanced by Baldwin, he suggested that the individual interprets reality via an intellectual structure characterized by action schemes (knowledge about what can be done with things) and abstract rules (how things can be related). As children develop, this intellectual structure changes. Thus, from one age to another, children interpret and perceive the world differently.

Development, in Piaget's view, is a function of both maturation (biological growth) and learning (experiential growth). In one sense he believed development is predetermined. Biology influences the rate and direction of development; this influence is both innate and inescapable. But the biological component of development is only half of the story; appropriate learning experiences are required to promote the growth and elaboration of the intellect.

In order to explain why development occurs, Piaget proposed that individuals attempt to maintain a state of cognitive equilibrium. Individuals construe their world, or try to make sense of it. If one's experiences are inconsistent with his or her understanding of how the world operates, the individual experiences a state of cognitive tension. This tension leads the individual to alter his or her intellectual structure to make it consistent with experience.

Factors that contribute to destabilization (hence creating the precondition for development) are both biological and environmental. In spite of Piaget's acknowledgment of the fundamental role of biology in the developmental process, his attitude about what constitutes the intellectual structure is strikingly Lockean. In fact, Piaget (1980) was emphatic in his disavowal of the nativist label. Though acknowledging specific reflexes that are extant at birth and that, in a very simple way, allow children to operate on and abstract some simple understanding of the environment, Piaget maintained that children's basic understanding of the world is a consequence of experience. These experiences represent necessary and sequential lessons, one lesson built upon the other.

Whereas Piaget's concept of the intellect has its Lockean features, this is so only insofar as the rules or operations that underlie the intellectual structure are concerned. These rules represent laws of the universe, an external reality that children come to appreciate. Piaget also believed that through the operation of a more advanced set of rules, children come to experience the dialectic quality of the mind. Inhelder and Piaget (1958), for example, described how adolescents may derive a set of rules to explain why an object eventually stops after it is impelled down some path (attributing stopping to friction and gravity). By operating upon these rules (in this case by negating them), they can derive the law of inertia (that is, in the absence of those factors that cause slowing—gravity, friction, and so on—an object will continue to travel at a steady rate perpetually).

More will be said of Piaget's theory in the following chapters. For the present, it should be noted that his theory is a unique blend of Kantian and Lockean ideas, which has produced a cognitive psychology quite different in flavor from that which arose in America. By the mid-1960s, Piaget's theory was widely popular in Europe and had begun to attract an international following. In America a number of psychologists (Elkind, 1961a, b; Flavell,

1966) began to replicate and evaluate the work coming from the Genevan school (Piaget was director of the Jean-Jacques Rousseau Institute at Geneva University in Geneva, Switzerland), elevating both its popularity and respectability in North America.

SUMMARY

If cognitive psychology doesn't reflect the revolution in scientific thought that some believe it does, it has at least made a profound impact on the way that we think about many of the more traditional ideas of interest to psychologists. Typically those who study cognition are interested in how information is acquired, maintained, and used in the course of mental activity. With respect to cognitive development, our interests shift to an examination of age-related changes in perception, memory, and conceptual processes (how information is used).

Historically, psychology has operated under two different views of man; these have been referred to as the Lockean and Kantian positions. The Lockean model encourages the perception of human nature as reactive and mechanical. It advocates the notion that to understand behavior, we must look to antecedent events to discover how experience (things external to man) structures the whole (behavior). Quite the opposite is postulated by the Kantian position, wherein human nature is seen as proactive, since man constructs reality and knowledge. To understand what we know, it isn't sufficient to examine the external environment; we must look within ourselves to discover those uniquely human qualities and characteristics that structure thought.

Traditional American learning theory was distinctly Lockean in its treatment of psychology, and it is in part from this heritage that contemporary information-processing theory stems. Attempts to explain the complexity of human thought and learning within this rigid Lockean paradigm led to theoretical revisions that redirected attention to internal mental states and structures. This redirection of attention to cognitive processes, coupled with the growth of research in artificial intelligence arising from developments in computer technology, produced a particular brand of cognitive psychology. It is one that regards the individual as a complex, information-processing system. Our attempts to understand this system have led to speculation about the components of the system and the rules by which it operates.

In Europe a different history produced another brand of cognitive psychology. As presented in this chapter, the European heritage was a blend of both Lockean and Kantian themes. Typical of European psychology was the speculation about the structure and processes of the mind. From this history emerged a theory advanced by Jean Piaget. Piaget advocated that to some degree development is predetermined by biological forces. But, in addition to these influences, children also need experiences from which they can learn an orderly set of lessons about their world and the way it operates. Development is the sequential unfolding of higher levels of knowledge, characterized and, thus, limited by biological states or stages.

2

An Information-Processing
View of Cognition
and Development

This text is organized around two contemporary theories of cognitive development introduced in the last chapter: information-processing theory and Piagetian theory. That two or more theories can exist simultaneously to account for a common set of phenomena is sometimes confusing to students new to the ways of science. In order to clear this confusion, the first part of this chapter is devoted to a discussion of the assumptions underlying scientific investigation and the nature and evaluation of theories. In the latter half of this chapter, a framework will be presented for understanding information-processing theory, one of the accounts of cognitive development that will be used for organizing information presented in the remaining chapters of this text.

ASSUMPTIONS UNDERLYING THE STUDY OF BEHAVIOR

The effort to understand ourselves is based on the assumption that we live in an orderly and understandable universe. Science is a set of principles and procedures that we believe will lead us to understand whatever aspect of the universe we choose to study, be it the stars, the atom, or ourselves. Intuitively it is easier to believe we can understand matter than it is to believe we can understand human behavior. We see, touch, and manipulate matter, but so many of those things that interest us about humans defy precise definition and observation.

Our activities, thoughts, and behaviors are indeed varied; however, if we are to study human beings, we must accept the premise that they can be understood. To persist in the study of human behavior without this assumption would be an exercise in futility. Although we believe that ultimately answers to our questions will be known, in a more immediate sense we also assume our "answers" are tentative.

This tentativeness comes from an awareness that psychology is still young. As such, there is an ever-expanding set of questions to be asked about behavior and thought, and with this proliferation of questions and knowledge comes a variety of ways to make sense of what we know.

Psychology itself was born of a desire to gather new kinds of information about questions debated philosophically for a long while. The early psychologists believed that by using empirical (data-based) methods they might gain more definitive answers to their questions. Alas, since the establishment of psychology as a science over 100 years ago, our questions have multiplied much faster than our answers. And, as an answer to one question was sought, the search recommended many other questions for our consideration. We are indeed complex beings.

The assumption that man is knowable seems contradicted by the recognition that we are also extremely complex. But we shouldn't confuse complexity with unpredictability. Any novel endeavor is shrouded with mystery and unknowns. A new job seems a mishmash of poorly understood procedures and a variety of things to be learned about later on. With time, the mystery fades as we make sense of procedures and discover the intricacies and nuances of our positions and thereby gain a sense of mastery and competence.

We can think about the study of psychology this way too. Although philosophers have pondered the nature of the mind for over 2000 years, only since 1879 (generally cited as the year in which the first psychology laboratory was established by Wilhelm Wundt in Leipzig, Germany) have we studied human behavior and mental activity empirically. For a good part of psychology's history we have excluded from our domain of inquiry issues related specifically to mental activity; those kinds of questions have been tackled systematically only within the last 20 years. It would be a great surprise (and disappointment) if we had those definitive answers. The proliferation of questions about our being is a healthy and encouraging sign that cognitive psychology is a vital and robust young science. We shouldn't expect too much in the way of definitive answers just yet; we haven't been at this thing we call psychology very long, especially that aspect of it concerned with cognitive development.

ON THE NATURE OF THEORIES

When observing any new event, it is not unusual for two people to see it quite differently. Anyone who has traveled abroad has likely debated among their fellow travelers why particular customs persist. Westerners fail to understand why indigent families in underdeveloped, Third-World countries continue to have large families. Without an understanding of underlying cultural attitudes about family, religion, and the absence of national pension plans for the aged (one's children are one's social security), for example, we fail to understand behavior. In our ignorance, we overlook important pieces to a puzzle or see the pieces in the mosaic fitting together in different patterns.

That scientists attempt to unravel the complexities of human experience doesn't suggest that their conclusions are any more absolute. They are skilled in the construction of viable explanations of events, and they know how to subject these explanations (or theories) to critical tests. The strength of their theories is evaluated on several grounds. First, good theories must be logical and consistent with past observations. Second, good theories must predict behavior. Those theories that predict accurately (that is, are supported by empirical tests of hypotheses deriving from the theory) gain credibility. Those that don't are weakened and are either abandoned for better theories or are modified to account for new, previously unanticipated phenomena.

Because of the complexity of the human mind, the scientist interested in its development is beset with an enormous riddle. It is a riddle that currently can be explained more than one way. Two of these explanations are information-processing and Piagetian theory. These theories have helped to clarify our understanding of the developmental process and guide speculation and research in development. Let's consider the nature of information-processing theory.

STRUCTURE OF THE INFORMATION-PROCESSING SYSTEM

In the last chapter you learned that the brand of cognitive psychology that evolved in America was a mix of contributions from a diverse set of disciplines (for example, mediated stimulus-response (S-R) theory, verbal learning research, psycholinguistics, and artificial intelligence). As such, no one figure nor any single theoretical model came to organize cognitive research in America. This diverse set of ideas has been loosely collected into something called information-processing theory. Despite the diversity of information-processing theory, a common thread winds through it. Information-processing theory is concerned with how information is taken into the organism, interpreted, represented, transformed, and acted upon. We are, in fact, interested in how information is processed. In order to process information, we must assume there is a structure to the intellect. This structure has been characterized by three basic systems: perceptual, mnemonic, and conceptual (Kinsch, 1970).

Linking the organism and the external world are the senses, specialized nervous tissue responding to physical energy. When sensory receptor cells are stimulated with sufficient energy, we experience sensations. While sensations are obviously important to the information processor (they are the raw material of our cognitions), of greater concern and interest to information-processing theorists is what we make of our sensations. That is, how does the information processor use or interpret these data? Thus, the first system of importance to those interested in information processing is the perceptual system. Perception occurs as we give meaning to our sensory experiences. It is clear that we do more than detect shades of gray, hues, angles, lines, frequencies, and amplitudes; we perceive those dimensions as organized, recognizable, and meaningful units of information.

Just what are the units of information that constitute our perceptual experience? Information-processing theorists write about a system that works with unitary bits of information (borrowing from computer language). But that which constitutes a bit of information is arbitrary. A bit may consist of a line in a particular configuration (/), a single letter (N), a word (NOW), or an entire sentence (Now is the time for all good men to come to the aid of their country). What we individually recognize as a meaningful bit of information varies as a consequence of our level of experience with a particular problem or situation, our individual states, and a number of other situational factors. For example, when studying expert and amateur chess players, Chase and Simon (1973) noted that experts recognize patterns of pieces on the board as single bits of information. Amateurs, on the other hand, attend to the positions of single pieces. How we represent information—i.e., what we take in as the fundamental unit of meaningful information—has important implications for the operation of the information-processing system. The human organism is a limited capacity system. We can respond only to a limited amount of information at any one time. But if we take in larger amounts of information as unitary bits, our ability to operate upon our experience is greatly increased.

As it is currently constituted, information-processing theory is characterized by two different, but complementary, approaches to understanding cognitive activity. One approach attempts to synthesize or construct elaborate models reflecting how specific kinds of information are perceived, remembered, or used. An alternate approach attempts to decompose the intellectual system in an examination of the components and operations that produce performance. After Posner and McLeod (1982), we'll refer to the first approach as a synthesis or systems modeling approach and the latter as an analysis approach.

A Synthesis Approach to Information Processing

One of the outcomes of the computer revolution has been the consideration of logical steps, decision rules, and sequences required to accomplish various tasks. By carefully elaborating sets of instructions in the form of computer programs, we can instruct machines to do some rather remarkable things.

Using a less remarkable example, we could program a computer to play a simple game. In this case, consider a program that will allow the computer to discover a whole number between 1 and 10 in a minimal number of guesses—a variant of the old Twenty Questions game.

If I were to solve this problem, I'd ask questions that would systematically halve the number of alternatives with each question asked. A diagram for a solution strategy using this technique is shown in Figure 2-1. In writing a computer program to solve this problem, I can use my strategy as a model. Thus, I'd ask my game partner, "Is the number odd or even?" I can also program the computer to ask this question. Using a computer language called BASIC, I write what is called a print statement (for example, 10 PRINT "Is the number odd or even?"). The print statement instructs the computer to print on the video monitor everything that is within the quotation marks. (The number preceding the statement is a line identification number. It informs the computer where it is in the program.) In other words, I can create a condition wherein the computer can send a message to someone else.

Next, I need some information or feedback from my game partner. We can also communicate with the computer by allowing a space in the program for feedback. We do this by including a dimension statement (20 DIM A$). This statement tells the computer to reserve space for incoming information (input).

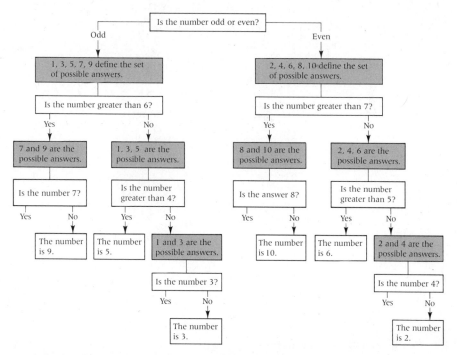

Figure 2-1. A tree diagram representing the logical steps required to discover a whole number between 1 and 10 and a computer program (next page) that will do the same.

```
10    PRINT "IS THE NUMBER ODD OR EVEN?"
20    DIM A$
30    INPUT A$
40    IF A$ = "ODD" THEN 270
50    PRINT "IS THE NUMBER GREATER THAN 7?"
60    DIM B$
70    INPUT B$
80    IF B$ = "YES" THEN 210
90    PRINT "IS THE NUMBER GREATER THAN 5?"
100   DIM C$
110   INPUT C$
120   IF C$ = "NO" THEN 150
130   PRINT "THEN NUMBER IS 6"
140   GOTO 999
150   PRINT "IS THE NUMBER 4?"
160   DIM D$
170   INPUT D$
180   IF D$ = "YES" THEN 999
190   PRINT "THE NUMBER IS 2."
200   GOTO 999
210   PRINT "IS THE NUMBER 8?"
220   DIM E$
240   IF E$ = "YES" THEN 999
250   PRINT "THE NUMBER IS 10."
260   GOTO 999
270   PRINT "IS THE NUMBER GREATER THAN 6?"
280   DIM F$
290   INPUT F$
300   IF F$ = "YES" THEN 430
310   PRINT "IS THE NUMBER GREATER THAN 4?"
320   DIM G$
330   INPUT G$
340   IF G$ = "NO" THEN 370
350   PRINT "THE NUMBER IS 5."
360   GOTO 999
370   PRINT "IS THE NUMBER 3?"
380   DIM H$
390   INPUT H$
400   IF H$ = "YES" THEN 999
410   PRINT "THE NUMBER IS 1."
420   GOTO 999
430   PRINT "IS THE NUMBER 7?"
440   DIM I$
450   INPUT I$
460   IF I$ = "YES" THEN 999
470   PRINT "THE NUMBER IS 9."
999   END
```

Figure 2-1. (continued).

Next we'd include an input statement (30 INPUT A$). This statement places the computer in a receptive mode; it can't go on until it gets an answer to its question, and neither can I. (A$ is the name we assign to whatever input is received.)

Once I've received some feedback, I evaluate it and plan my next move. If the answer to my question is "odd," I'd want to work with a new set of numbers—only the odd ones. Likewise, if the answer is "even," I'd want to work only with even numbers. The computer can also evaluate its input using "if-then" statements (for example, 40 IF A$ = "ODD" THEN 270). After comparing the input with the "if-then" statement, it will either proceed to another point in the program (line 270) or continue to the next line (line 50). Figure 2-1 contrasts a tree diagram of my solution to this problem with a computer program that will also solve the problem. (The "GOTO" statement is another command that can be given to the computer to send it to another place in the program.)

You will notice that when I'm finished writing the program, it reflects a particular style or strategy. In fact, it serves as an illustration of how I solve this kind of problem. If we were to run this program, the computer would play this game in an identical manner to the way I play. This should be of little surprise; after all, the program was modeled after my own performance. What I've done is to synthesize, via a computer program, a description of how I process information.

Researchers working in artificial intelligence have attempted to do something very much like the previous demonstration—to synthesize information-processing models that simulate human mental functioning (Simon, 1979). Typically these models are cast as running computer programs. As you saw in the example, it is assumed that human intelligence is characterized by a set of decision rules. By identifying the rules that govern mental activity, we can construct programs that react as humans might to specific problems and situations.

Developmental models of human information processing have also been constructed (Klahr, 1980, Klahr & Wallace, 1976; Klahr & Siegler, 1981; Siegler, 1982). Klahr, for example, has characterized the information-processing system as structured by production systems that become more elaborate with age. These production systems may be thought of as rule books. Given particular situations, there are a set of rules to play by. In golf, for example, when the golfer steps to the tee, a number of conditions are checked (distance to the green, wind velocity and direction, height of the grass, and so on). If a particular set of conditions exist (we can say that the conditions are satisfied), a particular action is taken. In this example, the golfer selects a specific club and hits the ball. The consequences of that production are evaluated in light of another set of conditions until some goal state is reached—the ball is put in the hole.

For specific tasks it is possible to construct production systems reflecting how children of different ages solve problems. Klahr has identified four types of decision-making models exemplifying children's performance on a balance beam problem. The problem requires children to predict which way a two-armed balance will tip as weight is added to the opposing arms. In the simplest solution (Model I, Figure 2-2), children attend only to how much weight is placed on either side of the balance without regard to distance. They reason that the balance will tip toward the greater weight. A production system characterizing this reasoning is shown in Table 2-1. The conditions represented on the left-hand side of the table are assumed to be maintained in some short-term working memory, and when they are satisfied, an action is triggered as indicated by the arrow. You can see that if one set of conditions is satisfied

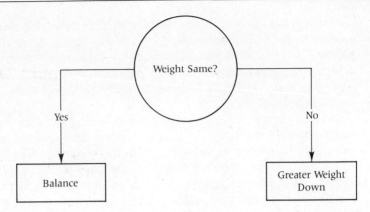

Figure 2-2. Model I for balance scale prediction. *(Adapted from Klahr, 1980)*

(same weight on both sides of the balance), one action is taken (children will say that the beam will balance). If another set of conditions is satisfied (there is a heavier weight on one side of the balance), a different action will be taken (children will say that the beam will tilt toward the heavier weight). More sophisticated forms of reasoning require more elaborate production systems.

One of the problems with this approach to human information processing is that it uses a model that has been criticized as rigid, inflexible, and limited to descriptions of activity within specific and well-circumscribed tasks (cf. Pascual-Leone, 1980). Thus, these models fail to explain the more interesting aspects of human intellectual functioning—how we decide what is the problem to be solved prior to executing a particular processing routine. Some of this criticism may abate as research in artificial intelligence produces programs that are capable of detecting patterns and, consequently, that model the more flexible and adaptive qualities of human intelligence (Klahr, 1980; Klahr & Wallace, 1976; Newell, 1973). Other criticisms of this approach have observed the omission of the human qualities of motivation and emotion. Here, too, programs may be developed in the near future to include these dimensions in performance models (cf. Colby, 1973).

The synthesis approach to studying information processing has also been criticized for having limited developmental application. Aside from constructing elaborate models of children's performance on specific cognitive tasks, there has been little emphasis on accounting for the transitional mechanisms that move children from one developmental level to another (cf. Pascual-Leone, 1980). Klahr (1980) has suggested that developmental change may occur as children retain some temporal record of what occurs during a process-

TABLE 2-1. Production System for Model I.

Model I
P1: (Same weight) → (say, "balance")
P2: (Side *x* more weight) → (say, "side *x* down")

(Adapted from Klahr, 1980)

ing episode. Presumably, they may become aware of conditions not previously included in a production system. This awareness leads to the inclusion of new conditions in the production system. Returning to the golf example, if you were to hit the ball a number of times, you might become aware of other conditions that affect your play (for example, the way the club is gripped, the distance you stand from the ball, and so on), that would be incorporated into the production system. Others (Fischer, 1980) have proposed more complete sets of rules that appear to explain changes in ability levels both within and across skill levels. Apparently these transformational rules are general laws for transforming knowledge used by children at all age levels.

An Analysis Approach to Information Processing

An alternate approach to the study of human information processing involves an analysis of the components and elementary processes or operations that are needed for cognitive activity. This orientation presumes that cognition is characterized by a finite number of elementary operations that combine to produce mental activity.

Posner and McLeod (1982) have suggested that basically four different kinds of mental operations constitute cognitive activity. *Structures* are one type of operation and represent enduring characteristics of the information-processing system. Structures correspond to specific domains of cognitive activity. As the stomach is structured to digest food, so specific cognitive structures may exist for such activities as processing language, recognizing objects, and solving problems. When we read, for instance, there appear to be a set of structures that are activated in some hierarchical order. First, we detect distinctive orthographic features and arrange these features into recognizable letters, words, and sentences. In addition to the activation of structures for letter and word recognition, other structures that are semantic in nature are activated, allowing us to derive meaning from print (Rumelhart, 1977).

Whereas structures are general systems used to respond to specific types of problems or computations, another set of operations, called *strategies,* are used to vary the efficiency with which structures operate. That is, under various conditions we use our intellect with greater or lesser ease. Expectations about what is being read (a strategy) have important consequences for facilitating or inhibiting the perception of words and letters in context (cf. Posner & McLeod, 1982). The strategy you adopt for processing written information may lead you to anticipate particular orthographic and syntactic forms.

Strategies and structures are domain specific—that is, they are applied to specific types of mental tasks. But there are other operations, usually discussed under the rubric of individual differences, that also influence cognition; these are *traits* and *states.* Traits are stable characteristics of the individual that uniformly affect information processing over a broad range of activities. Since these traits are enduring qualities of our personality, we bring them to bear on any task. For example, some children are impulsive (prone to make hasty and inaccurate responses), while others are reflective. Thus, on reading tasks or any others that require measured attention and concentration, impulsive children will make considerably more errors than reflective children (Meichenbaum, 1977).

State or situational factors also affect information-processing abilities of children and adults. Information processing, for example, is affected by the degree to which situational factors produce distraction. Older children seem better able to alert themselves to the requirements of the task and to disregard distracting information than are younger children (Smith, Kemler, & Aronfreed, 1975).

Those who have opted for studying the components of the information-processing system have generally concluded that the basic structure of this system is developed by the age of 5 years, if not sooner (cf. Hagen, Jongeward, & Kail, 1975; Klahr, 1980; Naus, Ornstein, & Hoving, 1978; Ornstein, 1977). If the basic information-processing system is developed by the age of 5, to what is development after this age attributable? It is, after all, obvious that much development occurs after that age.

The answer advanced by these theorists is that development can be explained by (a) the increased familiarity of children with the structures available to them and (b) the acquisition of specific strategies that allow them to use specific structures and operations with greater flexibility and efficiency. Ornstein (1977), for example, argues that memory improves as strategies are acquired for improving the organization, rehearsal and retrieval of information in memory. Whereas the basic structure of memory (the amount of information that can be stored, the speed with which information can be accessed, and so on) is believed to be invariant, the amount of information that can be retained and the durability of this information can be improved by learning a variety of mnemonic strategies.

SUMMARY

Information-processing theory is primarily concerned with an examination of the structure of the processing system and the transformation or change effected on information as it flows through the system. Two approaches have characterized research in this area. One of these approaches, the analytic approach, attempts to study the diversity of operations or processes that influence mental activity. The other approach attempts to synthesize models that simulate human performance on specific conceptual tasks.

The analysis approach proposes that the basic structures of the intellect are developed relatively early in life (approximately by 5 years of age). Development is attributed to the acquisition of strategies that allow children to use their intellectual structure more efficiently. Whereas the analysis approach has attended to cognition in a larger sense—exploring the variety of strategies, structures, and individual differences that characterize human cognition—the synthetic approach has been more narrowly focused. Those working within this approach have meticulously developed models that exemplify patterns of information processing exhibited on specific tasks.

One of the major difficulties with the synthesis approach is that it has failed to account sufficiently for transformational mechanisms that lead to higher states of knowledge. (Indeed this criticism can be extended equally well to much of the work stemming from the analysis approach.) Whereas developmental changes have been found in processing styles, there has been little explanation of why these changes occur. Current thinking on this matter offers several solutions. One lies in the application of some standard set of transformational rules (apparently available at all ages) that allow children to combine knowledge states at one level to generate higher states of knowledge. Another theory proposes that, as children grow older, they learn, either through self-discovery or direct instruction, a variety of strategies or tricks that increases the ease and efficiency with which information is used and manipulated.

3

Piaget's Theory of Cognitive Development

The developmental theory advanced by Piaget reflects the turn-of-the-century preoccupation of European intellectuals with evolutionary theory. Evolutionary theory had a profound impact on science and society, being in opposition to both the spontaneous view of creation (touted by theologians) and other popular views of conception and development (advanced by scientists). With the exposition of evolutionary theory, the scientific community's attention was directed toward developmental processes. Although Darwin's thesis was concerned with species development, others soon began to see evolution in the organism itself. A German biologist and philosopher named Ernst Haeckel, for example, proposed that the embryo of each individual passes briefly and rapidly through the phases of its own entire species evolution (Katchadourian, 1977, pp. 9–10).

Piaget's View of Intellectual Structure

Interest in the biological development of species and individuals stimulated speculation about psychological development as well. Historically, a precedent had been set for the idea that psychological development consists of the progressive attainment of higher levels of mental life from lower ones (as in the theories of Freud, Hall, and Baldwin). Thus, as Piaget began to formulate his own theory of cognitive development, the models were abundant both within biology (where he had his formal training) and psychology (where his predilections eventually led him) for an intellectual structure that develops in a sequential and orderly, stagelike fashion with higher forms of intellect developing from lower ones (Piaget, 1963, pp. 13–20).

It occurred to Piaget that as physical structures place limitations on what children of given ages can do, intellectual structures might also place upon them similar limitations. Whereas children 5 years of age are not likely to lift a 300-pound barbell, neither are they likely to understand differential algebra. The structures available to children, be they physical or intellectual, are insufficiently developed to handle these more adultlike tasks. Furthermore, it is unlikely that practice alone would allow children to perform in an adultlike fashion. In spite of the most rigorous physical regimen to which one might submit 5-year-olds, it is doubtful that they would ever lift a 300-pound weight; their physical structure is simply too immature to support such weight. Likewise, it was reasoned that intellectual training would be unlikely to produce any significant intellectual insights if the intellectual structure had not developed to the point that such insight was possible.

The intellectual structure, as defined by Piaget, consists of an abstract set of behavior patterns or rules. With age, the nature of this system changes both in its degree of abstraction and in the extent to which the system accurately represents properties and relationships that hold in the external world. Piaget observed that during infancy, children behave as though they have available to them a number of organized behavioral patterns. These behavioral patterns are either innate (reflexes) or learned (habits). Piaget called the cognitive component of these behavior patterns *schemes.* Schemes are abstract representations of action patterns—reaching, sucking, looking, and so on. The presence of schemes allows children to generalize some behavioral pattern to new objects and situations.

As children mature, schemes change. At older levels schemes become increasingly more abstract and are characterized by rules about how things might be transformed, combined, classified, and so on. In other words, children's thought is characterized by operations that can be performed on things.

Adaptation and Organization

Piaget believed that change in the intellectual structure occurs as a consequence of two complementary processes—adaptation and organization. The process of *adaptation* refers to the interaction between the organism and the environment. Adaptation occurs when experience produces in the organism change that is beneficial to survival. *Organization,* on the other hand, refers to the internal process of integrating changes into the operation of the total system. The organism is an intercoordinated system, and changes in any aspect of the system necessitate the adjustment of the whole (Piaget, 1963, pp. 3–8). The adoption of these two principles reflects Piaget's training in biology. Processes that account for biological growth were used as models for intellectual growth.

The process of adaptation involves two phases of activity— assimilation and accommodation. The first is *assimilation.* An organism survives by ingesting substance into its system, breaking it down, and fitting it to its own needs and uses. As we assimilate physical materials into our bodies, Piaget reasoned, we also assimilate information into our intellectual structure. That is, we take information about our experiential world and distort it to fit our existing intellectual structure. We try to make sense of our world, to understand it given the set of rules and relationships that we have worked out about the nature of things around us. For example, it is not uncommon for preschool children to believe that all older males and females are mothers and fathers. As children meet others, they are incorporated into this system of male-female, older-younger, parent-child relationships. The existence of some general underlying intellectual structure also explains the persistence with which young children adhere to their views and react with incredulousness when corrected. The stubborn streak that parents frequently see in their young children may be less a characteristic of personality than the expression of their children's perspective or "world view." Children, according to Piaget, don't see the world as adults do.

As a consequence of both maturation and learning, children gradually realize that their way of viewing the world is incorrect. Presumably, the inconsistency between what children believe to be true, on the one hand, and empirical, contradictory evidence confronting them, on the other hand, produces a state of tension that results in an alteration of their intellectual structure. This alteration makes the structure consistent with experience, reduces tension, and makes the intellectual system more effective. This type of change—change in the structure of the intellect as a consequence of experience—is also a part of adaptation and is called *accommodation.* Referring again to the example of parenthood, in time children encounter a number of instances wherein adults deny the parenthood attributed to them. One might suppose that the inconsistency between children's beliefs and the feedback they receive from some adults would be disconcerting and tension producing. Cognitive ambiguity is resolved if children modify their relational system, limiting the attribute of "parenthood" to only those individuals who care for and have custody of younger children.

Adaptation then is the interplay between the two processes of assimilation and accommodation. As mentioned earlier, adaptation is attained when there is an equilibrium between assimilatory and accommodative processes. Piaget (1963, p. 7) observes that adaptation is accomplished only when it results in a stable system and it is the nature of the organism to seek this state of equilibrium. It is the tendency to seek equilibrium that produces development.

Thus, part of development is the simultaneous attempt to fit experience to preexisting ways of reacting to the world (assimilation), and another involves the alteration of one's conceptual system to make it consistent with experience (accommodation). The process of alternating states of stability (equilibrium) followed by formative instability (disequilibrium) produces a spiral of ever higher levels of cognitive development.

As a process, organization is inseparable from adaptation. It is, however, the internal aspect of the growth cycle. Whereas adaptation is concerned with the interpretation of information from without, organization is a process by which the organism coordinates changes in the components of the intellectual system. Again, if we relate this concept to biological systems, we see that various body parts grow at different rates, and with each growth spurt the individual must coordinate the consequences of that new growth with the operation of the rest of the body. Likewise, as new conceptual understandings are acquired, there is the necessary coordination of these understandings with the intellectual structure as a whole.

FOUR STAGES OF DEVELOPMENT

As mentioned earlier, Piaget believed that development occurs as a consequence of both maturation and learning. Through maturation new alternatives or options become available to the individual. (Adults, for example, have the physical size and stamina to lift heavy weights, if they wish.) Maturation, although necessary for development, is not sufficient for the development of schemes and operations. Maturation merely expands the range of experiences from which children can profit; children must be presented with an opportunity to use their intellect if it is to develop. (Although most adults have the physical size to lift heavy weights, this ability is not realized unless one exercises in a persistent and well-planned fashion.)

Biology also determines the orderly sequence of stagelike development that is part of organization. Each stage is characterized by a unique intellectual structure that has a pervasive, organizing effect on all aspects of intellectual functioning. Although structurally unique, each level of development is dependent upon the attainment of knowledge at lower levels.

Piaget identified four basic stages of development: the sensorimotor period, the preoperational period, the period of concrete operations, and the period of formal operational thought. In the following sections we will consider the general quality of thought characterizing each stage, attending to major advances and limitations in children's thought. At this point we won't consider in too much detail the skills and abilities specific to children at these various stages of development. A more detailed examination of the research pertaining to these stages will come in subsequent chapters.

The Sensorimotor Period

The first stage of development is characterized by a progressive integration of motor and perceptual schemes, which culminate in a more objective understanding of one's self and surroundings. This sensorimotor period extends from birth to 24 months. Development in this stage is particularly important because it provides a base for all later learning. That is, during this stage the infant acquires a knowledge about four fundamental properties of the external world—knowledge of objects, time, space, and causation (to be discussed in some detail in Chapter 5). The period itself is characterized by six substages.

First substage. In the first substage (0–2 months) an infant's behavior is governed primarily by reflexes rooted in his or her genetic structure. Piaget believed that even these reflexes had schematic counterparts. Furthermore, and typical of Piaget's reasoning, the use of the reflexive schemes doesn't imply that infants are merely reactive. It was his belief that the existence of a scheme creates a need for its use (a condition referred to as *functional assimilation*). Thus, infants might exercise schemes simply to gain the pleasure of their use. It is important that schemes be used because through use they are strengthened and adapted.

One set of reflexes that is particularly important to the infant immediately after birth and during the first few months of life is that related to feeding. If infants are stimulated in the area of the mouth, they reflexively begin sucking. But infants also exercise innate sucking schemes automatically; infants can be observed sucking in the absence of any apparent stimulation. Over the course of the first two months of life, infants extend the range of objects to which sucking schemes are applied, sucking on blankets, toys, and fingers (Piaget referred to this as *generalizing assimilation*). It can also be noticed that under specific conditions, children apply schemes only to specific objects. Thus, when infants are hungry, they may reject a blanket, a finger, or a toy, but suck vigorously when presented a nipple (Piaget calls this *recognitory assimilation*).

Through assimilation, the reflexive schemes are adapted—extended to a variety of objects or to specific objects during the first few months of life. Infants at this stage are merely exercising the reflexive schemes they are born with; that is, these schemes don't undergo accommodation (change as a consequence of experience) until the next stage (Piaget, 1963, p. 41). Even so, through generalizing and recognitory assimilation, there are significant changes in infants' behavior. They eventually recognize the nipple (not as an object, but in the form of a selective response) and act as if they know where it is located. Reflexive behavioral schemes are organized so that when infants are hungry, they engage in behaviors that rapidly bring them in contact with the nipple. Furthermore, the entire feeding activity becomes a highly organized behavior pattern, involving the coordination of several reflexive visual and motor schemes.

Second substage. During the second substage (2–4 months), infants' behavior is increasingly less reflexive as it is modified through experience. These changes in behavior involve the incorporation of novel body movements into preexisting reflex schemes; the behavior patterns can be characterized as habits. Piaget calls such behavior patterns *primary circular reactions*. These behavior patterns develop through chance as infants engage in activities that produce interesting results. The fortuitous pairing of action with the pleasure gained from exercising a scheme increases the probability that the activity that produces pleasure will be repeated. Habitual thumb-sucking is an example of a primary circular reaction. An infant may accidentally bring his or her hand to the mouth, which triggers the sucking reflex, thus exercising the sucking scheme. As a consequence of activities that brought the hand to the mouth, infants are able to exercise the sucking scheme. As this particular behavior pattern is repeated a number of times, it becomes more refined, involving fewer body parts (in time only the thumb may be sucked). It should be noted that the initiation of these behavior patterns is unintentional—that is, infants don't demonstrate behavior suggesting that particular motor activities are initiated with the intent of producing some goal state (Piaget, 1963, p. 91). Whereas reflexive schemes found in stage one are now adapted by experience, they are nonetheless, triggered by stimulus events rather than intention.

Third substage.   As infants grow, they become more active and mobile. Consequently, they extend the range of things and events they experience. During the third substage (4–10 months), infants develop a new kind of habit pattern referred to as *secondary circular reactions,* connoting a shift toward the reproduction of activities involving objects. Like the primary circular reactions preceding this phase, secondary circular reactions begin as children make chance connections between the use of schemes and activities that produce interesting outcomes involving objects. A child may accidentally pull a string attached to a mobile as it hangs over its crib. Pulling the string produces movement in the mobile that exercises the child's visual schemes. With the activation of these schemes, there is a desire to repeat their use (through functional assimilation). Thus, infants are motivated to act to repeat interesting events—to assimilate again the movement of the mobile into the visual schemes. Infants, for example, will pull a string attached to a mobile not once but a number of times in succession, delighting in the movement that such activity produces.

At this stage, however, infants still have not discovered means-end relationships. Consequently, they do not act intentionally to reproduce activities previously associated with objects. Infants must rediscover relationships between actions and objects (Piaget, 1963, p. 151). An infant who looks at, handles, and sucks on a rattle may continue to incorporate the object into visual, haptic (touching), and sucking schemes; however, if the object is temporarily removed from sight, the infant doesn't intentionally act to recover the lost object. The need to repeat an act occurs only through discovery; in true acts of intelligence, discovery arises from the need to exercise schemes. Intentional behavior is the hallmark of true intelligence and is found for the first time in the next substage.

Fourth substage.   In the fourth substage (10–12 months) greater refinement and coordination occur in infants' secondary schemes. The coordination of these behavior patterns produces systematic, goal-oriented behavior. That is, rather than the fortuitous discovery of pleasurable activity associated with objects found in substage three, infants at substage four initiate behaviors that lead to specific goals. This behavior reveals for the first time practical intelligence. By this substage infants know what objects are for and desire to apply familiar schemes to them. The need to apply a scheme initiates an activity to recover an object so the scheme can function. Infants who are playing with a toy that temporarily slips behind a cushion will now attempt to find it. These infants don't abandon their desire to use schemes simply because the object allowing the scheme to function is out of sight. Instead infants use other familiar schemes (striking, pushing, pulling) to recover objects or to remove whatever barrier prevents them from having some desired object. This intentionality is characterized by the coordination of secondary schemes (for example, the generalization of a scheme to clear an obstruction in order to incorporate a toy into another scheme). Stage four behavior, however, is limited to the intercoordination of familiar schemes. Infants haven't begun to explore the various functions or properties of objects nor have they explored alternative means to obtaining goals. These explorations await the fifth substage of sensorimotor development.

Fifth substage.   In the fifth substage (12–18 months), infants show a growing curiosity and expansion of knowledge about the nature and property of objects (Piaget, 1963, p. 264). Behavior is initiated to discover new properties of objects; these behavior patterns are referred to as *tertiary circular reactions.* Schemes are no longer modified by environmental exigencies; they are altered through the child's own intentional exploration and manipulation. No longer do children use toys and other objects in highly circumscribed habit patterns as they did in substage three; they now apply habitual schemes to a variety of objects, noting that different objects behave differently when specific schemes are applied. For example, not all objects behave the same when dropped—a vase shatters while a rubber ball bounces. Thus curious infants at this substage delight in repetitive experimentation with objects, dropping spaghetti from high chairs, watching mashed potatoes ooze through their fingers, or custard dribble from their spoons.

   In addition to discovering new properties of objects, infants also develop new schemes for assimilating objects into action schemes. Infants may discover that an object can be attained not only by reaching, but also by pulling toward them a blanket on which an object rests (Piaget, 1963, p. 264). Thus, in the fifth substage of sensorimotor development infants expand both their knowledge about objects as well as knowledge about how to attain goals.

Sixth substage.   The final substage of sensorimotor development represents the culmination of the first five substages and marks a transition into the next stage of cognitive development. Prior to this substage, infants could discover new means-end relationships, but these relationships were discovered through direct perception and active manipulation of objects. In the sixth substage infants develop the capacity to consider mentally means-end relationships, allowing them to produce solutions to problems through sudden insight. Infants may see a toy out of reach, pause for a moment considering other objects around them, then take a stick and use it to pull a desired toy within reach (Piaget, 1963, pp. 235–236).

The ability to construct means-end relationships mentally is a consequence of both invention and representation. Invention no longer represents, as Piaget puts it, "sensorimotor groping," but the ability to mentally and spontaneously reorganize schemes that are accommodated to yield new solutions. To invent, the child must also be able to represent objects and actions symbolically (Piaget, 1963, p. 355). As early as the fourth substage, children begin to develop the notion that objects exist when out of view (a rudimentary form of representation). Such knowledge, however, is dependent upon an immediately preceding action effected on the object. In this last substage representation is detached from interaction with objects.

With the culmination of the sensorimotor period, children have developed a special competence about the world. They have developed the knowledge that permanent objects exist within some spatio-temporal framework in a world of causal relationships. Despite the remarkable achievements that have characterized development within the first two years of life, it is but a foundation for more sophisticated forms of knowledge acquired in the later stages of development.

The Preoperational Period

Semiotic function. The advent of the preoperational period (2–7 years) reflects a remarkable intellectual advance. Prior to substage six of the sensorimotor period, intellectual activity was limited to direct perceptual and motoric interaction with the external world. The preoperational child, however, has the ability to represent and, consequently, the ability to manipulate and act upon things in their absence. This representational ability is increasingly symbolic. It is a consequence of what Piaget calls *semiotic function*, the ability to use symbols or signifiers (things that stand for other things). The operation of semiotic function can be found in several activities, including deferred imitation, symbolic play, drawing, mental imagery, and language.

The availability of semiotic function has several advantages over sensorimotor functioning. First sensorimotor intelligence is limited to the speed at which activity can be performed. Through representation, preoperational children can exceed the limits of space and time to represent long action sequences rapidly. Second, sensorimotor functioning is limited to the here and now; representational ability frees thought from the immediacy. Third, sensorimotor intelligence proceeds in a linear fashion, from act to act. With the onset of representational ability, children can represent a series of objects or actions simultaneously (Piaget & Inhelder, 1969, p. 86).

Semiotic function itself is rooted in imitation and has its beginnings in early infancy. Infants assimilate gestures made by adults into their own schemes. If they have a scheme for the gesture, the scheme is activated and infants may repeat the gesture (Piaget & Inhelder, 1969, p. 55). Later in infancy, infants advance to a phase in which they imitate gestures that are new to them. These imitations are immediate replications of action patterns, although their imitation implies some internalized action scheme for a motor act. The evolution of symbolic activity is seen by Piaget (Piaget & Inhelder, 1969) as an advance from representations of actions (as in deferred imitation) to representations that are more symbolic and, hence, more closely aligned with thought (as in symbolic play, drawing, mental imagery, and language).

Deferred imitation represents a type of representation that is tied to the internalization of figural action patterns. It is present in children during the last half of the second year of life and involves the delayed imitation of overt action. A child may, for example, observe another throwing a temper tantrum; the following day the first child may throw a tantrum for the first time. The child has represented the actions observed and later incorporated this representation into his or her own behavior.

Clearly the rich fantasy life of the children engaged in symbolic play readily testifies to another level at which children's behavior becomes more symbolic. Preschool children create imaginary playmates, turn mud into tasty pies, or transform blocks of wood into buzzing, clacking, gyrating contraptions, symbolizing all kinds of things. Objects and actions are now used to represent other objects and events symbolically. Children place their hands under their heads to symbolize a pillow and close their eyes to symbolize sleep. Symbols are acquired as a consequence of generalizing assimilation. The child extends a set of schemes previously associated with one object (that which is signified) to another (the symbol), and thus the symbol attains meaning.

The development of mental imagery (another manifestation of semiotic function) occurs as children accommodate action schemes associated with objects and events. For example, Piaget believed that when we perceive something, a complex set of activities occurs; this may involve such processes as visually scanning the shape of an object and detecting the color, texture, and position of the object in space. Perception is an active process, and as a consequence of applying these perceptual schemes, we recognize things. As representational skills develop, individuals reinstate in some abbreviated form the various schemes that were used when the real object was present (Piaget & Inhelder, 1969). The internal activation of these abbreviated schemes constitutes the mental image (Ginsburg & Opper, 1969, p. 77).

One final, yet highly significant, manifestation of semiotic function is children's use of language. By the age of 2 years, children are clearly using language to refer to things not present. When a child says, "Mommy, want milk," he or she represents a wish for an object not present—an object has been signified by a word. It is important to note that language is but a manifestation of semiotic function and is not by itself responsible for representational ability that accompanies preoperational development. Language, however, is an important form of semiotic functioning. Unlike other symbols that children must create (images, drawings, and so on), language is a symbol system intact and one that is commonly used by an entire group of individuals. Consequently, language is a symbol system that can begin to socialize thought.

Limitations of intellectual ability.   Despite the appearance of semiotic function, the preoperational child's intellectual ability is limited. For example, children at this stage are unable to conserve—that is, to realize that the composition of an object does not change as a function of superficial changes in its appearance. Suppose that we were to show two balls of clay to a 4-year-old. Also suppose that the child initially judges the two balls to consist of equal amounts of clay. Next, and in full view, we flatten one of the clay balls, and again ask her if there are equal amounts of clay in the ball and the flattened mass. Curiously, we'd probably find that she no longer believes that they are equal— the child doesn't conserve substance.

In explaining children's reasoning on these tasks, Piaget found several logical deficiencies in preoperational children's thinking. One of these deficiencies is the child's inability to reverse the direction of thought. As adults we realize that if something can be subtracted from a quantity, then an equal amount can be added to it to regain the state in which it began. Likewise, we realize that if some substance is transformed, then an equal but opposite transformation can bring the substance back to its original appearance. Young children apparently don't appreciate this simple rule of logic.

Another deficiency in preoperational children's thought is in their inability to decenter. They have a tendency to focus their attention to one salient feature of the stimulus. Referring to the previous example, children at the preoperational level may attend to the height of the clay ball without simultaneously attending to its width (hence judging the flattened mass to contain less clay than the ball). These children apparently don't coordinate two dimensions at once.

Children's thought at this stage is also characterized by an attention to states rather than transformations leading to states. One might liken this limitation to the difference between a slide show and a motion picture. In the former, one is aware of only static, discrete states; in the latter, change and sequencing. In the conservation of substance problem, the visible transformation of the clay represents a dynamic sequence of events. An appreciation of the sequencing involved in the transformation provides evidence for the continuity of substance. For young children the beginning and end states of a transformation are seen as discrete and separate, rather than opposite ends of a continuum. As such, there exists in the mind of the child the possibility that the two masses of clay can indeed be different.

A final limitation on preoperational children's thought is egocentricity. Young children operate as if they are unaware that others may see something differently than they. These childen act as though their perceptions must be the same as everyone else's, and everyone else's the same as their own. Such a world view would obviously limit their willingness to alter their own perception or interpretation of the world. A young child viewing a scene may infer that another viewing from a different perspective sees an identical picture.

Whereas preoperational children are capable of symbolic representation, their intellectual structure doesn't reflect a knowledge about fundamental relationships existing within the external world. The gradual accommodation of schemes based on children's own actions and perceptions to those that are more decentered (that is, less egocentric and more general and abstract) frees children from a figural perception of reality to one that appreciates transformations and conservations (Piaget & Inhelder, 1969, pp. 92–97). This level of intelligence is found in the period of concrete operational thought and reveals in children's thinking a system of rules allowing them to discern relationships between elements and properties of objects in the physical world.

The Period of Concrete Operational Thought

The development of a rule-based system of thought is the hallmark of operational thought. Operations are internalized, reversible actions or rules, perhaps best thought of as mathematical functions (for example, combine ($+$), reverse ($-$), order ($<$), and substitute ($=$)). The period of concrete operational thought ranges from 7–12 years. Children's thought represents not only the ability to understand and use logical operators, but also the existence of groupings, or coordinated systems of internalized sets of reversible operations.

As an example, children at this stage demonstrate an ability to construct and manipulate class hierarchies. They can sort a set of objects into subcategories, appreciating the subordinate and superordinate relationships involved in classification. This ability is dependent upon the operation of one grouping (Grouping I), which allows children to (a) add classes together to obtain a higher order class of objects, (b) realize that a particular result can be obtained by grouping items in a number of different ways, (c) understand that nothing added to or taken away from something produces no change in the system, and (d) realize that for every element in the system, there is another element that cancels it out.

Although the intellectual structure is now rule based, its operation is limited to things that exist in the real world—tangible, concrete things. In this period, when children are presented with the conservation of substance problem, they judge mass to be unchanged despite superficial changes that occur in its appearance. However, when asked to reason about more abstract relationships (deriving a summary rule to explain why some objects float and others sink), their reasoning belies the degree to which their thought is tied to the physical world (they may explain that things float because they are light and others sink because they are heavy). Concrete operational children are, furthermore, baffled when confronted with contradictions in their arguments. They are unable to understand that other conclusions based upon observations not present in their experience are also possible. It isn't until the last stage of development that children's intelligence is structured so that a complete set of solutions to problems can be formulated and the truth of each systematically assessed.

The Period of Formal Operational Thought

As children, now adolescents, enter the stage of formal operational thought (12 years–adulthood), Piaget and Inhelder (1958) believed that their intellectual structure allows them to reason in an almost scientific manner. During the concrete operational period, children are able to reason about things encountered in the real world. But this reasoning is often unsystematic and incomplete. During the formal operational period, thought becomes characterized by an expanded set of rules that allows the individual to manipulate elements and operations so that all possible solutions to problems can be considered. Systematic tests can be constructed to evaluate hypotheses, and the results can be evaluated in such a fashion that conclusions drawn about relationships are true. (That is, the conclusions are both necessary and sufficient; there can be no other possible explanation of the phenomena considered.) These skills reflect the acquisition of an expanded set of logical operations (16, to be exact) that are more logical than mathematical in nature; that is, reasoning takes on the form of propositional logic rather than the mathematical quality that characterized operations during the concrete operational period. As with operations in the concrete operational period, these operations are believed to relate only two elements at a time. The possible combination of elements can be arrayed in the form of a truth table, indicating all possible results that might occur as a consequence of any pairing or combination of pairs (Table 3-1). This ability belies a hypothetical-deductive structure for testing events and, consequently, inferring relationships that exist between them.

Suppose that we were attempting to determine what factor or factors affect the speed at which a pendulum oscillates. We can isolate two factors: the length of the pendulum (long, and short) and the weight (heavy, and light). There are obviously four possible combinations of length and weight that will produce one of two outcomes; either the pendulum will swing fast or slow. Having derived the set of all possible combinations of elements and outcomes, we can arrange an experiment to test the truth of the propositions that have been elaborated, and, consequently, we can infer the relationship between the two elements. As seen in Table 3-1, the length of the pendulum is the necessary and sufficient condition affecting the oscillation of the pendulum.

In addition to the 16 logical operations that are available to adolescents, another set of operations known as the INCR group (identity, negation, correlativity, and reciprocity) also structures their thought. The presence of this group allows adolescents to manipulate the conclusions drawn from experiments, or to operate upon operations. As illustrated in Chapter 1, adolescents can derive the law of inertia only after isolating those factors that are responsible for bringing a moving object to rest (a moving object slows because of gravity or friction or other related factors). By applying the rule of negation

TABLE 3-1. A Truth Table: The Pendulum Swing Experiment.

Length of pendulum	Weight of fob	Possible outcome: Rate of swing	Truth value of the proposition
long	heavy	fast	false
long	light	fast	false
long	heavy	slow	true
long	light	slow	true
short	heavy	fast	true
short	light	fast	true
short	heavy	slow	false
short	light	slow	false

(*Adapted from Ginsburg & Opper, 1969*)

(that is, by altering the relationship that has already been discovered), one reverses all of the elements and operations of the original proposition and thereby derives the law in question (in the presence of no gravity, no friction, and none of the other related factors, an object will move perpetually).

NEO-PIAGETIAN POSITIONS

It is the nature of scientists to rework useful theories. Piaget's theory has certainly been a powerful tool; however, as is typical of most theories under constant scrutiny, a number of criticisms developed. One criticism leveled at the Piagetian approach is that it describes in rich detail the quality of children's thought, but fails to explain how these changes in structure evolve (Flavell & Wohlwill, 1969; Ginsburg & Opper, 1969). Although Piaget discussed the mechanism of adaptation as the process that accounts for development, his most explicit statements on this matter focused on development within the sensorimotor period (Piaget, 1963). He was less specific about how this process operates to advance development between stages. As such, Piaget is generally credited with a theory of development that richly describes the quality of thought within stages but neglects to specify how development from lower to higher stages occurs.

Piagetian theory is also predicated on the assumption that intellectual structure organizes thought. Intellectual structure, then, should have a pervasive influence over the manner in which children interpret any task or situation. Actually, it has been found that there is much asynchrony in development; this is quite the opposite of the synchronous development that Piagetian theory predicts across tasks tapping common operations (Brainerd, 1978a). Piaget recognized this unevenness in development and introduced the concept of *horizontal décalage* to describe it but the term is largely descriptive rather than explanatory.

Largely in response to these two basic criticisms (failures to account for developmental transitions and horizontal décalage) a neo-Piagetian position has developed. The neo-Piagetian position attempts to (a) predict developmental sequences; (b) explain, rather than describe, the developmental process; and (c) to account for the asynchronies that are found in the developmental process.

Characteristic of these neo-Piagetian positions is the postulation of an executive system (some higher level set of schemes or skills that govern the process by which the subject uses information) and the specification of age-related restrictions on processing capacity (Case, 1974; Pascual-Leone, 1970, 1980). In addition, individual difference variables are taken into consideration when behavioral predictions are made. Specifically, the theory suggests that one's information-processing capacity (or M-power) increases proportionally with age (Table 3-2). During a problem-solving task, an invariant amount of processing space is occupied by information, which must be available to the individual, about what is to be done and how the task is to be accomplished (this space is designated by some constant e). In addition to space that must

TABLE 3-2.   M-Power as a Function of Age and Developmental Stage.

Age (years)	Developmental substage	M-power
3 – 4	Early preoperations	$e + 1$
5 – 6	Late preoperations	$e + 2$
7 – 8	Early concrete operations	$e + 3$
9 – 10	Middle concrete operations	$e + 4$
11 – 12	Late concrete—Early formal operations	$e + 5$
13 – 14	Middle formal operations	$e + 6$
15 – 16	Late formal operations	$e + 7$

(*Adapted from Case, 1974*)

be allocated to an executive scheme, an additional amount of space must be available for elements that define the problem (information about relationships between states of objects and transformations effected on objects). All tasks can be characterized by the number of elements that must be manipulated and coordinated if a problem is to be solved. Obviously, if the child's capacity limitation is exceeded by the number of elements that must be coordinated, the child will fail the task. But even for children whose central processing capacity exceeds the number of elements that must be manipulated, performance may be imperfect due to individual differences. That is, some children habitually fail to use their maximum capacity. More will be said about these neo-Piagetian theories in Chapter 9; for the present we will say only that these theorists, while maintaining the developmental and qualitative flavor of Piaget's theory, have redefined a few of Piaget's basic concepts to make a more functional theory.

SUMMARY

Piaget's theory of cognitive development emphasizes the role of both maturation and learning. The organism is predisposed to develop in a preplanned sequence that is under genetic control. In order for children to develop, they must have the opportunity to interact with the environment, because it is through this interaction that they construct knowledge about reality.

During the first stage of development, the sensorimotor period, children construct a knowledge about the basic properties of their world—a knowledge of objects, time, space, and causality. Knowledge about the world during this stage is primarily perceptual. Things are known as they are experienced. Toward the end of the second year of life, children begin to reveal a new way of thinking that reflects children's ability to represent objects, people, and events in their absence. This representational ability marks entry into a second stage of development known as the preoperational period. Although representational thought is clearly an advance over the experiential-based reasoning which characterized the sensorimotor period, preoperational children lack a rule-based system of thought that would allow them to manipulate the content of their thoughts. Consequently these children continue to be swayed by the appearance of things. Thought, though freed from direct experience, is nonetheless influenced by perception.

By about 7 years of age, children begin to reason about object properties and relationships between objects in such a way as to reveal the development of a system of rules or operations. In spite of illusory transformations in the appearance of objects, concrete operational children make judgments about reality using these rules. With the attainment of formal operational thought in early adolescence, children elaborate a more complete set of operations and acquire the ability to manipulate the operations themselves. Thus, they acquire the capacity for more systematic, abstract, and flexible reasoning.

As a reaction to criticisms leveled at Piaget's theory, specifically with respect to the issue of horizontal décalage and the lack of specifications about the mechanisms responsible for development from one stage to the next, a number of psychologists, referred to as neo-Piagetians, have modified Piaget's theory. The modification has introduced the notion of age-related changes in system capacity, individual difference factors, and executive functions. These modifications have extended the range of phenomena that can be explained by developmental theory while retaining the developmental flavor and many of the concepts found in Piaget's theory.

4

An Information-Processing Account of Perceptual Development

As information users, we attempt to make sense of our experience from moment to moment. This analysis is predicated upon the availability of a variety of sensory information. We humans process information through five major senses: audition, vision, gustation (taste), olfaction (smell), and the cutaneous senses (pressure, pain, and temperature). Two other types of information are also experienced—kinesthetic (the position or location of our various body parts) and vestibular (the position of the body in three-dimensional space). Although the latter are often referred to as the minor senses, they are minor only insofar as we are often unaware of them. We rely most heavily on visual and auditory information for our survival. Consequently, the remainder of this chapter will focus on sensation and perception within these two modalities.

THE VISUAL AND AUDITORY SENSES

Our sense of vision occurs as light waves, varying in intensity and frequency register on light-sensitive receptor cells in the anterior portion of the inner eye (Figure 4-1). More specifically, light enters the eye through the cornea (the clear transparent outer covering of the eye), passes through the pupil (the opening created by the expansion of the iris), and passes through the lens (a clear, disk-shaped mass of tissue that can be flattened or bulged through the tensing of ciliary muscles attached at its edge). From the lens, light passes through the aqueous humor (the fluid filling the inner portion of the eye) and strikes the inner layer of the eye called the retina. The retina is composed of two types of receptor cells, rods and cones. The cones work primarily at high light intensity and allow for sharp, color vision; rods function under low light intensity and provide us with a colorless, blurred vision. Although rods and cones are found throughout the retina, the greatest concentration of cones occurs in the fovea (a small portion of the retina upon which the incoming visual image is projected). When stimulated, cells in the retina discharge a neural message that is transmitted along the optic nerve to the visual cortex in the anterior portion of the brain.

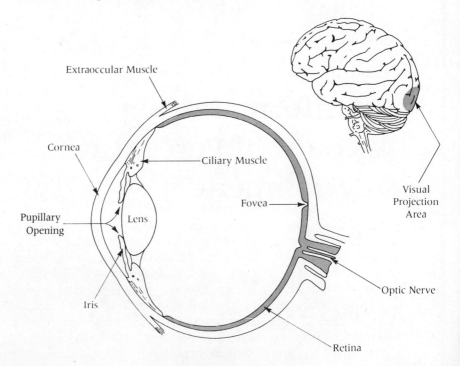

Figure 4-1. Anatomy of the eye.

At birth, the eye is structurally ready to differentiate all aspects of light energy, but the immaturity of the visual system limits the neonate's, or newborn's, visual ability. For example, the cornea is more spherical and the eyeball shorter than it is in the adult, producing hyperopia or farsightedness (Allik & Valsiner, 1980; Spears & Hohle, 1967). Hyperopia persists until approximately 6 years of age, when the eyeball begins to elongate, reaching its adult configuration by approximately 12 years of age (Spears & Hohle, 1967).

The tendency toward hyperopia is compensated by the accommodation (the adjustment in shape) of the lens. This accommodation, however, is controlled by the ciliary muscles, which are not completely matured until about the fourth month of life. Because neonates can't alter the shape of the lens, they have a fixed focal point (the place where vision is sharpest) about 20 cm from the eye.

The neonate's eye is immature in a number of other respects. For instance, the retina is not completely differentiated. Cone cells in particular are not fully dispersed and may not be until about 4 months of age; consequently, the fovea is underdeveloped for the first few months of life. The optic nerve is not entirely myelinated (coated by a fatty sheath), and the infant does not have full control over the extraoccular muscles, which move the eyes in their orbits.

Although neonates respond to the various dimensions of light energy (frequency and amplitude), the immaturity of their visual system likely alters the quality of information available to them. Although they are sensitive to brightness (the psychological sensation arising as a function of the amplitude of the light wave), pupillary constriction and dilation to changes in brightness are sluggish. Infants also respond to color (the psychological sensation arising from the frequency of the light wave), but they don't show the same spectral sensitivity as adults (Bornstein, 1978; Spears & Hohle, 1967). Because of foveal immaturity, poor binocular coordination, the shape of the cornea, and the inability to accommodate the lens, visual acuity (or sharpness of vision) is also poor. Estimates of visual acuity range from 20/850 to 20/150 (Reese & Lipsitt, 1970; Spears & Hohle, 1967). Another way of saying this is that, at best, infants see at 20 feet what the typical adult observer can see at 150 feet.

Despite these early limitations, the maturation of the visual system is quite rapid and likely facilitated by experience with the lighted world. Within four to six months following birth, the visual system develops to a point that the type of sensory information available to infants is roughly the same as that available to adults (Cohen, DeLoache, & Strauss, 1978).

The sensation of sound occurs following a variety of energy transformations effected by various components of the ear (Figure 4-2). Sound waves varying in frequency and amplitude enter the external auditory canal and strike the eardrum, causing it to vibrate. These vibrations set in motion three small bones (the ossicles) in the middle ear, which vibrate against the oval window. The oval window connects with the cochlea, a spiral-shaped cavity in the skull filled with fluid and lined with hairlike auditory receptor cells. As the oval window vibrates, it sets in motion a wave pattern that ripples through the cochleal fluid, stimulating specific receptor cells, causing them to fire and send

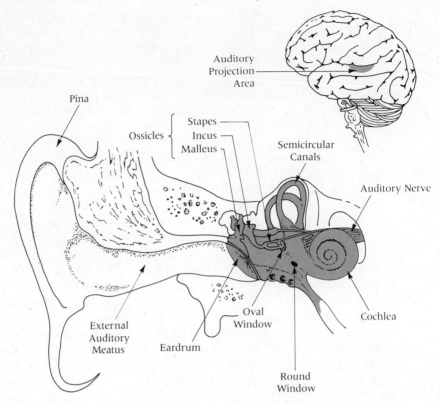

Figure 4-2. Anatomy of the ear.

a neural message through the auditory nerve to the auditory cortex of the brain.

The cochlea is fully developed and enervated four months prior to birth (Northern & Downs, 1974); thus, at birth the auditory system is anatomically complete and functional. A fluid, however, fills the middle ear, reducing the efficiency with which acoustical energy is transmitted from the outer to the inner ear. This obstruction produces a conduction hearing loss of about 40 dB (or what an adult might sense if hearing with a bad head cold). Within the first few weeks of life, this fluid is resorbed into the surrounding tissue or drained through the eustachian tube. As might be expected from this description, with some amplification newborns are sensitive to the various properties of sound (Stratton & Connolly, 1973).

Although only the integrity of the visual and auditory systems have been discussed, the other senses are also well developed at birth (Reese & Lipsitt, 1970). Since human infants have access to a wide variety of sensory information, we may begin to consider what they make of it; that is, what do they perceive?

In keeping with the general plan of this text, this question will be approached from both an information-processing and a Piagetian perspective (Chapter 5).

As will be apparent through the course of this chapter, the information-processing approach to perception typically takes an exteroceptive orientation; that is, attention is directed to what it is about the external world that is perceived by the child. This approach presumes that the external world can be characterized by a number of features or attributes and that it is the child's task to use that information in some meaningful manner.

Those of you who've had the opportunity to observe and interact with young infants have probably paused to wonder what they make of their experience. In lay conversations with parents we hear many claims for the neonate and infants' perceptual acumen. Some parents, for example, report that they are recognized by their infant within the first month of life. A little thought will reveal how remarkable this feat would be. The recognition of another is a rather complex task, requiring a variety of knowledge. Infants would need to differentiate themselves from other things in their environment, differentiate humans from other objects, and differentiate specific humans on the basis of subtle variations in face, posture, body shape, and voice pattern (cf. Yarrow, 1972).

Parents, understandably, are not the most objective students of their infants' behavior; their reports are often tainted by the pride of parenthood. The question of what infants perceive is nonetheless valid. Its answer has important implications for the types of experiences that we might want either to provide infants (should we attempt to teach infants to read?) or to avoid (early maternal separation or neonatal isolation). Many students of newborns are coming to characterize the neonate as arriving in this world in an information-hungry state. Much like a radio scanner, infants seem to sweep their surroundings for information to process (Haith, 1980; Haith & Goodman, 1982). Some of this information appears to be immediately organized and responded to in a meaningful manner, but much of the meaning given to experience awaits further learning and/or maturation.

METHODOLOGY

Prior to considering further the perceptual abilities of infants, it might be profitable to consider how researchers study infant perception. The task is a difficult one for it consists of asking nonverbal organisms a question about what they prefer and recognize as meaningful within their environment. Methods that capitalize on a range of neonatal responses and behavioral tendencies have been developed to study infant perception. Since the neonate and young infant can't communicate verbally, we must communicate nonverbally. The methods developed to communicate with young infants are quite varied.

Some researchers have used physiological measures to assess perceptual and sensory ability. In this technique indices such as electrical activity in the brain or in specific receptor cells, respiration and heart rate, and other physiological processes are monitored in the presence or absence of specific stimulus events. From changes in these indices relative to some baseline (a period of normal responding), we can judge whether the infant has perceived a change in the stimulus condition. From the nature or direction of change, inferences are sometimes drawn about the infant's perception of the event (that is, his or her psychological experience).

Other researchers have relied upon a procedure whereby eye movement or scanning patterns are recorded by sophisticated monitoring devices. Using these techniques, we can gain precise information about what infants look at; however, as with physiological measures, we can only infer what infants know about what they have seen.

There are other techniques that ostensibly allow us to understand how infants interpret their experiences. These techniques involve comparisons of responses made to sets of stimuli. In one technique introduced by Bower (1966), infants are trained to make an operant response to a conditioned stimulus. For example, they may be trained to make a head turn to a 1-m cube presented 3-m away. If a head turn is made when the cube (the conditioned stimulus) is present, the infant is rewarded. If the infant doesn't turn his or her head when the conditioned stimulus is shown, a head turn is elicited by stroking the infant's cheek, which is again followed by reinforcement. After the infant reliably makes an operant response (the head turn) in the presence of the conditioned stimulus, a set of test conditions are introduced; these involve totally new stimuli or the original conditioned stimulus, presented at different orientations or distances to the infant. A head turn to any of the test stimuli reveals that the infant has recognized it as the same as the conditioned stimulus, the object to which the infant has been trained to turn his or her head.

Perhaps the most common techniques for studying the perceptual abilities of infants are the fixation and habituation paradigms. In the *fixation paradigm* we measure the amount of time that infants spend looking at visual targets or listening to auditory stimuli. It is assumed that infants will spend more time looking at or listening to something they find interesting. In this paradigm, stimuli may be presented either individually or in pairs. When pairs are presented, differences in the amount of time looking at one stimulus versus the other indicates not only that infants detect differences between the two, but also presumably that they prefer one over the other.

A variation of this procedure is the *habituation paradigm*. Habituation is a decline in response rate to a stimulus following its repeated presentation. It is presumed that if infants have habituated to one target and another is presented in its place, an increase in responding or renewed interest (dishabituation) shows that children recognize the second stimulus as different from the first.

VISUAL PATTERN PERCEPTION

Work by European ethologists such as Lorenz (1965) showed that many animal species are predisposed at birth to respond to certain stimulus patterns with species-specific behavioral and psychological responses. The greylag geese, for example, are innately predisposed to respond with escape behavior and distress to the shadow of a hawk, a natural predator of theirs. From this research it is tempting to extrapolate to the human experience. That is, are there certain stimulus patterns that we humans find more meaningful than others in our early lives?

There are actually many kinds of patterns that adults find meaningful. Some of these patterns are fixed, relatively invariant features of our environment—for example, contours and shapes of objects or predictably arranged patterns of features, as with the human face. Other patterns are more fluid, but nonetheless recognizable. We recognize the activity someone is performing by his or her body posture, movement, and facial expression. It may be that these movement patterns are some of the earliest patterns that infants recognize. Their recognition would seem to facilitate the dichotomization of the world into a dimension of animate and inanimate objects, and perhaps even facilitate the development of a concept of self.

Animate and Inanimate Objects

One of the more immediate tasks confronting newborns is to distinguish between animate and inanimate things in their environment (Gelman & Spelke, 1981; Yarrow, 1972). The recognition that some things are animate while others are not has obvious adaptive value. Animate objects can do things for infants; inanimate ones can't.

Do young infants acknowledge the difference between animate and inanimate objects? There is some reason to believe that they do. Fox and McDaniels (1982) believe that young infants have an innate ability to detect movement patterns that are typical of human organisms, although this ability is not demonstrated until approximately 4 months of age. To examine this phenomenon, they placed small lights at the joints of a human form running in place and performing other activities. These dot patterns were recorded on videotape. The tape, showing biological movement, and another, of randomly moving dots, were shown to infants of 2, 4, and 6 months of age. Fox and McDaniels found that the 4- and 6-month-olds preferred to look at the dot patterns depicting biological movement. They reasoned that their failure to find an interest in biological movement by younger infants may be due to the immaturity of their visual system.

The ability to detect motion patterns that are typical of animate objects is important to the development of a knowledge about animate and inanimate things. But, in addition to appreciating movement patterns typical of living beings, we must also learn to anticipate certain kinds of behaviors from animate objects. Animate things act volitionally. Consequently animate things can take on agency roles—they can do things. Inanimate objects are disposed to recipient roles; they are the things on which agents act. Apparently the agent–recipient role of animate and inanimate objects is relatively well established by 2 years of age. Two-year-old children react with surprise when a chair appears to move on its own, but not if it is moved by a person (Golinkoff & Harding, 1980). Younger infants are less likely to show such surprise (Golinkoff & Kerr, 1978). Children apparently need time to categorize objects as animate and inanimate and to develop expectancies about how those objects should act.

Although more sophisticated knowledge about the animate properties of certain objects comes later in infancy, knowledge about the animate properties of specific objects (for example, human figures) may be acquired at a much earlier age. Very young infants, for example, show distress when confronted with an impassive and unresponsive human figure. It would even seem that young infants expect an interactive response from the human form (Trevarthen, 1977). Although there isn't complete agreement about when infants acquire these expectancies about human forms, it is likely that this understanding is developed by at least 4 months of age (Walker, 1982).

One consequence of detecting reliable and predictable patterns of movement may be the development of self-knowledge—the recognition of the self as a special entity within one's surroundings. Several researchers (Damon & Hart, 1982; Lewis & Brooks-Gunn, 1979) report that by 3 months of age infants begin to respond differentially to their own images in a mirror or as they see themselves live on a television screen. Mirror images or live video images always move contingently with one's movement. Infants presented with contingent and noncontingent moving images preferred to look at those that moved contingently. Apparently infants recognize that they are the source or cause of the contingently moving images, reflecting a rudimentary self-awareness.

Knowledge about other patterns of features also develops by about 4 months of age. Actually infants discriminate patterned stimuli much earlier than this. For example, complex patterns or those with high contrasts are preferred over others (Banks & Salapatek, 1981; Nunnally & Lemond, 1973). However, evidence for an awareness that certain patterns have specific functions or meaning doesn't appear until approximately 3 or 4 months of age.

The Human Face

Some of the most intriguing work in pattern perception research has studied infants' response to the human face. Early studies suggested that within the first few months of life, infants have definite preference for facial patterns (Fantz, 1963). From this research came the idea that infants might be innately predisposed to find the human face interesting and meaningful. Such a conclusion is appealing, since such preferences would facilitate attachment and socialization (Yarrow, 1972).

Although these early studies provided fodder for speculation about innate pattern recognition, they didn't necessarily support the unambiguous conclusion that human faces *per se* are any more interesting or meaningful to infants than other kinds of complex pattern stimuli. The human face, after all, is a complex set of features organized in a vertically symmetrical fashion. Is it some dimension other than facialness that infants find interesting? In an attempt to answer an aspect of this question, Haaf and his colleagues (Haaf, 1977,

1974; Haaf & Bell, 1967; Haaf & Brown, 1976; Haaf, Smith, & Smitley, 1983) have systematically compared the dimension of facialness (the degree to which patterned stimuli resembles the human face) and complexity (the number of features in patterned stimuli) in infants' preference for visual stimuli. In their procedure, infants are shown one of four stimulus patterns (Figure 4-3), which vary in the degree to which they maintain facialness or vary in complexity. If infants are responding to the facialness of the targets, they should spend more time looking at stimuli that resemble the face (stimulus A) than other stimuli (B, C, and D). On the other hand, if complexity is the dimension that infants respond to, a different pattern of results should obtain (more time spent looking at stimulus B than D, A, and C). Haaf has shown that children 15 weeks of age and older do prefer to gaze at those stimuli that bear a resemblance to the human face; however, preferences prior to 15 weeks of age seem determined by the complexity of the stimulus alone.

Another dimension of facialness once suspected of eliciting infants' interest

Stimulus	Degree of Facialness	Amount of Detail	% Fixation Time
A	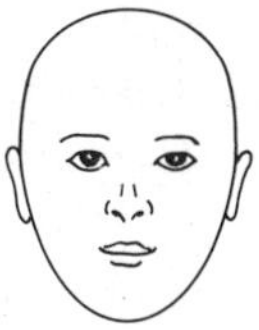 1	3	.33
B	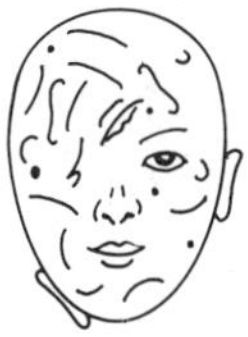 2	1	.28
C	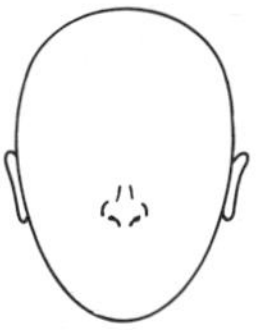 3	4	.19
D	 4	2	.20

Figure 4-3. The experimental stimuli, rank orderings of stimulus characteristics, and mean percentage fixation time scores for 36 Ss. *(Haaf & Bell, 1967)*

is vertical symmetry. Using an habituation–dishabituation paradigm, however, Maurer and Barrera (1981) found no preferences for faces prior to 2 months of age. These infants also did not discriminate facial from other symmetrical or asymmetrical patterns. Research shows that infants discriminate symmetrical patterns after 3 months of age, but they don't prefer vertically symmetrical arrangements until after 12 months of age (Bornstein, Ferdinandsen, & Gross, 1981; Fisher, Ferdinandsen, & Bornstein, 1981). Other research using a combination of physiological indices, fixation time, and facial expressions of interest measures support the idea that by 2 months of age infants are more interested in real human faces compared to mannequins, which are preferred to nonhuman forms (Langsdorf, Izard, Rayias, & Hembree, 1983).

The failure to find responses to facial patterns prior to 2 months of age may be due to the manner in which infants scan visual targets. When shown stationary targets, for example, infants tend to direct their gaze to the periphery of an object or to areas of high contrast (for example, the hairline); thus, they are insensitive to information within the target itself (Banks & Salapatek, 1981; Maurer & Salapatek, 1976; Salapatek & Kessen, 1966). By at least 3 months of age, infants systematically scan the interior of targets, and at the same time, they begin to discriminate subtle differences between human facial patterns. For instance, they have the ability to make discriminations between individual faces and even facial expressions (Barrera & Maurer, 1981a,b; Cohen, DeLoache, & Strauss, 1978). In one study Cohn and Tronick (1983) had mothers interact normally with their 3-month-old infants or to simulate a depressed mood state. Infants not only responded differentially to the two mood states, but their behavior in each maternal mood state was qualitatively distinct. When mothers were affecting a positive mood, infants spent more of their time looking at their mothers in playful interaction. When mothers affected a negative mood, infants became more negative in their interaction, showing strong protests and wariness. Not only did these infants discriminate between sad and happy faces, their response implied a meaningful interpretation of the expression seen.

The research discussed thus far shows that very early in life infants find particular stimulus patterns more appealing than others. Complex patterns and those having high contrast gradients capture the young infants' attention. It would, however, be misleading to suggest that young infants recognize these patterns as meaningful. At birth, infants may be biologically predisposed to attend to specific aspects of their visual world, but due to immaturity of the visual system, it is likely that infants don't attend to a large amount of visual information. At least by 2 months of age, the visual system has developed to the point that infants are processing a wide variety of visual information and have begun to interpret some of this information in a psychologically meaningful manner. Infants begin to discriminate faces from other patterned stimuli, and by 3 and 4 months of age begin to anticipate that human figures should behave in some predictable fashion. Within the brief span of 4 months, infants become rather sophisticated connoisseurs of their visual experience.

VISUAL CONSTANCIES

If we are to use visual information effectively, we need to appreciate not just pattern information, but also how objects in our visual field appear at varying distances and orientations. The information we receive about objects in our visual field shows them to vary as a function of their distance (far objects project a smaller retinal image than near objects) and their orientation to us (an object seen from the side projects a different retinal image than the same object viewed from the front). Although objects and people project different retinal images depending upon their distance and orientation, we realize that they maintain a constant size and shape—we experience their constancy. Experiencing visual constancy has an obvious advantage to limited capacity, information-processing systems like ourselves. Its experience reduces the amount of information we must remember. If we didn't experience visual constancy, we'd have to learn an infinite amount of information about how individual objects look at different angles and distances. Fortunately, at a relatively early age, infants also realize that objects maintain a constancy of shape and size. Both habituation and conditioning procedures have shown reliable shape constancy by 2 to 3 months of life (Bower, 1966a; Caron, Caron, & Carlson, 1979; Day & McKenzie, 1973). Research that has examined infants' appreciation of size constancy places the attainment of this knowledge somewhat later. Using a conditioning technique, Bower (1974) reported infants experiencing size constancy by 2 or 3 months of age; although, tests conducted with the habituation paradigm haven't found evidence for size constancy prior to 4½ months of age (Day & McKenzie, 1981; McKenzie, Tootle, & Day, 1980).

Depth Perception

Related to the work in size constancy is that which has examined depth perception in infants. (Many of the cues that allow us to detect size are also important in the perception of depth.) This work has generally supported the idea that depth is experienced very early in an infant's life, although the interpretation of depth cues may change with age.

Some of the earliest work in children's depth perception was reported by Walk and Gibson (1961). Their research examined the response of animals to a visual cliff (Figure 4-4), a "swimming pool"-like device with a shallow and a deep side. The surface of the pool is made of clear glass with an opaque centerboard dividing the deep and shallow sides. The sides and bottom of the cliff are covered with a checkerboard pattern to accentuate cues for depth. Walk and Gibson found that the young of most species (including human infants between 9 and 12 months of age) responded to depth cues, showing distress when placed over the deep side of the cliff.

Evidence of depth perception is also found in very young infants. Campos, Langer, and Krowitz (1970) found that infants as young as 1½ months of age discriminated between the deep and shallow sides of the cliff. To assess depth perception in these infants, their heart rates were monitored as they lay on their backs. They were then placed face down on either the deep or the shallow

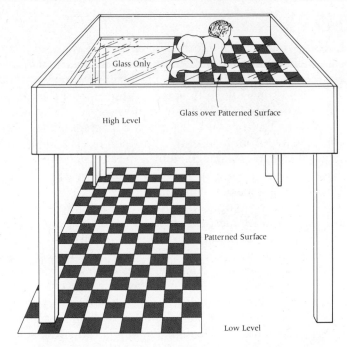

Figure 4-4. The visual cliff and apparatus. *(Walk & Gisbon, 1961)*

side of the cliff and any changes in their heart rate recorded. Both 1½-month-old and 3½-month-old infants showed a decline in heart rate to the deep side of the cliff. Younger, but not older, infants showed an increase in heart rate to the shallow side. The differential responding to shallow and deep sides of the visual cliff shows that these infants did recognize differences in depth, although the direction of heart rate change is curious. Heart rate deceleration is commonly associated with an orienting response (implying that infants were quieting themselves to attend to more information); on the other hand, heart rate acceleration is associated with a defensive response. It may be that these infants found the deep side of the cliff interesting, while the younger infants found the shallow side threatening. Infants may perceive depth early in life, but their psychological response to depth may change with age (Campos, Hiatt, Ramsey, Henderson, & Svejda, 1978; Schwartz, Campos, & Baisel, 1973).

Binocular and Motion Parallax

There are many cues that give rise to the perception of depth (for example, the convergence of parallel lines on the horizon, textural cues, and shading). We rely upon two primary cues: binocular parallax and motion parallax (Bower, 1966b). *Binocular parallax* occurs as a consequence of having two eyes set slightly apart. As such we receive information from our two eyes from slightly different angles. The integrated images of these two perspectives give rise to a three-dimensional image or the experience of depth.

Motion parallax is experienced as we move about—near objects move faster than far ones. This phenomenon is apparent while traveling. We see fence posts in the foreground zip by in a blur while a farmhouse on the horizon moves very slowly out of view.

From studies of infants' response to binocular and motion parallax, we find that they too rely upon motion parallax as a primary cue for depth. Walk (1968) tested infants' reaction to the visual cliff when both eyes were open (allowing for binocular cues) and when one eye was covered (allowing only for motion parallactic cues). He found that even when infants (9 to 10 months of age) were deprived of binocular cues, they continued to avoid the deep side of the cliff. Motion parallax, it would seem, is a sufficient cue for depth perception in older infants, and similar conclusions have been drawn by Bower (1966) in testing for depth perception in 2-month-old infants.

Even though young infants experience depth, there is also evidence that the ability to use depth cues improves with age. Walk (1978) believes that the ability to perceive depth may be innate, although experience modifies and improves this basic ability. Noting developmental improvement in infants' ability to respond to the absolute depth of a cliff (older infants perceive shallow depths better than younger infants), Walk concluded that with age infants are better able to use motion parallactic cues. Other research suggests that the ability to profit from motion parallactic cues continues to improve throughout childhood, perhaps up to the age of 12 years (Carpenter, 1979; Degelman & Rosinski, 1979).

PART VERSUS WHOLE PERCEPTION

Reflecting the direction of early Gestalt research, a long-disputed issue in perception has been whether or not things are perceived as organized wholes or as collections of component parts. In their review of this literature, Reese and Lipsitt (1970) concluded that it depends upon the nature of the stimuli. If the figure is very complex or poorly defined, then children will favor part processing. On the other hand, if the figure is simple or well defined, whole processing is favored. More recent research on this issue also suggests that individual differences affect children's part–whole perception.

Zelniker (Zelniker & Jeffrey, 1976; Zelniker, Renan, Sorer, & Shavit, 1977), for example, examined the perceptual styles of children who are impulsive (prone to rapid responding) and reflective (more deliberate in their responding). Zelniker maintains that impulsive children are prone to attend to the individual components or parts of a stimulus field more so than reflective children. To support their position, Zelniker et al. (1977) had impulsive and reflective children in the second grade solve Twenty Questions problems. The children were given sets of pictures that could be grouped along a number of dimensions. The task (as it always is in the Twenty Questions game) was to find the picture that the experimenter was thinking about with as few guesses as possible. The experimenters asked the children to sort the pictures into as many categories as they wished. Then the children asked if the designated picture might be in one of the piles. After feedback, children were allowed to resort their groupings, if they wished, and to guess again which pile the card might be in. Children proceeded in this manner until the problem was solved. It was reasoned that if the impulsive children were attending to a greater number of parts or components of the stimulus set than reflectives, then they would also sort the stimulus set into more piles on the first sort; this was in fact found.

Research with young infants also shows that, like older children, they too are capable of whole processing (Haith, 1980, Experiments 4 & 5; Milewski, 1979). But again stimulus factors influence perception. In a series of experiments by Schwartz and Day (1979) it was observed that infants based their form or shape recognition on relationships between the components of a simple figure rather than the individual components that constituted the item. In one experiment (Experiment 6), for example, 5-month-old infants were repeatedly shown a triangular shape. Following habituation to the shape, a series of test patterns were introduced (Figure 4-5). If sides or corners (that is, the components of the shape) were missing (as in patterns B and C), a significant amount of dishabituation occurred, implying that infants perceived these new patterns as different from the first. When pattern D was shown, which implied the shape of the object by virtue of the functional relationship

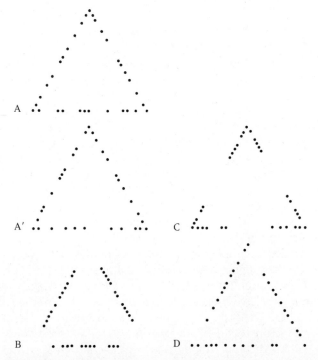

Figure 4-5. Set of incomplete triangles. *(Schwartz & Day, 1979)*

existing between the position of the three lines, no dishabituation occurred. It would seem that infants saw the last pattern as the same as the first, providing evidence for whole, rather than part, processing (also see Bertenthal, Campos, & Haith, 1980). However, a response to the stimulus as a whole figure depends upon the complexity of the form or shape. As found with older children, when figures are more complex, whole processing is also abandoned by infants (Schwartz & Day, 1979, Experiment 3).

AUDITORY PERCEPTION

Earlier we observed that, unlike the visual system, the auditory system is anatomically well developed and fully functional prior to birth. Given the maturity of the auditory system and prenatal experience with sound, we may expect that young infants would demonstrate a relatively well-developed knowledge of sound stimuli, and they do. Infants discriminate the varied and complex features of their auditory environment. They discriminate not only frequency and amplitude, but also tonal patterns (Bartoshuk, 1962). They are sensitive to the rearrangement of notes within a series (Melson & McCall, 1970), and the pitch at which sounds are presented (Kessen, Levine, & Wendrich, 1979). Other work shows that they are sensitive to the temporal characteristics of sound patterns. Chang and Trehub (1977), for example, monitored the heart rate of 4-month-old infants as a series of six tones were presented. The tones were grouped into a pattern of two tones, a slight pause, followed by the last four tones. After heart rate habituation to this series, a new pattern was presented. Significant dishabituation occurred in response to the new temporal grouping, providing evidence that these infants had perceived the temporal regularities of tones. Although young infants can discriminate temporal regularities of auditory stimuli, this ability improves with age. Davis and McCroskey (1980), for example, found developmental improvement (up to 8 years of age) in the ability to detect fine differences in the separation of tones.

The ability to discriminate differences between tonal and temporal patterns of stimuli would seem prerequisite to discriminating speech sounds. As these abilities have been demonstrated in young infants, it should come as little surprise that infants are also capable of making very fine discriminations between speech sounds or phonemes (Aslin, Pisoni, Hennessy, & Perey, 1981; Bower, 1974; Eimas, Siqueland, Jusczyk, & Vigorito, 1971) and the pitch of phonemic patterns (Eimas & Miller, 1980; Miller & Eimas, 1979). Eimas et al. (1971), for example, trained 1-month-old infants to suck on a nipple in order to turn on a tape recording of the sound "pa, pa, pa . . ." After the children had habituated to the recording, a new sound ("ba, ba, ba . . .") was played. With the phonemic change from a voiced (*p*) to an unvoiced (*b*) stop consonant, there was a dishabituation in children's rate of sucking, demonstrating their detection of the difference between the two phonemes. Similar findings have been obtained with Japanese infants in the discrimination of the (*l*) and (*r*) phonemes, phonemes that are easily confused by Japanese adults (Bower, 1977, p. 134.).

When discussing infants' preference for visual patterns, we saw that the human face is preferred by infants to other types of stimuli and responded to in a meaningful fashion by at least 3 or 4 months of age. A similar preference might also be postulated for particular kinds of auditory stimuli, specifically natural language. In fact, research on infant auditory perception supports the idea that natural language is inherently interesting to young infants (Hutt, Hutt, Lenard, Bernuth, & Muntjewerff, 1968). Several studies have reported that newborns are more responsive to a female voice than to other types of auditory stimuli (Freedman, 1971; Glenn, Cunningham, & Joyce, 1981; Kagan & Lewis, 1965).

Perhaps even more remarkable than data showing infantile preferences for vocal rather than nonvocal auditory stimuli is that which shows them to be responsive to even finer aspects of human speech patterns. Condon and Sander (1974) observed that while infants listen to adult speech, they seem to synchronize their body movements precisely to these sound patterns. Infants ranging in age from 12 hours to 12 weeks were filmed while listening to a variety of sounds including natural speech (both Chinese and English), disconnected vowel sounds, and rhythmical tapping sounds. Half of the infants were filmed with these sounds present and half when they were not. Naive observers rated two videotapes—one showing children responding in the presence of sounds, and another as they reacted in the absence of sounds but with the sound track from the first tape dubbed in.

Only infants actually exposed to sounds were observed coordinating their body movement with natural speech. If infants were moving when speech began, they immediately synchronized the movement of their head, arms, legs, and even toes and fingers to the speech pattern. A body movement would begin as a syllable began and stop when it ended. (We do this too. You might notice the next time you're talking with someone how you or the person you're talking with bobs his or her head, taps a foot, swings a leg or rocks the body in synchrony with the conversation.) Synchronies of body movement and sound occurred only for natural language; they didn't occur for disconnected vowel sounds or rhythmical tapping sounds. Neither was there any observed synchrony between body movement and the dubbed audio track, supporting the conclusion that these synchronies were real phenomena, not merely coincidental.

THE COORDINATION OF AUDITORY AND VISUAL PERCEPTION

Despite the precocity that seems to characterize the young infants' ability to perceive their auditory and visual worlds, there is some question whether they are able to coordinate these two types of information in a meaningful fashion. An early study by Aronson and Rosenbloom (1971) has often been cited in support of the idea that a coordination of auditory and visual information occurs early in life. In their study Aronson and Rosenbloom had mothers talk to their 1-month-old infants. For some of the infants, the mother's voice came from a location near her, while for others the mother's voice was displaced to the mother's left or right. Children who received the displaced voice reportedly became more distressed, crying and fussing more than infants whose mother's voice was proximal to her. Other research has been critical of this study. In fact, replications under more rigorous experimental conditions have found no indication of distress in infants 1 to 7 months of age when the mother's voice was displaced (Condry, Halton, & Neisser, 1977; McGurk & Lewis, 1974).

One of the problems with the preceding research paradigm is that it requires a coordination of not only visual and auditory information, but also spatial information (something that is difficult for young infants, cf. Clifton, Morrongielo, Kullig, & Dowd, 1981). Other research that has observed infants' reactions to auditory and visual information when spatial information is held constant shows that infants as young as 3 months of age display more positive affect if both visual and auditory information are presented simultaneously (both a face and a voice are presented) compared to conditions where either visual or auditory information is presented alone (Broerse, Peltola, & Crassini, 1983). It would also appear that infants as young as 3 to 4 months of age detect and anticipate the pattern of movement in a talking face, detecting a regularity between speech sounds and facial movement (Mendelson & Ferland, 1982; Walker, 1982).

It would appear that at birth, or very shortly thereafter, infants meaningfully interpret their visual and auditory experience. Currently it appears that they coordinate their auditory and visual experience when these two information sources are presented in a naturally occurring context (for example, a talking face). As with other aspects of auditory and visual perception, the ability to coordinate auditory and visual information improves throughout childhood, especially for boys (Alexander, 1977).

THEORIES OF PERCEPTUAL DEVELOPMENT

The early part of this chapter has dwelled on what it is that children perceive. In addition to documenting the perceptual abilities of children, however, we would also like to explain them. How do children come to perceive the world as they do? In this regard, information-processing theorists have attempted to identify what is recognized in the external world. Do we learn to recognize things by their unique features—learning what specific properties give something its identity? Or do we recognize something if it shares attributes common to some idealized exemplar or prototype of a class of objects?

Differentiation Theory

One view of perceptual development, referred to as *differentiation theory* (Gibson, 1969) regards the physical world as rich and varied in features.* Perceptual development is believed to involve the discrimination of those features,

---

*Although E. J. Gibson's work is discussed under the information-processing approach, she has recently been openly critical of this approach to perception (cf. Gibson & Levin, 1979). Her more current work focuses upon infants' perception of invariant perceptual features and the adaptive value of such perception (Gibson, Owsley, & Johnston, 1978).

which allows us to distinguish among objects and things in our world. The assumption is made that things in the physical world are initially undifferentiated. With practice, however, we learn to detect features that distinguish sensory phenomena.

The importance of distinctive features in perception is both intuitively and empirically demonstrable. In order to call our attention to important terms or ideas, book editors italicize or print in boldface type. Students who are studying a chapter of a text highlight important passages with transparent colored ink. The purpose of all of these efforts is to make specific parts of the text more distinctive from other material, hence making them more discriminable. Empirically, it has been demonstrated that when "same–different" judgments are made to pairs of stimuli, discriminations are easier if there are a greater number of distinctive features separating the pairs of items. Highlighting distinguishing features or reducing the number of irrelevant and distracting features serves to enhance their discriminability.

There is good evidence that our perception of meaningful differences changes with age. In one classic experiment which demonstrated developmental changes in children's recognition of distinctive features, Gibson, Gibson, Pick, and Osser (1962) asked children to compare a set of stimuli to a standard. These stimuli consisted of the standards and transformations effected on them (Figure 4-6). Children ranging in age from 4 to 8 years of age were asked to compare each item in a stimulus set to a standard and select matching items.

Gibson and her colleagues found that not all of the transformations were noticed by children. Alterations in the figure's perspective were often judged to be identical to the standard. On the other hand, figures with parts separated or closed-in were almost always perceived as different from the standard. Shifts in perception were also found with age. Younger children tended not to perceive rotations or reversals; older children did.

In a more recent study Murray and Szymczyk (1978) also found age-related improvement in the use of distinctive features to recognize objects, but even young children had better object recognition when pictures to be recognized conserved more distinctive features. In their study they asked 4- and 6-year-old children and adults to identify sets of incomplete pictures (Figure 4-7). Incomplete pictures conserved either 75% or 25% of the distinguishing characteristics of the pictures. Adults recognized more of the figures than children, although for all ages, stimuli that conserved 75% of the distinctive features were recognized more frequently than those maintaining only 25%. All age groups use distinctive features to recognize objects, and this ability improves with age.

The improvement with age in the ability to use distinctive feature information implies that with experience we learn to distinguish dimensions of feature variability. Pick (1965) reported a study demonstrating the kind of learning that might characterize the manner in which children learn to appreciate featural differences. In her study kindergarteners were trained to sort through a set of cards, picking out those that were the same as the standard. This training continued until children could sort through the deck without

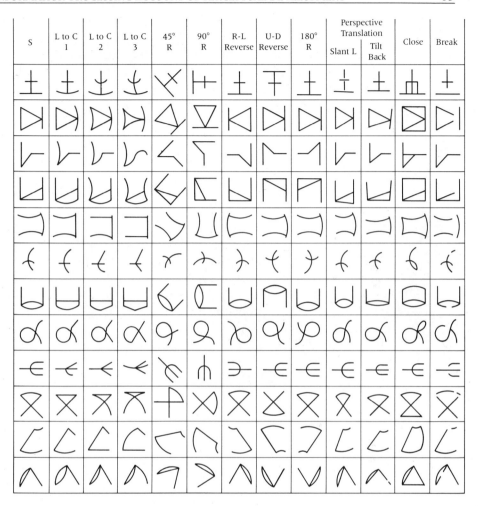

Figure 4-6. The standard forms (far left) and their transformations. *(Gibson, Gibson, Pick, & Osser, 1962)*

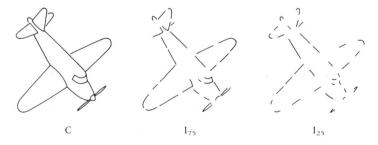

C   I₇₅   I₂₅

Figure 4-7. An example of picture stimuli used by Murray & Szymczyk in 1978. C is a complete representation, I_{75} contains 75% of the distinctive features, and I_{25} contains 25% of the distinctive features. *(Murray & Szymczyk, 1978)*

error. After training, children were assigned to one of two groups. One group (the distinctive features group) was asked to sort through another set of cards, selecting only those that matched a new standard. The transformations of this new standard, however, were within the same dimensions that characterized the training set. Another group (the prototype group) used the same standard as in the training condition, but sorted through a set of stimuli that had different transformations than those experienced during training.

If children learn to recognize objects by learning about distinctive features, then we would anticipate that the distinctive feature group would perform better on the second sorting task. This was indeed found. Although both of the groups receiving training performed better than a group that received no training, the distinctive features group performed the best.

A more recent version of differentiation theory has been proposed by Garner (1979). Garner has redefined what characterizes a distinctive feature. He believes that a stimulus has properties that are both dimensional (existing to some degree in all stimuli of a class) and featural (existing within a set of stimuli). The distinction between dimensions and features is important because, according to this theory, different error patterns should occur when comparing stimuli that vary either dimensionally or featurally. For example, if stimuli vary along a dimension, then all stimuli have the same amount of some attribute, as in the following set of letters: p, q, b, and d. All letters have the same features, a vertical line with a loop attached. They vary, however, along two dimensions: (a) a loop to the right or left and (b) a loop on the upward or downward portion of the vertical line. Given a recognition task in which letters are presented for very brief durations (7 msec or less), letters with the same features, but varying along the same number of dimensions, should be confused with equal frequency (p should be confused as often with q, d as often with b, and so on).

On the other hand, asymmetrical error patterns should be found for letters that vary only with respect to features, as with the "letter" set: |, ⌐, ∟, ⌐. With the rapid presentation of these letters, individuals should be prevented from scanning all relevant features. Those with fewer features should be recognized more accurately than those with more features. In fact, research with college students has confirmed these expectations (Garner & Haun, 1978).

Garner's work helps to clarify what it is about stimuli that we perceive. It also suggests that earlier research may have misrepresented the nature of changes in perception. To date there hasn't been a developmental test of Garner's ideas, although such an endeavor would help to expand our knowledge about what it is that children learn as they make finer discriminations about their perceptual world. Garner's work seems to indicate that detection of featural differences is primarily dependent upon the complexity of features and processing time. Given age-related changes in attention (see Chapter 5), scanning strategies (Elkind & Weiss, 1967; Vurpilot, 1968), and the amount of time needed to decode and enter information into the information-processing system (Hoving, Spencer, Robb, & Schulte, 1978), it may be that the ability to respond to featural differences reflects an improvement in the use of the processing system itself. On the other hand, developmental changes in recognition of dimensional differences may result from discrimination learning as originally proposed in differentiation theory.

Prototype Theory

An alternative to a distinctive features explanation of perceptual development is a *prototype theory*—the idea that perception occurs by comparing experiences to a prototypical exemplar of a class of objects or things. If the object shares most of the characteristics of the prototype, then it is recognized as a member of that class of objects. The recognition of objects on the basis of prototype comparisons is dependent upon the existence of a system for classifying sensory experience.

Like the acquisition of knowledge about distinctive features, knowledge about prototypes is acquired through experience. By working with things that can be grouped together to form a class of objects, we develop an understanding about the general structure of the class. Consequently, exemplars that have never before been experienced can be readily identified as class members on the basis of prototype comparisons. Posner and Keele (1968), for example, showed adults slightly, moderately, or extremely degraded dot patterns. These subjects were asked to sort the dot patterns into groups and were told when they were correct. Subjects, however, were never told what pattern to use for sorting. After subjects were able to sort the patterns without error, they were given a new set of distortions based on the previously sorted patterns. Adults sorted the new set with a high degree of accuracy. They had abstracted from their training experience prototypes that were used to organize subsequent sorts.

It would seem that as adults we use prototypes for identifying many objects and things that are encountered in daily living. We have little difficulty recognizing things as automobiles, although we experience an international smorgasbord of differently sized, shaped, colored, and styled four-wheeled vehicles. Children make use of prototypes in their perception of things as well.

Studies that have examined the use of prototypes by children have often required them to identify objects in distorted (broken-line patterns) or unfocused, blurred pictures. This research has shown that with age, children become more adept at this type of recognition (Bruner & Porter, 1964; Gollin, 1961, 1965; Murray & Szymczyk, 1978). There is some question about how these prototypes develop. One possibility is that with age there is a greater elaboration and specification of semantic knowledge (that is, what things are), and hence better prototypes (Saltz, Dixon, Klein, & Becker, 1977). With more elaborate prototypes, less information is needed to identify objects accurately.

Another possibility is that adults and young children use different strategies for learning about objects. Adults, it would seem, are prone to look for commonalities among sets of objects, even when instructed not to (for example, after instructions to remember specific characteristics of individual items). Younger children (preschoolers) seem as capable of abstracting prototypical information on tasks such as that described by Posner and Keele; however, when instructed to attend to the specific characteristics of objects, they are less likely to spontaneously abstract prototypes. Under instructions to attend to specific item characteristics, young children err more frequently when sorting new exemplars into categories and in recognizing prototypes. Their ability to recognize previously presented items, however, is quite good. Adults show the opposite pattern (Boswell & Green, 1982).

As we grow older, we may occasionally pay a penalty for abstracting prototypical information, or for categorizing our experiences. Although our ability to abstract prototypical information from experience facilitates the identification of new members of a class of objects, a parsimonious way for generalizing knowledge to experience, we may become less sensitive to the uniqueness of things that we experience. The danger of this rubrication (categorizing people, objects, and self) was observed by Maslow (1968). Perceiving ourselves and our surroundings within contrived categories limits and narrows our ability to perceive more fully and richly the uniqueness of our lives and the world around us. It dampens our pursuit of self-realization.

Maslow's thesis is an interesting one and, depending upon your perspective, a possible prescription for a more meaningful life. Our tendency to abstract prototypical information about our experiences, however, may be an unavoidable consequence of the human experience. Very early in life infants begin to make inferences about how things are alike and use this information to respond in a meaningful manner to objects they experience. Strauss (1979) not only demonstrates the ability of 10-month-old infants to abstract prototypical information about objects, but also reports how these prototypes are formed. One way to create a prototype is to average the values in a set of forms. Assuming that we saw a set of faces with noses ranging from short to long, a prototype based on the average of these values would lead us to recognize as most familiar a new face that had a nose of average length to those previously experienced. We might also create prototypes from the most commonly experienced exemplars (modal prototypes). If in our experience with faces we saw primarily faces with either long or short noses, we should find new faces with either long or short noses most familiar (rather than some average length nose). Strauss found that after infants had habituated to a set of faces, they showed greater interest (dishabituation) to new faces similar to a modal prototype. That is, they found the modal prototype faces more different from past experience than the average prototype faces. Apparently these infants had averaged the features in the previously experienced faces to create a prototypical exemplar of what they had seen.

A corollary to the idea that perception improves through the organization and development of prototype knowledge is the idea that training children to use prototypes should improve perception. The study reported by Pick (1965) suggested that prototype learning is less effective than distinctive features learning. Other research has suggested that this is not necessarily the case. Caldwell and Hall (1970) argued that young children may have misunderstood what was being asked of them in Pick's study. In order to ensure that children understood the nature of the matching task, Caldwell and Hall provided children with overlays during a training period. They were told that if the overlay and the figure matched exactly, only then was it to be considered the same. Following training, children were given a transfer task. Children who received overlay training did better when given the same standard with different trans-formations, and poorer when given a different standard, but transformations within the same dimensions as in training. It would seem that children will learn to discriminate distinctive features—or abstract prototypes—depending upon the experimental task, instructions, and their understanding of what it is that is being asked of them.

The attentive reader has probably become a bit skeptical of the value of drawing a distinction between distinctive feature and prototype learning. Most contemporary theorists are comfortable with the notion that both processes occur simultaneously to promote perceptual development (Oden, 1979; Reese & Lipsitt, 1970, p. 375; Stevenson, 1972, p. 267). It was observed by Kelly (1955) that in order to know something, we need to know how it is like some things but different from others. This would seem to apply to perceptual learn-ing. When confronted with some bit of sensory information, we must compare it to a set of information that has been stored in memory if we are to identify what that object is. Likewise, if we are attempting to compare two similar objects, we must be familiar with dimensions along which we know objects to differ—to look for features distinguishing them.

THE INFORMATION-PROCESSING VIEW OF PERCEPTION: A CRITIQUE

As with any area of psychological research, criticism can be made of both its methodology and theory. Methodologically, the research cited in this section has suffered on several accounts. First, a variety of methods for studying per-ception have led us to a diverse set of opinions about when particular abilities exist and of what those abilities consist. These data are often difficult to compare, especially in light of little information about the reliability or validity of these procedures (cf., Banks & Salapatek, 1981).

Valid and reliable procedures should allow us to draw unambiguous con-clusions from our results. Our procedures should measure what they purport to measure with consistency. In perception research we presume that our methods tap important dimensions of perceptual ability. But consider a prob-lem endemic to many of the methodologies used in infant research. Attention is directed specifically to the habituation–dishabituation paradigm, although the argument can be extended to other paradigms equally well. It is assumed in this research that if a stimulus is presented repeatedly, the infant will habi-tuate to it. It is also assumed that if another stimulus is presented and disha-bituation occurs, then the infant has perceived the second stimulus as different from the first. But, if no dishabituation occurs, we conclude that infants don't discriminate between the two events (Olson, 1976), and from this we infer that they have perceived the second stimulus as the same as the first.

In any research we always test the null hypothesis. Specifically, we test the proposition that there is no difference between two conditions or two events. Scientists are very conservative people; they try to stack the deck against themselves when conducting research. They are looking for very large differences, differences or changes that are so great that they would be very unlikely to have occurred by chance alone. We reject the null hypothesis when we find significant differences between two events (for example, as when we find dishabituation). By rejecting the null hypothesis, we accept the research hypothesis—that infants respond differently to two stimulus events. From this result we feel safe in concluding that the two stimuli are perceived differently.

If, however, we find no difference in children's response to two stimulus events, we are compelled to accept the null hypothesis. When we accept the null hypothesis, we can conclude only that we have failed to find a difference. We shouldn't extrapolate anything more from this result—that the subject perceives two stimulus events as the same. Intuitively it may seem reasonable to draw such a conclusion, but to do so is to violate a fundamental principle of statistical interpretation. Infants may perceive something as different, but for a variety of reasons respond in a similar fashion to two events, as might be the case if infants found the new stimulus as uninteresting as the one to which they habituated. Thus, it would be equally logical to conclude that infants found the second stimulus no more interesting than the first, as it would to conclude that infants didn't recognize a difference between the two. From nonsignificant results, we really can't say why infants fail to make a differential response (Sophian, 1980). Acknowledging this criticism, Carter and Strauss (1981) see no great problem in the use of these data given that null results are predicted and replicated. With some caution, they believe that null results are interpretable.

Methodologically, there is another concern that should be raised about this research. This concern lies with the nature of the population on which perceptual research has been conducted. In the interest of providing a basis for this concern, consider that young infants sleep for approximately 18 hours a day. Their sleep–wake cycles are not as regular as adults, but are spaced irregularly throughout the day. In light of this pattern we can appropriately question how infants' states (whether they are awake or asleep) affect the measurement of behavior. Pomerlau-Malcuit and Clifton (1973) have demonstrated, for example, that the infants' state affects the direction of heart rate change in response to a stimulus event. Given the frequency with which infants sleep, it might also be valuable to question how experimenters obtain the cooperation of young infants (or for that matter young children) for long periods of time as is typical of perception research. Bower (1966) has commented that his conditioning procedure takes approximately one hour. He confesses candidly, "The problem in experiments with infants is boredom; after a while even peekaboo [a game played with the infant to reinforce a response] loses its charm" (p.87). It is disturbing that a lack of information on the state of infants in these experiments or attrition that might have occurred during the experiment due to fussiness or boredom is lacking in a number of published studies (this is particularly true of early research). Although these difficulties need not invalidate the findings to date, it may be fruitful to question whether those infants who are more alert, more cooperative, and awake for longer periods of time are typical infants. It is possible that these data represent the behavior of a special group and, hence, misrepresent the behavior of typical infants.

In spite of the existence of a variety of theories of perceptual development (Gibson, 1969), much of the research in perception, as it relates to infants and neonates, has been largely atheoretical. Researchers, it would seem, have been more interested in describing what infants can do and when they can do it, rather than attempting to explain why or how they come to perceive as they do (cf. Banks & Salapatek, 1981; Gibson & Levin, 1979). As such, much of this early work has been disjointed and focused on cataloging a range of responses occurring under varying stimulus conditions, rather than attempting to discern some general pattern or principles in perceptual development that would allow us to predict heretofore unobserved behaviors.

Currently, there is a renewed interest in building theories of perceptual development. Both Haith (Haith, 1980, Haith & Goodman, 1982) and Banks and Salapatek (1981) have recently offered theoretical accounts of neonatal and infantile visual perceptual development. Both theories propose a number of innate principles or rules that govern perceptual organization. Haith (1980), for example, has proposed that we are born with a set of five rules that govern our reaction to visual stimulation (for example, there are rules for searching for patterns under different light conditions and rules that govern which aspects of patterns and shapes the infants will attend to). This view puts to rest the notion that the infants respond to light in a primarily reflexive fashion. Rather, there is the belief that newborns have basic abilities, plans, strategies, or rules that increase their contact with the visual environment. The infant is not simply an information responder, but an information seeker (cf. Banks & Salapatek, 1981; Linn, Reznik, Kagan, & Hans, 1982).

SUMMARY

William James, one of the founding fathers of American psychology, once described the world perceived by the newborn as a "blooming, buzzing confusion." Our current knowledge about the perceptual world of the neonate and infant would lead us to alter this judgment considerably. Young infants do make some sense of their auditory and visual environment, although it is not entirely clear just what kind of sense they make of it. We find that young infants have distinct preferences for particular kinds of stimuli, both visual and auditory. Some of these preferences would appear to involve social stimuli (human faces and voices). Additional work has addressed what it is about these stimuli that infants find interesting. Prior to 3 or 4 months of age, infants apparently attend to complex and high contrast visual patterns; however, at least by 4 months of age infants respond to the human face and show appropriate affective responses to subtle changes in facial features and expression. With auditory stimuli, infants have a preference for voices over other kinds of stimuli and at a relatively early age (3 to 4 months) coordinate auditory and visual information under naturally occurring conditions.

Information-processing accounts of perceptual development have typically assumed that the external world is richly structured. Perceptual development occurs as one learns to discriminate and respond to meaningful dimensions of one's environment. One view proposes that stimuli can be characterized by distinctive features. Through the discrimination of distinguishing features, it is believed that we recognize objects in our surroundings. The alternate view proposes that perception is based on prototype matching. That is, an object is believed to be compared to some idealized exemplar and, if it conserves most of the properties of the exemplar, it is recognized as being one of those things. There is evidence for the operation of both of these processes in perceptual development. In fact, contemporary opinion views these two processes as complimentary rather than antagonistic.

5
A Piagetian View of Perception

In the previous chapter we characterized the information-processing approach to perception as primarily exteroceptive, or directed toward discovering what characteristics of the world are perceived and responded to by the infant or child. The approach is based upon the notion that real things exist outside the body and have well-defined, specific properties that can be discovered and known. The Piagetian view of perception is quite different. It proposes that perception is a construction of reality. Thus, rather than focusing on the attributes or characteristics of the physical world that give rise to perception, the Piagetians have turned their attention inward to examine the manner in which individuals structure experience.

Perception itself is believed to involve two components. One of these is the *figurative component,* or the phenomenon itself (sometimes referred to as the schemata or schema) and the other is the *operative component,* or the intellectual scheme or operation that organizes perception. The figurative component is always subordinate to the operative component. Perceptual development is not the mere sharpening of the child's ability to recognize the external world more clearly (that is, refining the schema); it is an improvement in one's operative structure, or the scheme (Piaget & Inhelder, 1969).

Because perception involves the activation of schemes, perception can be equated with action. Since schemes are internalized action patterns, perception implies the exercizing of these schemes. Perception is essentially an act of assimilation—the application of some organized action pattern to an object, person, or event. It is through the application of schemes that things are recognized, and it is through the accommodation of these schemes and their coordination that perception develops (cf., Piaget, 1963, p. 71).

The structure of the intellect therefore governs what is perceived. We begin to develop a knowledge about our world, to structure our intellect, very early in life. It is during the sensorimotor period that children begin to develop a knowledge about four primary concepts: object, space, time, and causality. An examination of the evolution of these concepts reveals (from the Piagetian perspective) a clue to understanding what infants and children perceive and also how that perception changes with age (cf. Laurendeau & Pinard, 1970, p. 10; Piaget & Inhelder, 1969, p. 29).

METHODOLOGY

The methodology advocated by Piaget is often in stark contrast to that typically used in research stemming from information-processing theory. As seen in the last chapter, information-processing theory has attempted to examine perception by relying upon rigidly administered procedures in relatively well-controlled laboratory environments. A standard set of tests are administered to infants and children in a systematic and planned manner. Tests of Piaget's theory have relied upon a clinical methodology that, in contrast to that described in the previous chapter, is more flexible. For instance, it advocates an examination of children's knowledge in more naturalistic environments, and using test materials and problems that are familiar to children. In administering problems to infants and children, the examiner typically demonstrates some event to the child and the child is then either verbally or nonverbally required to explain his or her understanding of what he or she has experienced. The examiner is free to adapt or modify the situation as needed to ascertain the child's interpretation of an event in order to obtain a more accurate sample of a child's behavior. It is assumed that the responses that the child gives to these tasks reflect the manner in which the child's intellect is structured.

THE PERCEPTION OF OBJECTS

Perhaps the most important knowledge to develop during the sensorimotor period pertains to knowledge about objects (Flavell, 1963). Piaget's ideas about what children know about objects was gained by observing their reaction to objects that were visible or as previously visible things were hidden. To truly understand what an object is, Piaget reasoned, infants need to know that things exist independently of actions effected on them—that is, that objects have identities of their own that are independent of seeing, hearing, touching, smelling, and tasting.

To assess this knowledge, Piaget devised a procedure whereby experimenters subject objects to a series of occlusions, first partially then totally hiding them, and observing with each displacement how children respond. In the first two substages of the sensorimotor period, infants show no active search for objects that have been either partially or totally hidden. To children at this stage of development, it would seem that an object is merely something to be incorporated into an action pattern. Objects aren't yet differentiated as things separate from self. Once an object is removed from sight, it is as though it ceases to exist. Gratch and Landers (1971), for example, gave infants (6 months of age) toys and proceeded to cover the toys with a blanket. Infants responded to the occlusion as though the object never existed. It didn't matter if the infants were touching the toy; covering it resulted in their apparent loss of interest in the object. On the other hand, if the object was covered with a transparent sheet, infants continued to respond to the toy.

By about 6 months of age, children enter the third stage of sensorimotor development, showing a new way of responding to objects. In this stage infants begin to associate objects with actions previously carried out on them, schemes involving objects (secondary circular reactions) are repeated and coordinated. It is through the coordination of these action schemes associated with objects that shape and size constancy are believed to develop. By coordinating haptic (touching) schemes and visual schemes, infants come to realize that objects maintain a constant size and shape regardless of their visual appearance. These constancies are inferred from infants' recogniton of partially hidden, familiar objects (Piaget, 1954; Piaget & Inhelder, 1969). If an infant sees a familiar toy partially covered by a blanket, he or she will reach for it; however, if that same toy is shown to the infant, then totally covered, the infant will fail to look for the toy.

During the fourth stage infants begin to acquire a sense of object permanence. If familiar objects are now totally hidden, infants will look for them where they have last been found. Piaget reasoned that infants fail to separate objects from the action of looking for them (Piaget, 1954). The representation of an object is still tied to perception and action. If after the infant searches for and finds an object in one location, the object hidden in the first location is then visibly displaced (that is, while the infant watches, the object is moved to a new location and hidden again), infants will search for the object in the location where it was last found (this is often referred to as the stage four *perseverative error*).

In the fifth stage of sensorimotor development, infants no longer make the perseverative error and, following a visual displacement, will look for an object in the last place that it was hidden. A truly objective concept of object develops in the sixth stage when infants demonstrate persistent searches for hidden objects, even when displacements of an object are not visible to them. This behavior reveals a representation of object that is independent of both the child's perception and action. One might reason that children would at this stage truly appreciate a game of hide-and-seek. By approximately 18 months of age, children know that objects exist independently of their perception or interaction with them.

Contemporary research in object permanence has examined factors that contribute to infants' demonstration of knowledge about objects. This research has generally found that whereas object permanence develops in the direction described by Piaget (cf. Gratch, 1975), a number of factors influence infants' performance. For example, higher levels of object permanence are found when infants are asked to find persons rather than inanimate objects (Bell, 1970) and when objects are familiar rather than unfamiliar (Jackson, Campos, & Fischer, 1978; Lingle & Lingle, 1981). Other research suggests that the manner in which objects are hidden influences object concept. Better performance may be found when objects are hidden behind something than when they are hidden under something (Bower, 1974; Jackson et al., 1978; although see Lucas & Uzgiris, 1977 for an alternate opinion). Also, better performance is found if objects are hidden behind or under something rather than inside of something (Dunst, Brooks, & Doxsey, 1983).

In addition to the variety of factors in the test situation that influence performance on object permanence tasks, other research shows that the child-rearing environment also influences the development of object knowledge. Chazan (1981) has reported that several maternal care-giving variables are significantly related to how rapidly infants develop person and object permanence. Mothers who provide a positive affective environment seem to have babies who more rapidly develop knowledge about person permanence. A similar conclusion was drawn by Bell (1970), who found that infants with closer emotional ties to their mothers were more advanced in their knowledge of object concepts in general than infants who were either indifferent or ignored their mothers.

By the time that infants are 18 months of age, they have developed a relatively stable concept of object permanence. Nonetheless, qualitative changes in intellectual structure continue to distort children's perception of object properties throughout childhood. Preoperational children, for example, tend to perceive objects as variable in what are invariant dimensions of change (as in their perception that the quantity of a substance changes as the shape of the substance is altered). An accurate perception of objects precludes such distortion and is dependent upon the development and integration of a variety of logical operations—which doesn't occur until about 11 years of age.

THE PERCEPTION OF SPACE

As acknowledged in Chapter 2, Piaget believed that the intellect is an inter-coordinated system of knowledge. When considering the four concepts that develop during the sensorimotor period, we must remember that they don't

stand in isolation to one another, but are mutually responsible for an understanding of the world. Thus, a discussion of knowledge about objects, for
example, is inseparable from a discussion of knowledge about space. By their
very nature, objects occupy positions in space. Therefore, how infants respond
to objects carries implicit information about their knowledge of space.

As with very young infants' knowledge of objects, their knowledge of space
is also limited. Infants understand positions as practical spaces (Piaget, 1954).
These spaces represent independent and uncoordinated reference points between
the infants and their experience. It would be as though we had vision independent of sound, touch independent of sight, and so on. Thus, there are as
many practical spaces as there are activities (for example, touching, seeing,
hearing, smelling, tasting). Only with the third stage of sensorimotor development do these practical spaces begin to be coordinated. The development
of the infants' ability to manipulate objects brings together information from
a variety of practical spaces. The coordination of practical space facilitates not
only the development of a concept of object, but also the elaboration of a
more functional sense of space and location.

Spatial reasoning by stage four infants is characterized by several qualities.
One characteristic of infants' spatial knowledge is that they tend to be confused
by proximity. Objects that occur close to one another may be perceived as
fused rather than occupying separate spatial positions. Lucas and Uzgiris (1977,
Experiment 1) tested this notion by having infants observe toys hidden behind
or under screens. Prior to the toy's being hidden, the toy was placed in front
of one screen (a), and a second screen (b) was then moved to hide the toy.
After the toy had been hidden, screen (b) was moved with the toy to the
infant's right. The most frequent response made by infants in the weeks preceding a search for the object behind screen (b) was a search for the object at
(a). These results suggest that young infants tend to fuse object location with
adjacent landmarks, rather than recognizing that different objects occupy different locations in space (also see Butterworth, Jarret, & Hicks, 1982).

Another characteristic of infants' representation of space is that it is egocentrically referenced (that is, judgments about the location of things are based
upon the self or bodily cues) rather than allocentrically (judgments are based
on external landmarks). Infants who have lost something may remember it
as having been to the right, and consequently direct a search to the right—
despite subsequent changes in the infants' orientation to the space around
them.

As with contemporary work in object permanence, recent research in infants'
spatial perception reveals that a number of factors affect their performance on
spatial localization tasks. For example, it would appear that infants are more
likely to use allocentric frames of reference in familiar versus unfamiliar surroundings (Acredolo, 1978). Furthermore, the salience of the perceptual environment has much to do with whether or not young infants will use allocentric
or egocentric frames of reference (Acredolo & Evans, 1980; Bremner, 1978;
Goldfield & Dickerson, 1981). In one study, Acredolo and Evans (1980) sounded
a buzzer to signal the occurrence of an event to the infants' right or left. Eleven-

month-old infants who had been trained to anticipate an event either to the right or left were turned 180 degrees and the buzzer sounded again. Anticipatory head-turning was recorded. Infants oriented correctly to the position where the event had occurred during training if that place had been visually distinct (a salient landmark was provided near the anticipated event). Acredolo and Evans also found that even 6-month-old infants responded less egocentrically if the environment was rich with salient landmarks.

A truly objective concept of space occurs as infants realize that they and other objects are arrayed in some intercoordinated, three-dimensional space. Furthermore, the perception of space is progressively organized by an allocentric frame of reference. In the spatial orientation task just mentioned, Acredolo (Acredolo, 1978; Acredolo & Evans, 1980) reports that 16-month-old infants almost always orient in the direction of an anticipated event, even when there are no salient landmarks to mark the location of a previous event.

The infant's ability to use an allocentric frame of reference doesn't imply that spatial perception is entirely decentered and adultlike by the end of the second year of life. In fact, preschool children are often deficient in their reasoning about space and location; their judgment is frequently influenced by their own perspectives. The ability to see something from another's point of view may not appear until about 7 years of age or the period of concrete operational thought. Piaget and Inhelder (1956) and Laurendeau and Pinard (1970) report that the intellectual structure of preoperational children limits their ability to shift perspectives on spatial judgment tasks. In one series of experiments, Laurendeau and Pinard (1970) presented children between the ages of 4 and 12 years with three-dimensional displays consisting of three cones of different sizes and colors (Figure 5-1). Children were asked to select from various pictures those that showed how a toy man would see the display from a perspective other than their own (Figure 5-2). It was found that young preoperational children tended to choose pictures that showed how the array looked from their own perspective. As children become less egocentric and are better able to coordinate several dimensions simultaneously (for example, coordinating right and left, and front and back), their ability to perceive scenes from a variety of perspectives improves.

As with object knowledge, task factors have also been found to affect children's spatial reasoning; however, it would also appear that these factors don't entirely explain children's performance. Liben, Moore, and Golbeck (1982) had preschoolers reconstruct the arrangement of furniture as it typically occurred in their classroom (a familiar environment). Reconstructions involved the actual furniture in a real classroom and toy furniture arranged in a model of the classroom. Children displayed much better spatial knowledge when arranging furniture in the real classroom. It would appear that children have better spatial knowledge when that knowledge is tapped in ecologically meaningful situations. These researchers note, however, that even in these real-life situations, children's spatial knowledge was not uniformly perfect and in some instances quite poor. Something more fundamental than task variables (where children are tested and with what materials) apparently mediates children's performance.

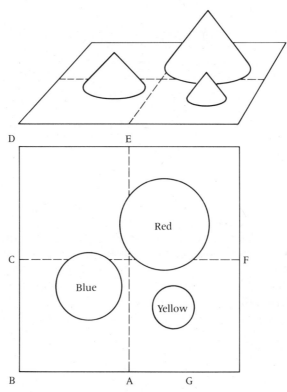

Figure 5-1. Stimuli used in perspective-taking task seen from front and above. Letters A through F indicate positions from which children are asked to judge the perspective of a toy man. *(Laurendeau & Pinard, 1970)*

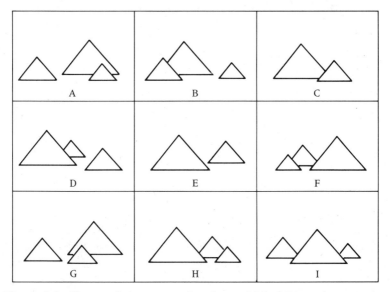

Figure 5-2. The set of nine perspectives from which children choose in the perspective-taking task. *(Laurendeau & Pinard, 1970)*

How children develop spatial knowledge is, of course, central to the Piagetian position. The Genevans believe that an active, rather than passive, learner is needed for adaptation. Again, there is some support for this aspect of the theory in current research. Feldman and Acredolo (1979), for example, found that preschoolers developed much better spatial knowledge if allowed to explore novel environments on their own compared to when they were led through a physical space by an adult. Independently and actively exercising their intellect through interaction with the physical world, children learn valuable lessons about the world in which they live.

THE PERCEPTION OF TIME

Although we are often unaware of it, the appreciation of time permeates our day-to-day activities. Of course, we live in a time-conscious and scheduled society, which exacerbates our sense of conventional time (hours, minutes, and seconds); however, there is another level at which an appreciation of time plays a major, but less conspicuous, role in our lives. We'll call this *logical time*. Logical time refers to knowledge about the position that events occupy in the continuum that constitutes our existence.

It is this aspect of time that Piaget (1969a) referred to in his discussion of the development of temporal knowledge. A mature understanding of logical time results from the coordination of two dimensions: succession (when things begin and end) and duration (how long something lasts). As adults we can reason about simple problems involving temporal relationships because we understand and coordinate these two dimensions. For example, Bill and Jim work at the same office and drive the same distance to work every day. Jim arrives at work before Bill. From this simple bit of information we appreciate that it took Bill a longer period of time to get to work than it did Jim. To use logical time in its simplest form, we don't need to know exactly how long it took Bill and Jim to get to work; we can imply duration from the succession of events themselves. Likewise, if we know that it takes Bill and Jim the same amount of time to arrive at work, but that Jim arrives before Bill, then Jim must have left for work before Bill. That is, if duration and distance are held constant, then succession can be implied. A more sophisticated understanding of logical time can be had as we begin to coordinate succession and duration. Given a constant distance, Jim may arrive at work before Bill. This outcome may eventuate if (a) Jim leaves for work before Bill, (b) it takes Jim less time to get to work than Bill (they both leave at the same time), (c) Jim leaves for work later than Bill and it takes him less time to get there, or (d) Jim leaves for work earlier than Bill and it takes him less time to get there.

Having noted the nature of logical time, we can begin to appreciate the infant's use of that knowledge. For the sensorimotor infant, temporal information is used only in a practical sense. During the first few stages of sensorimotor development, infants effect habitual action schemes in sequence. However, only from the fourth substage of the sensorimotor period, according to Piaget (1954), do infants demonstrate an appreciation of logical time. During this stage infants act purposefully, ordering action schemes and exercising one so that another might also be used. For example, an infant may pull away a cloth so that a toy can be grasped.

With the acquisition of semiotic function at the end of the sensorimotor period, children can partially reconstruct a series of events from immediate memory. As children observe a simple series of displacements, they can symbolically represent that series and, consequently, respond appropriately to the place where an object was last hidden. Children can also coordinate a series of purposeful behavior patterns. Piaget (1969a), for example, describes a child who comes to a closed door with both hands full. The child pauses for a moment and then (a) puts the objects she was holding on the floor, (b) opens the door, (c) picks up her possessions, and (d) walks through the open door. This act is quite different from an earlier one wherein a child lifts a cloth to get at a toy. In the earlier stage it is presumed that the action of looking for something is linked with the object that is found. In this case actions and objects are clearly disassociated as an intermediate set of actions is sequenced (putting something down, opening the door, and picking up) in order to get through the door.

Although preoperational children demonstrate practical uses of logical time, their understanding of it is quite confused. In his research on the development of knowledge about logical time, Piaget (1969a) had children reason about the amount of time (in a relative sense) that it would take two toy cars to travel down two parallel tracks. The tracks were either aligned or staggered, and the beginning or end points at which the two cars were started and stopped was varied, as was the rate at which the cars traveled. Piaget found that preoperational children (prior to about 7 years of age) tended to confuse time, distance, and speed. The toy car that was further down the track was believed to have traveled faster and for a longer duration. Getting somewhere first implied that it had started before something else; being last implied that it had started after something else.

With age, children begin to differentiate before and after in time from before and after in space. As development progresses into the concrete operational period, Piaget believed, the concepts of time, distance, and speed become differentiated. Several studies examining Piaget's ideas on the development of the concept of logical time have generally been supportive (Friedman, 1978); however, the differentiation of time from distance and speed may come a bit later than posited by Piaget (somewhere between 11 years of age and adulthood; Siegler & Richards, 1979).

Other studies have been less supportive of the Piagetian position. In a set of experiments by Levin and his colleagues (Levin, 1977; Levin, Israeli, & Darom, 1978; Levin, Gilat, & Zelniker, 1980) it is argued that contrary to Piaget's belief, knowledge of succession and duration do not develop simultaneously and, furthermore, the demonstrated confusion of duration with spatial succession does not reflect the young child's inability to understand duration independently of succession. The confusion noted by Piaget is believed due to the strong perceptual cues exerted by physical succession. For example, in one study (Levin et al., 1978) children were tested under two conditions. Children (kindergarten, first- and third-graders) were asked to judge the succession and duration of two lighted bulbs (which one came on first, went off last, or was on the longest) or two toy cars traveling down two parallel paths. In both stimulus conditions, even the youngest children separated succession from duration, judging more accurately about succession. Furthermore, the accentuation of perceptual cues for succession (in the toy car problem) significantly interfered with duration judgments across age levels.

THE PERCEPTION OF CAUSALITY

A final knowledge developing during infancy is causality. There is no doubt that an appreciation of causality requires the coordination of events in time; however, there is the additional need to draw inferences about events occurring in time. Causes must precede effects. Piaget believed that children demonstrate a very primitive form of causal knowledge by about the third stage of sensorimotor development. At this stage, Piaget (1954) believed, infants have a magico-phenomenalistic notion of causality. They have an almost magical sense about what causes something to happen, failing to appreciate intermediate relationships that exist between their actions and the effect of those actions on objects. Young infants may look at mobiles and rock their bodies, as if their movement alone were sufficient to make the mobile move. Even adults carry vestiges of this magico-phenomenalistic notion of causality. What golfer, for example, hasn't hit a drive and then attempted to bring an errant slice back onto the fairway with the lean of the body?

By the end of the sensorimotor period, infants have obtained a practical sense of causality. They are capable of attributing causality to events beyond their immediate observation and establishing links between events that are independent of their own activity. Piaget (1954) described a child trying to open a gate. The gate, however, was jammed by a chair placed behind the gate and not visible to the child. Not to be thwarted, the child went around the fence to the opposite side of the gate and triumphantly removed the chair. From some effect (a stuck gate), Piaget reasoned, the child had deduced the cause (something was obstructing it).

In spite of the development of a more objective and useful kind of causal knowledge that eventuates toward the end of the second year of life, the child's understanding of cause and effect remains quite different from adults. Preoperational children's reasoning about causality is quite subjective. Piaget observed that young children believe that the causes of events are those things that occur contiguously, or near, in time (phenomenalism). Cause and effect are not entirely separate and may be perceived as interchangeable. Furthermore, causes may be justified in terms of some natural order (finalism). Things have purposes that justify their existence. Or, cause of things may be perceived as due to the actions of higher beings (artificialism) or the possession of life (animism) or human strength and qualities (dynamism) by objects in the phenomenal world.

In studies by Piaget (1930) and Laurendeau and Pinard (1962), children (between the ages of 4 and 12 years) were asked to explain the causes of a number of phenomena (for example, "What makes clouds move?"). Young children justified events on the basis of finalism, animism, and dynamism. For example, when asked why some objects float while others sink, children reasoned that boats are made to float, or that objects float because they don't want to sink or because the water is strong and won't let them down. Nails sink because, as one child explained, "there is a man here [in the nail] and he likes to go to the bottom" (Laurendeau & Pinard, 1962).

As children grow older, differentiating and coordinating the various dimensions of the physical world, their perception and attribution of causality also change. Boats float because they're not heavy for their size; marbles sink because they're heavy and small. Though at times inaccurate due to an, as yet, incomplete and uncoordinated set of rules about relationships between properties of objects, children begin to base their perception of causality on physical attributes of objects and the relationships that, in fact, obtain between properties of objects.

PIAGETIAN VIEW OF PERCEPTUAL DEVELOPMENT: A CRITIQUE

Piaget has suggested that knowledge is based in the acquisition of four primary concepts: object, space, time, and causation. Since perception is rooted in knowledge about things (that is, schemes), perception must change with age as a function of stage-related changes in children's operative knowledge. Criticisms that have been leveled at this particular view of perception can be summarized in the form of three general issues. First, it may be asked whether or not intellectual structures do in fact organize perception. Second, it may be questioned whether perceptual development occurs in the steplike, stage-related fashion posed by Piaget. And, third, it can be asked whether perception is best characterized by constructive processes or, as discussed in the preceding chapter, by the discrimination and discovery of properties or features inherent in the phenomenal world.

Does Intellectual Structure Organize Perception?

At the heart of Piaget's theory of development is the idea that intellectual structure organizes the perception of reality. Limitations in knowledge should influence performance across a variety of tasks and situations. But many critics of Piagetian theory have observed that there is too much unevenness in development and, thus, the notion that intellect structures performance is weakened (cf., Cornell, 1978). It is quite apparent that the results obtained on Piagetian tasks are easily influenced by both the testing environment and test materials. On object permanence tests, performance has been shown to vary as a function of (a) how an object is displaced [for example, under or behind (Jackson et al., 1978), or in or under something (Lloyd, Sinha, & Freeman,

1981); (b) what the object is hidden under (Rader, Spiro, & Firestone, 1979); and (c) the properties of the object that is hidden, for example, person versus object (Bell, 1970; Lamb, 1973), familiar versus unfamiliar object (Lingle & Lingle, 1981), and whether the infant is emotionally attached to the object (Lingle & Lingle, 1981)]. On spatial judgment tasks, allocentric responding is more likely to be found if children are tested in familiar versus unfamiliar environments (Acredolo, 1978; Liben et al., 1982) and when landmarks are distinctive (Bremner, 1978; Goldfield & Dickerson, 1981). Levin (1977; Levin et al., 1978) has demonstrated that stimulus factors influence estimates of time duration, and Siegler (1976) has shown that children's ability to reason about physical causality is also influenced by task characteristics. Given the current state of knowledge, the influence of intellectual structure on perception wouldn't seem as pervasive as might be anticipated. However, it is necessary to remember that task factors alone do not explain all of children's performance. Inevitably strong developmental effects are found regardless of task variables. Furthermore, developmental trends are found even on tasks that should be familiar to children (Liben et al., 1982).

Does Perceptual Development Occur in a Steplike Sequence?

This particular issue seems best addressed at two levels. The first concerns the necessity of postulating stages; the second relates to the age levels at which specific behaviors are found. The idea that development progresses in stages presumes that there are qualitatively distinct states of knowledge at points along a developmental continuum. Furthermore, it is assumed that knowledge develops in some systematic and predictable fashion. Research that has examined the evolution of the concepts of object, space, time and causality has generally supported the direction and pattern of development originally proposed by Piaget. However, to describe a pattern of development doesn't necessarily imply that development is stagelike (Brainerd, 1978a, see Chapter 9 for an extended discussion on this matter). Others who have studied development during infancy don't find evidence for clearly defined, qualitatively distinct stages in the evolution of conceptual knowledge. Cornell (1978), for example, has criticized object permanence literature, arguing that the concept of object is better characterized as a continuous acquisition of knowledge about when things are permanent (as when they are hidden behind or under something) and when they are impermanent (as when things are eaten). A similar argument has been proposed for the development of spatial knowledge (cf. Lasky, Romano, & Wenters, 1980).

Although it is wrong to equate developmental stages with age, there is and should be a reliable relationship between the two. Older children should reason about developmentally more advanced concepts better than younger children. Furthermore, if young children's performance is affected by cognitive structure, then we shouldn't expect training (cf. Burns & Brainerd, 1979) or minor alterations in stimulus conditions to produce substantial changes in their performance. Whereas strong developmental effects are found in perceptual research, a variety of research also shows that young children perform tasks suggesting rather sophisticated levels of knowledge. Several studies (Acredolo & Evans, 1980; Bremner, 1978; Reiser, 1979) have shown that some very young infants (6 months of age) will use allocentric frames of reference for locating objects in space if there are salient landmarks in their perceptual field. Levin (Levin, 1977; Levin et al., 1978, 1980) has shown that school children discriminate physical succession from duration on time judgment tasks. With regard to children's understanding of causality, Hood and Bloom (1979) report that 2- and 3-year-old children use causal expressions appropriately, showing clearly that they distinguish cause from effect. And, if we are willing to accept an interpretation by Lewis and Brooks-Gunn (1979), infants as young as 3 months of age detect causation. Observing response contingent movement (as when looking in a mirror), infants seem to recognize that the reflected images move as a consequence of their own actions.

A factor that contributes to the range of variability observed in children's competencies is the methodology that characterizes Piagetian research. The clinical approach, by its very nature, yields conservative estimates of children's abilities (Brainerd in Hood & Bloom, 1979; Cornell, 1978). In order to demonstrate competence within a particular domain of knowledge, children must first understand the nature of the task (what is expected of them) and, comprehending the task, they must make an overt motor response (reaching for, uncovering, or verbally reporting something) that is often unrelated to the knowledge domain in question. Thus, the clinical method requires a coordination of diverse knowledge and action systems that may produce the systematic underestimation of what children know or perceive.

In addition to problems in assessing competency based upon children's motor responding, another problem involves developing instructions that clearly communicate to children the nature of the task. Children who are given perspective-taking tasks, for instance, are strongly affected by the type of instructions they receive (Huttenlocker & Presson, 1979). Gelman (1978) has also suggested that the types of questions that are asked of children on some Piagetian tasks may be biased against more sophisticated responses. She points out that, as regards questioning children about causality, it is likely that children haven't had much opportunity to learn why rivers flow, or what causes wind and rain (do most adults know?). Lacking such knowledge, children may be compelled to rely upon animistic explanations of phenomena. Children may also misinterpret what it is that the experimenter is requesting. Indeed, if asked to explain what makes a bicycle go, "The child might say he thinks the pedals are responsible for the bicycle's movement because he takes the question to be one about causal agent and not one about force" (Gelman, 1978, p. 312).

In defense of the Piagetian position, some caution should be observed in concluding that young children, who are performing feats apparently requiring sophisticated knowledge, actually have that competence. By continuing to simplify tasks, we are likely to continue to find what appear to be earlier levels of conceptual understanding (cf. Antell & Keating, 1983). Liben et al. (1982) regard successful performances no more revealing competence than performance failures are revealing of incompetence. It is possible, these researchers argue, to find what appear to be sophisticated levels of conceptual understanding in much of what infants and children do. Whether these performances represent some underlying competence in the Piagetian sense is quite another matter.

Is Perception Constructed from Action?

The Piagetians believe that perception is constructed—that perception is the assimilation of objects into action schemes. By exercising schemes, we know about things. Furthermore, it is through action that schemes themselves are developed. Piaget (1963), for example, believed that through the coordination of information about things assimilated into visual and haptic (touching) schemes, children construct knowledge about the constant shape and size of objects.

The idea that perception is based in action has a long history in psychology. Hebb (1949) proposed the notion that perception occurs through the application of habitual scanning patterns. In a frequently cited experiment, Held and Hein (1963) demonstrated the practical importance of activity in the development of visual perception. In their study, pairs of kittens were exposed to varying degrees of sensorimotor experience. During development, one member of the pair was allowed to move about a constant visual environment and a yoked control received essentially the same experience while passively restrained. On tests of visual perceptual ability the active member of the pair exhibited better visual perception than the passive member. For example, active members discriminated deep from shallow when placed on a visual cliff, the passive member of the pair did not. After a 48-hour period of freedom in a lighted room, however, even the formerly passive member of the pair exhibited normal depth perception.

Others have been equally emphatic about the role of activity in the perceptual development of infants and children. Zaprophets (1965) has suggested that motor activity directed at objects serves to create motor images that facilitate object recognition. Zaprophets' research has shown that between the ages of three and seven years of age there is an increase in active systematic scanning of both tactile and visual stimuli. Other research has shown similar developmental trends for infants (Schofield & Uzgiris, 1969).

One area in which activity is believed to play a major role in perception is infants' knowledge of objects. It will be recalled that stage four children tend to commit the perseverative error, that is, after finding an object hidden at one location (A), they will search at (A) in spite of a visible displacement of the object to a new location (B). It is assumed that this response reflects the fusion of the action of looking for the object with the object itself. Schemes for assimilating objects are not differentiated from schemes involving the child's own actions. Although there is good evidence that children make this error (Gratch, 1975; Harris, 1975), its explanation has varied. Several accounts suggest that spatial localization errors rather than deficiencies in object concept are responsible (Butterworth, 1977; Butterworth et al., 1982; Evans & Gratch, 1972;

Lloyd et al., 1981) and that actions carried out on objects have nothing to do with children's perception of them (Butterworth et al., 1982).

The notion that perception is a consequence of actions carried out on things also suggests that an increased opportunity to experience and integrate information from a variety of sensory domains should promote better concept knowledge. Following this line of reasoning, Harris (1971) examined the role of haptic and visual exploration in the development of object knowledge. Infants (12 and 8½ months of age) were shown an object that appeared from behind a screen. For some of the infants the object was placed in a transparent box, allowing them only to look at it. For the remaining infants, the object was placed in an open box, and the infants were allowed to manipulate the object as well as look at it. After a short time the object was hidden behind the screen. It was found that for both age levels, children who were allowed to see and manipulate the object searched for it when it was hidden. Older children, however, were more likely to search for a hidden object after just seeing it. This suggests that for young infants, object knowledge is facilitated by a combination of visual exploration and haptic manipulation. In a similar study, just the opposite conclusion was drawn. Gottfried, Rose, and Bridger (1978), for example, subjected 6 to 9-, and 12-month-old infants to one of three object familiarization sessions. Infants were (a) shown a toy (visual), (b) shown a toy and allowed to touch it (visual/haptic), or (c) shown a toy that was encased in a clear plastic cube which they were allowed to manipulate (visual/manipulation). On a subsequent habituation–dishabituation test of visual recognition, superior object recognition was found in the visual condition. In fact, children who were allowed to manipulate the toy showed poor object recognition, suggesting to these researchers that manipulation may in some cases interfere with the acquisition of knowledge about objects (at least as measured by visual recognition).

Other studies have taken exception to the conclusions drawn by Gottfried et al. (1978), noting that object manipulation may be very important to the acquisiton of some kinds of knowledge. Ruff (1982), for example, believes that object manipulation may be important to knowledge about the three-dimensional properties of objects. Other research has indicated that if young infants are to be asked to remember properties of objects, it may be necessary to reinstate the conditions under which they are familiarized with objects. For example, if an infant becomes familiar with an object by both looking at it and manipulating it, then greater object recognition should occur if an infant is given the object both to look at and manipulate. Likewise, if the infant is allowed only to look at the object, greater object recognition should occur if the object is only shown (Mackay-Soroka, Trehub, Bull, & Corter, 1982).

Thus, there is evidence supporting the idea that some of what infants perceive is based in activity and other research suggesting that this is not the entire answer. Although haptic exploration of objects may facilitate the acquisition of some types of information (for example, three-dimensional versus two-dimensional knowledge) about objects, it may not be the case that it necessarily produces better knowledge than other types of learning.

Despite the long history of this issue, the role of activity in perception is yet to be resolved. Indeed, theorists have posited that the development of object permanence (Cornell, 1978; Moore, cited in Gratch, 1975) and spatial localization (Lucas & Uzgiris, 1977) can be equally justified by both Piagetian or discrimination-differentiation accounts of perceptual development. Certainly there is good evidence that activity facilitates the elaboration of perceptual skills; however, the extent to which activity is necessary for structuring and thereby determining perception is as yet unknown.

SUMMARY AND SYNTHESIS

This chapter has advanced the notion that perception, like other mental activity discussed by Piaget, is structured by some underlying system of intellect. The operative component of the intellect, or schemes, determines the nature of the perceptual trace, or, the schemata. Knowing about things, according to Piaget, implies action at two levels. First, he believed, children structure their world through interactions with things, and through interaction they adapt and organize schemes to promote the development of the intellectual system. Second, through the assimilation of objects into schemes, children recognize or perceive the objects. The application of schemes (through visual scanning, haptic manipulation, and so on), gives meaning to our sensory experiences.

As with the preceding chapter on information-processing views of perception, the current chapter has focused on infancy, although it is apparent that perceptual development continues throughout childhood. Nonetheless, it is within infancy that we acquire a basic knowledge about our world. Piaget believed that perception is based in the development of four fundamental concepts: object, space, time, and causality. Through this knowledge, we recognize and respond effectively to our environment. The tack taken by information-processing theorists has been to focus on how infants respond to various information modalities, primarily visual and auditory. The two orientations are quite different in what they accept as the content of perceptual research. One attempts to discover what it is that individuals know about the world that leads them to structure their perception as they do; the other directs attention to what is perceived and responded to in the external world.

By and large, sensorimotor research supports the pattern of development documented by Piaget; however, a variety of situational and task factors influence children's performance on tasks assessing their knowledge of objects, space, time, and causality. We find that under certain conditions or when children are asked to reason about specific kinds of information, they demonstrate competencies at ages much younger than anticipated by Piagetian theory. With respect to when children demonstrate knowledge about particular properties of objects, there is some concordance between Piagetian and information-processing research. Both positions, for example, posit that knowledge about size and shape constancy emerges reliably by about 4 to 6 months of age. These two positions are also similar in their prediction when information from various sensory modalities is integrated. Research reviewed in the previous chapter suggests that infants as young as 3 months of age may develop expectancies about specific objects (people) in their environment and appreciate the interactive properties of sight and sound. Piaget (1963) believed that this type of integration occurs during the third substage of sensorimotor development (or approximately 4 months of age).

Just how sensory experience is perceived is a principal source of difference between these two positions. The Genevans believe that perception eventuates through the modification of innate, reflexive action schemes. These modifications occur as a consequence of active exploration and interaction with the environment. Perception is action and perceptual development is construction.

A growing number of information-processing theorists believe that several perceptual abilities (for example, perception of size and shape constancy, and depth) are, by contrast, innate rather than constructed. They also believe that perceptual refinements occur through the discrimination of distinctive environmental features and/or the abstraction of prototypical information from sensory experience. Although experience is obviously important to perceptual development in both Piagetian and information-processing theory, there is a question of how much and what kind of activity is necessary. Piaget emphasized the need for infants to vigorously and actively explore the environment visually and haptically. Information-processing theorists, on the other hand, appear less committed to the role of activity in perceptual development. For example, studies assessing the development of knowledge about distinctive features or prototype development have used relatively passive techniques (picture-sorting tasks and habituation–dishabituation paradigms). The question of how much activity is needed for perceptual development is difficult to answer and is not so easily reduced to a comparison of procedures that allow children to wander about a room versus study it from a chair. Even visual scanning involves considerable activity. Consequently, it would be unfair to conclude that information-processing theorists advocate a passive organism in the process of perceptual development.

Thus, we find that there are a number of points of correspondence between these two theories. In fact, there is considerable overlap between these two theories in their explanation of how perceptual development occurs. Piaget believed that schema are modified through both generalizing and recognitory assimilation. That is, we come to extend a set of common behaviors to different objects (generalizing assimilation) as well as to restrict certain behavior patterns to specific objects (recognitory assimilation). A parallel to these two processes is found in prototype (extending a common response to a diverse set of objects) and distinctive features learning (responding to specific features of objects) advocated by information-processing positions. The Piagetian approach does add something beyond that advanced by information-processing theories; this is the belief that perception (and other cognitive processes) is subordinate to the underlying intellectual schemes. Information-processing theories propose that perception is but an initial activity to be performed within a sequence of events, or a hierarchy of functions, as information enters and flows through the processing system. Although this system is coherent and organized, it is commonly presumed that there is no general intellectual structure (in the sense used by Piaget) that changes with age that affects the quality of activity within the system.

6

A Multistore Model
of Memory

In this and the next two chapters we will consider another aspect of the cognitive system—memory. Theories of memory must account for the acquisition, storage, and retrieval of information. It is not such an easy task to define precisely what constitutes memory in relation to other aspects of the cognitive system. Consider the problem of differentiating between perception and memory. Perception involves a meaningful response to or recognition of some stimulus event. Recognition, however, requires some memory involvement, be it the detection of critical features, matching a stimulus to a prototype, or assimilating an object into a scheme. All of these processes assume some *a priori* capacity that allows us to interpret and respond to sensory experience.

Likewise, some models of memory include systems that appear to account for perceptual phenomena (for example, the sensory register of the multistore model), in addition to components more typically associated with memory.

That these overlaps should occur between components of the cognitive system need not be disconcerting; in fact, they are probably unavoidable. Decisions to discuss particular phenomena as perceptual, mnemonic, or conceptual often reflect convention rather than a theoretical necessity.

THREE STORAGE SYSTEMS

In the course of your experience with young children, you've probably noticed that they don't remember very well. The question we'd like to answer is, why not? One explanation suggests that children don't voluntarily use a variety of strategies or tricks to better retain and retrieve information from memory. This particular explanation is a developmental adaptation of the multistore model of memory.

The multistore model of memory (Atkinson & Shiffrin, 1968; Broadbent, 1958; Waugh & Norman, 1965) distinguishes between structural (or invariant) systems of memory and control processes (operations that can be learned or developed in order to alter the way that memory functions). Structurally, memory is believed to consist of three discrete storage systems: a sensory register, a short-term store, and a long-term store (Figure 6-1). These storage systems can be thought of as discrete bins through which information passes or is placed to either (a) hold information temporarily for incorporation into

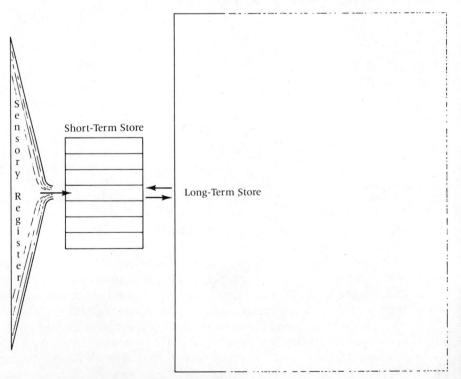

Figure 6-1. A multistore view of the structure of memory.

the system, (b) keep information in consciousness for mental work, or (c) retain information for use at some later point in time. Multistore theorists believe these stores have four distinguishing characteristics: (a) the trace duration (how long a piece of information can stay in each store before it decays or is forgotten); (b) the capacity of each store (how much information can reside within it); (c) the code of information storage (the modality or format in which the information is represented); and (d) the control processes that are unique to each storage system.

Those who have assumed a multistore model of memory have generally concluded that the structure of memory is complete by about 4 years of age and remains invariant over the life span. The development of memory during childhood is explained by improvements in children's ability to use control processes (Hagen, Jongeward, & Kail, 1975; Naus, Ornstein, & Hoving, 1978; Ornstein, 1977). By 12 or 13 years of age, it is believed that children have acquired a variety of mnemonic strategies, allowing them flexibility in the use of memory; however, prior to that time, the failure to use control processes severely limits young children's memory functioning.

SENSORY REGISTER

Information coming from the external world enters the information-processing system through the senses. This information is believed to be temporarily registered in some large capacity register from which we selectively process some of it. The sensory register is generally believed to hold large quantities of information, but this is for very brief periods of time—for less than a second (Colehart, 1975). In order to grasp the kind of memory being described, you might think of the image that lingers with you as you walk into a darkened room and rapidly switch the lights on and then off. For a very brief moment after the lights have been turned off, it seems as though an image (or icon) of things in the room still exists. But in an instant the image fades. Thus, we must selectively process some of this information if we wish to transfer it to a more durable short-term store for further interpretation and processing.

Trace Duration

The lifetime of information in sensory register is very brief. Unless this information is scanned and transferred to short-term store, it will be forgotten altogether.

As might be anticipated, a specialized apparatus is required for studying the nature of sensory register storage. For studying the retention of visual information an apparatus known as a tachistoscope is used to present visual stimuli for very brief durations (less than a second). In examining iconic (visual) memory, either single-item or multi-item visual displays are shown to subjects. Single-item displays (a single letter) are generally presented in conjunction with pattern masks (a set of random lines). These masks occur at varying intervals prior to (forward mask) or after (backward mask) the presentation of a visual target to camouflage the icon (the visual image that remains of the target, see Figure 6-2). The use of masking techniques provides information about the durability of the icon (see Hoving, Spencer, Robb, & Schulte, 1978, for a discussion of methodological problems in these types of studies). The backward mask provides information about the rate at which an icon decays. Masks presented too soon after the presentation of the target should camouflage the icon, preventing its recognition. A forward mask is used as a control for the effects of performance factors (practice, fatigue, and motivation).

Similar techniques are used to study echoic (auditory) memory. Brief sounds are presented in rapid succession, and the subject must identify either the first or the second sound. Recognition of the last sound is analogous to the forward masking procedure and recognition of the first, the backward masking procedure (that is, the latter sound should mask the first).

Studies examining iconic memory and using single-item displays have generally found that the speed at which an icon is processed increases with age. Hoving et al.(1978) note that young children (preschool age), compared to

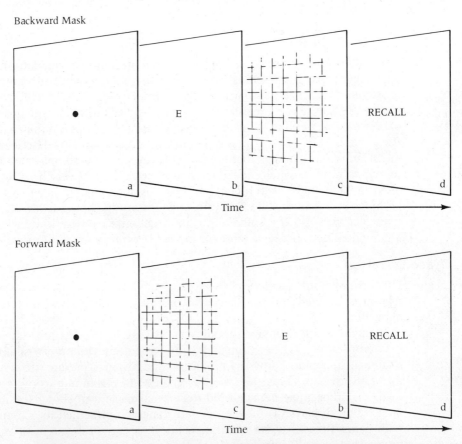

Figure 6-2. Backward and forward masking procedures (a, fixation point; b, stimulus card; c, pattern mask; d, recall cue).

older children (elementary school age) and college students, may require longer delays between the presentation of the target stimulus and the backward mask in order to reach a level of recall accuracy comparable to a no mask control. Lasky and Spiro (1980) for example found that 5-month-old infants required up to a 2000-msec delay between the cessation of a target and an intervening mask if the target was to be processed sufficiently to be recognized. Because age differences aren't found under forward masking conditions (Wellsandt & Meyer, 1974) or are much smaller (Liss & Haith, 1970), it is concluded that younger children process the contents of sensory register more slowly than older children.

Similar conclusions have been drawn regarding the operation of echoic memory. Massaro (1973) found that backward masks interfered with adult information processing if the mask was presented before a 250-msec delay; thereafter, performance with and without the mask was essentially comparable. Infants (8 to 9 weeks of age), however, need more processing time. Their sound recognition is interfered with if a second sound is presented before 400-msec following the offset of the first sound (Cowan, Suomi, & Morse, 1982). As with visual information, infants and younger children need more time to process auditory information. Curiously, adults may intuitively respond to this need in children and infants. Adults slow their speech in talking to infants and children (Snow & Ferguson, 1977). Observations of adults interacting with infants also suggests that objects are presented to infants more deliberately and at slower rates. Furthermore, many learning activities involving adults and children are implicitly structured to slow the pace at which both visual and auditory information is presented (as in reading from picture books). This feature of adult–child interaction should facilitate information processing given the limited speed at which children process information in sensory register.

Iconic memory can also be studied using multi-item displays, requiring either full or partial reports of items in the displays. When full-report procedures are used, the subjects are asked to report as much about the display as they can. Young (preschool) children, not surprisingly, report less information than adults. Haith, Morrison, Sheingold, & Mindes (1970), for example, asked 5-year-olds and adults to recognize items that had been briefly presented in displays of 1 to 4 items. Whereas adults showed a systematic increase in the amount of information recognized as a function of increasing set size, young children did not. With set sizes of between two and four items, children recognized an average of only 1.6 items.

An obvious problem with full-report procedures is that a number of non-memory-related factors can influence recall (reporting without assistance the contents of memory) or recognition (selecting from a set of items those that were in the display). For example, young children are slower to respond than older children and they are less fluent. Both of these factors would contribute to the poorer performance of young children on multi-item, full-report tasks. To correct this problem, a partial-report procedure is used. In this technique the subject is shown an array of items; following some variable delay interval, a probe signals the subject to identify the item occupying a position in an array. When this procedure is used, children and adults recall comparable amounts of information with delays up to 150–200 msec; however, for both there is a rapid loss of information over this period (Sheingold, 1973). (See Figure 6-3.) For adults there is a relatively stable retention of information after 200 msec, but there is a continued loss of information by younger children. This pattern of information loss has suggested to some that adults actively process iconic information to prevent its further decay, while young children don't (Haith, 1971; Morrison, Holmes, & Haith, 1974; Sheingold, 1973). Again, as with research utilizing single item displays, young children don't process the contents of the sensory register as efficiently as do adults.

The exact reason why children don't process the contents of sensory register as efficiently as adults is not entirely clear. There is some suggestion that at least some of the problem may have nothing to do with the operation of memory itself, but may be connected with stimulus and task familiarity. Adults (especially college students) may acquaint themselves with task demands more quickly than children. Lawrence, Kee, and Hellige (1980) found no age differences in the recognition of information from iconic memory using a task that minimized verbal encoding and response demands.

When processing sensory information, we attend to a number of dimensions. When processing visual information, for example, we may attend to both identity (what it is) and spatial characteristics (where it is). Studies appear to show that whereas young children have difficulty retaining identity information, their ability to retain spatial information alone is much better. Finkle

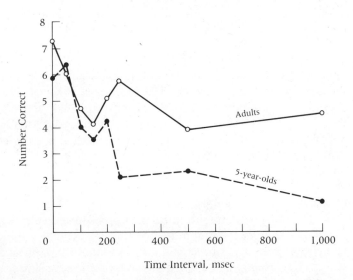

Figure 6-3. Average number of items correctly reported by 5-year-olds and adults as a function of delays between stimulus offset and probe onset. *(Sheingold, 1973)*

(1973, Experiment 1) briefly presented dot patterns to kindergarteners, third- and sixth-graders, and college students. Following tachistoscopic presentation of the dots, subjects were asked to reconstruct the patterns. Although older subjects did better than younger subjects, across age levels the number of positions recalled correctly continued to increase as more dots were added to the pattern. This pattern of performance differs markedly from the data reported by Haith et al. (1970) who found that children recalling the identity of items in a display reported an average of 1.6 items only. When both item and position information are recalled, processing of position information is apparently sacrificed at the expense of processing identity information. With the introduction of one bit of identity information into an array (a geometric form is substituted for a dot in a pattern of dots), there is a decline in children's recall of position information (Finkle, 1973, Experiments 2 & 3)(Figure 6-4). It is likely that young children have difficulty sumultaneously processing identity and position information. When both must be processed, young children attend to what is in the visual field rather than where it is. This type of processing hierarchy may reflect young children's need for additional time to identify what things are (Maisto & Baumeister, 1975). It is unknown whether we differentially process features in other modalities. Such an examination would, however, be profitable. In order to appreciate language, for example, we must process a variety of acoustical information (place of articulation, stress, intonation, and pitch). Some research suggests that at least with acoustical information, even young infants are capable of simultaneously processing more than one acoustical feature (Eimas & Miller, 1980).

Capacity

It is virtually impossible to discuss a traces duration without also considering the amount of information that can be held in sensory register; data from tachistoscopic research provides information about both. When partial-report procedures are used, sensory register capacity approximates the total number of objects in the display, thus giving rise to the assumption that the capacity of this system is quite large (Sheingold, 1973, Figure 6-3). These capacity estimates hold for all age levels and are unaffected by the type of information processed (Haith, 1971).

Code

It is generally believed that the modality in which information is stored in sensory register is similar to the sensation that gave rise to it (Broadbent, 1958). That is, if information is presented visually, this information is represented iconically, or if auditorily, then echoically, and so on. The research reviewed in Chapter 3 revealed that infants are responsive to all dimensions of their sensory world; hence, it would be fair to conclude that even very young infants are capable of representing a variety of information in sensory register in a manner similar to adults.

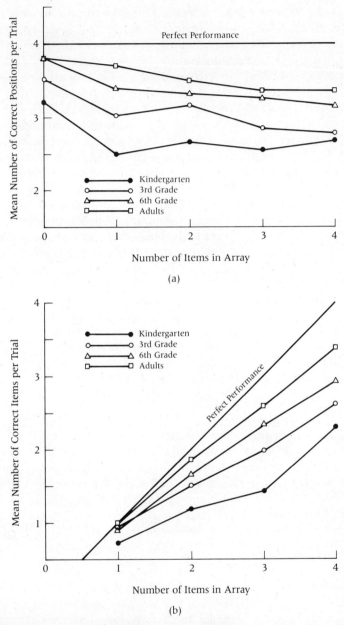

Figure 6-4. Mean number of positions (a) and items (b) reported correctly as a function of number of items in an array. *(Finkle, 1973)*

Control Processes: Selective Attention

Although the nature of sensory register functioning is similar across age levels, we've also seen that children don't process the contents of this store in such a manner as to prevent it from decaying or to facilitate its transfer to a more durable short-term store. Haith (1970) has suggested that adults might visu-ally rehearse the contents of sensory register to prevent the decay of infor-mation from this memory, although there hasn't been much additional spec-ulation about this visual rehearsal process. Another process that is much more important to the operation of sensory register is selective attention.

There is at any moment a great quantity of information impinging upon our sense organs. Currently you're attending to a specific set of visual infor-mation (letters, words, and sentences). But, there is a quantity of other infor-mation available to you. If you scan your various senses, you'll become aware of a variety of auditory stimulation (the humming of neon lights, someone talking, noise from traffic in the street) and other less obvious sensations (odors, pressure on various parts of your body, and tension in muscles and joints). Due to information-processing limitations, we can't attend to all of these sources of stimulation at once. If we are to be efficient information processors, we must attend only to information that is appropriate to the particular activity or task at hand. Adults are very adept at selectively attend-ing. We don't, for example, have much difficulty following a conversation at parties despite a variety of competing auditory distractions. Young children are not so capable.

An examination of the development of selective auditory attention reveals a progressive improvement in children's ability to listen selectively (Geffen & Sexton, 1978; Hiscock & Kinsbourne, 1980; Maccoby & Konrad, 1966; Sexton & Geffen, 1979). A variety of research has also attempted to localize the nature of this selective attention deficit. Two possibilities have been suggested. The first, which was originally proposed by Broadbent (1958), is that selective attention occurs through the selective filtering of information. That is, as we grow older, we attenuate or filter out unwanted sources of information. Another explanation of selective attention is that with age we become more adept at focusing on the central task itself (Doyle, 1973; Lane & Presson, 1982). Doyle (1973) found support for the latter interpretation by examining the degree to which 8-, 11-, and 14-year-old children filtered unwanted information or were able to focus on a central message in a selective listening task. Children were asked to listen to lists of simultaneously presented word pairs, repeating the words in one list while ignoring those in another. As might be anticipated, young children made more intrusion errors than older children. When given a recognition test after the shadowing task, older children also recognized more words from the shadowed list; however, there were no age differences in the recognition of words from the distractor list. These results led Doyle to conclude that young children are distracted by competing messages. Their major problem, it would seem, is one of focusing on the central task. The better performance of older children in this case appears unrelated to an improvement in an ability to filter out unwanted information, since there was no interaction between age and recognition of words from the distractor list. This pattern of results has been found in several other studies with both verbal (cf., Anooshian & McCulloch, 1979) and visual information (cf., Zukier & Hagen, 1978). Furthermore, since the effective use of information is attributed to the skillful use of selective attention, it might be anticipated that training children to attend selectively would improve memory performance. In fact, it does (cf., Vliestra, 1978).

Although young children appear to lack the ability to attend selectively, this may in part be a function of the types of tasks that children have been asked to perform (for example, tracking a list of words presented in one ear, or remembering where a picture is in a serial memory task). There is evidence that in more naturalistic settings (television viewing) preschool children demonstrate the ability to shift their attention appropriately between sources of information, while monitoring a source of information (for example, a television program, Pezdek & Hartman, 1983).

A consideration of children's use of the sensory register, reveals that whereas the basic system operates much like that of adults, young children are deficient in their ability to process information stored in this memory. The reason for this inefficiency is as yet not entirely known. It may be related to developmental changes in the speed with which children begin to process the contents of sensory register or the acquisition of strategies (selective attention) that facilitate the operation of the sensory register. Or it may be a function of nonmemory factors (task and stimulus familiarity). The development of selective attention, nonetheless, does facilitate the efficiency with which children incorporate information into the system.

SHORT-TERM STORE

It is presumed that some information, having been processed in sensory register, is eventually passed into short-term store. The multistore model also allows that information enters the short-term store from long-term storage as well. The short-term store can be likened to a workbench, a conscious space where mental work is done. A problem with this store is that its capacity is limited, and information can reside there (without some additional effort on our part) for less than a minute. But, as you will see, we acquire a number of tricks or strategies to work around these space and time limitations.

Trace Duration

It is estimated that the amount of time that information resides in short-term store, without some active attempt to prolong its duration, is about 10 to 30 seconds. The rate of decay or forgetting from this store can be assessed by presenting subjects with information followed by recall several seconds later. The interval between stimulus offset and recall may be filled by a distractor activity (counting backwards from some number) or may be empty (subjects may do whatever they like during the delay interval). With adults, it is found that recall is very high if the retention interval is unfilled, but drops if the interval is filled and recall is delayed beyond 20 sec (Peterson & Peterson, 1959). In studies with children, recall following a 20-sec delay is poor even when the retention interval is unfilled (Rosner & Lindsay, 1975). Unlike adults, young children are deficient in their ability to prevent the loss of information from short-term store; however, the duration of unprocessed information seems to be about the same for children as adults.

Capacity

The amount of information that can be retained by adults in short-term store has been estimated to range between four and nine items (Mandler, 1967; Miller, 1956). In comparison to adults, young children have an even smaller capacity. A summary of some capacity estimates by age and type of information remembered are shown in Table 6-1.

Code

The modality in which information is represented in short-term store is quite varied in adults. Whereas Atkinson & Shiffrin (1968) emphasized the importance of auditory-verbal codes (cf. Baddeley, 1966; Conrad, 1971), others have shown that information can also be represented visually (Paivio & Csapo, 1969; Proctor, 1978) and semantically (Wickens, 1970). Studies with preschool children reveal that they too are capable of representing information in a variety of ways; however, unlike older children and adults whose coding preferences tend to be echoic, they prefer visual-iconic representation. That is, while we do mental work, we have a tendency to talk to ourselves. There is an overwhelming tendency to verbalize our experience silently. Young children don't seem to be so disposed; on the contrary their thoughts may be filled with pictorial representations.

One line of evidence for this preferred visual mode of encoding comes from research using a serial-memory probe task. In this task, card sets with items of varying degrees of visual and verbal similarity are shown to subjects. Brown (1977), for example, presented preschool children with four sets of letters. Sets consisted of letters of low visual and low auditory similarity (ORTY), low visual and high auditory similarity (DETV), high visual and low auditory similarity (KMVX), and high visual and high auditory similarity (BDGP). In the serial probe task a set of cards is presented to the child, one card at a time. As the card is shown, it is placed face down in front of the child. The last card in the set is a match for one of the cards that has already been presented, and the child must identify it. In Brown's study, it was found that kindergarteners made more errors when recalling visually similar letter sets compared to auditorily similar ones. This finding supports the notion that young children prefer to represent information iconically in short-term store. This phenomenon is well documented and occurs across a variety of situations. To cite one further example, Hayes and Shultze (1977) had preschool children remember a series of pictures that were visually similar (knife, arrow, nail, and pencil), nominally similar (whale, nail, pail, and snail), or unrelated (ring, key, pan, clock). It was found that children had greater difficulty remembering sequences of visually similar pictures as compared to unrelated pictures. No such confusion was found for pictures with similar names. In light of these and other

TABLE 6-1. A Sampling of Studies Reporting the Average Number of Items Recalled as a Function of Grade (Age).

| | | Preschool | | Grade | | | | | | | | | | |
Source	Materials	3 yrs	4 yrs	K	1	2	3	4	5	6	7	8	H.S.	Col.
Terman & Merrill (1937)	Forward digits (serial recall)	3	4				5		6					8–9
Farnham-Diggory (1972)	Motor activities (serial recall)			4.3		5.1			5.7					
Flavell et al. (1970)	Words (serial recall)		3.5	3.6		4.4		5.5						
Conrad (1971)	Letters (serial recall)		3.2			3.8	4.1	4.4		5.9				
Belmont (1972)	Colors (Immediate probed recall)							2.8		3.8			3.8	4
Paivio et al. (1975)	Pictures (serial recall) (free recall) Words (serial recall) (free recall)													7.2 9.8 8.5 9.7
Liben (1979)	Pictures (Free recall, semantically categorized lists)						9.3		11.6		11.8			

studies (Cramer, 1976; Hayes & Rosner, 1975; Ingison & Levin, 1975), it would seem reasonable to conclude that preschool children prefer to encode visually when information is presented in a visual form; older children and adults may recode the same information in an alternate form, often an echoic-auditory one.

In spite of preschool children's preference for visual representation, it is also apparent that they adapt their coding strategies to task demands. In a demonstration of this ability, Tversky (1973) showed preschoolers a series of pictures, each followed immediately by either another picture or a word. Children were required to respond "same" if the second stimulus was either a nominal (picture-word) or an identical (picture-picture) match and "different" if otherwise. Tversky reasoned that if children encoded the second stimulus in the modality of the first, then the amount of time needed to make a response would be faster than if the first and second stimulus had been encoded differently. In 80% of the trials the second stimulus occurred in a predictable modality (either a picture or a word); thus, children could anticipate the modality in which the second stimulus would occur. In this situation it would be to the children's advantage to recode the first stimulus in the modality in which the second stimulus was likely to occur. Indeed, an examination of children's responses revealed faster reaction times on trials in which the second stimulus appeared in the expected modality compared to those trials when it did not. These children had shifted their mode of encoding to facilitate their performance on the task (cf. Hoving, Konick, & Wallace, 1975).

Preschool children's tendency to process information within a visual modality is also found in their responses to what is perhaps the most conspicuous source of audiovisual information in their lives, the television. Although some studies have shown that young children process more auditory than visual information while watching television (Anderson & Levin, 1976), other studies have reported that it is the visual message that children remember. In fact, children are often unaware of auditory messages. In one study, Hayes and Birnbaum (1980) showed preschoolers cartoons with sound tracks that were either appropriate or inappropriate to the visual portion of the program, or they showed the visual or auditory portions of the program only. They found that children remembered better information that was unique to the visual, rather than the auditory, portion of the program. It was also observed that in the condition where visual and inappropriate auditory information was presented, few children detected an inconsistency. Although young children seem to comprehend more of the visual portion of television programs (cf. Pezdek & Hartman, 1983, Experiment 1), this doesn't mean that auditory information is an insignificant source of information to younger children.

Several studies have suggested that the auditory message may serve as an attentional device, directing children's attention to key aspects of a televised program. Children's attention to programs is directly related to their comprehension of the program, and curiously, altering aspects of the audio portion of programs produces more inattentiveness in children than alterations in the continuity of the video portion. Apparently young children are quite sensitive to the auditory tract, using it as a guide for attending to specific segments of the visual track. Calvert, Huston, Watkins, and Wright (1982) found that salient auditory features (vocalizations and sound effects) elicited preschoolers' attention and enhanced their comprehension of program content. Whereas it may be that young children have better factual memories for visually presented material (Beagles-Roos & Gat, 1983; Hayes & Birnbaum, 1980; Hayes, Chemelski, & Birnbaum, 1981; Pezdek & Hartman, 1983), it also seems that sound serves as a salient attentional cue for bringing children's attention back to task and signaling important facets in an information-laden situation.

Structurally, we find that the operation of the short-term store is relatively similar across age levels. Children are able to retain information in this store for about as long as adults (provided adults are prevented from processing its contents), and both adults and children represent information in a variety of codes (although we find some age changes in preferred modes of encoding). Children have less short-term capacity than adults, although, capacity as well as other aspects of short-term store functioning do appear to be affected by children's failure to use a variety of control processes.

Control Processes:
Rehearsal, Chunking, Imagery, and Subjective Organization

It should be obvious that we can retain information in some working memory for periods much longer than 30 sec. If you were asked to remember a strange telephone number, a name, or an address—and barring the availability of paper and pencil—you'd probably begin to rehearse, or to repeat the information over and over. By rehearsing, we believe we temporarily delay the loss of the to-be-remembered information from memory. Also we have the impression that the more we practice this information, the more resistant to forgetting it becomes. In fact, rehearsal was originally believed to be an important process for transferring information to long-term, permanent memory (cf. Atkinson & Shiffrin, 1968; Rundus, 1971). The longer information resided in short-term store (the more rehearsal it received), the more likely it was believed that it would be transferred to the long-term store. Consequently, much of the early work in the development of short-term memory focused on the presence of rehearsal in children's attempts to remember.

An examination of young children's performance on tasks requiring memory reveals that they don't spontaneously rehearse; this failure to rehearse has consequently been linked with their poor performances on short-term memory tasks. The old adage "in one ear and out the other" may not be an entirely inappropriate description of young children's short-term memory.

Early work by Flavell (Flavell, Beach, & Chinsky, 1966; Flavell, Friedrichs, & Hoyt, 1970) found that kindergarten children used little rehearsal in learning a series of pictures, although there was a progressive increase in the use of rehearsal throughout the elementary school years. Other studies seeking to understand children's use of rehearsal have taken a more indirect route, studying what words within a list children remember (Atkinson, Hansen, & Bernbach, 1964; Cole, Frankle, & Sharp, 1971; Ornstein, Naus, & Liberty, 1975).

If we were to plot the frequency with which words are recalled as a function of their presentation order, we'd find that adults recall more of those words from the beginning of a list (*primacy effect*) as well as those from the end of the list (*recency effect*). Children's recall, while showing a recency effect, doesn't typically show primacy. It is generally assumed that the primacy effect reflects recall from long-term store, whereas recency reflects recall of the contents of the short-term store. Furthermore, the argument has been made that primacy is a function of the more frequent repetition of earlier occurring items (Dark & Loftus, 1976; Rundus, 1971). In an examination of children's word retention strategies, Ornstein, Naus, and Liberty (1975) have found that older children (sixth- and eighth-grade), compared to younger children (third-grade) both rehearse more and in their rehearsal sets include a greater number of words.

Although there is little evidence that young children rehearse spontaneously in list-learning tasks, it is possible to train them to use rehearsal to delay forgetting and improve memory. Several researchers (Asarnow & Meichenbaum, 1979; Ornstein, Naus, & Stone, 1977) have had children learn word lists, encouraging them to rehearse using multi-item rehearsal sets or allowing them to study in any manner they wish. These studies have shown that as early as 5 years of age children's memory can be improved through rehearsal training.

Whereas cumulative rehearsal may be effective for extending the amount of time that information can be maintained in short-term store, other control processes are currently believed to be more important in improving the operation of the short-term store and the transfer of information to a more permanent memory. Generally these processes reflect voluntary attempts by the memorizer to consolidate and organize information entering and residing in this store (Rundus, 1977). One strategy to increase the capacity of short-term store involves grouping (or chunking) bits of information together to form larger units, which themselves become unitary bits of information. For example, if you attempted to memorize the sequence 6-1-4-7-2-3-2-1-2-5, you'd probably have some difficulty as the span exceeds or borders on the capacity of most adult's short-term memory. In order to simplify this task, you might combine the digits into larger but fewer units: 61-47-23-21-25, or as is done with telephone numbers: 614-723-2125. By chunking, there are fewer units of information to be remembered, but in an absolute sense, more information is retained.

In one study demonstrating this process, Rosner (1971) instructed children (first-, fifth-, and ninth-graders) to learn a series of pictures by either rehearsing items in sequence or chunking (making up ways that pictures could be put together). The performance of children receiving chunking or rehearsal instructions was compared to a group that received standard free-recall instructions. Over a series of trials, first-graders failed to profit from either rehearsal or chunking instructions. Chunking instructions, however, facilitated the retention of item information for both of the older age groups. The failure of chunking to facilitate young children's memory suggests that mnemonic strategies involving stimulus consolidation may be difficult for young children. Another technique for facilitating memory involving the elaboration of interactive visual images seems to support this notion.

It is known that it is easier to remember words eliciting high imagery (ice cream) than it is to remember words eliciting low imagery (justice) (Rohwer, 1970). Instructing older children and adults to produce interactive visual images of to-be-remembered information facilitates learning (Kosslyn & Pomerantz, 1977) and is the basis for the remarkable feats of memory performed by mnemonists (Lorayne & Lucas, 1974). One memory technique based on imagery, called the keyword technique (Raugh & Atkinson, 1975) consists of transforming to-be-remembered words into visual images consistent with the words' meanings. When learning foreign vocabulary, for example, one might translate the Spanish word *huevo* into an image of an egg (the English equivalent) floating on a wave. This particular technique has been found to be extremely effective for teaching older elementary school children a variety of technical terms and aiding them in recalling historical events, places, and people (Jones & Hall, 1982; Shriberg, Levin, McCormick, & Pressley, 1982) and remembering faces and names (McCarty, 1980). Whereas young children appear to have better factual knowledge of information presented visually (rather than auditorily), they seem less likely to profit from imagery instructions than are older children and adults (Reese, 1970; Rohwer 1970).

Currently much attention is being given to another elaborative process for facilitating the operation of memory. This process is subjective organization. The importance of subjective organization has been known for some time. Ancient Greek orators, for example, associated parts of lengthy oratories with specific locations and used these locational cues to assist them in recalling their speeches (Bugelski, 1970). Sir Francis Galton described a similar technique for retrieving long sequences of information, pairing information with shops and places along a path that he walked regularly (Crovitz, 1970). Both of these techniques imply the imposition of order upon a stimulus as it is entered into memory and subsequently the use of these organizational cues to retrieve it.

One way to study subjective organization is to have subjects recall lists of words with varying degrees of category similarity. It is anticipated that lists constructed of conceptually similar words will be easier to organize and that recall will reflect this organization—recall will be clustered into sets of categorically similar words. Developmental studies show that older children use the categorical properties of word lists to facilitate recall (Lange, 1973; Laurence, 1966; Vaughan, 1968) and that they cluster to a greater degree than younger children (Galbraith & Day, 1978; Rossi & Wittrock, 1971; Vaughan, 1968). As might be anticipated, increasing the salience of categories by blocking lists of words into categories elevates the frequency with which category clustering occurs during recall (Yoshimura, Moely, & Shapiro, 1971).

The research reported in this section shows that young children fail to use a number of control processes or strategies for delaying the loss of information from the short-term store or expanding its capacity. It has also been demonstrated that some types of training (rehearsal) or task structuring to call attention to specific organizational properties of word lists improves memory (blocking related words in a list). Other types of strategies relying upon the spontaneous organization and elaboration of information (chunking and interactive imagery) are not as amenable to training. Whereas a significant aspect of memory functioning entails getting information into the information-processing system (processes described to this point), an equally important aspect of any information-processing system is the retrieval of information, or accessing the contents of a memory store.

Retrieval from Short-Term Store

Retrieval has been studied using a task developed by Sternberg (1969) in which subjects are shown a series of items that are committed to memory. A probe is then presented, and subjects must state whether or not the probe is part of the memorized set. On each trial a new set of items is committed to memory; the sets vary between one and six items. When checking the contents of memory, Sternberg observed that four different types of searches were possible. A search might either be serial or parallel. In serial searches, subjects would compare the probe individually with other items in the memory set. In a parallel search the item would be compared simultaneously to all items in a set. Whether a search is parallel or serial can be inferred from an examination of the amount of time it takes to identify an item as part of a set as the number of items in the memory set is increased. Serial searches would vary as a function of set size, whereas parallel searches would be unaffected. If a search is serial, it may either be self-terminating or exhaustive. A self-terminating search would be stopped as soon as a match to a probe is found; an exhaustive search would be continued until the probe has been compared to all items in the set. In verifying the presence or absence of an item in a set, exhaustive searches would produce equivalent reaction times to probes whether or not they were part of the set. Self-terminating searches would produce shorter response latencies to probes that were in the set.

A number of experiments using this technique have shown that search strategies are similar across age levels. For all ages, searches have been found to be serial and exhaustive (Hoving, Morin, & Konick, 1970); furthermore, the rate at which memory is searched remains constant across age levels (Harris & Fleer, 1974; Hoving et al., 1970; Silverman, 1974). These data suggest that the manner in which memory is scanned is an automatic process rather than under some developmental control.

Although we find similarities across age levels in the manner in which children scan the contents of memory, there are developmental changes in the ability to generate effective retrieval strategies—strategies that are apparently influenced by task and situational demands. Wellman, Somerville, and Haake (1979) had preschoolers search for missing objects on a playground or in cupboards in a classroom. Searches were strongly influenced by the environment in which the search was conducted. On the playground, searches were much more logical, taking into consideration information about where the object was last seen. In the classroom, searches through cupboards were exhaustive; children disregarded information about where the object had been last seen. It would seem that young children modify their search behavior depending upon the amount of effort required for the search. Under conditions that might require much work (searching for something on a playground), more logical strategies are adopted. Anooshian, Hartman, and Scharf (1982) have supported this notion but note that children's ability to remember sequential and event information are also important determinants of children's ability to conduct effective searches.

The need for children to be able to generate or use retrieval cues to retrieve information successfully is also supported in developmental trends in recall and recognition tests of memory. A number of studies using recognition tests (which reprovide the memorized information) have shown that age differences in memory performance are either attenuated or nonexistent (cf. Brown, 1973; Murphy & Brown, 1975). Providing children with retrieval cues has also facilitated their level of recall (Kenniston & Flavell, 1979; Kobasigawa & Middleton, 1972). These findings have led some experts to conclude that the failure of young children to retrieve information from memory does not necessarily reflect their inability to use retrieval cues, but their failure to produce them.

In this past section, we've considered the development and operation of a temporary working memory. But our ability to retain and retrieve vast amounts of information from a more distant past reveals the operation of a more permanent memory system, the long-term store. It should be apparent that not all information we process through the short-term store becomes a part of long-term memory. Can you recall or recognize, for instance, your license plate number? Some of you probably can, but others like me can't, even though we've undoubtedly written these numbers down a couple of times when we've filled out credit applications or motel registrations. That information has been in our working memory, but for some of us, we've failed to transfer it to long-term storage. The question of how information is transferred from the short-term store to the long-term store is the subject of considerable debate. The multistore theorists in the past have argued that cumulative rehearsal is the key to transferring information to long-term memory (Atkinson & Shiffrin, 1968; Dark & Loftus, 1976; Rundus, 1971). The more frequently an item is rehearsed in short-term memory, it is argued, the more likely it will be transferred to the long-term store. Therefore, if you write your license plate number frequently, as you might if you bought gasoline with a credit card, you'd be more likely to have this information in long-term memory.

LONG-TERM STORE

The long-term store is generally characterized as a large capacity system capable of holding information for lengthy periods of time—possibly indefinitely (Atkinson & Shiffrin, 1968). We store a variety of information in this store and do it in a highly organized fashion.

Code and Organization

It should be of no surprise that we retain a variety of information in the long-term store. Information is stored here about odors, textures, temperatures, locations, sounds, shapes, and so on. We can give meaning to all of these. In addition to the variety of information held in the long-term store, these memories are highly structured. When we are accessing the contents of long-term store, this organization allows us to recover information quickly. For example, the capacity to read proficiently attests to the rapidity with which we perceive some set of orthographic features, match them to some information about letters or features in long-term store, and give meaning to these groupings.

It is also apparent that children impose organization upon the contents of their long-term stores, although the nature of that organization may change with age. In a study demonstrating these organizational tendencies, Kellas, McCauley, and McFarland (1975) asked fourth-, sixth-, and eighth-graders to judge if a word was a member of one of two category pairs (for example, state–flower or tree–flower). It was reasoned that if children were able to impose organization on this task, they would unify the two latter categories (tree–flower) to form a derived category (plants) from which to make judgments. If such organization occurred, it was expected that judgments would be quicker to the categorically similar than to the dissimilar pair. In fact, at all age levels this is exactly what was found.

It is generally believed that information is organized hierarchically in the long-term store. The nature of this organization has been the object of considerable research. One idea about how information is organized in long-term store was proposed by Collins and Quillian (1969). Their model (sometimes referred to as the specificity model) assumes that words are stored in a network (Figure 6-5), with various kinds of information stored at different nodes. Information stored at each node is specific to things defined by that node. Thus, if in this hierarchy there was a node for birds, we would associate with it information about wings, flying, and feathers (characteristics unique to birds). We might have other nodes for specific kinds of birds (for example, canaries) and at those nodes store additional information specific to them (canaries are yellow, small, and are songbirds). This model could be tested by discovering how rapidly one can verify a sentence as either true or false. Questions asking about properties contained at specific nodes ("Are canaries yellow?") should be verified faster than questions asking about properties contained several nodes removed ("Do canaries breathe?").

Anderson and Bower (1973) have proposed a different view of how information might be organized in the long-term store. Their model (sometimes called the saliency model) assumes that words are linked in semantic memory on the basis of associations. Suppose, for example, that a subject is presented with a pair of sentences, "The child hit the landlord" and "The minister praised the landlord." After hearing these sentences, we could predict that the subjects (the child and the minister) should be equally associated with the object (the landlord), as would the actions associated with the landlord (hitting and praising). If associations have been drawn between the elements of these sentences,

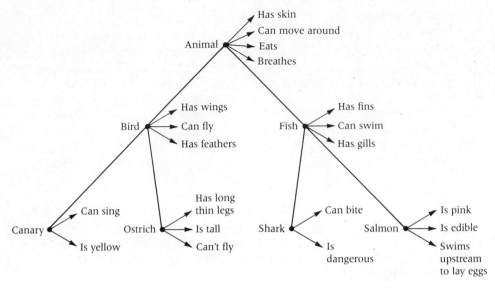

Figure 6-5. Illustration of the hypothetical memory structure for a three-level hierarchy. *(Collins & Quillian, 1969)*

then providing subjects with sentence blanks such as, "The child praised the _____" and "The minister hit _____" should be equally effective (though inaccurate) in cuing the recall of the direct object *landlord*.

In an assessment of these two views of long-term memory organization, Nelson and Kosslyn (1975) presented sentences varying in degrees of saliency (characteristics highly associated with the direct object), and specificity to 8-, 11-, and 13-year-old children and college students (Table 6-2). These subjects were asked to indicate whether sentences were true or false. It was found that at all age levels, response latencies were shorter to highly salient sentences than to those with low saliency. Curiously, sentences with low specificity were responded to faster than those with high specificity. These results suggest that for all age levels, long-term memory is organized on the basis of associations. Work by Chi and Koeske (1983) also shows that children's semantic memory reflects a structure based around interitem associations. Less well-known information is characterized by fewer item interconnections or associations.

TABLE 6-2. Examples of Sentences Varying in Saliency and Specificity.

Saliency	Specificity	Sentence
High	High	A leopard has spots.
High	Medium	An orangutan can climb.
High	Low	A peacock has a tail.
Medium	High	A peacock has a crest.
Medium	Medium	An eel can swim.
Medium	Low	An iguana has skin.
Low	High	An eel can twist.
Low	Medium	A leopard has feet.
Low	Low	A mink has a nose.

(From Nelson and Kosslyn, 1975)

The research reviewed thus far suggests that across age levels the contents of long-term memory are highly organized along associative dimensions. In spite of these similarities, the types of associations drawn by children are likely quite different than those of adults. In word association tests, for example, it is found that adults give common associations in response to words (Palermo & Jenkins, 1966). Children's responses to these word associations are much more varied and idiosyncratic (Palermo, 1971; Palermo & Jenkins, 1966).

There are two explanations of how children come to organize information in a way that their organizational schemes resemble those of others in their culture. The integration view posits that young children have formed categories in which relevant items have been excluded. Children's concepts are fragmented and incomplete (Figure 6-6). As children grow older, formerly fragmented categories are combined to represent more adultlike conceptual groupings. Studies of children's sorting behavior, for example, have found that older children include more items into category sorts than younger children (Saltz, Dixon, Klein, & Becker, 1977; Saltz, Soller, & Siegel, 1972) and include a greater number of peripheral (less obvious) category members into conceptual groups (Rosch, 1973).

The opposite view to integration is differentiation. This position holds that conceptual organization is a consequence of deleting irrelevant items from conceptual groupings (Figure 6-6). In support of this view it has been observed that in naming items that belong to categories, older children are more consistent with respect to what they deem to be appropriate category members. Young children tend to generate a more diverse set of responses (Neimark, 1974; Nelson, 1974).

While differing in their approach to conceptual development and organization, these two processes likely operate simultaneously. Rosner and Hayes

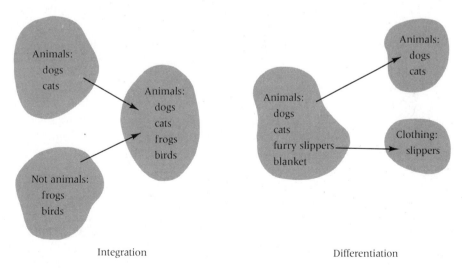

Integration   Differentiation

Figure 6-6. An integration and differentiation view of semantic development.

(1977) had preschoolers and fourth-graders name instances of a general category (animals) and specific categories (farm animals, zoo animals, pets). They found that preschoolers generated fewer instances of both general and specific categories. Whereas there were no differences between the two age levels in the appropriateness of items included in the general categories, younger children did include more inappropriate items into specific categories. The inclusion of inappropriate items into specific categories reveals that differentiation must occur as these children develop and organize conceptual hierarchies. An examination of omissions and misinclusions to the general class also revealed that the preschoolers were less likely to include certain subcategory items into the general class, thus revealing the need for integration in conceptual development as well.

THE MULTISTORE MODEL OF MEMORY: A CRITIQUE

As will undoubtedly be the case with any conceptual model, the multistore model of memory, popular in the early 1970s, became the frequent target of criticism toward the end of that decade (Postman, 1975). Much of that criticism centered around the necessity of postulating the existence of separate memory systems and the role of cumulative rehearsal in committing information to a more permanent memory store.

Is There a Sensory Memory?

Evidence for the existence of the sensory register has derived, in part, from a comparison of research using either full or partial reports of tachistoscopically presented visual fields. Full reports are generally assumed to reflect recall from short-term store. As evidence for this, it is noted that the absolute quantity of information reported under this procedure remains constant (at about 4.5 items) over time, thus suggesting that recall is from a more durable though limited storage system. Partial reports are assumed to provide information about the operation of sensory register. As evidence, researchers point to initially large amounts of information that can be recalled immediately following the offset of a visual field and the rapid rate of information decay during delays of up to 300 ms. The quality of recall under partial- and full-report procedures is quite different and therefore seen as support for the presence of two memory systems.

Others have argued that the differences obtained on these tasks are mere artifacts of the methods employed. Holding (1975), for example, attributes superior immediate recall under partial-report procedures to cue anticipation. He suggests that by anticipating what is to be cued, subjects can attend to a limited set of information and thereby improve their recall accuracy. Holding also argues that full-report procedures may produce poorer recall because of output interference—the recall of past items may inhibit current item recall.

There are, however, several problems with Holding's objections. First, the partial-report procedure is designed to reduce cue anticipation. Most studies have presented position or identity probes randomly, thus negating any advantage that could accrue from anticipating what or where something might be probed. Second, it has been observed that contrary to Holding's claim, output interference is negligible in tachistoscopic experiments (Colehart, 1975). And third, none of Holding's explanations of the superiority of partial-report procedures adequately account for the rapid decline in recall accuracy that occurs in this procedure with recall delays of up to 300 ms (Colehart, 1975; Hoving et al., 1978).

Are There Short- and Long-Term Stores?

One of the major arguments for a distinction between short- and long-term stores comes from clinical studies of individuals with organic brain damage and the effects of a variety of drugs on memory performance. Damage to portions of the hippocampal region of the brain produces a cognitive disorder in patients in whom pretraumatic memory is intact; however, posttraumatic long-term memory is very poor. These individuals are able to retain information for about 30 sec and interruption of rehearsal processes used to delay the loss of information from memory produces rapid forgetting (Milner, 1970). A similar phenomenon has been observed in individuals suffering from Korsakoff's Syndrome (Talland, 1965).

This research implies that these individuals are unable to transfer information from short-term to long-term storage. Similarly, varying levels of neurochemical transmitters in the brain have distinct effects on short-term memory. Injecting subjects with the drug, scopolamine, for instance, produces a loss of short-term memory, although long-term memory is unaffected. Such evidence provides a compelling physical demonstration of the separation of short- and long-term stores. However, it may be premature to conclude that these data conclusively demonstrate the existence of separate memory stores. Research with Korsakoff patients, for example, reveals that they are capable of acquiring simple motor skills and that they demonstrate normal or near normal levels of classical conditionability (Knight & Wooles, 1980).

Another criticism that has been leveled against the existence of separate storage systems is that the empirical evidence offered to support their distinctiveness is unconvincing. Craik and Lockhart (1972) have criticized the presumption that short- and long-term stores can be characterized by unique code, duration, and capacity characteristics. Research examining each of these characteristics, they conclude, reveals a greater overlap of characteristics between stores, than separation between them.

How Does Information Get from Short-Term Store to Long-Term Store?

One of the more important control processes associated with the multistore model of memory is rehearsal. Multistore theorists originally argued that the amount of time that information resides in short-term store or the amount of repetition that information is given while in short-term store has a direct bearing on the likelihood that it will be transferred to a more permanent long-term store.

Perhaps the most damaging case against cumulative rehearsal as the mechanism for the transfer of information from short-term to long-term store comes from studies on incidental memory. These studies have essentially shown that in a number of situations, whether or not an individual is intending to remember something has little to do with his or her retention of that information. Memory in these situations would appear to be explainable by processes other than intentional ones, such as rehearsal. In one such study (Craik & Watkins, 1973, Experiment 1), subjects were shown a series of words and were asked to report the last word in the list that began with a particular letter. Subjects could essentially ignore words that did not begin with the critical letter. Within lists, the amount of space between the monitored word (the last one having the pertinent letter) and the one that replaced it was varied. It was assumed that when more space intervened between a monitored word and its replacement, the word would be given more rehearsal. Within the multistore model, it would be predicted that items that were rehearsed more would be found more frequently in a final, free recall. Final free recall, however, did not show any effect due to rehearsal. These results were interpreted by Craik and Watkins as evidence against rehearsal as the mechanism responsible for the transfer of information from short-term to long-term store.

Despite the trend toward discounting cumulative rehearsal as an important factor in information retention, other studies suggest that in some instances cumulative rehearsal is useful for the long-term retention of information. Dark and Loftus (1976) had subjects study word lists, which were followed by variable retention intervals before recall. During some intervals, subjects were required to rehearse, and during others the retention interval was filled by a rehearsal-preventing task. After a number of study-test lists had been presented, subjects were given an unexpected final recall of all previously presented words. It was found that in the final recall, words that were rehearsed during the delay intervals were remembered better than words from lists where rehearsal had been prevented. Furthermore, the probability of recalling a word in final, free recall was directly related to the length of the retention interval; longer rehearsal intervals produced higher levels of final recall. It would appear that a case can be made for the value of rehearsal in the long-term retention of information after all.

SUMMARY

The multistore model characterizes memory as a system of three distinct and separate memory stores; these are the sensory register, short-term store, and long-term store. These storage systems can be differentiated on the basis of structural characteristics—code, trace duration, and capacity, and control processes. Although the structure of memory may be intact and invariant by a young age (at least by 4 or 5 years of age), changes are believed to occur in the use of control process that allow for a more efficient use of memory. The improvement in the use of these processes accounts for the development of memory ability. In retrospect, much of what has been reported in this chapter supports this position.

The structural aspects of the memory system appear similar across age levels. Developmental improvement in memory functioning would appear related to the better use of control processes such as selective attention in sensory register, rehearsal, chunking, and subjective organization in the short-term store, and the organization of information in the long-term memory store.

A number of criticisms have been leveled at the multistore model of memory and have focused on the necessity of postulating distinct and separate memory storage systems as well as the importance of cumulative rehearsal in the transfer of information from some short-term memory space to some long-term store. Although rebuttals have been offered in defense of the model, another set of data to be discussed in the next chapter has presented the multistore model of memory with a serious challenge, suggesting a radically different model of memory.

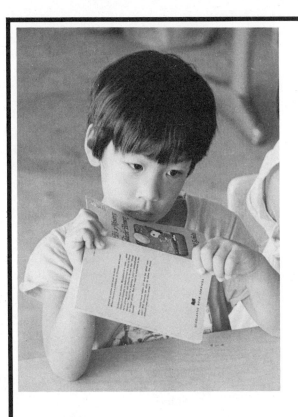

7

A Levels-of-Processing Model of Memory

Anyone who has studied for a test should appreciate how little is remembered following rote memorization. Mechanically memorizing some content verbatim, without assimilating it into an existing system of knowledge and experience may make the information temporarily available, but little is remembered after a lengthy delay—save for the painful recollection of the effort required for this type of preparation. What we seem to remember best are events, people, places, and things that have been important to us, or information that we have been able to relate to an existing set of knowledge. We remember meaningful things, and we forget less meaningful ones. This relatively simple intuition of how our memory operates reflects the underpinning of a second model of memory to be considered in this chapter: the *levels-of-processing model of memory*.

SEMANTIC AND NONSEMANTIC LEVELS

Within the levels-of-processing model, it is assumed that information coming into the information-processing system is processed in a hierarchical fashion—in a series of processing stages. These processing stages are believed to represent varying depths of analyses. Information may be thought of in a variety of ways. When attending to the word *car*, we can consider its nonsemantic, physical features—for example, how the word is spelled (*c-a-r*)—or how the word sounds (/k//a//r/). Or we can attend to its semantic properties—for example, a car is a type of transportation, a passenger vehicle with four wheels. Consequently, we can process or encode information about shallow, physical features or deeper, semantic ones (Figure 7-1). It is assumed that retention is a direct function of the depth to which information is processed. Memory then is thought of as a continuum of encodings ranging from traces based upon the less permanent encodings of physical features to more durable encodings of semantic features (Craik & Lockhart, 1972).

You will recall from the previous chapter that multistore theorists for a time believed rehearsal to be an important mechanism for transferring information to a more permanent memory. Levels-of-processing theorists also believe rehearsal is important for retention; however, they distinguish between two kinds of rehearsal. On the one hand, these theorists recognize the existence of rehearsal characterized by rote repetition. This type of rehearsal is called Type I processing or maintenance rehearsal. Although maintenance rehearsal may be important for keeping information in an immediate memory, it is of little consequence for the long-term retention of information.

A second type of rehearsal recognized by the levels theorists is Type II processing or elaborative rehearsal. This type of rehearsal involves the elaboration or processing of information to develop a memory trace that includes semantic associations. It is believed that only elaborative rehearsal produces long-term retention.

With a set of experiments conducted by Craik and Tulving (1975), a paradigm was established for levels-of-processing research. The paradigm consists of showing to subjects a list of words, one word at a time. Prior to being presented a word, subjects are asked a question about the word to which they must answer either yes or no. Several kinds of questions are asked. They may be about nonsemantic features ("Does the word begin with the letter *c*?" or "Does the word rhyme with 'lar'?"). Questions may also be asked about semantic properties of words ("Is it a type of vehicle?" or "Would the word fit the sentence: 'The _____ was parked on the street'?"). It is assumed that questions fix the level at which words are encoded. Word lists may be presented under intentional (subjects are told that they will be asked to remember words after list presentation) or incidental conditions (subjects are told only that they are participating in a word recognition task; they are uninformed about the final recall or recognition task).

Research from both intentional and incidental recall and recognition tests supports the notion that semantically encoded words are remembered better

PHYSICAL

CAR (n) 1:a. vehicle moving on wheels, a carriage, cart, wagon;
b. a chariot of war; c. a vehicle adapted to the rails of a railway
or street railway; d. automobile; 2: the cage of an elevator.

SEMANTIC

Figure 7-1. A levels-of-processing view of memory functioning.

than those nonsemantically encoded (Craik & Tulving, 1975; Till & Jenkins, 1973; Walsh & Jenkins, 1973). There are a number of reasons why semantic elaboration facilitates retention more than other types of encoding. Eysenck and Eysenck (1979) suggest that nonsemantic orienting activities may direct the learner's attention to parts of the stimulus (the first letter of words or the last syllables), thus detracting from an encoding of the entire stimulus. Other explanations (Eysenck, 1978; Fisher & Craik, 1977) have suggested that semantic elaboration is more likely to facilitate retention because there are a greater number of features at that level that can be coded uniquely and that can serve to distinguish to-be-remembered items in memory. Because physical encodings share a more restricted set of features (there are only 26 letters in the

alphabet and 33 phonemes in the English language), there are fewer discriminating attributes and greater possibilities for confusion in memory.

As with the multistore model, the levels-of-processing model accounts for
children's memory performance with the same processes responsible for adult
memory functioning. In fact, children, like adults, remember semantically
encoded words best. The improvement in children's memory performance is
attributed to their growing appreciation of semantic features of items, the
amount of semantic elaboration they are able to impose upon situations, and
their ability to generate suitable and compatible cues for retrieving the contents
of memory.

Demonstrations of semantic involvement in children's memory have been
many. Geis and Hall (1976), for example, presented lists of words printed on
cards to first-, third-, and fifth-grade children. As a word was shown to the
child, the experimenter asked a question about it that could be answered with
a "yes" or a "no" response. Three types of questions were asked: some asked
about the case type of words ("Is it in big letters?"), others about rhyme
characteristics ("Does it sound like 'larms'?"), and still others about semantic
characteristics ("Are they part of your body?"). After all the words had been
shown, children were given an unexpected recall test. For all age levels,
semantically encoded words were recalled better than nonsemantically encoded
ones (Figure 7-2). Geis and Hall concluded that obligatory semantic encoding
facilitates children's recall across age levels equally. (Encoding is obligatory in
the sense that the experimenter, by nature of the questions asked about words,
requires subjects to attend to specific stimulus features.)

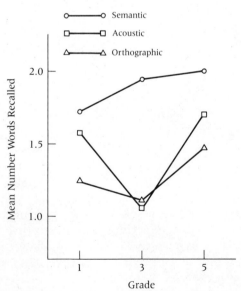

Figure 7-2. Mean number of words recalled as a function of grade level
and orienting activity to words. (*Geis & Hall, 1976*)

When optional, or voluntary, encoding strategies can be eliminated or minimized (as in incidental memory tasks) developmental differences in children's memory are reduced. Although semantically encoded words, compared to nonsemantically encoded ones, have been found to be remembered best across a wide range of ages (Geis & Hall, 1976, 1978; Ghatala, Carbonari, & Bobele, 1980; Murphy & Brown, 1975; Owings & Baumeister, 1979; Waters & Waters, 1976), there are conditions under which this phenomenon may be less likely to occur. Weiss, Robinson, and Hastie (1977) assessed second- and fourth-grade children's incidental recall of picture-word cards and found that older children remember more of the semantically encoded words than younger children. No age differences were found in the recall of nonsemantically encoded words. These data suggest that under certain conditions (types of questions asked about words, types of stimulus materials used, or list length) younger children may be less sensitive to the semantic properties of words or prone to engage in less semantic elaboration than older children.

SPREAD OR DEPTH OF ENCODING

In an extension of the levels-of-processing concept, Craik and Tulving (1975) proposed that it may be more appropriate to talk of a spread of encoding rather than some continuous hierarchical set of analyses conducted on information. Spread of encoding is a more flexible concept than is depth of encoding, suggesting that a memory trace may be developed that includes additional information within the dimension of orienting activity as well as information from other dimensions (Figure 7-3). The concept can be likened to what happens when ink is dropped into a glass of water: there is a dispersion of dye in all directions. So it would seem with spread of encoding. Whereas an orienting activity may fix the depth at which a trace begins to be elaborated, there is a spread of encoding, or an activation of associations including other semantic and nonsemantic features.

Support for a spread-of-encoding interpretation of memory is based, in part, on a comparison of performance on incidental and informed memory tasks. When performance on these two types of tasks is compared in relation to the type of orienting activity directed at words, the pattern of recall is similar (Craik & Tulving, 1975, Experiments 3 & 4). Recall is best when words are associated with semantic questions. Although there are seldom interactions between instruction type and orienting activity, intentional recall is frequently better than incidental recall. Thus, it would appear that some additional elaboration of the stimulus trace is carried out in the intentional recall condition at both the semantic and nonsemantic levels. Furthermore, studies that have manipulated the meaningfulness of stimulus words have found that those that are more meaningful are remembered better than those that are less meaningful following nonsemantic as well as semantic orienting activities (Hunt, Elliott, & Spence, 1979). Apparently, nonsemantic orienting activities activate some network of associations, and richer networks (including both semantic and

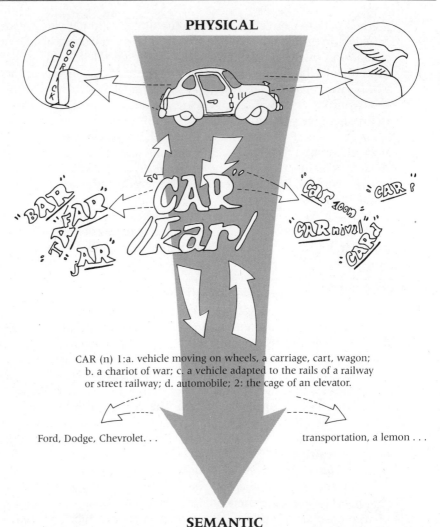

PHYSICAL

CAR (n) 1:a. vehicle moving on wheels, a carriage, cart, wagon;
b. a chariot of war; c. a vehicle adapted to the rails of a railway
or street railway; d. automobile; 2: the cage of an elevator.

Ford, Dodge, Chevrolet. . .   transportation, a lemon . . .

SEMANTIC

Figure 7-3. A spread-of-encoding view of memory functioning.

nonsemantic features) facilitate memory. Additional support for a spread of encoding is found in the "congruity effect." Across a variety of situations, words with "yes" responses are always remembered better than those with "no" responses. These questions, it would appear, provide a more meaningful encoding context that induces the information processor to construct more elaborate memory traces.

One curious observation of Geis and Hall (1976) and Weiss et al. (1977) was that, contrary to expectations, their data failed to reveal the congruity effect (Geis & Hall, 1978 report such an effect but only with twice-presented items). This failure led to some speculation about whether or not children would construct more elaborate memory traces. In fact they do, although we find developmental improvement in this tendency.

The failure to find the congruity effect in these earlier studies was largely due to a methodological problem related to the order in which words and questions were presented (Ghatala et al., 1980). By showing words prior to questions (as was the case in the studies cited earlier), children apparently spontaneously gave words a more "meaningful" analysis—thus, attenuating any effect for congruity. When questions precede words (thus, more specifically fixing the type of processing that would be given them), the congruity effect is obtained. Spontaneous elaboration occurs more frequently with older (ninth-grade) than younger (second-grade) children. Whereas some degree of elaboration occurs at all age levels, older children are more likely to elaborate stimulus information to a degree that it becomes more resistant to forgetting (Ghatala et al., 1980).

Although research shows that a spread of encoding occurs within semantic and nonsemantic domains (Craik & Tulving, 1975; Kunen, Green, & Waterman, 1979), it is also likely that elaboration occurring within semantic domains is more beneficial to memory than elaboration within nonsemantic ones. Eysenck and Eysenck (1979), for example, presented lists of words to subjects asking questions of either semantic ("Is the item edible?") or physical ("Is the letter A in the word?") properties of words. Elaboration was extended by asking questions involving two features instead of one ("Is the item edible or solid?" or "Does the word contain an A or an I?"). Their results showed that additional elaboration significantly increased the recall of semantically but not physically encoded words.

Research with children also shows that elaborate semantic encoding facilitates retention. For example, preschoolers have better memories for pictures and sentences when they are presented for learning in a semantically organized manner (Emmerick & Ackerman, 1976). Increasing semantic similarity of words in lists (Wetherick & Alexander, 1977) or having children verbally construct relationships between nouns (Ackerman, 1982; Pressley, 1982) also produces heightened levels of recall in children across age levels. Recall is also better if words come from familiar knowledge domains (Chi & Koeske, 1983).

Whereas semantic elaboration facilitates memory across age levels, older children are more likely to profit from inducements to elaborate semantically. Baumeister and Smith (1979) assessed preschool and fifth-grade children's ability to learn sets of nine pictures under conditions designed to enhance thematic elaboration. One list (a) consisted of three subsets of three objects that formed a theme (for example, a cow next to a bucket and a milking stool). In another list (b), these objects were spatially blocked into subsets of three objects, but not explicitly organized. Another list (c) included spatially blocked subsets of three thematically unrelated items (Figure 7-4). It was found that the structure of the list affected the two age groups' recall differently. On their first recall trials, older children profited from the semantic theme in lists a and b, recalling these lists better than all others; younger children showed no differences in recall between lists.

Why older children profit from semantic encoding more than younger children is not entirely clear. One possibility is that the older children are better

List a

List b

List c

Figure 7-4. Examples of items used in Lists a, b, and c. (*Baumeister & Smith, 1979*)

able to consider not only the meaningfulness of single items, but also the meaningful relationships between a number of items (Ackerman, 1982; Buss, Yussen, Mathews, Miller, & Rembold, 1983). For example, a young child might see a dog under a table chewing on a bone and process the contents of the event (dog, table, bone) separately, failing to elaborate a unified, cohesive memory trace for the event. Such an explanation is compatible with an observation made previously—that young children do not profit in memory from instructions to elaborate interactive images. This is also consistent with Piaget's observation that preschool children view the world as discrete scenes rather than appreciating the transformations that occur between states of objects.

To summarize, like adults, children also profit from activities designed to direct attention to more meaningful, semantic features of information to be committed to memory. Although children at all age levels experience this facilitation, as children age, they are more apt to elaborate information spontaneously or profit from contexts that prompt such processing.

ENCODING SPECIFICITY

In order for a memory model to be complete, it must address the issue of information retrieval. Thomson and Tulving (1970, 1973) have suggested an encoding specificity notion of retrieval that complements the levels-of-processing formulation of memory functioning. When we try to remember something, we attempt to generate retrieval cues. The effectiveness of our effort is believed to depend upon how closely the cues we generate reinstate the context in which we learned something—that is, how closely the cue resembles the encoded trace. If, for example, you associated a word in a list with the cue "It's a form of transportation," the statement "A form of transportation" would be a more effective retrieval cue than would the statement "Rhymes with 'lar.' "

In assessing this principle (Thomson & Tulving, 1970, Experiment 2), subjects were presented with a set of low-associate word pairs. They were trained to anticipate the use of one of the words as a retrieval cue for recalling its mate (the target). At recall, and for some subjects, retrieval cues were provided that were originally paired with the target word (congruent-low associates). Thomson and Tulving found that recall of target words was best when the retrieval cue was congruent with the encoding context compared to when incongruent high-associate retrieval cues were provided—thus, supporting the encoding specificity explanation of retrieval.

Further research by Fisher and Craik (1977) provided further support for the idea that recall is facilitated by retrieval cues that are congruous with the encoding context. In an incidental recall task, subjects were given cues that reinstated the context in which information was encoded or cues that were different. As can be seen in Table 7-1, recall was best when the retrieval cue and the encoding context were congruous.

Again, like adults, children also remember best when they are provided with retrieval cues that reinstate the learning context (Ceci, Lea, & Howe, 1980; Ceci & Howe, 1978; Ross & Killey, 1977). Ceci and Howe, for example,

TABLE 7-1. **Proportions of Words Recalled as a Function of Encoding Questions and Retrieval Cues** (*Fisher & Craik, 1977, Experiment 1*)

	Encoding Question							
	Positive Responses				Negative Responses			
Retrieval Cue	Rhyme	Category	Sentence	M	Rhyme	Category	Sentence	M
Rhyme	.40	.43	.29	.37	.26	.28	.28	.27
Category	.15	.81	.46	.47	.10	.28	.11	.16
Sentence	.10	.50	.78	.46	.08	.18	.08	.11
M	.22	.58	.51		.15	.25	.16	

used a procedure similar to that of Tulving and Thomson. In their study, 7-, 10-, and 15-year-old children learned lists of paired associates. After the list had been studied, children were shown a list of cue words, all high-associates of the target words. Some of these associates were congruent, while others were incongruent with the original word pairs. It was found, as predicted, that recall cues that were congruous with the encoding context led to higher levels of recall than those that were incongruous.

Although children across age levels are abetted by retrieval cues that are congruent with the encoded trace, retrieval environments that are congruent with the encoding context are more useful to older children. Geis and Hall (1978) presented children (first- and fifth-graders) with a standard incidental memory task with attention directed to semantic and phonetic properties of words. At recall, cues were provided to children that either reinstated the encoding context or were different. For older children, congruity between the retrieval cue and encoding activity produced higher levels of recall than it did for younger children. It should be noted, however, that even for younger children congruity facilitated recall.

The message of the level-of-processing research is very clear in its prescription for improving children's memory performance. If we wish to help children remember their lessons, we must encourage them to relate their lessons to a network of associations and experiences that they have already acquired. Furthermore, we should strive to fashion a learning experience that is likely to be consistent with the context in which the child will be called upon to retrieve knowledge.

LEVELS-OF-PROCESSING MODEL OF MEMORY: A CRITIQUE

Despite its much heralded arrival, the levels-of-processing model of memory has come under attack for a variety of reasons. Perhaps the most problematic is the model's lack of an independent predictor of depth or spread of encoding. Furthermore, the same criticisms leveled at the multistore model regarding arbitrariness in defining key concepts are equally applicable to the levels model.

Is It Possible to Measure Depth or Spread of Encoding?

One of the more objectionable features of the levels-of-processing model of memory is that there is no independent measure of encoding depth, aside from intuitive decisions based upon the qualitative nature of the orienting activities directed at to-be-remembered information (Baddeley, 1978; Eysenck, 1978). Differential retention of information following qualitatively different orienting activities or retrieval environments is used as both evidence for and a definition of depth, spread, or encoding specificity.

One solution to the problem of defining depth has been to measure the amount of time needed to respond to orienting questions. Deep analyses, it has been suggested, should take more time than shallow ones (Craik & Tulving, 1975; Fisher & Craik, 1977). Processing time, however, has also been shown to be an inadequate measure of depth for both theoretical and practical reasons (Eysenck, 1978). The Craik and Lockhart model rejects the assumption that processing invariably proceeds from physical to semantic attributes (Craik & Lockhart, 1972, p. 676), and, furthermore, experimental evidence shows that processing time does not always correlate well with retention (e.g., Craik & Tulving, 1975, Experiment 5).

How Do We Determine at What Level Information Is Processed?

The paradigm used in levels research implies that levels of encoding can be fixed by a question directed at some aspect of the information to be remembered. Such a notion is a bit simplistic. There are a variety of features that can be used to represent information in memory, and the separation of these features into semantic and physical domains is often subjective and arbitrary rather than based upon sound scientific criteria (Baddeley, 1978; Eysenck, 1978).

It may also be wrong to assume that orienting activities directed at words, under either intentional or incidental memory conditions, actually fix the level at which that information is processed. It has been demonstrated that when adults are asked to consider nonsemantic properties of words, semantic associative information is also encoded and vice versa (cf., Nelson, Reed, & McEvoy, 1977; Nelson, Walling, & McEvoy, 1979). Similar observations have been made with children. Ceci, Lea, and Howe (1980) have shown that if children remember an attribute of an item (meaning, color, or location), it is likely that information about other attributes associated with it will also be remembered. Multiattribute encoding would appear to be common to subjects over a wide age range.

What Role Does Intentionality Have in the Memory Process?

One of the more interesting notions to be advanced out of the levels-of-processing research is the idea that intentionality—whether or not someone tries to remember something—has little to do with what is remembered (Glass, Holyoak, & Santa, 1979, p. 141). The notion certainly runs counter to our intuition about how memory operates. Such an assumption also seems at variance with the finding that on memory tasks adults spontaneously use a variety of mnemonic strategies (rehearsal, subjective organization, imagery, and chunking) to improve their performance.

Early research on this matter supported the notion that intentionality had little effect on memory. Nonsignificant differences in performance were found between intentional and unintentional recall; in both cases the type of analysis given to words did influence retention (cf. Hyde & Jenkins, 1973; Walsh & Jenkins, 1973). A reexamination of the methodology used in these experiments, however, reveals that information from the primacy and recency positions were excluded from data analysis—precisely those positions where intentional recall is best (Rundus, 1971).

Other studies have reported better recall of words under intentional, compared to incidental, memory conditions (Craik & Tulving, 1975, Experiments 3 & 4; Nelson et al., 1979, Experiments 1 & 2). Although intentional recall is frequently found to be best, the pattern of recall under intentional or incidental conditions is always the same; semantically encoded words are recalled better than those encoded nonsemantically. Explanations that have been offered for the intentionality effect are vague at best. As noted earlier, Craik and Tulving (1975) suggested that under intentional recall conditions subjects carry out some additional elaboration of words; others (Nelson et al., 1979) decline to speculate on the matter.

The lack of attention to or interest in intentionality seems typical of the levels research. To overlook this effect, however, is to downplay what is apparently an important aspect of memory function. What is it that informed learners do to remember information? Some researchers believe that intentional learners consolidate information that has been committed to memory, consequently facilitating long-term retention and recall (Masson & McDaniel, 1981; McDaniel & Masson, 1977). Other research indicates that informed subjects may elaborate qualitatively different traces in anticipation of the memory task. Two experiments conducted by Gross and Montes (1981) revealed that in addition to encoding that occurs following specific orienting activities directed at words in a list, informed subjects also elaborate a memory trace to include attributes that were likely to facilitate an anticipated recall task.

Intentionality is also important in children's approach to memory tasks. We know that preschool and older children have higher levels of attention following instructions to "remember" compared to instructions to "look at" something (Wellman, Ritter, & Flavell, 1975; Yussen, 1975), and instructing older children to remember something produces better recall (Appel et al., 1972; Wellman et al., 1975; Yussen, 1975). Other studies have shown that under intentional learning conditions, children may actually alter their information-processing styles. Hayes, Chemelski, and Birnbaum (1981), for example, found that under informed conditions, preschool children recognized more visual material from a television program than did children who viewed the program in an incidental memory condition. Curiously, no such differences were found for the retention of auditory information.

Is Retrieval Cue-Specific?

In presenting their idea of memory functioning, it is apparent that Craik and Lockhart (1972) were primarily interested in the acquisition, rather than the retrieval, of information from memory. In fairness to the two theorists, it was not their intent to advance a complete model of memory but rather a framework for memory research. Nonetheless, the emphasis placed on encoding processes and the lack of attention placed on retrieval processes in this type of reseach has been duly noted (Baddeley, 1978; Eysenck, 1978; Fisher & Craik, 1977).

In accounting for retrieval within this model, it has been popular to use the encoding specificity principle (Craik & Tulving, 1975; Fisher & Craik, 1977; Geis & Hall, 1978). Despite evidence that retrieval environments reinstating the encoding context produce higher levels of recall than those that don't (Ceci

& Howe, 1978; Fisher & Craik, 1978; Gross & Montes, 1981; Thomson & Tulving, 1970), others have been critical of the principle. Santa and Lawmers (1974), for example, suggest that much of what has been taken as evidence of encoding specificity may be artifactual, a mismatch between what subjects expect of the task and what they discover the task to be.

SUMMARY AND SYNTHESIS

The levels-of-processing and the multistore models of memory have offered two unique explanations for memory phenomena. It is apparent that one's faith in the existence of one or another model will depend on how much stock is placed on particular kinds of evidence. Multistore theorists believe that there is sufficient separation between particular processing characteristics to suggest the existence of unique, discrete storage spaces in memory; levels-of-processing theorists don't. The levels-of-processing theorists have no problem in accepting evidence for the operation of some short-term memory (the same evidence that the multistore theorists use to support the notion of a short-term store). A major feature of this type of memory is the use of cumulative rehearsal as a process for prolonging the duration of information in working memory. Multistore theorists, of course, attribute considerable importance to cumulative rehearsal as a mechanism for transferring information from the short-term to the long-term store. The levels theorists, while acknowledging the process as important for retaining momentary knowledge, attribute it little importance in the long-term retention of information; for long-term retention, information must be elaborated to some semantic level. Whereas levels theorists place considerable emphasis on encoding or elaborative processes, they have paid scant attention to the role of voluntary processes in memory, perhaps a reflection of their disagreement with the multistore model and the importance they give to encoding processes, be they intentional or incidental.

To deny a role to either cumulative or elaborative rehearsal in the long-term retention of information in memory would likely be premature. It would seem that in those cases where semantic-associative analysis is appropriate, semantic processing significantly facilitates the acquisition and retention of information. But in other cases, evidence, intuitive and otherwise, suggests that some of what we know is acquired through cumulative rehearsal. There is much information that we use daily that does not avail itself to any particular semantic analysis (at least not in any traditional sense, cf. Postman, 1975). For example, we remember locker combinations, telephone numbers, addresses, names, dates, and motor movements—all of which may have low levels of meaningfulness. In such cases, perhaps the best way, or even the only way, to commit this information to memory would be through cumulative rehearsal or practice.

When explaining developmental memory within the multistore framework, we observed that development comes from an improvement in the use of control processes—that is, voluntary strategies applied to memory tasks. The levels-of-processing approach is a bit different, suggesting that retention is primarily a consequence of analysis. Although all age levels supposedly remember as a consequence of subjecting information to deeper levels of analysis, older children apparently engage in more elaborate analyses or profit from the availability of semantic themes more than younger children. Both theories are in agreement that young children are particularly deficient in their ability to produce appropriate retrieval strategies for accessing information in memory.

The multistore model of memory, while lacking in its demonstration of the effectiveness of cumulative rehearsal as a method for making information more resistant to forgetting over a long period of time, has served to identify a number of processes that are spontaneously used by children to organize and store information. Levels-of-processing research has observed age-related improvement in children's spontaneous semantic elaboration of information; unfortunately, the model has been less specific about the role of other voluntary strategies used by children to improve memory functioning. Memory development is apparently something more than mere cumulative rehearsal and, by the same token, something more than just semantic elaboration.

In both models of memory reviewed to this point, attention has been given to a detection and representation of the stimulus itself. That is, both models are based on the assumption that the stimulus has some real properties that are responded to and represented by the organism. In the Piagetian treatment of memory, quite a different tack is taken; in this case memory is an interpretation of experience. Memories do not necessarily accurately represent things as they exist, but are constructions of things. Memories, as such, are figments of the child's imagination, figments that are based in the developmental structure of the intellect itself.

8

A Piagetian Model
of Memory

Information-processing models of memory have typically assumed that information processors faithfully commit aspects of stimulus events to memory. We might liken this to the registration of some photographic image, a copy of reality. As we have seen in the last two chapters, these theories also assume that the basic structure or processes responsible for memory function operate across age levels. A second way of thinking about memory has been to presume that memories don't faithfully represent aspects of the stimulus event, but are constructions and reconstructions of the event. We might liken this to an impressionistic painter's depiction of reality. The picture isn't a copy of reality, but rather an interpretation of it. This latter position describes the Piagetian view of memory. This view of memory has important developmental consequences as constructions are based on one's knowledge state or the way in which one perceives reality. Obviously, as perception of reality changes with stage-related change in cognitive structure, the products of memory should also change with age.

MEMORY IN A BROAD AND NARROW SENSE

Piaget and Inhelder (Piaget & Inhelder, 1973; Inhelder, 1969), have observed that memory improves over time—that is, specific memories of past events are actually better over some period of time rather than worse as traditional notions of long-term memory would predict. Children who have poor short-term memory for a set of ordered sticks, for example, may recall these items arranged in their original serial order at some later period in time.

In explaining this phenomenon, Piaget and Inhelder distinguish between memory in a broad sense and memory in a narrow sense. Memory broadly defined refers to what one understands about his or her world based upon past experiences. This knowledge reflects the operation of intellectual schemes. It is referred to as the operative component. In its broadest sense, memory is an aspect of intellectual structure. Memory schemes are distinguished from intellectual schemes only as they are used to comprehend the characteristics of things that have occurred in the past. Because intellectual structure is believed to change with age, children's memory also changes with age—children's operative level will influence how they comprehend the past.

As the term is used in the narrow sense, memory refers to a more traditional usage, the product of mnemonic activity, or that which is recollected about things. This aspect of memory is referred to as the figurative component and it is a construction of reality (Liben, 1977). It may consist of some perception, an imitation, or image and represents what might be regarded as the memory trace. The figurative aspect of memory doesn't exist independently of the operative component. Objects and things are known through their assimilation (or incorporation) into intellectual schemes. These schemes represent the mnemonic basis for knowing. Consequently, that which is remembered about something is dependent upon the children's level of operative development. What infants remember about a bottle is different than what older children remember. Infants apply sensory and motor schemes to objects, assimilating them into habitual action patterns (grasping and sucking). By applying schemes to objects, infants recognize them. By accommodating schemes, infants distinguish bottles from other things. Older children, on the other hand, through an expanded set of schemes and operations, can internally represent actions associated with objects (thereby enabling them to imitate the functions of a bottle—for example, pretending to drink from a bottle) and ultimately can conserve more complex relationships that hold between objects (that the liquid in a bottle will remain parallel to the horizon in spite of changes in the bottle's orientation). What we know about things, and consequently what we remember about them, is dependent upon our conceptual understanding of the world about us.

As you may have gathered from this discussion, that which is remembered about something is not an exact copy of reality. Like perception and other products of cognition, memory is an interpreted event, both when information is committed to memory and when the memory trace is retrieved. In their theorizing about memory, the Genevans have tended to direct attention to the operative aspects of memory, examining the effects of operative change on memory performance. Theoretically, changes in operative level should produce reliable changes in the kind of information children remember about past events.

THE LONG-TERM IMPROVEMENT OF MEMORY

There has been ample empirical demonstration of the long-term improvement of memory as predicted by Piaget's theory, although its significance depends upon the criteria against which this improvement is measured (cf. Liben, 1977). Piaget and Inhelder (Piaget & Inhelder, 1973; Inhelder, 1969) have reported on a body of research demonstrating that children's recollection of past events improves over time; as would be predicted, this improvement is specific to stimuli incorporating some operative feature. Memory for information that has no operative component shows a degradation over time. Inhelder (1969), for example, described an experiment in which children (3 to 8 years of age) were shown and told to remember a pattern of ten sticks of unequal length arranged in order of size (thus conserving the operative concept of seriation). Recall was assessed one week later and six to eight months later by having children draw the sticks as they remembered seeing them. Drawings were scored for the presence of one of three recall patterns: (a) no seriation (children recalled the sticks of equivalent size), (b) incomplete seriation (some seriation occurred, with recall evidencing bundles of large and small sticks), and (c) complete seriation (children recalled the set as fully seriated).

After children had drawn the sticks from memory at six or eight months, they were asked to arrange another set of sticks in order of ascending size (to assess their knowledge of the operative concept of seriation). On the basis of their performance, children were categorized as preoperational (the concept of seriation was not found in their organization of sticks), transitional (children ordered sticks by size, but in bundles of three or four items), empirical seriators (children ordered the sticks through trial and error), and operational seriators (children had a clear concept of seriation, rapidly organizing the sticks in a series).

In this study it was assumed that young children who had not acquired a scheme for seriation (preoperational children) would show no seriation in their recall (both after one week and after longer durations). As children develop a scheme for seriation (as in the transitional, empirical, and operational seriators), they should show a greater tendency to include seriation in recall. Supporting these predictions, Inhelder reports that children's recall corresponded closely with their level of operational development (Table 8-1). The

TABLE 8-1. Percentage of Subjects within Each of Four Operational Groups Who Produced Each of Three Types of Drawings of Seriated Sticks during Recall[a]

	Memory Types		
Operational Stages	No Seriation	Some Seriation	Complete Seriation
Preoperational	83	17	0
Transitional	0	65	35
Empirical seriation	0	27	73
Operational seriation	0	0	100

[a]Inhelder, 1969, p. 341.

majority of preoperational children (nonseriators) failed to include seriation in recall. The transitional children had begun to include seriation in recall and the operational seriators consistently included seriation in recall. Comparing recall at one week and several months later, Inhelder reports an improvement in 74% of the drawings of all children (the remainder showed no improvement, but neither did they show any regressions); 90% of the drawings of the older children (5 and 8 years of age) showed improvements. Similar results were obtained in the recall of horizontal liquids, numerical and spatial configurations, situations involving causal inferences, and configurations having some abstract organizational principle.

In a related study, Blackburne-Stover, Belenky, and Gilligan (1982) showed how operative development is also related to our recollections of reasons for past decisions. They studied women who decided to terminate a pregnancy. Women who had experienced operative development over the period of a year gave different accounts of why they decided to terminate a pregnancy compared to their reasons given a year before. Curiously, these women couldn't recall the reasons given a year earlier. Women who hadn't experienced operative development gave similar reasons at the initial interview and a year later, and had no difficulty recalling the rationale for their decision a year earlier. Something apparently happened to the memory of women who experienced operative development.

Whereas subsequent tests of Piaget and Inhelder's prediction of long-term memory improvement with age have been substantiated (Liben, 1977), the amount of long-term improvement has often been less than that reported by the Genevans. Furthermore, there is a nagging problem of regressions in memory performance, which were largely ignored by Piaget. In one of the earlier replication studies (Altemeyer, Fulton, & Berney, 1969), kindergarteners were provided with either an ordered or an unordered series of ten sticks to be recalled one week and six months later. Of those children who were shown the ordered array, 43% showed an improvement in drawing sticks (including in their drawing some indication of order or pattern). This is substantially less improvement than found by Piaget and Inhelder, but nonetheless an impressive gain. (Piaget and Inhelder included in their sample a wider age range of children, thus increasing the likelihood of finding operative improvement in recall.) Unlike the study reported by Inhelder, however, 25% of the children showed memory regressions during the six-month interval. Furthermore, of those children who were presented the unordered array, 41% recalled this stimulus as ordered or patterned several months later, calling to question whether in fact this improvement was in truth mnemonic.

Other studies that have assessed improvement in children's recall of stimuli conserving the concept of seriation have shown mixed support for a long-term improvement of these memories. Dahlem (1969), using a reconstruction test (sticks were given to children to be arranged as they remembered seeing them), found that children who reproduced constructions accurately either immediately or after a one-week delay also reconstructed the stimulus accurately six months later. It was also observed that with time there were a number of improvements in reconstructions; however, regressions were as common as improvements. Liben (1975b) used a cued-recall procedure (at the test pictures omitting operatively relevant features were present, and children were asked to complete the picture as they remembered it in the past). (See Figure 8-1). She found that kindergarteners' recall of operative features improved, although a comparable number of regressions occurred as well.

Studies that have examined the long-term improvement of children's memory for stimuli involving other operative concepts have shown the same pattern—some improvements and some regressions. Furth, Ross, and Youniss (1974), assessing children's recall for water levels in a tilted glass (thus conserving the concept of horizontality), reported that over a six-month interval

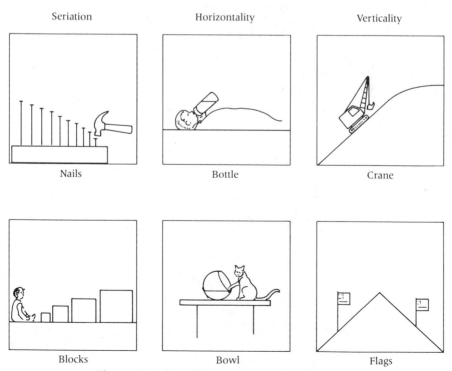

Figure 8-1. Stimuli for memory task. (*Liben, 1975*)

17% of the children in their study reproduced operatively improved drawings. It should be noted that they also found that 56% of these children showed regressions in performance. Liben (1974, 1975b) reports that with older children, there is a long-term improvement in some children's recall of stimuli that conserve horizontality; however, again, there is about as much regression as there is improvement. Although research supports the notion that there is some long-term improvement in memory, whether or not one accepts these improvements as support for the Genevan position depends upon the criteria to which they are compared. Piaget and Inhelder (1973) propose that compared to what one might expect to find in children's memory for events over a long period of time (no improvement or regression), the degree of improvement that occurs demonstrates the importance of operative factors in long-term memory. How else, the argument goes, can we account for these improvements? Others (Liben, 1977), as we shall see, are critical of this particular criteria for gauging improvements in long-term memory.

RECOGNITION, RECONSTRUCTION AND RECALL

In addition to proposing long-term memory improvement with age, the Genevans have also proposed three distinct types of memory; these are recognition, reconstruction, and recall (or evocation). These memories represent more than different methods of studying memory; they are qualitatively distinct kinds of memory, having different developmental onsets and different figurative characteristics.

Recognition is believed the earliest type of memory and can be found in the first few months of life. Recognition is inherent in every sensory-motor habit as infants assimilate familiar objects into habitual actions schemes associated with them. The content of these early memories is therefore perceptual. Recognition is not only the earliest memory to develop, it is also extremely important in promoting an accommodation of mnemonic schemes. In recognition the original model is always reinstated for the viewer's inspection; as such schemes can be more easily altered to represent objects accurately (Ross & Kerst, 1978).

Reconstructive memory is intermediate to recognition and recall. This form of memory requires a reproduction of relationships that exist between various elements in some set of objects or events. Reconstruction is a kind of recall by action, and inherent in this type of memory is deferred imitation. This is the child's ability to represent actions of others, the self, or objects symbolically; this ability develops during the second year of life. Reconstruction also facilitates the accommodation of intellectual schemes. Because the components of the object to be reconstructed are available to children, all that need be applied are actions to objects. Since children manipulate objects better than they do images, it is easier for them to accommodate these action schemes (cf. Liben, 1977). Furthermore, the manipulation of materials assists memory by reactivating schemes formerly applied to stimuli.

Recall is the developmentally most advanced form of memory. In order to recall, children must remember both objects and relationships between them. Consequently, mental imagery is the basis of this type of memory. Due to the need for more advanced symbolic representation, this type of memory should not be observed until the preoperational period (or, about 18 to 24 months of age).

In brief, the Genevan position sees memory to be evolving in a developmental sequence. This sequence is characterized by the emergence of qualitatively different kinds of representation, which reflect the basic nature of intellectual development. Recognition, for example, relies on perception; reconstruction on imitation, and recall upon mental imagery. Because development proceeds from habitual action patterns, to the representation of action sequences, and finally to symbolic representation, there is a necessary order in memory development. Early memories conserve this basic order (are based in the application of action schemes to things), and consequently recognition and reconstruction are easier than recall. Recall works just the opposite— relying upon mental imagery to reinstate some supporting action schemes related to the imagined object; consequently, recall is more difficult (cf. Ross & Kerst, 1978).

Developmental support for the qualitative separation of these three memories comes from several kinds of evidence. If these memories are unique, we should be able to observe a reliable sequence in their development; children should first use recognition, next reconstruction, and then evocation. In addition to this sequencing, we should anticipate that performance on tasks requiring the use of earlier developing memories (recognition and reconstruction) should be easier than tasks requiring recall. Children of any age should find recognition easier than reconstruction, and reconstruction easier than recall. Finally, because different intellectual abilities are prerequisite to each of these memories, infants without sufficient intellectual maturity should be unable to use more sophisticated types of memory.

With respect to the general pattern of memory development, the sequence evolves much as was described by Piaget. A review of research on infant memory shows a preponderance of studies on recognition memory. Research in reconstructive memory and evocation has typically involved preschool and elementary school children. This pattern to memory research may represent an implicit belief by experimenters that infant memory is primarily based in recognition. In any case, there are obvious methodological problems in developing paradigms that would allow us to assess other kinds of infant memory. (Later in this chapter we'll consider some tangential data that suggest that such paradigms might exist.)

Without a doubt children and adults find recognition memory much easier than reconstruction, and the latter easier than recall (Piaget & Inhelder, 1973). Liben (1974), for example, had children reproduce pictures with operative content after one week and again six months later. After children had drawn stimuli from memory at six months, they were given a recognition test. Recognition performance was always better than recall. Another study by Murray and Bausel (reported in Liben, 1977) revealed that over a four-month interval, a significant number of regressions occurred in children's recall of operatively defined stimuli; however, when recognition memory for the same content was assessed, there was virtually no deterioration. Finally, Brown (1975b) asked kindergarten and second-grade children to recognize, reconstruct, and recall sequences of three pictures presented in a thematically organized context or an unorganized sequence. She reports that for both types of picture sequences, the anticipated order of difficulty between recognition, reconstruction, and recall was always conserved.

THE PIAGETIAN MODEL OF MEMORY: A CRITIQUE

As might be anticipated, there has been considerable skepticism about several aspects of the memory theory proposed by Piaget and Inhelder. We will focus on several issues addressed in these criticisms. First, we need to consider the nature and significance of long-term memory improvements. Second, and related to the first issue, is whether or not improvements in long-term memory really reflect memory development, or whether these improvements reflect an operative influence at some other level of cognition (for example, perceptual). Third, we need to consider whether memory does evolve from recognition to recall. Is it possible, for example, that a variety of memories are available and used at ages much earlier than Piaget's theory predicts?

Does Memory Improve with Time?

Perhaps the most interesting and controversial notion to come from Piagetian research on memory is the idea that children's long-term memory actually improves with time. In the broad sense in which Piaget defines memory, it is necessary that memory improve; that is, if one acknowledges age-related changes in operative schemes. As intelligence becomes operatively more advanced, memory schemes must also reflect these changes (Inhelder, 1969, Piaget & Inhelder, 1973).

Whereas long-term memory improvement has been well documented, recent reviews of this phenomenon have been critical of the methodology used to establish improvement and the criteria used to evaluate it. Methodologically, early research confounded the effects of repeated testing or exposure to test stimuli with the effects of operative development (Liben, 1976, 1977; Maurer, Siegel, Lewis, Kristofferson, Barnes, & Levy, 1979). Studies controlling for effects of repeated testing and monitoring operative development independently of the memory performance are rare (cf., Liben, 1981; Maurer et al., 1979).

One of the more critical problems vexing this line of research is which criterion to use in evaluating long-term memory improvement. Piaget and Inhelder compared performance to that which would be predicted by trace theories (that is, no improvement). Using this criteria, they found impressive improvements in long-term memory. Liben (1977), however, argues that this is the wrong criteria against which to evaluate change. If, for example, improvement is due to random or chance factors, just as much improvement as regression should be anticipated. A more critical test of long-term memory improvement would be a significant improvement in memory relative to regression. Even if we use this criterion, the data reported by Piaget and Inhelder are impressive, revealing few if any regressions. However, data from non-Genevan research programs often reveal as much regression as improvement in long-term memory.

Whereas methodological problems and scoring criteria may foster the appearance of significant long-term memory improvement, the basic notion of long-term memory improvement can be criticized at a more theoretical level. Piaget (1968) has stated that the memory trace is a construction rather than an exact copy of reality. Memory traces will not conserve information about operative properties of objects and events unless children have within their intellectual structure some corresponding operational scheme that can assimilate this information. If children haven't developed a concept of seriation, then the memory trace shouldn't conserve this information either. Nonetheless, the Piagetians believe that later reproductions of this trace will be seriated if the scheme for seriation has subsequently been acquired. Operative memory schemes serve to decode or comprehend objects and events experienced in the past.

Something in this argument is a bit peculiar, at least in the traditional way that memory is understood. It is difficult to understand why children whose figurative image of a set of seriated sticks is just a set of sticks (with no information about pattern or seriation) should later "remember" that seriation was part of this past event. The memory trace does not conserve this information. Although studies have demonstrated that scrambled sticks (Altemeyer et al., 1969) and other operatively incorrect stimuli (Liben, 1974) are at some later point recalled in an operatively improved fashion, one might also ask whether or not memory has actually been involved and certainly whether memory has improved. Apparently, operatively advanced schemes have organized retrieval, but at least with respect to the retention of the original memory trace, memory has deteriorated. The tendency for children to include operatively advanced concepts into spontaneous drawings also confounds the issue of whether long-term memories are actually memories at all (Liben, 1975a). As one example of this, Figure 8-2 shows the development of the operative concept of verticality in one child's drawings over a two-year period. As children grow older, they are more likely to conserve verticality; they become more likely to place a chimney perpendicular to the horizon rather than to the slope of the roof.

Contrary to Piaget and Inhelder's (1973) claim that operative improvement is the only way to explain long-term memory improvement, there are other demonstrated instances of memory improvement that can be explained by factors other than operative development. We find that on some memory tasks subjects demonstrate a phenomenon known as *hypermnesia*. With repeated recall, subjects show a progressive improvement in recalling information previously committed to memory. This phenomenon appears to be related to the

Figure 8-2. Child's spontaneous drawing of a house with chimney at (a) 4 years, 6 months; (b) 5 years; (c) 5 years, 5 months; (d) 6 years.

consolidation of trace information over time (Erdelyi & Kleinbard, 1978) or simply practice in retrieving information from memory (Roediger & Payne, 1982).

Children's long-term memory improvement may also be explained as a consequence of improvement in memory retrieval skills. Children may encode more information about a memory trace than they report. With better retrieval strategies, they may gain access to more information about the memory trace. Murphy and Brown (1975) have, for example, demonstrated that young children are able to retain accurate memories for pictures over long periods of time, provided that retrieval demands are minimized through the use of recognition tests.

Are Piagetian Studies of Memory Really the Study of Memory?

The foregoing discussion has implied that what has been taken for long-term improvement in memory may be attributed to nonoperative cognitive phenomena. Another possibility is that long-term improvement in performance may not be a consequence of operative influences on memory, but an operative influence on perception. Liben (1981), for example, had children both copy and recall pictures that incorporated the concept of verticality (that trees growing on a hillside grow perpendicular to the horizon rather than to the slope of the hill). Children were originally tested with respect to their operative knowledge for verticality and then asked to copy a picture of a tree growing on the side of a hill. Following copy, children were asked to draw the picture from memory immediately after copy, one week later, or five months later. Those children who drew operatively correct pictures understood the concept of verticality prior to testing and demonstrated operatively correct copies of the stimulus. Children who had more advanced knowledge of verticality copied and remembered the drawing more accurately. However, there was no improvement in recall beyond that which was found in copy, suggesting to Liben that operative level does affect children's reproduction of past events, but that the locus of this effect is perceptual rather than mnemonic.

Are Recognition, Reconstruction, and Recall Determined by Genetic Factors?

It has been noted several times in this chapter that recognition produces higher levels of performance than recall. The Genevans propose that this advantage accrues to the fact that recognition memory and reconstruction conserve some natural genetic order of development—actions are carried out upon objects, assimilating them into perceptual schemes, which facilitates their recognition (cf. Ross & Kerst, 1978). Recall, however, requires the reinstatement of a mental image, which only then can be acted upon. As the description suggests, this process is much more elaborate, cognitively demanding, and intellectually advanced than recognition or reconstruction.

As noted earlier, much of infant research has focused on recognition memory, a memory demonstrated by infants at least as young as 3 months of age. These infants, however, also may be able to reconstruct and recall events from memory.

You will recall from an earlier discussion that reconstruction is based in deferred imitative abilities, or the ability to represent some observed sequence and map these actions onto one's own behavior. Piaget (1963) believes that this ability doesn't develop until about 8 to 10 months of age. Consequently, reconstructive memory should be unavailable to very young infants. Meltzoff and Moore (1977, 1983), however, report that very young infants, from several hours to several days old, are capable of imitating facial gestures. These findings suggest that neonates are capable of coordinating actions and matching what they see to their own actions, thus implying some abstract representational basis for infants' behavior and memory.

In addition to evidence for primitive reconstructive memory in 1-month-old infants, other research suggests that within the first 3 months of life, infants are even capable of recall. Consider the research in infant discrimination learning. There is good evidence that infants learn discriminations very early in life (Siqueland & Lipsitt, 1966). Consider also the nature of this type of learning. In discrimination learning the infant learns that in the presence of one stimulus $(S + d)$, but not another $(S - d)$, reinforcement $(S+)$ can be obtained for some response. An increase in response rate in the presence of $S + d$ but not to $S - d$ reveals that the infant has learned the discrimination. This type of paradigm is not unlike a paired-associated learning paradigm in which a learner associates one word with another and then uses one of the words as a cue to recall the other on a subsequent test of memory. In this case the $S + d$ serves as a cue to make some response. Recent research on infant discrimination learning reveals the durability of these associations and provides a demonstration of a simple type of long-term, cued-recall memory (Davis & Rovee-Collier, 1983; Fagen, Yengo, Rovee-Collier, & Enright, 1981; Rovee-Collier & Sullivan, 1980; Sullivan, Rovee-Collier, & Tynes, 1979). Fagen et al. (1981) trained 3-month-old infants over a two-day period of time to kick their legs in the presence of one mobile $(S + d)$ but not another $(S - d)$. The $S + d$ was arranged such that if the infant kicked its legs, it also shook the mobile, which also served as a reinforcer $(S+)$. Twenty-one days after discrimination training had ended, the infants were again shown either the $S + d/S+$ or the $S - d$ as a reminder of what had occurred during discrimination training. The experimenter moved the $S + d/S+$ at a rate comparable to that produced by an infant at the end of discrimination learning. For those infants receiving the $S - d$ as a reminder, the mobile was suspended in a stationary position in front of the child (as it had occurred during training). Twenty-four hours later, children were given a long-term cued-recall test, being shown both the $S + d$ and the $S - d$. Compared to children who received either the $S - d$ reminder or no reminder at all, children receiving the $S + d/S+$ reminder one day earlier showed significantly higher rates of kicking when shown the $S + d$. In fact Fagen et al. report that the $S + d$ reminder produced a condition of complete retention of the original discrimination. Providing infants with the original reinforcer (the moving mobile) served to remind the infant of the original discrimination. This phenomenon would seem to imply the existence of a memory system dependent upon symbolic and representational skills, one that allows the child not only to recognize something from the past $(S + d/S+)$ but also to recall what to do with it (kick one's legs).

SUMMARY AND SYNTHESIS

Piagetians have defined memory in both a broad and a narrow sense. Broadly defined, memory refers to intellectual schemes that shape the construction of a memory trace and its reconstruction when it is recollected. Narrowly defined, memory refers to the content of memory or the memory trace. Because intellectual structure changes during the developmental years, it is also believed that the content of memory changes. Furthermore, the Piagetians believe that three qualitatively distinct memories exist: recognition, reconstruction, and recall. It is believed that these memories have different figurative components and different developmental onsets.

Whereas we find support for improvement in memory over time, there are questions about the significance of improvement and to what improvement is due when it is found. A number of critics of the Piagetian position have contended that the zero improvement criteria against which Piagetians have gauged memory improvement is inappropriate. When compared to regressions in memory, for example, memory improvement is less impressive. Some discussion has also focused on whether improvement in memory is actually due to memory at all. That is, the operative improvement in recollections of a stimulus event may be due to a number of nonmemory-related factors (for example, the spontaneous inclusion of operatively advanced elements in children's drawings, improvement in communication skills, and methodological confounding). Other research has challenged the Genevan contention that there is a developmental sequence to the acquisition of qualitatively different kinds of memory. Whereas it is certainly true that performance is better on recognition than recall tasks, current research suggests that very young infants are able to rudimentarily represent stimulus events (actions and objects) in order to imitate (the basis of reconstruction) and perhaps even recall them.

In the course of the past three chapters we've considered several models of memory functioning and development. Typical of all three approaches is an interest in the process by which information is assimilated into memory. The multistore model specifies a processing system that is accompanied by a variety of control processes that can be used to make the basic system operate better. The levels-of-processing model proposes that information is evaluated in a series of processing stages and that deeper levels of processing facilitate retention. The position advocated by Piaget and Inhelder suggests that information is modified in accordance with operative schemes. Because of differences in the operative structure of younger and older children, children will remember different things about their world.

Accounts of how memory changes vary between approaches. Both of the information-processing positions propose a system or structure that remains basically invariant with age. On the other hand, the position advanced by Piaget and Inhelder suggests that the mnemonic structure itself changes with development. The multistore model and the levels-of-processing model both suggest that developmental improvement in memory comes from learning to use the system or structure of memory better. For example, the multistore model proposes that with age children can better attend, acquire, and retain information in some short-term store, and organize and retrieve this information at some later point in time. The levels-of-processing model proposes that older children are better able to elaborate memory traces (enrich the trace with semantic information) and use retrieval processes that serve to facilitate performance. Only in Piaget and Inhelder's position is there the belief that the memory structure itself changes with age. These changes account for developmental memory improvement with advanced operative schemes serving to decode or comprehend past events. This belief is apparent in Piaget's interest in both the operative effects on memory (*memory* in the broader sense) and his belief that recognition, reconstruction, and recall represent a rough developmental sequence, which defines the evolution of memory (*memory* in the narrower sense), with each phase having different figurative properties.

The importance of the encoding process is found in all three theories. Like the Piagetian model, the multistore model acknowledges a reliable change in the way that children represent information—the memory trace is likely to be different in younger than in older children. These two theories, however, have quite a different view of the nature of the memory trace. The multistore theory assumes that the to-be-remembered item consists of a bundle of memory attributes and that the individual selectively attends to and codes information about one or several attributes. The Piagetian position focuses on the operative components of the stimulus. Due to limitations in operative development, children are predisposed to perceive and encode specific features in the stimulus event; memory is reconstructive rather than reproductive.

The levels-of-processing model of memory places great importance on encoding processes in memory retention. Unlike the Piagetian position, this model of memory suggests that children at all age levels process information similarly—they encode or represent information through some series of processing stages. Encoding perceptual or structural features of a stimulus event is believed to contribute little to the long-term retention of information; processing information semantically, however, creates a more durable memory trace. In this latter regard, the Piagetian and the information-processing positions are in opposition. The Piagetian model predicts that recognition will be easier due to the fact that it relies upon a perceptual component. It is not anticipated that any semiotic functioning need occur for this type of memory to operate. And, in fact, it is exactly for this reason that recognition memory is better. Recall, which is dependent upon the reinstatement and maintenance of mental images (some symbolic representation of things), is more difficult. The levels-of-processing theories propose that perceptual analyses lead to relatively transient memories; it is only with the semantic elaboration of information (we may assume the operation of semiotic function here) that it becomes more permanent. Whereas it is not disputed by either the multistore or the levels-of-processing theorists that recognition memory is easier than recall, their account of this superiority is quite different from that offered by Piaget and Inhelder. That is, in their account of this superiority, recognition memory is viewed to be one that is memory assisted; it provides a retrieval environment with a rich domain of retrieval cues that serve to facilitate retrieval of the original memory trace.

The research reviewed in this chapter provides little support for the view that memory improves as a consequence of operative development. Nonetheless, Piaget and Inhelder have added to our thoughts about what a theory of memory development should be; their ideas may have some merit. A number of theorists believe there is something to the notion of stage-related changes in children's knowledge base. The research reported in this chapter shows that operative effects do express themselves either at the time that information is perceived and encoded (cf. Liben, 1981) or when that information is retrieved (Altemeyer et al., 1969; Liben, 1974, 1975b). The idea that children represent or encode information differently with age is not a novel idea; the work by Piaget and Inhelder, however, goes beyond the simple documentation of these changes and attempts to identify their origin.

9

An Information-Processing Approach to Problem Solving

In the past several chapters we've considered a number of ideas about how information is recognized, acquired, and stored; these are important functions of any information-processing system. We are, however, much more than repositories for large quantities of information; we are information users. "I think, therefore I am" in more than one way would seem a fitting (however trite) epithet for what may be the ultimate purpose of mankind—to solve problems.

Adults and children are confronted daily with problems to solve. We may need to discover what factor or factors are responsible for some negative outcome. For example, why does a lamp no longer work (a faulty switch, a broken

145

bulb, a blown fuse, and so on)? Or, in some instances, why do things turn out well or produce positive results? For example, why did one perform well on a test (study time, attitude, interest, health, and so on)? Young children are also confronted with these kinds of problems—getting something from a shelf that is out of reach, discovering what makes a toy run, or perhaps drawing inferences from what others say.

In Chapter 2 we observed that there are two frameworks in which to study problem solving: analysis and synthesis. An analysis method studies the various components and processes involved in problem solving. It is presumed that performance is affected by the interaction of a variety of structures (mnemonic, perceptual, and conceptual) as well as individual difference variables (anxiety, cognitive style and so on). The synthesis, or systems modeling method, on the other hand, is directed at the specification of precise rule systems, algorithms that define the problem-solving process. These models are often described with running computer programs that are taken as self-validating models of how problems are solved. We will consider research from both of these positions shortly, but first let's consider the attitude behind the information-processing approach to problem solving. Specifically, what do these methods consider the important questions in problem-solving research, and to what do they attribute age-related changes in problem solving?

Of primary interest to the information-processing methods is the discovery of what children know about logical problem-solving rules. Information-processing theory characterizes problem solving as the sequential application of a set of rules—rules that are both logical and necessary to problem solution. Furthermore, it is presumed that the coordinated use of information gained from the application of these rules reflects a strategy—that is, a systematic plan for evaluating information en route to problem solution. There are different strategies for solving problems, and certain strategies are more typically used at some age levels than others. A child who wants to find out why a toy no longer works will need to isolate a number of factors that affect the toy's operation (does it have a battery, are the batteries dead, is the motor broken, and so on). Having elaborated a set of hypotheses, the child will need to conduct a test to isolate the factor(s) that prevent the toy from operating. Some strategies (for example, isolating some variables while holding others constant) will be more effective than others (randomly manipulating factors).

Two explanations are offered for why children demonstrate the use of some rules while not others, and for why we find age-related changes in strategy. One suggestion for why children fail to use logical rules during problem solving is that, while knowing a rule, they fail to apply it because of limitations in other subprocesses underlying problem solving. We know, for example, that there are changes in children's ability to avoid distraction, to discriminate or attend to a number of features in multidimensional stimuli (perceptual factors), and to rehearse, organize, and store information (mnemonic factors). All of these could markedly influence rule use or the integration of information gained from rule use. Another reason for their failure to use logical rules is that they simply may not have acquired them. Both of these positions generate clear predictions about how children will perform in problem-solving situations. First, in situations that require sophisticated subprocessing skills (on tasks requiring resistance to distraction or having an increased memory demand), we would anticipate that children would use fewer logical rules and apply them less systematically. Under conditions that minimize subprocessing demands, logical rules should be used more frequently and more adequately. It would also be anticipated that training children to use logical rules should increase the frequency with which they are applied to problem-solving tasks if problem-solving failures occur through ignorance of problem-solving rules. Generally, research with children has supported both of these expectancies, but with some interesting qualifications.

AN ANALYSIS METHOD FOR PROBLEM SOLVING

It is presumed in cognitive research that problem solving of any kind is intentional rather than a mere consequence of reinforcement history. That is, when we attempt to solve problems, as for example in the detective game Clue or Mastermind, we realize that there are a finite number of possible solutions. In the game of Clue the answer will be one of five rooms, one of six murder weapons, and one of eight suspects. In the game of Mastermind the solution will involve some combination of colored pegs. We play both games by asking questions and evaluating feedback. The game is won when we, or someone else, discover the answer to the riddle. If you've played either one of these games, you'll recall that the manner in which you approached either game was systematic, not haphazard.

The study of hypothesis-testing behavior has a relatively long history in psychology. Bruner, Goodnow, and Austin (1956) were of the first to observe that when solving problems presented in a variant of the Twenty Questions game (trying to guess what someone else is thinking with as few questions as possible), problem solvers used different types of strategies. Some problem solvers, for example, tended to formulate a set of all possibly relevant answers to a problem and to eliminate information successively from that set as more information about the problem and its solution became available (we call this strategy focusing). Others generated trial-to-trial guesses about possible problem solutions, seemingly ignoring information from past outcome trials (we refer to this strategy as scanning). As you may be able to discern, focusing is the more efficient strategy. By focusing, we can narrow the field of potentially correct alternatives very rapidly with each new bit of information.

The Blank-Trials Procedure

The recognition that problem-solving behavior is strategic led to a curiosity about what types of rules are used when solving problems. In order to examine rule use, researchers developed several new experimental paradigms. Levine (1966), for example, developed the *blank-trials procedure* in which problem solvers had to discover some experimenter-defined solution to a problem defined by a deck of cards. Every card in a deck has two pictures on it, each the exact opposite of the other (Figure 9-1). Each time a card is shown, problem solvers are asked to point to the picture that they believe has the answer (one of eight possible values that the experimenter has in mind). Following some choices, the problem solver receives feedback (he or she is told whether the choice was correct or not); however, on other trials they receive no feedback (these are therefore referred to as blank trials). Typically feedback is given on the first, and thereafter every fifth, trial on each problem.

By examining performance on these problems, we can gather a variety of information on hypothesis-testing behavior and the use of logical rules and strategies. For example, we can arrange a set of four blank-trials in a row and, from the pattern of responses, infer whether or not children are testing hypotheses. There are, in fact, eight possible response patterns possible over a set of four blank-trials. Problem solvers may choose pictures that are on the right or the left side (4-0 response patterns), pictures alternating between right and left (2-2 response patterns), or one picture on one side and three on the opposite side (a 3-1 response pattern). Referring to Figure 9-1, you'll see that these 3-1 response patterns correspond to and are assumed to reflect the use of simple hypotheses. All other response patterns (4-0 and 2-2) are presumed to be nonhypothesis patterns.

Hypotheses				Sequence of Stimulus Pairs	Hypotheses			
square	dotted	red	large		circle	striped	blue	small
left	right	left	left		right	left	right	right
left	left	right	left		right	right	left	right
left	right	right	right		right	left	left	left
right	right	right	left		left	left	left	right

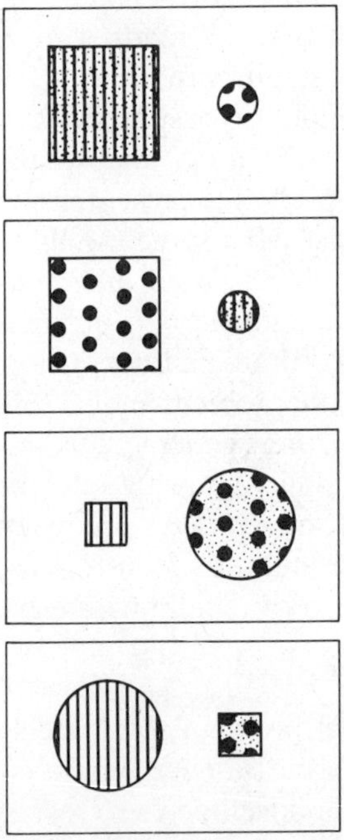

Figure 9-1. A stimulus sequence that permits the inference of eight simple hypotheses from 3−1 (three responses to one side and one to the opposite side) patterns of responding during a blank-trial probe.

In addition to inferences about the use of hypothesis, the blank-trials procedure also allows us to examine whether or not problem solvers use a variety of logical rules. For instance, in order to solve these problems efficiently, you must (a) test hypotheses that are consistent with the immediately preceding feedback trial, and you must use (b) the win-stay rule and (c) the lose-shift rule. If you're testing an hypothesis and you receive feedback that confirms your hypothesis, you should keep it and use it to guide subsequent choices (win-stay). On the other hand, if your hypothesis leads you to choose an instance that is disconfirmed (you're told that you're wrong), you should change your hypothesis (lose-shift). Furthermore, if you received disconfirmation and you decided to change your hypothesis, it would be best if you chose a new hypothesis from the alternate set—the set that by necessity must contain the correct answer (this is called the local consistency rule).

The use of hypotheses and logical rules should also be accompanied by a plan or strategy for solving problems, and there are several strategies that could be used. Gholson, Levine, and Phillips (1972) identified three of these. Focusing and hypothesis checking or scanning have been mentioned previously. The third is dimension checking. Those who are focusing would construct some hypothesis statement about all possibly correct answers on the first outcome trial and on successive outcome trials compare this original set to current information, eliminating from it disconfirmed information. Using such a strategy, you can solve blank-trials problems such as those depicted in Figure 9-1 in a minimum of three outcome trials. Subjects who are hypothesis-checking test values independently of one another. The problem solver retains a hypothesis until it is disconfirmed and largely through trial and error selects hypotheses until the correct solution is found. Dimension checking is generally regarded as a strategy that is intermediate in sophistication to focusing and hypothesis checking. The problem solver imagines a list of dimensions and proceeds through the list, testing one dimension at a time. When a hypothesis is tried and disconfirmed at or after the second outcome trial, the problem solver should realize that it is logically impossible for other hypotheses within the same dimension to be correct; thus, that dimension is abandoned and another tested.

The Introtact Probe Procedure

Whereas the blank-trials procedure has been a common technique for assessing problem-solving behavior, it has several untoward qualities that limit its use with young children. First, it is an extremely time-consuming procedure and, second, due to scoring prescriptions, some of the data pertaining to rule and strategy use must often be excluded from analyses. In an attempt to resolve these dilemmas, the paradigm has been modified a bit to make it more amenable to collecting more information on how individuals solve problems but in a shorter period of time. These methodological features are particularly valued when working with children. The modified version of the blank-trials procedure is called the *introtact probe procedure* (Phillips & Levine, 1975). The modification is a relatively simple one; instead of the blank-trial probe, problem solvers are simply asked to state what they believe to be the answer to the problem.

Hypothesis Testing, Rule Knowledge, and Strategy Use

Research that has used the two problem-solving tasks just described and variations on the Twenty Questions game has focused on two fundamental issues. One of these has to do with whether or not children use hypotheses and logical rules at levels above chance. That is, when children use an hypothesis-testing pattern or a logical rule correctly, do they use it consistently enough to conclude that they really understand the value of its application? Or, does use occur so rarely that when it is found, it is likely a chance phenomenon? Another concern of this research is in the documentation of age-related changes in children's knowledge and use of hypotheses, rules, and strategies.

To date, problem-solving research shows that children don't spontaneously use hypotheses at above chance levels until about the second grade (Eimas, 1969; Gholson et al., 1972). Approaching these tasks, preschoolers and kindergarteners tend to apply nonhypothesis testing patterns or use hypotheses that are inappropriate to solution. On blank-trial problems, for example, it is not uncommon to find young children responding by position—selecting all of the stimuli on the right or left, or alternating choices between right and left. Their solutions apparently lack an awareness that problems have solutions defined by a set of answers specified by the experimenter (Gholson et al., 1972; Olson, 1966). When hypotheses are tested, they are often stereotyped—children persist in their use despite evidence that they are inappropriate. This tendency is found in young children's everyday behavior too. A preschooler looking for her mother may stand at the door of the bathroom for minutes saying, "Mommy, you in there," failing to search in other locations when no response from the bathroom is forthcoming.

Although most second-grade children solve problems by testing hypotheses, it is also found that the frequency with which they use them increases markedly during the early elementary school years. In fact, by the fourth grade nearly 80% of the time children spontaneously test hypotheses on blank-trial problems, and by the sixth grade, this figure rises to approximately 95% (Gholson, 1980).

We also find a reliable developmental progression in children's use of logical rules. By the time that children begin to use hypotheses spontaneously at above chance levels, they also use several logical rules. Second-graders, for example, select hypotheses that are consistent with immediately preceding feedback (Eimas, 1969; Gholson, 1980; Phillips & Levine, 1975). This need not be surprising since hypothesis testing implies the selection of some value that has relevance to solution. If children are, in fact, testing hypotheses while solving problems, at the very minimum we should anticipate that they would choose feedback consistent hypotheses. We also find that when young children are required to volunteer hypotheses, as in the introtact probe technique, even kindergarteners select hypotheses that are consistent with feedback (Cantor

& Spiker, 1978). Thus, although kindergarteners may not spontaneously generate hypotheses during problem-solving tasks, they do know what hypotheses are and how to use them correctly.

With the use of other problem-solving rules, similar developmental patterns emerge. By the second grade, children tend to use the win-stay, lose-shift, and local consistency rules at above chance levels; however, the latter two rules tend to be used less consistently by younger children. Kindergarteners have particular difficulty abandoning disconfirmed information (using the lose-shift rule), and this is true of their performance on both the introtact and blank-trial probe procedures (Cantor & Spiker, 1978; Gholson, 1980). Whereas kindergarteners may know what hypotheses are, even when they are required to use them, they seem either ignorant of or unable to apply other logical rules that would allow them to use information more efficiently.

Strategies are plans that guide choice behavior during problem solving. In the use of strategies, striking changes are found in children's coordination of information during problem solving. Using a variation of the Twenty Questions game, Mosher and Hornsby (1966) found that 83% of an eleven-year-old sample asked questions that were very general in nature and eliminated large numbers of items in a single question ("Is it bigger than a bread box?"). On the other hand, 98% of a six-year-old sample asked questions that were item-specific ("Is it the bread box?"). Asking the former type of question obviously reflects a more efficient strategy for playing this game. We also find similar trends toward more efficient strategy use on the blank-trials and introtact problems. On the blank-trials problems it is rare to find any strategies used by kindergarten and preschool children. As mentioned earlier, their responses are largely position choices. Or if they test a hypothesis it is typically a stereotype—there is a tendency to maintain their original selection in spite of feedback informing them that their choices are wrong. During the early elementary school years, children begin to use hypothesis-checking or scanning strategies, shifting to the use of dimension-checking strategies, and finally to the more advanced strategy, focusing, by early adolescence (Gholson, 1980). Using the less demanding introtact procedure, we find a higher frequency of dimension-checking and focusing strategies used by children at younger ages, although the relative order previously noted appears to be conserved (Phillips & Levine, 1975).

By the second grade, most children attempt to solve problems by testing hypotheses. Although kindergarteners and preschoolers don't use hypotheses spontaneously, they do know what hypotheses are and how to use them in certain contexts. They are, however, unable to coordinate this information in a meaningful fashion to solve problems efficiently and accurately. The application of more advanced problem-solving rules appears above chance by the second grade, although the lose-shift and the local consistency rule are used less frequently by younger children. The ability to coordinate the use of a variety of logical problem-solving rules in the form of strategies develops in the early elementary school years. These strategies show a reliable evolution from the less efficient hypothesis-checking (scanning) strategy to the more efficient focusing strategy.

Having documented these developmental changes in the use of logical rules and strategies, we need to consider why these changes occur. At the outset of this chapter two possible explanations were entertained. One of these is that subprocessing deficiencies may attenuate the application of a variety of logical rules, and the other is that children may need to learn how to use specific logical rules.

PROBLEM SOLVING AND SUBPROCESS DEFICIENCIES

One of the explanations for why younger children are less efficient information processors than older children and adults focuses on the known deficiencies in other cognitive systems that support problem-solving efforts. In our review of perceptual and mnemonic abilities of children, we saw reliable age-related changes in ability to acquire and store information. It is reasonable to assume that deficiencies in each of these areas would alter the manner in which children approach a problem-solving task. A child who doesn't attend to a sufficient amount of detail in the stimulus field is distractable, has a limited memory capacity, or stores information in a particular fashion may be prone to rely upon less efficient solution strategies or use logical rules inefficiently. Theoretically, training children to attend to relevant features of stimuli (perceptual training) or altering the task so that such deficiencies are less disruptive to the problem-solving effort should improve children's problem solving.

Perception and Problem Solving

In considering young children's perception of stimulus events, we have noted that they don't (a) discriminate the stimulus field as accurately as do older children and adults, (b) resist distraction, or (c) decenter (consider several dimensions simultaneously). Rather, young children tend to focus on one salient dimension, disregarding others. These tendencies would seem to explain why kindergarten and preschool children persevere on a particular response and commit the lose-shift error. Several studies have attempted to assess the role of these factors in children's problem solving by providing children with stimulus differentiation training prior to problem solving.

In one study, Gholson and McConville (1974) presented kindergarteners with a set of three-alternative oddity problems prior to solving problems in the blank-trial paradigm. On the pretraining task, children were asked to point to a pair of stimuli that were the same and to identify the one that was different. Half of the children were told if they were correct, whereas the remainder were not. The stimuli on the oddity problems varied along the same dimensions and values as used in the blank-trial problems. It was found that children who had received stimulus differentiation training with feedback generated more hypotheses and were less likely to show stereotypic response patterns. A similar study (Gholson, O'Connor, & Stern, 1976) found that this particular type of training was particularly effective with concrete operational children. (The possible role of some operative factors in setting limits on problem-solving abilities is an issue we will consider later.) Following feedback training, these developmentally more advanced kindergarteners showed more strategy use (more dimension checking and hypothesis checking) than other concrete operational children who had not received feedback during pretraining. Stimulus pretraining with feedback had no effect on the problem-solving abilities of children who were preoperational.

In a study with preschool children, Gross (1977a, b) pretrained preschoolers to discriminate visually the various values that defined the stimulus figures used in problem solving. Then the preschoolers were asked to solve blank-trial problems. In order to extend the effects of training to the problem-solving task, prior to solving each problem, children were required to discriminate visually the values defining the first positive exemplar. Using this procedure, preschoolers used hypotheses at above chance levels and tended to use hypotheses that were consistent with feedback; however, neither the use of more sophisticated problem-solving rules nor problem-solving strategies were observed.

The effectiveness of stimulus pretraining in inducing better problem solving in young children seems marginal at best. Even when the introtact probe paradigm is used (which should promote higher levels of performance), stimulus pretraining has little effect on young children's performance. Spiker and Cantor (1977), for example, exposed kindergarteners to one of several training conditions prior to problem solving. In one of these, a familiarization condition, children sorted cards with pictures of the problem-solving stimuli into stacks defined by their dimensional values (red or blue, large or small). This type of pretraining produced no better performance than a no-training control group. Whereas this type of stimulus differentiation pretraining may in some instances induce children to generate hypotheses spontaneously, it does not appear particularly effective in prompting higher levels of strategy or rule use in very young children.

Memory and Problem Solving

In Chapters 6, 7, and 8 we noted a number of changes that occur to memory during childhood. It is apparent that children's mnemonic limitations could affect the manner in which they solve problems. We know that young children have a limited short-term memory capacity and a preferred mode of encoding different from older children. They also fail to use a variety of control processes—including rehearsal, chunking, interactive imagery, and subjective organization—to facilitate information retention. As with research reported on perceptual training, we have evidence that memory deficiencies reduce problem-solving efficiency in older children, although these difficulties don't appear to be the major factor limiting preschool children's problem-solving performance.

Studies that have examined the influence of memory on problem solving have generally manipulated the task to either increase or decrease memory requirements. In one sense, comparisons between children's performance on the blank-trial and introtact-probe problems suggest memory factors may alter task performance. You may recall that on blank-trial probes children must retain information over a series of nonfeedback trials; on introtact probes there is little delay between feedback trials, thereby presenting a mnemonically less demanding task. It is interesting to note that for all age groups studied, the introtact probe procedure has consistently produced better performance than that found in the blank-trial procedure.

Other studies have more clearly demonstrated the role of memory in children's problem solving. Gholson, Phillips, and Levine (1973) had second-graders solve blank-trial problems under three memory conditions. In one condition (+ 3 condition) feedback was presented immediately after the child had made a selection, and the stimulus card remained in view for three seconds before the next stimulus card was presented. In another condition (0 condition), feedback was presented immediately after the child had made a choice, and the stimulus card was removed immediately. In a final condition (− 3 condition), after the child had chosen one of the figures on the stimulus card, the card was removed and feedback was delayed three seconds. You can imagine that the memory requirements would be much greater in the 0 and the − 3 conditions. In fact, problem solving under these two conditions was much worse than it was under the + 3 condition. Under these two conditions, children showed poorer use of the local consistency rule and less efficient problem-solving strategies (that is, hypothesis-testing patterns observed were either hypothesis-checking patterns or hypothesis stereotypes).

Other studies have attempted to assess the effects of memory aids on problem solving, the presumption being that problem solving will be facilitated under memory-aided conditions if problem-solving inefficiency is related to mnemonic limitations. Eimas (1970a) examined second-graders' problem solving using the blank-trials procedure under one of three memory aid conditions. In one condition (memory aid), outcome information was left in front of the child with a plus sign next to the figure if the child had received confirmation or a minus sign if the figure had received disconfirmation. In another condition (memory-recoding aid), a plus sign was placed next to the figure with the answer regardless of the child's choice (whether the child had received confirmation or disconfirmation). In another condition (memory-recoding-attention aid), only positive outcome information was left for the child to see. Both the memory aid and the memory-recoding aid conditions produced better problem solving compared to a control group that had no memory aid available. These children used more hypotheses, were more feedback consistent in the selection of hypotheses, and used more focusing in solving problems. Curiously, the memory-recoding-attention aid condition produced no better problem solving than the no memory aid control condition.

We also find that both the amount and type of information to be remembered affect problem-solving performance. Bruner et al. (1956) demonstrated that even with adults, as the amount of information to be manipulated increases beyond some magnitude, adults begin to revert to less efficient problem-solving strategies. In fact, we find a similar phenomena with children. Using a variant of the Twenty Questions game, Eimas (1970b) found that children asked more constraint-seeking questions when displays defining possible answers to the problem had fewer items. It has also been found that increasing the saliency of information to be manipulated facilitates problem solving (Eimas, 1970b; Mims & Gholson, 1977; Van Horn & Bartz, 1968). Eimas, for example, found that children solved problems more easily with color-form figures than when problems were defined by the position that "O's" occupied in a matrix.

Whereas memory factors influence the problem solving of young elementary school children, it has yet to be demonstrated that these factors have much of an influence on younger children's problem solving. In one set of experiments (Gross, 1977a, b) preschoolers were subjected to several types of memory training prior to solving blank-trial problems. Prior to problem solving, some children were taught to name the various values that defined the problem-solving stimuli, other children were taught to rehearse verbally, and others were taught to construct stimulus figures that would be encountered in the problem-solving task. The gains from these types of manipulations were less than impressive. In fact, following verbal rehearsal pretraining, children tested fewer hypotheses than a nontask-related pretrained control group (cf. Parrill-Burnstein, 1978).

These data suggest that efforts to remediate subprocess deficiencies do promote better rule use in older (second-grade) children; however, even after these types of intervention, it is uncommon to find children spontaneously using more sophisticated strategies, such as focusing. Very young children (preschool and kindergarten) don't seem to profit from training. This suggests that younger children are ignorant of problem-solving rules and strategies for solving problems.

RULE INSTRUCTION AND STRATEGY TRAINING

Two different techniques have been used to teach children to use developmentally more advanced problem-solving rules and strategies. One of these methods involves direct rule or strategy training; the other uses indirect instruction through modeling.

Direct Instruction

Attempts to train children to use developmentally advanced rules and strategies have produced mixed results. Direct training has been found to be more effective with children beyond preschool and kindergarten years; although young children may occasionally profit from this instruction. For example, Anderson (1965, 1968) taught high IQ, first-grade children to use a focusing strategy and found that, compared to a nontrained group, those in the training group more frequently solved transfer problems. Using the introtact probe technique, Cantor and Spiker (1978, Spiker & Cantor, 1977) demonstrated that even kindergarteners can be taught a focusing strategy. This can be done, however, only after a pretraining procedure that teaches the children (a) that problems have solutions, (b) how to use the win-stay and lose-shift rules, and (c) how to use an hypothesis-testing strategy. It should be noted that even after the training just described, only 30% of the children who were subjected to this training condition actually used focusing on problem-solving tasks.

Thus, although young children can learn to use rules and evaluate information in a manner that characterizes the focusing strategy, it is not something that young children find particularly easy. Similarly, Parrill-Burnstein (1978) found that kindergarteners could be taught to solve blank-trial problems, with the most improvement coming after a systematic training program that taught children to identify hypotheses, to represent hypotheses visually, to test one of the isolated hypotheses at a time, and to evaluate feedback. Training each or a combination of these steps separately produced performance that was better than a nontrained control group, but not better than when all elements of the training program were combined.

Research on direct strategy training also suggests that specific types of training may be more effective with particular age groups. McKinney (1973a), for example, found that training 5- and 6-year-old children to use a scanning strategy reduced the number of trials that children needed to solve problems, but didn't increase the frequency of problem solution; there was no facilitation whatsoever when these children were trained to use a focusing strategy. Both types of training, focusing and scanning, reduced the number of trials that children needed to solve problems and produced higher frequencies of problem solutions.

Modeling

In addition to direct strategy and rule training, several studies have attempted to alter children's problem-solving behavior by modeling specific rules and strategies. Using such a procedure, Laughlin, Moss, and Miller (1969) found that third-, fifth-, and sixth-grade children were more likely to use constraint-seeking questions when solving a Twenty Questions game after observing an adult model using a similar strategy. Other studies have sought to examine what it is about the modeling condition that facilitates rule and strategy induction.

Denney (1973, 1975; Denney, Denney, & Ziobrowski, 1973; Denney & Turner, 1979) has experimented with several different types of strategy models. One of these, an exemplary model, simply demonstrates the types of questions that are asked in one strategy or another (constraint seeking or hypothesis seeking). Another modeling condition, cognitive model, uses a model that asks questions specific to constraint seeking and also verbalizes the various steps that must be taken to use that strategy, evaluating the information gained from each question. In general, this research has shown that (a) exemplary models are effective in eliciting constraint seeking in older (8 and 10 years old) but not younger (6 years old) children; (b) cognitive models are more effective in eliciting constraint seeking from young children (6 years old) than are exemplary models; and (c) providing children with cognitive models and requiring them to rehearse the rules of the strategy while they solve problems produces more constraint seeking in both younger and older children, but only with the older children does this modeling condition produce more concept attainment. Although younger children can be induced to use more sophisticated strategies, there is some question about their ability to evaluate what they have learned from its use. Children may mimic adult behavior but fail to appreciate its significance.

To briefly summarize, research has revealed a complex relationship between perceptual, mnemonic, and conceptual processes on problem-solving tasks. There is some indication that children's problem solving is mediated by sub-process deficiencies. Training children to differentiate stimulus dimensions or reducing memory demands improves problem-solving performance. But there may be a limit to how much performance can be improved by attenuating or remediating subprocessing deficiencies. With very young children, for example, training them to differentiate stimuli may induce them to use hypotheses, but this may be to little avail since they seem unable to coordinate information gained from their hypotheses to solve problems efficiently. Some of young children's difficulties in solving problems are therefore attributable to the absence of knowledge about rules and strategies requisite for efficient problem solution. Again, however, we find limitations on how much very young children can learn. Whereas it may be possible to induce them to use more sophisticated strategies (through modeling or direct training), preschoolers and kindergarteners are not particularly receptive to this intervention, either being unable to coordinate the amount of information needed to use more advanced strategies or unable to appreciate the value of strategies themselves.

While striking developmental changes in problem-solving performance are found on artificially contrived deductive reasoning tasks, it is also important to consider that comparisons of this kind may also inflate developmental effects. Older children aware that they are being tested may be more apt to use developmentally sophisticated rules and strategies; whereas, younger children, less familiar with problem-solving tasks of the kind used in problem-solving research, may be at a disadvantage. In fact, adults don't perform logically on certain problems (Wason & Johnson-Laird, 1972), and younger children in more naturalistic problem-solving situations spontaneously use more sophisticated solution strategies. In one study, Tschirgi (1980) had second-, fourth-, sixth-grade children and college students reason about a number of problems that might be confronted in everyday experience. In one instance, children were told a story of a child who wanted to bake a cake but ran out of ingredients. Margarine was substituted for butter, honey for sugar, and whole wheat flour for regular white flour. Children were told that the cake turned out either great or terrible. The child wanted to know why and suspected that it might be due to the honey that was substituted for sugar. The experimenter asked children how they could prove this. Tschirgi found that if the outcome had been bad (the cake tasted terrible), both adults and children were likely to state that another cake should be baked but substituting sugar this time for honey. (The youngest children did have a tendency to manipulate more than one variable compared to older children.) On the other hand, both adults and children tended to use less logical strategies when attempting to confirm positive outcomes. That is, rather than again opting for baking a cake with sugar rather than honey, they stated they'd bake a cake with honey while varying one or more of the other ingredients. In more natural settings, younger and older children seem to opt for similar strategies based upon the outcomes of their manipulations rather than the logical structure of their solutions.

In attempts to train children to develop more sophisticated solution strategies, informal experience with objects may be more beneficial than formal training programs. Smith and Dutton (1979), for example, allowed preschool children to play with apparatus relevant to the solution of a problem (joining two sticks together to retrieve a marble) or gave them specific training in the problem's solution. Compared to a group of children receiving no training, both those who were allowed to play with the apparatus and those who were solution-trained solved problems more rapidly. On a new task requiring an extension of the rule, children who played with the materials prior to problem solving solved transfer problems more rapidly and with fewer hints.

Thus, more naturalistic problem-solving contexts and training programs facilitate younger children's problem solving. This knowledge suggests that the poor performance of young children on problem-solving tasks is not entirely due to a lack of ability (competence), but also results from faulty interpretation of task requirements, failure to generalize knowledge to new tasks, or lack of motivation or interest in the types of tasks presented for solution.

AFFECTIVE FACTORS AND PROBLEM SOLVING

In addition to speculation about interactions that exist between perceptual, mnemonic, and conceptual systems, we might also consider how individual differences affect problem solving. We know, for example, that both state and trait characteristics of individuals exert powerful influences on task performance.

Whereas there is an extensive and growing literature on the nature of the interaction between systems of the intellect, much less is known about how state characteristics of the individual influence problem solving (cf. Spielberger, Gonzales, & Fletcher, 1979). Such an oversight is particularly curious given intuitive and empirical evidence that such factors as motivation and state-anxiety significantly affect scholastic performance during the elementary school years (Hill & Sarason, 1961; Sarason, Davidson, Lighthall, Waite & Ruebush, 1960) and problem solving in general (Meyers & Martin, 1974).

The disruptive effect of state-anxiety may occur at one of two levels. It may interfere with the operation of the conceptual system itself—interfering with the application and use of a particular set of rules and strategies—or, more likely, it may interfere with the use of subprocesses (perception and memory) that support conceptual processes. We know, for example, that state-anxiety attenuates memory in both adults and children (Mueller, 1975; Sarason, 1972; Sinclair, 1969) and disrupts children's attention (Nottelmann & Hill, 1977).

Whether state anxiety affects memory and attention, and consequently task performance, depends on the complexity of the task. On tasks that have high memory demands, e.g., tasks requiring general comprehension and recall of factual information, performance suffers as a function of high state-anxiety. However, on tasks requiring reasoning alone and without excessive memory demands (as on an open-book test), performance is little affected by state-anxiety (Carlson & Ryan, 1969; Sinclair, 1969). Furthermore, problem solving by high-anxious subjects (both adults and adolescents), improves when memory aids are provided (Leherissey, O'Neil, & Hanson, 1971; Sieber, Kameya, & Paulson, 1970). Other research has demonstrated that with adults, high-anxious problem solvers may fail to encode sufficient amounts of information about potential problem solutions and consequently are forced to rely upon less efficient solution strategies. If we're anxious, for example, we may focus on one salient solution and ignore others. A very nervous person might put a key into a lock that is jammed and continue to jimmy the key or pound on the door in utter frustration rather than considering alternative solutions. Reducing memory requirements by providing anxious individuals with memory aids results in a reinstatement of more efficient problem-solving strategies (Gross & Mastenbrook, 1980). We can see this in our everyday experiences, too. If we are anticipating a particularly hectic day, we can improve our effectiveness if we make a list of all of the various things that need to be done that day.

The specific influence of state-anxiety (or for that matter other state factors such as motivation) on children's problem solving is not well known. Considering the stress that many children feel within school and home (cf. Gardner, 1971), further research on this aspect of problem solving would be extremely useful.

Quite the opposite of the meager attention that has been given to the influence of state factors on the problem solving of children, there has been considerable attention paid to trait characteristics. Two such trait characteristics have received specific attention: Reflexivity–impulsivity and field-dependence–field-independence. Children who are reflective generally take more time solving problems and are prone to make fewer errors than impulsive children. Zelniker, Renan, Sorer, and Shavit (1977) have suggested that this cognitive style may influence the type of perceptual processing that is used by the child. Reflectives presumably attend to the parts of the stimulus field; whereas, impulsives process the stimulus field as a whole. Others (McKinney, 1973b) believe that this particular trait predisposes children to use particular types of conceptual strategies on problem-solving tasks. For example, reflectives tend to use constraint-seeking strategies and impulsives hypothesis-checking strategies. Cognitive-style factors have also been implicated in children's performance on a variety of Piagetian tasks. For example, both reflectivity and field independence have been found to facilitate performance on tasks requiring both concrete and formal operational skills (Barstsis & Ford, 1977; Brodzinsky, 1982; Case, 1974; Hill, 1980).

To this point, we have considered a method for the study of problem solving that views the problem solver as influenced by a number of cognitive and affective variables. I trust this review has conveyed the sense of complexity that characterizes the relationship. In the next section, quite a different method for problem-solving research will be presented. It is a systems-modeling method, which attempts to synthesize a linear set of rules and procedures that exemplify particular patterns of problem solving exhibited by children within a problem-solving situation.

A SYSTEMS-MODELING METHOD FOR PROBLEM SOLVING

Another method to understanding problem solving is the synthesis approach (Kail & Bisanz, 1982; Klahr, 1980; Klahr & Wallace, 1976; Siegler, 1981). Typically this method characterizes the development of problem-solving ability as the progressive attainment of more powerful problem-solving rule systems. We might liken this process to the purchase of increasingly more sophisticated calculators. We begin with a simple model that has a limited number of functions that prevents us from performing very sophisticated calculations. Over time, however, we upgrade our calculator, acquiring models with an increasing variety of functions that are flexible enough to use over a broad range of situations and problems. Siegler (1981), for instance, has proposed four rule systems that characterize general changes in children's approach to problems requiring a knowledge of equilibrium (Figure 9-2). Suppose that we were to present children with a balance beam problem (as described in Chapter 2). On this problem, children must determine whether or not a two-armed scale will balance or tilt to one side. Children using Rule I make judgments about problems based upon one dominant dimension only. On the balance beam problem, weight is characteristically the most salient dimension. Children using this rule will predict that the beam will balance if there is an equal amount of weight on either side of the balance or that it will tilt in the direction of greater weight regardless of the distance that weight is placed from the fulcrum. Children using Rule II will make judgments based on the dominant dimension too, but when weights are equal, they will consider the subordinant dimension (distance) in making judgments. For those children using Rule III, both the dominant and subordinate dimensions are considered, but when weight and distance are in conflict (that is, one side may have less weight, but the weight is placed further from the fulcrum), the child becomes confused and must guess at the solution. Finally, children using Rule IV always consider both dimensions and regard the task as one of proportionality, deducing some ratio between distance and weight and judging on the basis of this knowledge.

Given these types of rules, Siegler proposes that we can diagram the thought process of children operating under each rule system, given specific types of problems. On one type of problem, equality, both weight and distance are equal on either arm of the balance; consequently, children using any of the four rules should predict correctly. On dominant problems, the weight is greater on one side, but placed the same distance on either arm. Again we'd anticipate that children using any of the four rules will predict that the balance will tilt to the direction of the greater weight. On subordinate problems, equal amounts of weight are placed on either side but at different distances from the fulcrum. Children using Rule I should incorrectly predict equilibrium; children using all other rules should predict the beam to tilt to the direction of greater distance. On conflict-dominant problems, an unequal weight is placed at varying distances, but in a manner that the balance will tilt to the direction of the greater weight. On this problem all children but those using Rule III should predict correctly. Children using Rule III should guess at the solution, pre-

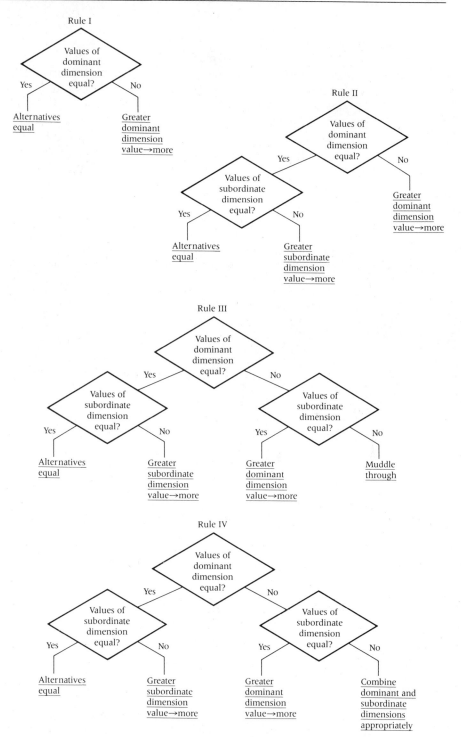

Figure 9-2. Modal rule models. (*Siegler, 1981*)

dicting no better than chance. (Since there are three possible guesses—balance, tilt left, and tilt right—the child has a 33% chance of being correct). With conflict-subordinate problems the weight and distances are confounded with the balance tilting toward the greater distance. In the conflict-equal problem, weight and distances are again confounded but counterbalanced (the balance maintains equilibrium). On these last two problems we would anticipate that children using Rules I and II will fail to predict accurately, children using Rule III will predict at chance, and those using Rule IV will predict correctly. On the basis of children's pattern of performance on these problems, Siegler grouped children by rule use. Data for each of these rule-users was then combined and averaged across problem type. As might be expected, the performance of groups defined by each of the four rules corresponded very closely to expected probabilities (Figure 9-3)—there was consistency in the performance of children classified as Rule I, II, III, and IV users. The use of particular rules also demonstrated a reliable age sequencing. On the balance beam problem, at 3 years of age none of the children demonstrated consistent

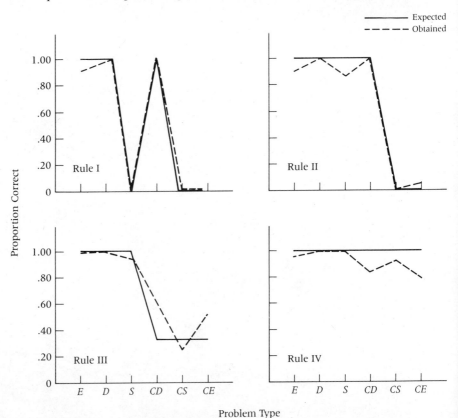

Figure 9-3. Proportion of correctly predicted results on the balance beam problem as a function of children's use of rules and problem type (E = equality, D = dominant, S = subordinate, CD = conflict dominant, CS = conflict subordinate, CE = conflict equal). (*Siegler, 1981*)

rule use. By 4 years of age, half of the children used Rule I, and nearly all used the rule by 5 years of age. Older children (8 and 12 years of age) generally used Rules II and III. Most of the college students used Rule III, with less than a third using the most advanced Rule IV.

Taking a similar tack to that of Siegler, Klahr (1980) has more meticulously specified the various conceptual processes that would be involved in the execution of any one of these rules. In so doing, he has characterized the problem-solving process as a set of productions (that is, a condition and an associated action). Conditions represent momentary knowledge states that when satisfied lead to some action, which in turn leads to another production, and so on until a final goal state is reached. The coordination of a set of productions is called a production system.

A production system involves predictions (*P*), expectancies (*E*) and changes in the contents of short-term memory (*SW*). These changes occur as a consequence of comparing expectancies with actual outcomes and revising or maintaining one's criteria for expecting certain consequences.

Let's consider the production system that would characterize Rule III behavior (Table 9-1). This production system is an imposing set of statements, but let's work through it. Remember that children using Rule III consider both the dominant dimension and the subordinate dimension, but when these two dimensions are in conflict, the children guess about how the balance will tilt.

On beginning the problem children are asked to predict how the balance

TABLE 9-1. Production System for Model III after Klahr, 1980

*P*1: ([predict] [weight is the same on both sides] → [made prediction] [expect balance to be level] say, "Balance.")

*P*2: ([predict] [weight is more on side 1] → [made prediction] [expect side 1 to lower] say, "Side 1 down.")

*P*3: ([predict] [weight is the same on both sides] [distance is more on side 1] → [made prediction] [expect side 1 to lower] say, "Side 1 down.")

*P*4: ([predict] [weight is more on one side] [distance is more on one side] → find that which is greater)

*P*5: ([predict] [criterion dimension is weight] [criterion dimension is more on side 1] [second dimension, distance, is more on side 2] → [made prediction] [expect side 1 to lower] say, "Side 1 down.")

*P*6: ([predict] [weight is greater on side 1] → [made prediction] [expect side 1 to lower] say, "Side 1 down.")

*P*7: ([predict] [distance is greater on side 1] → [made prediction] [expect side 1 to lower] say, "Side 1 down.")

*P*8: ([predict] [no information about weight or distance] → attend to the state of the balance beam)

*E*1: ([expect] → look at the beam)

*E*2: ([expect side 1 to lower] [see the direction to which side 1 tilts] → [saw the expected side lower] [result was as expected])

*E*3: ([expect side 1 to lower] [see the direction to which side 1 tilts] → [saw the expected side raise] [result was unexpected])

*SW*1: ([result was wrong] [conflict judgments resolved by criterion dimension of distance] → [old result was wrong] [change criterion dimension from distance to weight])

*SW*2: ([result was wrong] [conflict judgments resolved by criterion dimension of weight] → [old result was wrong] [change criterion dimension from weight to distance])

beam will react when it is allowed to move freely. With this command the first cycle of the production system is initiated. To make a prediction, children need information about the state of the balance beam. Let's presume that the two dimensions are in conflict (that is, there is greater weight on one side of the balance, but the lighter weight is placed further out on the other side of the beam). In the initiating cycle, the child has no information about the beam, thus only production (P8) is satisfied, which triggers the action (→) to attend to characteristics of the balance beam. It is presumed that upon initiating the second cycle, the child has encoded information about the balance beam, and with this information in short-term memory (summarized in parentheses), the individual satisfies productions (P4 and P2). Because P4 is a special case of P2, it fires and initiates a new cycle to find which is greater, weight or distance. The third cycle begins as this new information (that the left arm has more weight and the right arm more distance) is coded in short-term memory. The productions satisfied in this cycle are P2 and P4 (with P4 a special case of P2 having priority), and P5, P6, and P7 (since P5 is a special case of P6 and P7, it too has priority). Thus, P4 and P5 are in conflict—both productions are satisfied. Klahr reasons that since P5 is a more recent production, it has priority and executes its action. Because children at this level can't coordinate two dimensions simultaneously, and because weight and distance are confounded, it is assumed that their judgment is governed by some *a priori* criterion (weight or distance) for resolving conflict. Presuming that weight is the criterion dimension used by a particular child to make a judgment, a prediction is made that the side with more weight will lower.

During the next cycle the child observes what actually happens to the balance as it is allowed to move freely. Let's assume that the child predicted wrong and the balance tipped in the opposite direction. Presumably the child encodes this information in short-term memory, and in the fifth cycle the outcome is compared to the expectancy that is disconfirmed (E3). The last cycle reflects a modification of the system, as the unexpected result leads to a change in the criterion (weight changes to distance) that the child uses to make new predictions when weight and distance are again in conflict.

By specifying the nature of problem solving in such a precise manner, it is possible to simulate these problem-solving sequences with computer programs—as Klahr has in fact done. The operation of these programs and the generation of response patterns similar to those observed in children are presumed to validate the sufficiency of these models as typical processes underlying children's problem solutions.

INFORMATION-PROCESSING VIEWS OF PROBLEM SOLVING: A CRITIQUE

The criticisms of information-processing approaches to problem solving have focused primarily on what it is that has been studied. It should be clear that both the analysis and synthesis approaches attempt to discern age-related patterns in behavior characterized by rules, production systems, and strategies. Focusing as they do on descriptions of performance on well-specified tasks, these approaches have been less explicit about the mechanisms responsible for change. This research has also been criticized for underestimating the flexibility and adaptability of human thinking.

Specifying the Mechanisms of Change

Information-processing theories have been particularly vulnerable to the criticism that they have not attended to the issue of how children acquire more powerful rules, strategies, or production systems (cf., Beilin, 1980; Breslow, 1981; Pascual-Leone, 1980). Theoretical accounts of the mechanisms of change have indeed been vague. When discussing changes in production systems, theorists suggest that likely sources of transformation stem from the detection of recurrent irregularities or inconsistencies in one's experiences (Klahr, 1980) or in the growth of the capacity of the information-processing system (Kail & Bisanz, 1982). Presumably, with increased processing capacity the organism can include into the production system a greater number of productions or processing steps. This system growth might occur as a consequence of either an absolute growth in the capacity of the system itself (particularly an increase in short-term memory capacity) or the consolidation of productions or skills into higher-order processing units, thereby reducing the amount of information that needs to be stored and freeing up additional space for the addition of new productions or skills (Fischer, 1980).

Although it is true that synthesis approaches have devoted much of their attention to the description of processing routines specific to particular tasks, there has not been a complete absence of speculation about transition mechanisms. In fact, Fischer (1980) has proposed a complete set of transition rules accounting for development both within and between developmental levels.

Research reviewed under the analysis approach also suggests that it may be necessary to incorporate into our accounts of development, a maturational factor much like that advocated by the Genevans. Children don't necessarily profit from tasks that reduce subprocessing demands nor from rule and strategy training. These data have led some (Gholson, 1980; Gholson & Beilin, 1979; Gholson & Cohen, 1980) to speculate that operative knowledge may limit the degree to which children can profit from experimental intervention. For example, if preschool children lack operative knowledge (the ability to decenter, reverse thought, and construct class hierarchies), their performance should be characterized, as it is, by the inefficient use of logical rules and nonstrategic, stereotypical hypothesis patterns. These operative limitations apparently negate the effectiveness of training programs that require higher levels of operative knowledge (as would be the case in the use of focusing). Although training specific to children's operative level may facilitate the use of skills and strategies that are available to them, operative factors may place an upper limit on how much children will profit from training programs.

The Machine as a Metaphor

Another observation made by critics of the information-processing approach is that it treats the organism as a mechanical being—as in its appeal to the use of the computer as a metaphor for the human information-processing system. This comparison has been abrasive to some theorists who see in this characterization a passive, rigid, and nonadaptive organism (cf. Pascual-Leone, 1980). It is a characterization believed to misrepresent the flexible quality of human thinking. Kail and Bisanz (1982), however, argue that we must also remember that within this metaphor is the recognition that a variety of programs are available to sophisticated computers. It is the adaptive nature of these programs that make the system flexible. It is also noted that it is wrong to view the information-processing theorists' use of the computer metaphor as a direct comment on their attitude about the human organism. Indeed, an inspection of the attitude conveyed by these theorists about the information processor's performance on a variety of tasks reveals the belief that man is an active and constructive being.

The Concern with Task Performance

A final criticism of information-processing theory is that it is too task-specific. Whereas the theory has provided a precise explanation of performance on specific tasks, it has failed to produce a general theory that provides a set of abstract concepts that account for development across a wide range of problem-solving domains (cf. Pascual-Leone, 1980). Whether one wishes to start from the general and work toward the specific or vice versa seems a matter of preference. It is the information-processing theorists' belief that starting from the specific provides a basis for truly understanding some aspect of performance (Kail & Bisanz, 1982). It is presumed that by understanding the specifics of performance on particular tasks, we will eventually piece these specifics together to form an integrated understanding of the whole.

SUMMARY

Information-processing theories of problem solving have typically examined children's performance on sets of well-specified problem-solving tasks. Analysis approaches to problem solving have examined the relationships between a variety of cognitive and affective components of the intellect. We find that young children don't use logical problem-solving rules or strategies spontaneously prior to the second grade. Some, but not all, of the poor performance of young children on problem-solving tasks is attributable to deficiencies in the use of subprocesses (attention and memory) that support the problem-solving effort. It is also likely that many young children have not yet learned more sophisticated solution strategies. Some caution needs to be exercised in interpreting data from contrived experimental tasks, since we find that adults are sometimes less logical in solving problems in more naturalistic settings, whereas younger children may demonstrate more systematic solutions.

One of the main contributions of the analysis approach has been a revelation of the complexity of the relationship that produces performance. Although some trait characteristics of problem-solvers have been linked to problem-solving styles, little is known about state variables in children's problem solving.

The synthesis approach to problem solving has examined a complexity of another sort—the intricacy of the system of rules that constitutes any single task performance. Working with specific kinds of problems, researchers have identified rule systems that characterize the performance of children at various age levels and have translated these rule systems into sophisticated computer programs that mimic the performance of children on problem-solving tasks.

10

A Piagetian Approach to Problem Solving

Although Piaget was not the first to propose a theory of development, his particular opinion on that matter has affected our thinking like no other theory before. Regardless of your particular theoretical orientation, at some point you're compelled to consider how Piaget might have addressed a problem—and more often than not, how he did. Piaget believed that intelligence is affected by one's stage of development. Higher stages of intellectual development are marked by capacities and skills unavailable at lower levels; lower level skills, however, serve as a basis for higher order skills. Consequently, one's ability to interact with the world is revealed in progressively more elegant and efficient forms of reasoning.

This particular view of intellectual development leads to a consideration of a different set of issues and questions about problem solving than those studied in information-processing theory. Information-processing theorists are primarily interested in how children use a variety of logical rules on problem-solving tasks. Looked at from the Piagetian perspective, the more important question becomes, why do children use the rules they do? To understand how and why children solve problems in their own fashion, we must first consider the nature of the intellect.

If children are to perform a variety of intellectual tasks (solve problems, discover concepts, or categorize), they must first symbolically represent their world and, second, understand something about various properties of objects and relationships that hold between them. This latter ability presupposes the operationalization of thought.

As will be evident in the later section of this chapter, the non-Genevan position has been critical of the Piagetian construct of stage (and by extension the general age ranges within which specific abilities should be found). Non-Genevan research has focused on the age–stage issue almost to the exclusion of examining more specific questions posed by Piaget's theory—the nature and necessity of logical structures that presumably constitute intelligence and provide the basis for knowledge. The Genevans, on the other hand, have either ignored non-Genevan research or observed that critics have failed to understand the basic premises underlying their research. In fact, the exuberance with which non-Genevan researchers have attempted to demonstrate competencies in young children would seem to underscore the differences between these two schools of thought—a difference between wanting to know what children can do versus why they do it (Pinard, 1981).

THE OPERATIONALIZATION OF THOUGHT: DEVELOPMENT OF A SYSTEM OF RULES

As observed in Chapter 3, the hallmark of preoperational thought is the ability to use symbols. Symbolic thought or semiotic function is evident in children's use of language, mental imagery, deferred imitation, and symbolic play. Despite the intellectual achievement that semiotic function allows, it is a limited advance. The thought of the preoperational child is basically unidirectional, static, and dominated by the salient perceptual features of the physical world (see Chapter 3). In light of these limitations it is not surprising that preschoolers perform poorly on problems requiring analytical reasoning. Only with the accommodation of the intellectual structure to include transformational schemes—operations that allow children to recognize and appreciate the logical relationships that hold between elements in the world—are they able to manipulate thought itself.

The ability to manipulate thought develops through the attainment of operational structures. Operations are internalized action schemes corresponding to understandings about how things can be related to one another. Most importantly, these operations are reversible. It is Piaget's belief that a common set of operations underlies concrete operational thought. These operations are coordinated into cohesive and interdependent groupings, which allow children to reason about specific types of problems. For the purpose of this discussion, we will consider only problems of *classification, conservation,* and *seriation.*

Because similar sets of operations are believed to underlie concrete operational thinking, one might anticipate a synchronous evolution of problem-solving ability within each of these three areas. Longitudinal studies of concrete operational development suggest otherwise. Hooper, Toniolo, and Sipple (1978), for example, demonstrated that transitive knowledge (here subsumed under a discussion of seriation) predates knowledge of conservation. Other studies (Tomlinson-Keasey, Eisert, Kahle, Hardy-Brown, and Keasey, 1979) have found that seriation and numeration predict children's knowledge of conservation of weight and volume, which develop several years later. Although these variations don't diminish the importance of an operational structure in thought, they do suggest that structures, operations, and groupings develop at different rates and in a much less synchronous fashion than earlier believed (Piaget & Szeminska, 1952; Pinard & Laurendau, 1969).

Classification

Mature classification involves an awareness that common items form groups and that groups can be arranged hierarchically. A group may be a superordinate class for objects below it (animals) while itself being a subordinate group to other classes of objects (living things).

The ability to classify implies particular kinds of knowledge about classes and the properties that define them. Membership in one class, for example, precludes the simultaneous membership in another mutually exclusive class (for example, something can't be both long and short within the same organizational scheme; it is classified as either long or short). Second, all members of a class must be alike in some way. The property that defines class membership is referred to as the intention of the group. Third, classes may be described by a list of things that can be included in it (the extension of a class). And, fourth, by knowing what attribute(s) defines intention, we always know what things are members of a class; intention therefore defines extension.

Piaget (1954, Piaget & Szeminska, 1952) reasoned that knowledge of classification develops between the ages of 5 and 7 years of age. Late preoperational children, he recognized, could sort objects into hierarchically defined sets—first sorting by shape and further subdividing by color, and so on. The ability to sort categorically, however, does not by itself reveal a true understanding of the nature of classes. Critical to this knowledge is the understanding of class inclusion. This is knowledge about how an item's membership in one group is also related to groups that are both superordinate and subordinate to the one in which it is included.

To demonstrate the importance of this kind of understanding, let's assume that we have identified a child (about 5 years of age) who can group beads by composition (glass or wooden), size (large and small), and color (red and blue). Taking a handful of wooden beads, six of which are red and four blue, we ask the child to tell us if there are more red beads or more wooden beads.

Much to our consternation, the child may tell us that there are more red beads. This particular child apparently fails to understand that the subordinate class (red beads) is also a part of some higher class of objects (wooden beads) and as such can never have more items in it than the superordinate class.

The failure of preoperational children to understand class inclusion is attributed to several intellectual limitations that typify their reasoning. The young child is incapable of considering two elements simultaneously—in this case, that something could be both red and wooden at the same time. The young child is also distracted by the most salient features of the perceptual field, attending only to one dimension (the red objects) while neglecting other relevant dimensions. Children are also unable to work their way up and down the classification hierarchy, using it as an abstract system for manipulating objects rather than simply grouping them together.

Operations Underlying Classification

The ability to classify implies the internalization of a system of operations, a set of mathematicallike rules that allow children to infer relationships that exist between things in reality. The use of classification schemes implies the existence of a coordinated set, or *groupment*, of logical operations relating elements within a group. One groupment (Groupment I) is essential to understanding classification; each operation that is a part of it is integral to knowledge about classes.

One operation that is necessary for hierarchical classification is composition (addition). Adding two elements in a hierarchy forms a new class of objects. Combining red beads (r) and white beads (wh) forms a new class of objects, wooden beads (w), or $(r + wh) = w$. Reversibility is another operation that implies knowing that for every operation effected on the system there is another that reverses it—for example, $(r + wh) = w$ and $(w - r) = wh$. Another operation in this groupment is associativity. Classes of objects are considered in a binary manner, and, consequently, there are a number of ways that lower-level groups can be combined to form higher-order ones. Hence, associativity—$(wh + r) + g$ (glass beads) $= b$ (all beads) or $(w + g) = b$. Identity is another operation that is a part of this groupment. It is the operator that when added to or subtracted from anything in the system leaves the system unchanged. Or, taking the opposite of something from itself produces identity or nullifiability—for example, $(w + 0) = w$, $(w - 0) = w$, or $(w - w) = 0$. Finally, the use of class hierarchies also implies knowledge of tautology and resorption. Tautology refers to knowledge that combining any class with itself produces itself; wooden beads combined with wooden beads produces wooden beads $(w + w) = w$. Resorption refers to the understanding that a subclass added to a higher-order class is simply defined by the higher-order class $(w + r) = w$. Whereas these principles seem redundant, perhaps even simplistic and trivial, it was Piaget's belief that it is precisely from such operative knowledge that older children and adults so easily and accurately organize, understand, manipulate, and use hierarchical structure in problem solving.

Empirical Support for Piaget's Explanation of Classification

Empirical tests of Piaget's views on classification have tended to focus upon two primary questions. The first is a traditional concern of non-Genevan research—when can children sort or use classification schemes? The answer to this question seems to be that they can classify much earlier than originally proposed by Inhelder and Piaget (1964). Another age-related question is when do children show class inclusion? Rather than being a benchmark of concrete operational thought, class inclusion is not reliably demonstrated until later in that period. The final question that has been addressed with some regularity is, what is the basis for class inclusion? For example, is this ability dependent upon the application of operational schemes mentioned earlier, or is it explainable by other strategic behavior? For now, this question remains unanswered.

Early studies of children's classification behavior provided reasonable support for the view that children do not begin to use classification hierarchies until late in the preoperational period. Denney (1972) reported that of 36 children (2, 3, and 4 years of age), only 11 four-year-olds were able to sort stimuli along two dimensions and but only 2 of the 2-year-old children were able to classify perfectly. More recent research has successfully demonstrated that under certain conditions, even very young children can sort stimuli along two dimensions. Watson, Hayes, & Vietze (1979) trained children to sort stimuli varying along one dimension with two values. Following successful unidimensional sorting, 2½-, 3½-, and 4½-year-old children were provided with two-dimensional stimuli with two values each. It was found that only four of nine 2½-year-old children successfully sorted the two-dimensional objects, but 29 of 32 children in both the older age groups sorted these stimuli successfully. Despite this demonstration of bidimensional sorting or classification, it should be noted that stimuli were extremely simple (three objects, a blue square, a red square, and a red disk), and sorting was accomplished only after a lengthy training session.

In another demonstration of what appears to be classification behavior by young children, Sugarman (1981) observed the manner in which 1- and 3-year-old children interacted with sets of eight objects. These object sets were made up of either one dimension with two values (a set of plates and blocks) or two dimensions with two values each (red and blue plates and blocks). Children's spontaneous manipulation of objects was observed for sequential selections of objects within the same class (touching in succession plates then in another sequence blocks). This type of inspection of an array of objects set before a child was taken as evidence for classification behavior; indeed older children did more of it. Sugarman believes that this behavior suggests the use of classification schemes by very young children, but a more basic issue might be raised with respect to these results. Describing her procedure, she states that the array of objects was pushed toward the child and the child was told, "These are for you to play with." A more interesting question might be why, under these conditions, would we expect children to apply classification schemes? Is classification, for example, presumed to be a scheme that is activated spontaneously when one is presented with an unstructured task and a varied assortment of objects?

In addition to evidence that at least suggests very young children use hierarchical classification schemes, there is also convincing evidence that the objects that children are given to classify significantly affect their performance. Rosch, Mervis, Gray, Johnson, & Boyes-Braem (1976), for example, posit the existence of natural categories—certain basic levels of categorization that humans apply to their world. Objects forming natural categories have many attributes in common; those forming more abstract superordinate groupings have fewer. It is easier to define the attributes of a chair, for example, than it is to define what furniture is. Rosch et al. note that with sorting tasks, developmental differences in sorting accuracy accrue to tasks requiring sorts along abstract, superordinate dimensions. On the other hand, no developmental differences occur when subjects are asked to sort things into basic or natural categories.

Markman (1979a) has also argued for a finer distinction in what we consider to be classes of things. She suggests that there are both classes and collections of things. To know whether or not something is a member of a class, we don't need to know about the other things in that class. We ascribe class membership by knowing what attributes define the class (its intention). If the object has the relevant attributes, then it is a member of that class. On the other hand, in order to know if something is a member of a collection, we need to know something about that particular collection. Superordinate–subordinate relationships are diminished (if they exist at all) in a collection and, furthermore, there is a much stronger part–whole relationship. A collection exists through the relationship of its members. There is less of that type of relationship with classes; whether or not some particular object exists or not has little to do with the existence of that class of things as a whole. Whether or not I grind a particular rock into sand has little to do with the existence of a class of objects known as rocks and minerals. But if I have a particular rock collection, the loss of one of those rocks significantly alters the nature of my collection, perhaps even redefining what I have a collection of. Markman & Siebert (1976) have found that young children find it easier to classify things as members of collections than to classify things as members of classes, perhaps due to the abstract nature of properties that define classes.

Whereas it is clear that children are capable of classification much earlier than the age mentioned by Inhelder and Piaget, there is the remaining question of whether or not children actually have a logical understanding of class hierarchies. According to Piaget, to truly understand classification, children had to first understand class inclusion.

In an extensive review of class inclusion literature, Winer (1980) drew a rather surprising conclusion. Rather than finding evidence for class-inclusion abilities before the age established by Piaget (the beginning of the concrete operational period), he found just the opposite. Class inclusion, it would appear, is a type of knowledge that develops relatively late. For example, even by early adolescence, class inclusion is not understood perfectly. Although more precocious demonstrations of this ability can be found, it is more typical to find this ability developing late in the concrete operational period, and even then children have a hard time justifying their responses to class inclusion problems (Markman, 1978). Performance on these problems is clearly affected by the types of classes that children reason about (Inhelder & Piaget, 1964; Markman, 1979a) and the types of questions that are asked about classes (Hodkins, 1981). Nonetheless, a precise explanation of children's performance on class inclusion is yet forthcoming (Winer, 1980).

An alternative explanation of class inclusion to that offered by Inhelder and Piaget (1964) is that the strategy adopted by younger children may be one of empirical counting, rather than reasoning about the subordinate–superordinate relationships. Suppose, for example, we present a child with a set depicting six roses and two daisies, and we ask the child, "Are there more roses or flowers?" Now, the child who doesn't understand class inclusion will say that there are more roses. Wilkinson (1976) has argued that this error may have nothing to do with knowledge about superordinate–subordinate relationships. Instead, he has suggested that children may count items in groups— but with a special rule that says that no item can be counted twice. Having counted the roses once, children are prevented from counting them again when considering flowers. Thus, they count the remaining flowers (the daisies), compare the two sums, and give an incorrect response to the question. Miller and Barg (1982) have suggested that this may be a primitive strategy used with class inclusion problems; as children grow older, they come to justify more of their class inclusion judgments on the basis of operational principles as proposed by Inhelder and Piaget (1964). In fact, several researchers (Niebuhr and Molfese, 1978; Tomlinson-Keasey et al., 1979) have found that knowledge of a variety of logical operations predicts performance on class inclusion problems. At best, it would be safe to conclude that some operational knowledge is necessary for performance on class inclusion problems. Precisely what the nature and extent of that ability should be is not yet known.

Conservation

One of the classic benchmarks of entry into the period of concrete operational thought is the child's ability to conserve properties of objects. An objective understanding of reality, for example, requires that one realize that certain object properties remain invariant despite superficial alterations in an object's appearance. My car, for example, doesn't weigh less now than it did before its fender was dented. Likewise, an amount of clay doesn't weigh less when it is flattened into a pancake than when it is rolled into a ball.

The ability to conserve, like any other form of reasoning, is dependent upon the availability of logical operators. Conservation occurs through the coordination of three operations: identity, negation, and reciprocity. *Identity* implies an understanding that a property remains the same if nothing is added or taken away from it. *Negation* is an operation that allows children to reason that an alteration in one dimension can be reversed by an equal but opposite transformation. Finally, *reciprocity* implies a quantitative comparison by the child, a type of logical multiplication of the form "If something of a particular amount has been taken away from one dimension, an equal amount has been added to another dimension." Changes in one dimension have compensated for changes in another. The use of logical operators allows children to consider more than one dimension of an array simultaneously and to consider successive states of objects, comparing their present and past states using mentally reversible operations.

It was Piaget's belief that some common group of operations underlies children's performance on conservation tasks; however, he also acknowledged the effects of stimulus properties on performance. Properties of objects that were more easily dissociated from children's own actions, he reasoned, would be conserved earliest. Judging a substance's length, for example, is less dependent upon a child's involvement with an object than is judging its heft, or weight. Children's performance on conservation tasks should therefore reflect both the development of the operative component of intellect as well as influences exerted by stimulus properties (Elkind, 1961b; Flavell, 1963). As such, it is predicted and found that there is a reliable ordering in the attainment of conservation of various object properties. Table 10-1 lists varieties of propties and the relative ages at which they are conserved by children. For comparative purposes, both data from Piaget's original work and replication studies are reported.

Number and Continuous Quantity

Rather than reviewing the extensive literature that exists on these various types of conservation, the current discussion will focus on two forms of conservation—number and continuous quantity. This is done primarily for practical reasons, as the flavor and findings of research in these areas are similar to that found with other types of conservation. The majority of the studies examining children's knowledge of conservation have addressed several issues. First, and typical of the non-Genevan research, is the concern with the age at which children demonstrate conservation. Although we cannot equate stage of development with chronological age, Piaget (1954) did provide general age ranges in which we could anticipate certain kinds of knowledge. His research indicated that it would be unlikely to find children younger than 6 or 7 years of age conserving properties of objects. As you will see, various researchers have suggested that it is possible to induce conservationlike behavior in children as young as 3 or 4 years of age; however, whether or not these skills represent true conservation is questionable. More important than issues related to when children conserve is the issue of what skills or abilities underlie performance. The literature is again inconclusive on this matter. There is some evidence to suggest that conservation is dependent upon knowledge of specific logical operators, as suggested by Piaget; but there is another equally strong body of evidence suggesting that some logical operators originally described by Piaget may not be needed for conservation.

Conservation of number.   An examination of Table 10-1 shows that children generally conserve number by 6 or 7 years of age; thus, number is one of the earliest properties to be conserved. Although Piaget recognized that

TABLE 10-1. Age at Which More Than 50% of Children Passed a Test of Conservation Using Traditional Piagetian Tasks

Source		Type of Conservation					
	Number	Substance	Length	Continuous Quantity	Area	Weight	Volume
Piaget & Szeminska (1952)	6 yr*						
Piaget & Inhelder (1962)		8 yr (72%)				8 yr (52%)	10 yr (56%)
Piaget, Inhelder, & Szeminska (1960)			7 yr*	8 yr*	7 yr 6 mo*		11 yr*
Elkind (1961a)		6 yr				7 yr	11 yr (25%)
Lovell & Ogilvie (1960)		8–9 yr					
Lovell & Ogilvie (1961b)						10–11 yr	
Lovell & Ogilvie (1961a)							11–12 yr
Braine (1959)			4–5 yr				
Uzgiris (1964)		9 yr 3 mo				10 yr	10 yr 7 mo
Dodwell (1960)	6 yr 6 mo (65%)						
Beilin & Franklin (1962)			9 yr (82%)		9 yr (27%)		
Smedslund (1963)			8–9 yr (72%)				
Bruner (1964)				6 yr			

*Estimate based on typical age reported.

younger children distinguish between a greater and lesser number of objects in a set, he believed that it isn't until approximately 6 years of age that they begin to demonstrate an appreciation of the metric properties of numbers. The evolution of this knowledge can be seen in children's reasoning about transformations effected on two parallel rows of pennies. Each penny is matched to another in an opposite row. Children are first asked to judge whether there are an equal number of pennies in both rows. They generally agree there are. Then the spacing in one of the rows is altered (either elongating or shortening the row) and, again children are asked to compare the rows. Preoperational children judge the longer row to have more pennies (Elkind, 1964; Piaget & Szeminska,1952). Piaget believed that knowledge of number develops as children acquire operations needed to coordinate the dimensions of density and length simultaneously. Children with a logical understanding of number appreciate the additive and subtractive properties of sets and understand the notion of identity and compensation. A penny is equivalent to any other penny, and adding or subtracting any penny from the set results in an equivalent transformation. Barring addition or subtraction of something to a set, identity obtains. But, according to Piaget, this is not the entire story; identity alone is insufficient for conservation. Real conservation involves logical multiplication found in the form of compensation. Thus, the conserving child realizes that if length is increased, density is reduced by an equal amount. Conservation of number is more than the mere empirical counting of objects; it is an understanding of number based upon a more abstract knowledge of numeration.

As mentioned, we have some reason for believing that children conserve at younger ages than originally thought. Gelman (1972; Gelman & Gallistel, 1978) has provided evidence for early number conservation when the number of items in sets is not too large. In one ingenious procedure, 3- and 4-year-old children were asked to remember which of two plates had a greater or lesser number of toy mice arranged in a row on each plate (one of the plates had two mice, the other three mice). A trial occurred as the plates were covered and children were asked to keep track of the plate that had either the greater or lesser number of mice. As in the old carnival shell game, the two plates were shuffled about and the child asked to point to the plate that was the "winner" (the one they were tracking). After several trials, the experimenter secretly switched the winning plate with another. The new plate either (a) conserved the same number of mice, but with the row elongated or shortened; or (b) increased or reduced the number of mice, but conserved the length of the row. The children's reactions were noted as they selected and uncovered the "winning" plate. Simply changing the length of the row had no effect on children's responding; however, when they discovered an extra mouse or that one of the mice was missing, children showed surprise and often looked for the lost mouse, explaining that the experimenter had played a trick on them. In fact, using a technique similar to this, research has shown that even young infants may conserve number—that is, recognize the differences between two and three items (cf. Antell & Keating, 1983).

These data have been taken as evidence for the early conservation of number by young children. As such, it seems to call into question the presumption that young children are deficient in whatever schemes are necessary for number conservation. There is some doubt, however, whether conservation has actually been assessed in these studies. Silverman and Briga (1981), for example, argue that on these tasks young children's judgment may be based on some simple numerical counting strategy (much like that suggested to account for young children's class inclusion reasoning). Presenting 3-year-old children with larger set sizes produces nonconservation, even with designs like those discussed by Gelman. Large sets are difficult for young children to count and manipulate with simple addition and subtraction. With smaller sets, young children may be able to add and subtract one item (and thus reason something has changed), but not two or more. Thus, although very young children perform as though they conserve number, there remains some doubt about whether this performance represents true conservation (knowledge based on reversible operations).

Conservation of continuous quantity. Perhaps the most familiar of conservation tasks to students of child development is the test for liquid conservation. To assess this knowledge, researchers ask children to reason about what happens to the amount of water as it is poured from a narrow jar into a wide jar (conservation of identity) or to compare the amount of water in one jar to an identical quantity in another jar as it is poured from one jar to another (conservation of equivalence). As with the conservation of number, it was reasoned by Piaget that quantity is first judged in general terms of "bigger" or "littler" and on the basis of some salient perceptual cue (the height of the fluid in the container). Logical knowledge of liquid quantity, he believed, is based, again, on the ability to quantify two dimensions (height and width) and logical multiplication (understanding that changes in one dimension are compensated by changes in a second dimension).

Non-Genevan research has shown that under special conditions, very young children also appear to conserve liquid quantity. Elkind (1967), for example, noted that two types of conservation are involved in Piagetian tasks: the conservation of identity and the conservation of equivalence. Research has shown that identity is conserved much earlier than equivalence (cf. Hooper, et al., 1978). Other studies have demonstrated that children are apt to give conserving judgments if salient, perceptually misleading cues are kept from children's view. Bruner (1964) found that 45% of 4-year-old children and 83% of 5-year-old children stated that the quantity of liquid poured from one jar to another differently sized jar would remain the same if the jar into which the liquid was poured was screened from view. When children were shown the water level of the liquid in the jar into which liquid had been poured, all of the 4-year-olds stated that they had erred and said that the quantity of water had changed (nonconservation). Almost all of the 5-year-olds, however, stuck to their belief that the quantity of liquid hadn't changed (conservation). The latter performance can be compared to that of 5-year-olds tested in a more traditional fashion. For these children, only 20% judged the quantity of liquid to remain the same. Bruner's experiment shows that young children are strongly influenced by perceptually misleading cues in making judgments about conservation. Five-year-old children appear to be able to break the perceptual habit, and are able to judge conservation on the basis of knowledge about identity (nothing added, nothing gained). It is obvious that this form of reasoning isn't automatic for these children, and unless special conditions prevail (as in distracting children away from perceptually illusory cues), their judgment continues to be influenced by perceptual distortions.

Piaget (1967) has criticized the assessment of conservation by using tasks that tap the use of the identity operator alone. Tests of conservation based on identity alone, he argued, are likely to reveal pseudoconservation (performance that appears to show conservation, but isn't based in reversible operations). Children may predict that water poured from a narrow jar into a wide jar will remain constant in quantity, but, as soon as they are confronted with evidence of physical change, they should switch their response. Conservation, according to Piaget, involves a coordination of two dimensions, and the use of compensation in making judgments.

But is compensation really necessary for conservation? Bruner's (1964) early work revealed that even 5-year-old children retain a conserving judgment after being shown changes in water level—the perceptual cue to alter one's judgment from a conserving to a nonconserving one. Several recent studies also call to question the necessity of compensation in children's knowledge of conservation (Acredolo & Acredolo, 1979; Gladstone, 1981) and raise the possibility that knowledge of identity may be sufficient for judging conservation of substance. Acredolo and Acredolo, for example, had children estimate the level to which water would rise as it was poured from one jar (a wide one) into another (a narrow jar) and to predict if there would be equal amounts of water in each of the jars following the transformation (a prediction of conservation). Piaget's theory anticipates the following: (a) those children who predict that amount of water will remain constant over the transformation, but who give nonconserving responses when presented with the consequence of the transformation (rising water level), should, prior to the transformation, have predicted that the height of the columns of water in the two jars would be the same; (b) children who predicted that the amount of water would change over the transformation should have predicted a change in water level and maintained a nonconserving response when presented with the evidence of their prediction.

Acredolo and Acredolo note that in addition to these predictions, two additional predictions can be made if we assume that identity alone is responsible for children's knowledge of conservation. It may be, for example, that a child's choice is dictated by two competing response tendencies: to respond either to knowledge of continuous quantity (identity) or to other illusory cues competing for one's attention (water level). (Note that this analysis does not consider compensation necessary for performance.) This analysis would also lead to the prediction that (c) at least some of the time that children anticipate conservation, they will predict no change in water levels, and even when confronted with the actual change in water levels, will maintain a conserving judgment (if the identity operator alone mediates responding). Also, one might anticipate (d) that even after a child had predicted conservation and antici- pated a change in water levels, when shown the height of water level in a jar, the child could be compelled to switch to a nonconserving judgment. In fact, the results of this study showed clearly that children were capable of conserv- ing on the basis of identity alone. Approximately 36% of the responses children gave were of the kind described in c and d—response patterns that Piaget did not predict. Of these response patterns, approximately 27% showed conser- vation by identity alone (as in c). Whereas Piaget is correct in his recognition of the importance of an identity operator in children's reasoning about con- servation, this knowledge may be better described by the increasingly extended use of that operator in reasoning about substances and the gradual extinction of a type of reasoning based upon perceptually illusory cues.

Seriation

As with other kinds of knowledge, relational knowledge (the ability to reason about relationships that exist between objects) evolves from an egocentric, perceptually dominated form of reasoning to one that is based on operational knowledge. Piaget, in fact, studied a variety of relational knowledge, including knowledge of right and left and of brother and sister (Piaget, 1929). However, the most widely studied type of relational knowledge is that for items in a series.

Children's understanding of a series is assessed by presenting them with a set of rods of unequal lengths to be ordered in a stair-step fashion. Young children (3 years of age), while able to choose the smallest and the largest in a series, are unable to arrange the rods in any systematic fashion. The ability to order things in a series implies that children have acquired the logical oper- ator for seriation. Without this operator, children should fail to appreciate the order of a series and be unable to coordinate information in a series. By about 5 years of age, children can usually arrange rods serially, but their construction is labored and deliberate. Introducing new members into the set often results in confusions and misplacement of these elements. Piaget, Grize, Szeminska, and Vinh Bang (1977) have suggested that younger children may construct simple relationships between adjacent items—a knowledge that is empirical and not based in an abstract understanding of a series. A child may reason that A and B go together, and the B and C occur together; he or she may thus demonstrate the ability to order things without any real appreciation of the relative nature of items in a group.

By 6 or 7 years of age, series are constructed effortlessly by children, and new members can be inserted into the set with ease. The ease with which series are constructed suggested to Piaget that performance of these children is based on some operative understanding of a series. They realize that some items can be larger than some members while being smaller than others, and that items in a series are systematically related to others in the set. It is this reversible nature of the ordering operation that allows children to work with series effortlessly. With this knowledge, children can not only order items, they can reason about things within the series; that is, they can make transitive inferences. For example, children can reason that if *A* is greater than *B*, and *B* is greater than *C*; then it follows that *A* is also greater than *C*.

As with conservation, research on children's knowledge of a series has shown that they can seriate much earlier than 6 years of age. Koslowski (1980), for example, demonstrated that with a reduced set of rods (four rather than ten) very young children were capable of seriation. But, like so many other apparent competencies demonstrated by young children, the ability to order items doesn't necessarily imply that this ability is based on an operative understanding of seriation.

The idea that young children have a knowledge of seriation was bolstered by the work of Trabasso and others (Adams, 1978; Bryant & Trabasso, 1971; Riley & Trabasso, 1974), which demonstrated that children as young as 4 years of age could make transitive inferences about a five-item series. In one study Riley and Trabasso tested the hypothesis that much of young children's difficulty on transitive reasoning problems is due to an inability to retain sufficient information about the premises that were to be reasoned about. In a test of this hypothesis, 4-year-old children were trained to discriminate the lengths of five uniquely colored sticks. Some of the children never saw the lengths of the sticks, but saw only their tops. Feedback about the lengths of sticks in paired combinations was given verbally. For other children, feedback was given both verbally and visually; they were told about the size of the sticks and were shown the pairs. Discriminations were made between adjacent pairs ($A>B$; $B>C$; $C>D$; $D>E$). After training, children were tested on their knowledge of all possible pairs, taking the *BD* judgment as a critical test of children's ability to make a transitive inference. (Note that the *BD* comparison was never trained; a correct judgment would have to come from information gained from an integrated knowledge about the other pair discriminations.) It was found that when training was based on verbal feedback alone, 68% of the children inferred the *BD* relationship correctly, and if training was based on verbal and visual feedback, 88% of the children inferred the relationship correctly.

It is Trabasso's belief that children have knowledge about transitive relationships and that their ability to reason with this knowledge is much like that of adults—if other factors such as memory are held constant. Other work, however, has opposed such a conclusion on both empirical and logical grounds. Russel (1981), for example, had children solve transitive inference problems and probed their memory for premises following problem solutions. He found that virtually none of the children justified an incorrect conclusion on the basis of an incorrect memory for the premises. In one experiment (where memory for premises was actively probed by the experimenter), a third of those who inferred incorrect conclusions recalled the premises correctly. In a second study (where children were encouraged to justify their conclusions spontaneously), 15% of those inferring incorrectly remembered the premises accurately. The memory-deficiency interpretation of transitive inference would not appear to be a complete account of why young children fail transitive inference problems.

A similar critique of Trabasso's work has been offered by Breslow (1981), who also discounts the role of memory in children's transitive reasoning. Instead he offers an alternative explanation of children's performance on these problems. Citing some of Piaget's (Piaget et al., 1977) later work, Breslow suggests that children may construct knowledge of a series in a qualitative fashion. From this construction, they are able to reason later about things in that particular series and use these associations to make judgments about items. Children may, for example, form associations between contiguous members in the series. To exemplify this process, consider a novice learning the game of baseball. In the logic of baseball, we find that a hit that puts you on first is good, on second better, on third even better, and on home best. We have in effect a series, first < second < third < home. But to learn this "series," you really don't need to know anything about the relative value of bases. Presuming that you're on first, your main effort is to get to second. In a sense, you begin to form an association between first and second (second base comes after first). Similar associations could be made between second and third, and third and home. With this simple, qualitative representation in mind, you can begin to reason about things in that series. (But note that to do this requires no knowledge about the relative value of these bases.) You can tell what is between first and third and between second and home without having any knowledge about what each base is worth. But inserting new information into the series without any knowledge of relative value of items creates a problem. Suppose that the novice is now told that there is another base that we'll call "short base." Obviously this information has absolutely no meaning in the context in which the novice has learned the series. Inserting a new element into the series can be done in a meaningful fashion only if we have an operative understanding of the relationships in a series.

With the advent of concrete operational thought, children acquire a set of reversible operations (rules) for working with elements in a problem-solving task. The existence of operations allows children to experiment with elements to discover relationships that exist between object properties. About the age of 7, children show changes in their judgments about what happens to various object properties as illusory changes occur to the shape or arrangement of objects. We also find changes in the way children reason about categories and series of items. In each instance children become more agile in their judgments, apparently using an abstract rule system to reason rather than relying on the appearance of objects alone.

Although changes in reasoning are most apparent in young school-aged children, under certain conditions it is possible to find what appear to be instances of conservation, seriation, and knowledge of class hierarchy in much younger children. The appearance of what appear to be relatively advanced forms of thought in younger children has led theorists to question both the role of genetics in the developmental process and the necessity of specific operations (for example, compensation) in various kinds of reasoning. As reviewed in this section, the debate is far from concluded.

The intellectual powers attributed to concrete operational children are considerable. These powers, however, are limited to reasoning about concrete, real-world phenomena. Furthermore, the problem solving of these children is often unsystematic and incomplete due to a lack of a completely elaborated set of logical operators. The expansion of operational knowledge gives the adult the opportunity to reason in a much more flexible and thorough fashion.

FORMAL OPERATIONAL THOUGHT

The period of formal operational thought is the last stage of development described by Piaget. Piaget originally estimated that children enter this stage between 12 and 15 years of age (Inhelder & Piaget, 1958); later reconsidering this matter, he thought that formal operational thought might not occur until 15 or 20 years of age (Piaget, 1972). More recent studies indicate a transition from concrete to formal operational thought at about the time first suggested by Piaget.

Compared to the kind of thinking that precedes it, formal operational thought is more abstract and freed from the constraints of the physical world. Thought is characterized by the ability to generate possibilities and to operate upon those possibilities. Presented with a problem to solve, the formal operational adolescent can elaborate a set of possible solutions (hypotheses), devise a procedure for systematically evaluating the truth of each hypothesis, and construct a test to evaluate information derived from their experimentation—thus, arriving at a conclusion that is by necessity correct.

To understand the significance of this intellectual development, consider a problem in which children are asked to determine if there is a relationship between the type of drug that people take and whether or not they get better. We can represent taking the drug with the symbol (D), and not taking the drug with the symbol $(\overline{D})$; getting better with the symbol (B) and not getting better with the symbol $(\overline{B})$. Presented with this problem, concrete operational children are quite adept at elaborating the four possible products of these elements. Some people who take the drug get better (BD), and some people who take the drug don't $(\overline{B}D)$, some people who don't take the drug get better $(B\overline{D})$ and some people who don't take the drug don't get better $(\overline{B}\overline{D})$. But with these four combinations, concrete operational children stop. They construct the cross-products, but they don't entertain the possibility of operating upon the products of these operations. For example, all four conditions might eventuate. Some people who take the drug get better and some don't, and some people who don't take the drug get better and others don't: $(BD) + (\overline{B}D) + (B\overline{D}) + (\overline{B}\overline{D})$. In fact there are exactly 16 possible outcomes to this problem (Table 10-2). The elaboration of these possibilities implies the existence of a complete combinatorial scheme. We could substitute the logical symbols $(p$ and $q)$ for the values B and D and their negations $(\overline{p}$ and $\overline{q})$ and relate these values with logical connectors. Using these symbols, we can symbolically describe the conditions represented by 16 combinations of B and D. For example, suppose that we reason that by taking a drug one will get better. Notice that we should always find that whenever the drug is taken, one should get better (BD). Also note that by not taking the drug our health may or may not improve ($B\overline{D} + \overline{B}\overline{D}$); the statement doesn't say anything about the consequence of not using the drug, only what will happen if the drug is taken. In fact, the only condition that this statement cannot sustain is one in which taking the drug leads to continued illness ($\overline{B}D$). Therefore, if the claim is made that taking the drug will produce better health, we should anticipate the conditions: $BD + B\overline{D} + \overline{B}\overline{D}$. This is equivalent to saying that if you take the drug (p) then you will get well (q). This statement is known as one of reciprocal implication and is symbolized: $q \supset p$.

The remaining combinations and their logical counterparts are summarized in Table 10-2. The development of this completely elaborated combinatorial scheme is that which gives formal operational thought its thoroughness.

In addition to an elaborated set of operators, the formal operational adolescent develops a set of higher-order operations, a group of transformational rules that can be used to manipulate operations. This new set of operations is referred to as the INRC group (identity, negation, reciprocal, and correlative). Identity is an operation that when applied leaves any element in the proposition unchanged. Consider, for example, a balance beam problem in which the experimenter alters the balance by moving or adding specific quantities of weight at specific distances along one of the arms. The subject's task is to return the balance to equilibrium and explain why the solution works. The identity transformation simply reveals to the adolescent that whatever transformation was effected on the system, nothing happened (as would be the case if more weight was added to the side that was already tipped, the subtraction of this added weight would do nothing to right the system). The child can right the balance by subtracting added weight or adding that which is taken away (hence, negation). If weight has been added or moved in distance from the fulcrum, a transformation can be effected to the opposite arm by

TABLE 10-2.   The Combinatorial System (*Neimark, 1975*)

Name	Symbol	Combination*	Name of Complement	Symbol	Combination
Complete affirmation	$(p * q)$	$BD + \overline{B}D + B\overline{D} + \overline{B}\overline{D}$	Negation	(ϕ)	
Incompatibility	(p/q)	$\overline{B}D + B\overline{D} + \overline{B}\overline{D}$	Conjunction	$(p \cdot q)$	BD
Disjunction	(pvq)	$BD + B\overline{D} + \underline{BD}$	Conjunctive negation	$(\overline{p} \cdot \overline{q})$	$\overline{B}D$
Implication	$(p \supset q)$	$BD + \overline{B}D + \overline{B}\overline{D}$	Nonimplication	$(p \cdot \overline{q})$	$B\overline{D}$
Reciprocal implication	$(q \supset p)$	$BD + B\overline{D} + \overline{B}\overline{D}$	Negation of reciprocal implication	$(\overline{p} \cdot q)$	$\overline{B}D$
Equivalence	$(p \subseteq q)$ or $(p = q)$	$BD + \overline{B}\overline{D}$	Reciprocal exclusion or exclusive disjunction	$(pvvq)$	$\overline{B}D + B\overline{D}$
Affirmation of p	$p[q]$	$BD + B\overline{D}$	Negation of p	$\overline{p}[q]$	$\overline{B}D + \overline{B}\overline{D}$
Affirmation of q	$q[p]$	$BD + \overline{B}D$	Negation of q	$\overline{q}[p]$	$B\overline{D} + \overline{B}\overline{D}$

*Note: To shift from property combinations to propositional combination, $B = p$, $\overline{B} = \overline{p}$, $D = q$, $\overline{D} = \overline{q}$, $+ = v$.

adding a comparable amount of weight, or moving the weight an equivalent distance from its equal on the opposite arm (reciprocity). Additionally, adolescents can think proportionally, reasoning that a specific unit of weight is compensated by an equivalent distance on the balance arm. Adding one unit of weight to the left arm, for example, may be comparable to moving the weight on the opposite arm one unit of distance away from the fulcrum (correlativity).

Compared to research on concrete operational thought, that conducted on formal operational thought has been quite meager. Whereas Neimark (1975) identifies eight concept areas requiring formal operational knowledge (combinatorial operations, proportions, coordination of two systems of reference, the concept of mechanical equilibrium, the concept of probability, the concept of correlation, multiplicative compensations, and other advanced forms of conservation), only a few of these have received any sustained attention.

Like much of the early work on concrete operational thinking, the more recent research has been primarily replicative, establishing the lower age limit of formal operational thought. Since intellectual structure is believed to organize behavior, we would expect some rapid improvement in children's ability to solve formal operational problems with entry into this stage. Martorano (1977) seems to have found evidence of such a transition. She tested 6th-, 8th-, 10th-, and 12th-graders on ten formal operational problems. Although there were substantial differences in the difficulty of the various tasks, reliable shifts in performance occurred across tasks between the 8th and 10th grade. While there is considerable improvement in children's reasoning between 12 and 14 years of age, Martorano's data also reveal a continuing development of formal reasoning skills through late adolescence and early adulthood.

The attainment of formal operations has important practical as well as theoretical implications. In western culture it is assumed that until about the age of 18 years, youths are incapable of making decisions based upon sound, mature judgment. Consequently, decisions about health and welfare are placed in the hands of adults, who presumably possess the capacity to make better decisions.

Piagetian theory, on the other hand, suggests that by 14 or 16 years of age the logical structure of children's thought is not unlike the adult's. If this is so, there is good reason to reconsider legal age restrictions placed upon adolescents. In fact there are a number of legal precedents for such a reconsideration. Pregnant minors can obtain abortions without the consent of their parents if they can demonstrate maturity and after considering a variety of information about the consequence of abortion (*Bellotti* v. *Baird II*, 1979).

In light of these legal decisions, it may be questioned whether adolescents do indeed have the capacity to make logical decisions about their health and welfare. Actually, studies seem to show that they do. In one study (Weithorn & Campbell, 1982), 9-, 14-, and 18-year-old subjects were asked to reason about various medical and psychological dilemmas, deciding upon various treatment options after being presented with information about the relative merits and side effects of each treatment. Youths as young as 14 years of age demonstrated competence equivalent to adults on four standards: knowledge of choices available, expectation of a reasonable outcome from their decision, rational reasons for their choices, and an understanding of the risks and benefits, and alternatives to treatment. These data support the view that the reasoning powers of the adolescent are not all that different from the adult's and support the position that adolescents should be granted more responsibility for decision making.

Having found support for the idea that there is a shift in reasoning ability during the early adolescent years, we might consider the various abilities that characterize this level of intellect. In doing so, we'll focus on several types of concepts requiring formal operational structure: conservation of volume, combinatorial operations and isolation of variables; and proportion probability, and correlation. Much of this work has been directed at a replication of Piaget's work. From this research it would seem safe to conclude that children younger than 10 and 12 years of age seldom have success in the solution of formal operational problems, despite attempts to structure the task in their favor (although see Case, 1974). Other research has attempted to determine what types of skills, ability, and knowledge underlie performance on formal operational problems.

Conservation of Volume

In an earlier discussion of conservation, it was noted that various properties of objects are conserved later than others. This asymmetry in the development of knowledge about objects is believed to be in part a function of an individual's capacity to dissociate the object from its attributes (Pinard & Chassé, 1977). Being an inherent, yet intrinsic part of any object, volume is less dissociable and, hence, a property that is conserved much later in development. Elkind (1962) demonstrated that, of a sample of college students, 74% of the males and 58% of the females conserved exterior volume (how much water would an object displace if it were submersed); the conservation of interior volume (how much could a container hold) is achieved slightly earlier (Piaget et al., 1960; Pinard & Chassé, 1977).

Unfortunately, knowledge about the factors that precipitate these more advanced forms of conservation is meager. In one study that partially addresses this issue, Pinard and Chassé (1977) had adolescents judge the constancy of volume of objects after changes in the object's surface area (the surface area of an object was altered while its volume remained constant) or had them judge the constancy of surface area after changes in the object's volume (the volume of an object was altered as its surface area remained constant). It was found that adolescents don't show a reliable separation of knowledge about surface area from volume until about 12 or 14 years of age (again about the time that formal operational thought develops). They also report that although early formal operational adolescents realize that the surface area of an object is changed as its volume is distributed differently, not many of them realize that volume changes as a function of alterations in the surface structure of an object (indeed only 36% of the adults in their study conserved volume). Thus, the reliable conservation of surface area predates and may be prerequisite for later volume conservation (both internal and external). Although these data begin to demonstrate the evolution of these higher levels of conservation, little is known about the relative role of the combinatorial system or the INRC transformation in the development of this knowledge (cf. Neimark, 1979).

Combinatorial Operations and Isolation of Variables

Studies that have examined adolescents' ability to deduce sets of possible orderings or to derive a complete combinatorial scheme and to reason about these propositions have relied upon several procedures. In a chemistry experiment described by Inhelder and Piaget (1958), for example, adolescents are shown four flasks of colorless, odorless liquids and a fifth solution labeled "g." Adolescents are encouraged to discover and later to explain how to produce a yellow color by dropping some of "g" into any one or a combination of liquids. Adolescents are generally able to perform this task by about 14 or 15 years of age (cf. Martorano, 1977).

Other tasks used to assess combinatorial knowledge have children elaborate all of the various possible combinations of two bivalued dimensions. For example, what are all of the possible combinations of animal life that might be found on a newly discovered planet if all life forms could be categorized as either vertebrates or invertebrates and terrestrial or aquatic? Using a similar question, Elkind, Barocas, and Rosenthal (1968) found that most (52%) 14-year-olds generated 15 of these combinations (although they usually omitted the zero combination—no life forms). Martorano (1977) reports that by the tenth grade, 70% of the adolescents in her study succeeded on this type of task.

While adolescents are able to elaborate combinatorial schemes, the failure to find a greater number of adolescents elaborating complete schemes may simply be due to their failure to understand what is being asked of them. Consider, for example, the directions to the "possibilities of life on other planets" problem. I've given this problem to a number of my classes with exactly the same instructions described earlier. Invariably these college students perform the logical multiplication deriving the four possible classes of things, but well over half go no further. After explaining that there are actually sixteen possibilities, students usually complain that they were misled (cf. Neimark, 1979). In fact, when problem solvers are prompted to elaborate all possible solutions to a problem (Danner & Day, 1977; Stone & Day, 1978), they perform at much higher levels than when they are instructed in the traditional fashion.

Whereas it would appear that by 13 or 15 years of age, adolescents are fairly adept at elaborating combinatorial schemes and using that set of possibilities to isolate variables relevant to a problem's solution, this reasoning may be limited to an intuitive understanding of the principles of combination. When required to evaluate propositions—to reason about specific logical relationships—these same adolescents perform more poorly. Martorano and Zentall (1980), for example, had 8-, 10-, and 13-year-old children reason about which of two dimensions (length or diameter) affected the pitch of chimes. After training children to appreciate that two dimensions were being varied, children were asked to discover what it was about a chime (its length or diameter) that affects its pitch. To test for an understanding of the principle of controlling variables, the experimenters asked children to state which chimes would have to be compared to ensure that length did or didn't affect pitch. Another question was asked to discover if children could distinguish between a confounded and an unconfounded comparison. Although many children were able to use the control of variables principle to discover which of the two variables affected pitch, a significant number of these children failed to discriminate between confounded and unconfounded tests when a comparison was described to them. Whereas adolescents understand the basic principle involved in controlling variables, they have difficulty decoding propositional statements based on the same principles (cf. Lewis, 1981).

Proportion, Probability, and Correlation

Common to several of the formal operational problems is the need to set up ratios or to appreciate the proportions in which particular events occur. For example, to predict the direction that a balance beam will tilt, we would need to derive a ratio between units of weight and units of distance from the fulcrum where weights are hung. Whereas concrete operational children can physically restore the balance to a state of equilibrium, they are unable to predict how the beam will operate. In order to predict, children must construct a ratio between weight and distance and compare the ratios for both arms of the beam. (For example, presuming that the child has deduced that two units of weight are equal to one unit of distance, the child can reason that two units of weight hung one unit of distance from the fulcrum on the right arm are the equivalent of one unit of weight hung two units of distance from the left arm.) The formal operational child need not see the beam to reason about it; having established the ratio, the problem is merely a matter of ratio comparisons rather than an empirical test.

The solutions to problems involving the construction of proportions have shown a shift to formal operational reasoning by about 15 years of age (Lunzer & Pumfrey, 1966; Pumfrey, 1968). Problems concerned with proportionality appear to be more difficult than most formal operational tasks. In a comparison with ten other formal operational problems, tasks requiring the construction of proportions (shadows and balance beam) were of the more difficult (Martorano, 1977).

Another type of knowledge that seems to develop later in the formal operational period is that of probability and chance. Piaget and Inhelder (1975) studied children's knowledge about chance by having them predict the outcome of purely random events—for example, predicting the position of a set of black and white marbles after they had been shaken up and come to rest in a box. Knowledge of probability was assessed by having children predict the likelihood that certain events or combinations would occur if objects were selected randomly from a specified population. For example, in one task children were asked to predict the colors of pairs of chips drawn from a bag, the chips in the bag differing in color and the frequency with which their colors occurred. The probability of drawing a specific combination varied from trial to trial as chips were not replaced and additional chips were added to the bag on successive trials.

Obviously, a well-developed knowledge of chance would lead one to conclude that no predictions can be made about where marbles would be positioned after they had been tossed about—except that as more marbles are added to the box the number of different positions possible through random assortment increases. On the probability task, formal operational subjects should predict combinations that are most probable on a trial-to-trial basis, these predictions co-varying with the number and kind of chips remaining in the bag. In replicating Piaget and Inhelder's work, Green (1978) found clear evidence for stagelike development in children's verbal judgments about chance and probability. Formal operational judgments about these two events were found in most adolescents by 16 years of age.

Knowledge about correlated events can be assessed by asking children to interpret the significance of the frequencies with which two properties co-vary with one another. Suppose, for instance, that after observing 100 people, we find 47 who have blond hair (A) and blue eyes (B), 38 who have dark hair ($\overline{A}$) and brown eyes ($\overline{B}$), 15 who have dark hair ($\overline{A}$) and blue eyes (B), and none who have blond hair (A) and brown ($\overline{B}$) eyes. For this sample, we could conclude that there is a correlation between hair and eye color. We can ascertain correlation by constructing a matrix of possible events:

$$\begin{array}{c|c} AB & \overline{A}B \\ \hline A\overline{B} & \overline{A}\,\overline{B} \end{array}$$

By summing the diagonals, we can deduce the strength of the relationship. Ratios close to one should convince us that there is no relationship between the two properties; on the other hand, ratios close to zero should convince us that the correlation is very strong. Again referring to Martorano's (1977) data, correlations were apparently one of the easier formal operational problems to solve (70% of the 10-year-olds and 95% of the 12-year-olds solved these problems correctly). Neimark (1975), however, reported that in two experiments with student nurses, there was little understanding of correlation. It is quite probable that a number of task variables affect performance on these problems, e.g., familiarity with the variables that are correlated and clarity of instructions. Neimark in fact reports that in one study a third of the student nurses didn't even understand what the task was about.

THE PIAGETIAN VIEW OF PROBLEM SOLVING: A CRITIQUE

A Difference of Method

Methodologically, the Genevan program has been chided for its deviation from the more systematic, controlled experimentation that has characterized traditional American psychology. This deviation reflects a major difference between the information-processing and Piagetian theories. The clinical procedure, a trademark of Genevan research, was adopted by Piaget expressly for the purpose of establishing a data base from which an ecologically valid theory of development could be forged. When reading any of Piaget's numerous papers and books, one is impressed with the status of the narrative. The content of psychology is the whole behavior, as is clearly demonstrated in Piaget's meticulous description of children's behavior and verbal responses to particular tasks. There is throughout these works a persistent avoidance of quantification. It is in fact both the lack of structure in the adminstration of tests and the lack of quantification of results that have been so annoying to non-Genevan researchers.

Given the verbal requirements (both receptive and expressive) of the clincial method, there is a tendency to underestimate young children's cognitive ability (Brainerd, 1978a; Gelman, 1978), while possibly overestimating the ability of older children (cf., Neimark, 1979). As a consequence of the looseness with which Piagetian tasks are administered, it is also found that performance is particularly susceptible to a number of situational and task variables. A number of researchers, for instance, have noted that children's performance on conservation tasks is markedly influenced by the types of questions that are asked of them (Braine & Shanks, 1965; Hall & Kingsley, 1968; Neimark, 1979; Puffal, 1975).

An additional methodological problem lies with the manner in which Piaget has analyzed and interpreted his data. Perhaps in a reflection of his reluctance to quantify behavior, on those instances when Piaget did, there were sometimes flaws in both calculations and the accuracy with which data were reported. Flavell (1963) was one of the first to observe that Piaget often seemed to force "unwilling data" into "preset theoretical molds." In replicating Piaget and Inhelder's work on children's understanding of chance, Green (1978) found miscalculations in the trial-to-trial computations of event probabilities—a serious mistake considering that it was on the basis of these calculations that children's knowledge of probability was gauged.

Is the Stage Concept Necessary?

In addition to these methodological issues, a number of criticisms have been leveled at the structure of Piagetian theory. The most fundamental aspect of Piagetian theory is the necessity of stages, and relatedly, the idea that learning is stage-dependent. We shouldn't expect children to learn unless their intellectual structure has evolved to the point of allowing them to understand the lesson to be learned.

The concept of stage has been criticized at both a general level and also in the specific sense with which Piaget uses the concept (Brainerd, 1973, 1978b). It is noted that any stage theory must (a) describe a set of behaviors that undergo change, (b) state which antecedent variables are responsible for behavioral change, and (c) provide a procedure whereby behavioral change and variables producing it can be measured separately. The more difficult problem for stage theories is the latter—finding some way to assess change independently from the explanator "stage." To fail to do so results in circular statements such as, "Children don't conserve because they are in the preoperational stage, and we know they are in the preoperational stage because they don't conserve." Such a system of proof ill suits the requirements for theory validation.

Brainerd (1978b) has further criticized both the empirical and theoretical base from which Piaget argues the necessity of stages. Piaget (1960) believed that several criteria were sufficient for defining the existence of stages: an invariant sequence of development, specific cognitive structures for each stage, integration of preceding stages into later ones, consolidation of structures within stages, and equilibration (rapid changes in behavior followed by stabilization).

It was Piaget's belief that the most compelling evidence for stages is in their invariant sequencing. All children seem to develop through each of the stages in an orderly fashion; we never find children demonstrating concrete operational knowledge before preoperational knowledge. But Brainerd (1978b) rejects the idea that sequencing reflects some underlying, biologically predetermined maturational plan as proposed by Piaget. This sequencing, for example, may be only an artifact of the measurement procedure (referred to as a measurement sequence). Given the manner in which children's knowledge is assessed, it would be impossible for them to demonstrate any other pattern of development than that which is found. It would be impossible, for example, to expect children to construct proportions before they acquired the prerequisite skills of counting and grouping. Thus, to say that higher-order skills require prerequisite knowledge does not necessarily imply that intellectual development is also dependent upon an innate maturational blueprint.

The other major criteria for establishing the existence of stages is that each stage should be defined by a unique structure. Again Brainerd comments upon Piaget's somewhat casual definition of what constitutes the structure of thought at each stage (cf. Flavell, 1963; Parsons, 1960); the lack of behavioral counterparts for proposed underlying structures (cf. Flavell, 1963); the primarily descriptive nature of stage structure (there is no explanation offered for how higher structures develop from lower ones); and the non-uniqueness of structures at each stage.

A number of minor criteria have also been offered by the Genevans as evidence in support of the existence of stages. One is that later stages presuppose the existence of earlier ones, but Brainerd again recognizes this as a restatement of the sequencing issue addressed earlier. On this point, Fodor (1980) also detects a logical flaw in the theory itself. Implicit in the notion that higher stages evolve from lower ones is the belief that in order to develop to some higher level, one must first be able to conceptualize what that higher level is like. Fodor argues that if all learning is a process of hypothesis formation and confirmation, to get to higher stages, "the least you would have to do at Stage 1 is to characterize truth conditions on formulas containing concepts in Stage 2" (p. 148). But, as Fodor observes, Piaget's theory is staunchly constructist; stages and their logical structures are dependent upon active assimilation and accommodation. One's ability to interpret and interact with the environment is dependent upon intellectual structure. Consequently, there is no way that children with lower level structures could conceptualize some higher level knowledge and, consequently, be induced to accommodate or change their present state.

Two additional criteria offered for stage theory are consolidation and equilibration. It is suggested that development within stages is characterized by the mastery of skills that are acquired following the child's entry into a new developmental stage. Although some evidence exists for this phenomena (Moshman, 1977), Brainerd argues that like the integration issue, the matter of consolidation is irrelevant since, again, it concerns sequencing. Equilibration would predict that development should be characterized by rapid and abrupt changes in skill levels followed by periods of quiescence (consolidation). But a consideration of available evidence has led a number of investigators to conclude that individual development is better characterized as a continuous and gradual acquisition of concepts and skills rather than the "fits and starts" that would be expected were the phenomenon of equilibration important (cf. Brainerd, 1978a; Cornell, 1978; Flavell & Wohlwill, 1969).

As stage theory has been criticized in principle, so has the theory been attacked on empirical grounds. If stage-related intellectual structure limits the range of intellectual competencies, training programs designed to facilitate the development of competencies not expected of very young children should be ineffective. The research in this area, however, has demonstrated that training programs can effectively produce change in children's understanding of a variety of concepts. Preschool children can profit from training in conservation, the use of relational concepts, and transitive inference (Beilin, 1980; Gelman, 1978). Even when evaluated against the criterion for learning established by the Genevans (no prior knowledge of the concept, pre- to post-test change in knowledge states, generalization of the concept, logical explanation of one's response, and long-term retention of the concept; Inhelder, Sinclair & Bovet, 1974), the gains in concept knowledge acquired through training programs are impressive.

A NEO-PIAGETIAN POSITION

The recognition of many of the problems noted in the preceding section provided the impetus for a revision of various aspects of the cognitive-developmental theory proposed by Piaget. Whereas the neo-Piagetian position differs markedly from Piaget's original formulation, it is important to observe the areas of similarity between the two positions. Like Piaget, the neo-Piagetians are interested in describing some generalizable intellectual structure. Their interest, however, is directed toward an examination of factors that contribute to the evolution of skills over time.

Like Piaget, the neo-Piagetians maintain the importance of both the concept of stage and equilibration, but in an altered form. Piaget believed that stages are defined by groups of operations or habitual schemes of action. The synchronous development of schemes or operations organizes children's behavior across problem-solving domains. This rigid idea of the way in which the intellect grows within stages gave rise to the thorny problem of horizontal décalage—the unevenness of development within concept domains. The neo-Piagetians have proposed a solution to this problem with a reformulation of the stage concept (Case, 1974; Pascual-Leone, 1970).

In redefining the concept of stage, the neo-Piagetians have proposed that with age there is a change in children's processing power. That is, over time there are changes in how much information children can remember, consider, or manipulate at any one time. (You'll recall that we discussed these age-related changes in capacity in Chapter 6). Pascual-Leone (1970) dubbed this capacity M-power (see Table 3-2). These changes in M-power are believed to produce the stagelike patterns of development observed by Piaget.

Pascual-Leone (and other neo-Piagetians, such as Case, 1974) maintains the concept of equilibration as the force impelling development—but again with considerable elaboration upon the concept originally offered by Piaget. Both Piagetian and neo-Piagetian positions state that development involves conflict resolution. Piaget views this conflict arising from a perceived discrepancy between what one experiences and the habitual schemes that are applied to a particular situation or object.

Piaget's conceptualization of equilibration, however, poses a paradox: how do we explain how new intellectual structures develop from what are described as basically rigid, permanent, habitual schemes? How does the child come to conceptualize some higher form of thought while operating at some lower level? Presumably it is a tension that inspires children to accommodate their mode of thinking, but it would be difficult to conceptualize how this might be possible given the nature of intellectual structure proposed by Piaget. The neo-Piagetians (Case, 1974; Pascual-Leone, 1970, 1980) again believe they have the answer.

The solution to this paradox lies in the postulation of what Pascual-Leone (1980) refers to as performatory structures. That is, not all problem solving occurs through the assimilation of information into permanent intellectual structures. The performatory structure is a situation-free, temporary construction used to assimilate information in a novel fashion. Through these novel syntheses higher states of cognitive development are possible.

In order to understand the nature of this process, it is important to recognize that neo-Piagetians believe that any problem can be defined by a number of comparative steps. Consider the problem involving the conservation of equivalent substance in which children are shown two masses of clay that are equivalent in shape and judged by the child to be equivalent in amount ($A = B$). One of these balls of clay is transformed by being rolled into a sausage shape (B'). The child is asked to compare the two amounts, and state if they are still equal.

To perform this task, the child must coordinate three sources of information and apply an executive strategy (compare equality). That is, children must remember and recall (a) information about the relationship that exists between masses of equal quantity and shape (A and B), (b) information about the relationship that exists between an original mass (B) and its transformed state (B'), and (c) information about the nature of the transformation (that it is one in which quantity is preserved—identity). In addition to remembering these three elements, the child must do something with this information. We'll call this action an "executive" and represent it by the symbol (e).

Whether or not the child will conserve depends upon a number of factors, one being the M-factor. If children have limited processing capacity (below that required by the task), they will not conserve. They simply lack sufficient capacity to remember and coordinate all of the information relevant to the task. But Pascual-Leone (1980) also proposes that other individual difference variables may operate to affect performance. Some children don't process information as efficiently as others, being easily distracted by perceptually disorienting aspects of the environment. Literature on field-independence or dependence shows that there are individual differences in the degree to which individuals are distracted by the context in which something occurs. Some individuals, for example, are less prone to be misled by perceptual distractions than others. Consequently, although children may have sufficient M-power to perform a task, they may nonetheless commit errors, failing to use their M-power to the fullest.

Assuming that M-power is sufficient for reasoning about a problem, how does the child come to switch from a nonconserving judgment to a conserving one? As children grow older, it is assumed that they begin to decenter, considering more than one dimension of a stimulus at a time. The younger child with limited processing power will be strongly influenced by field effects (in the example, the effects exerted by either the width of the object or its length). But, with increased processing capacity, the older child can consider the object in several dimensions; although A is wider than B, B is longer than A. Pascual-Leone (1980) observes that children with sufficient M-power to recall these two results and who, through some temporary performatory structure come to compare or relate these two sources of information, will be "horrified" by the contradiction. Accepting the premise that we operate in an internally consistent fashion, he reasons that children should cease to judge equivalence by a perceptual strategy (since such a strategy provides contradictory results) and rely upon a different strategy, one that relies upon a memory for events prior to the transformation and a strategy based upon the use of the identity operator.

The utility of this neo-Piagetian model has been effectively demonstrated by Case (1974, 1977) on several occasions. In one study (Case, 1974), three groups of children were tested on the bending rods problem.* These groups consisted of 6-year-olds who were field-independent, nonconservers of substance ($m < 3 + e$); 8-year-olds who were field-independent, conservers of substance ($m = 3 + e$) and 8-year-olds who were field-dependent, conservers

*The bending rods problem is a formal operational task requiring the isolation and control of variables. Children solving this problem must be able to identify which of five variables affect the bending of rods of varied length, composition, and diameter that have differing quantities of weight attached to them at different distances from their base.

of substance ($m = 3 + e$). For four days, one-half of the children in each group were trained in the separation of variables. This training was designed to establish a well-practiced executive scheme (e) for the separation of variables, which defines the bending rods problem. Recognizing that the bending rods problem requires an M-power of $3 + e$, we can make a number of clear predictions about how children will perform on the criterion task. None of the younger children should solve the problem; they simply don't have sufficient M-power. Because both of the older groups have sufficient M-power, training should facilitate their use of the executive scheme; thus, the trained group should perform better than the untrained group. Furthermore, in the trained group, field-independent children should perform better than the field-dependent children. In the untrained group, and because of the interfering effects of perceptually misleading cues, field-dependent children should perform poorly on the bending rods problem. On the other hand, some of the field-independent untrained children should solve the problem. These results were obtained and provide a convincing demonstration of the predictive value of this theoretical formulation (also see Case, Kurland, & Goldberg, 1982).

SUMMARY AND SYNTHESIS

Piagetian theory has been around now for approximately 60 years. In the span of time that we judge events occurring within psychology, it would be fair to conclude that the theory has had good staying power. The reasons for its longevity are varied. The reasons we'd accept for that longevity would likely reflect our biases. Brainerd (1978a), for example, believes that Piagetian theory appeals to an intuitive belief about what we think development should be like. In spite of what he believes to be a lack of empirical evidence to support it, its acceptance has appealing implications for such ideas as educational "readiness," individualized programs of instruction, and psychological evaluation (see Chapter 13). Others regard the theory as a credible heuristic. Beilin, for example, compares Piaget's theory to other developmental theories and concludes "[in] the contemporary alternatives to Piaget's theory one finds relatively few major adversaries" (1980, p. 245).

A consideration of the literature reviewed in this chapter suggests a reliable shift with age in children's performance on tasks assessing operational knowledge. Whether or not the intellectual structure that underlies performances is as described by Piaget is quite another issue. Some of Piaget's observations seem to be quite accurate (as with the importance of certain operations or rules that govern particular knowledge states), while other research suggests that the necessity of specific operational knowledge for particular kinds of reasoning (as the need for compensation in deducing conservation) is not well founded. For other aspects of the theory we simply do not have enough evidence to judge whether or not the structure of the intellect proposed by Piaget is valid (as with most speculation about formal operational thought).

The revisions effected by Pascual-Leone and others have provided an interesting and profitable extension of Piaget's theory. This neo-Piagetian work has demonstrated that while retaining many of the fundamental concepts advocated by Piaget, the theory can be easily restructured to account for much of the data that the original theory could not (horizontal décalage) and provide a system that is testable, functional, and predictive.

A consideration of both the neo-Piagetian and information-processing approaches discussed in the preceding chapters, reveals a promising convergence. The work by Gholson (1980) has incorporated the concept of developmental stages into the traditional information-processing model of problem solving. Likewise, neo-Piagetians have freely incorporated research from traditional information-processing theory, especially with regard to their notion of an M-factor (which is clearly based on work stemming from information-processing models of short-term memory).

Whereas the two models show a trend toward convergence, ample differences exist between the two positions. On the one hand, the Piagetian and neo-Piagetian positions characterize the information-processing position as basically sterile and machinelike in its treatment of intelligence. They criticize the information-processing position for failing to provide a convincing explanation for how novel behavior patterns are acquired. Furthermore, they criticize the manner in which research is conducted, focusing as it does on problem solving within single-task domains. Little wonder, they conclude, that this position has not found stagelike patterns of development nor a structure of intelligence that generalizes across tasks. Whereas it is acknowledged that some information-processing theories have demonstrated the capacity to simulate problem-solving processes with computers, critics argue that this research has failed to demonstrate that these models are organismically valid (Heil, 1981; Pascual-Leone, 1980).

The information-processing theorists, on the other hand, criticize the degree of abstractness and generality with which the Piagetians and neo-Piagetians specify the operations that are believed to underlie task performance. Good models, they propose, should specify the rules and systematic processes associated with the use of information. The very strength of the information-processing position rests in its degree of specification, "its emphasis on precision" (Klahr, 1980, p.128). The weakness attributed to one theory is perceived as its own virtue.

11

Metacognition

If you want to perform well on any task, be it perceptual, mnemonic, or conceptual, it's important for you to be sensitive to your cognitive state—that is, to know if or when you know something. Flavell (1979) calls this the *metacognitive experience*. Furthermore, you should know what skills, strategies, or procedures to use on specific tasks; what things about yourself or others affect performance; and what factors pertaining to the task or environment affect your ability to attend, retain, and retrieve information, and solve problems. Flavell refers to this as *metacognitive knowledge*.

You may get a better grasp of the importance of this type of knowledge by trying to answer the following question, "Who was the president of the United States in 1959?" If you are a United States citizen, you probably recognized the question as one to which you might know the answer (assuming you have taken a course in modern American history). Were the question, "Who was the prime minister of England in 1959?", you'd likely dismiss the question as unanswerable and invest no further effort in its solution. Realizing that you either do or don't have sufficient information about a problem, or skills necessary to solve a problem, is an essential first step in approaching any task.

The mere recognition that you know something doesn't, however, guarantee that you can solve a problem or remember something—as is amply demonstrated by the "tip-of-the-tongue" phenomenon (Brown & McNeill, 1966). You may realize that you know someone's name, for example, but you are unable to recall it. Likewise, you may be given a familiar problem but be unable to remember its solution. People usually get stuck on the missionaries and the cannibals problem. (See Box 11-1.) They're unable to recall its solution, although they've solved the problem several times and "know" the solution.

BOX 11-1. THE MISSIONARIES AND CANNIBALS PROBLEM

The missionaries and cannibals problem consists of discovering a way to get three missionaries and three cannibals from one side of the river to the other without losing any missionaries. You can't ever have more cannibals than missionaries on one side of the river and you can't transport more than two individuals across the river at a time. Solution: (1) Cannibal and missionary cross river, missionary returns alone. (2) Two cannibals cross river, one returns. (3) Two missionaries cross river, a cannibal and a missionary return. (4) Two missionaries cross river, a cannibal returns. (5) Two cannibals cross river, a cannibal returns. (6) Two remaining cannibals cross river.

In previous chapters we've considered the performance of children on a variety of cognitive tasks—what children actually perceive or remember, or how they solve problems. In this chapter we will consider a different type of cognition—children's awareness of their own cognitive processes, an area that has come to be known as *metacognition*.

It should be emphasized that it would be wrong to presume that cognitive performance (what one does) is synonymous with metacognitive knowledge (what one knows). The relationship between the two is complex and variable (Flavell & Wellman, 1977). A variety of research has indicated that, whereas children may be aware of variables affecting performance or facilitating some cognitive activity, in an actual test situation, children may not use such knowledge to facilitate performance. Likewise, children may use a variety of sophisticated strategies to facilitate performance, but be unable to report their use. Flavell, Beach, and Chinsky (1966), for example, noted that of 31 children who were observed using labeling as a strategy while attempting to learn a list of pictures, only 23 spontaneously reported that they had used that strategy in a post-test interview.

These findings have presented a dilemma of sorts to students of metacognition. On metacognitive tasks employing performance measures, children's competence (their awareness that particular factors affect performance) may be obscured by a failure to use such knowledge on an actual task. And, as noted by Flavell et al. (1966), performance itself doesn't predict metacognitive knowledge. An overreliance on either performance or nonperformance verbal measures may either inflate or underestimate our assessment of children's metacognitive knowledge. As will be seen in the research reviewed in this chapter, this dilemma has been particularly troublesome and has occasionally led to misperceptions of children's metacognitive knowledge.

METAPERCEPTION

Metaperception, as the term will be used here, refers to an awareness of information content (stimulus input) and a knowledge of factors that influence perception. One area of metaperceptual research that has recently commanded interest from the developmental community is that of referential communication—that is, children's awareness of their listening skills and their ability to evaluate the informational adequacy of messages. Research to date suggests that young children aren't as sensitive to the information content of messages as are older children (Markman, 1979b).

When studying these abilities, researchers have typically presented children with sets of pictures. The experimenter then describes only one of the pictures in the set. The child's task is to identify the picture the speaker has described. Messages given to the listener are varied with respect to information content. Some descriptions are fully informative (information is sufficient to make a correct choice), some are partially informative (descriptions provide enough information to eliminate several but not all of the alternatives), and others are uninformative (descriptions provide no information that bears upon the choice).

When we receive an uninformative or partially informative message, we would be likely to ask for clarification; however, children younger than 9 years of age don't. It's unclear why they fail to request additional information, although several explanations have been suggested. One possibility is that young children simply don't distinguish between things that are more versus less correct. In ambiguous situations children may not thoroughly compare messages received to alternatives that are available. Instead they may simply choose the first referent that seems reasonable (cf. Flavell, Speer, Green, & August, 1981; Ironsmith & Whitehurst, 1978).

In other instances children may fail to realize that it is helpful to provide feedback to the speaker when they are in doubt (cf. Flavell et al., 1981; Ironsmith & Whitehurst, 1978). Or, young children, still limited in their own communication skills, may blame themselves for a failure to understand, not attributing equal responsibility to the speaker for communicating clearly. One might suppose that if the latter were true, children would defer to an adult speaker more often than a peer. Research, however, has shown that children fail to respond to inadequate messages whether the speaker is a peer or an adult (Flavell et al., 1981). Nonetheless, there is reason to believe that children are sensitive to age differences in the ability to attend to and decode messages. In fact, in natural settings, children as young as 2 years of age alter their communication to make it appropriate to the age of the listener and situation (Wellman & Lempers, 1977). Furthermore, Miller and Weiss (1982) have found that kindergarteners are sensitive to the fact that older children are better at selective attending than younger children.

We also find that a number of factors related to the task or situation influence children's knowledge of their perceptual state. Flavell et al. (1981) found that some messages may be too complex for children to understand and in these situations their metaperceptual knowledge is obviously poor. You might imagine how you might perform if you were sitting in on an advanced physics class (presuming you have no background in physics), and after a long discussion of some theoretical matter, the professor turns to you and asks you a question about the topic of discussion. Obviously your performance doesn't reflect your inability to evaluate the informational adequacy of messages; it represents an absence of an ability to make sense of any message presented in that particular context. Patterson, O'Brien, Kister, Carter, and Kotsonis (1981) varied both the complexity of messages and their informational adequacy and found that with simple messages, kindergarteners were able to discriminate between informative and uninformative messages. Only with more complex messages did older children (fourth-graders) discriminate better those messages that were informative from those that were uninformative. Thus we must qualify our judgment of children's ability to evaluate the information content of messages. Provided with appropriate materials and contexts, they do quite well (Pratt & Bates, 1982).

Not only does the context in which information is evaluated influence children's sensitivity to the informational adequacy of messages, young children are also sensitive to the idea that situational characteristics also affect the ability to attend to information. Miller and Zalenski (1982) found that on a nonverbal task, even 3- and 4-year-old children knew that attention would be better if children's interest was high and the surrounding environment quiet (cf. Yussen & Bird, 1979). When children's knowledge about attention is probed using a verbal task, however, their knowledge about factors affecting attention is much poorer (Miller & Weiss, 1982).

Research on children's metaperceptual knowledge reveals that young children are less sensitive to the informational content of messages than are older children. Much of this insensitivity may be due to the nature of the messages presented them. When provided with simple messages, very young children are able to discriminate informationally adequate from inadequate messages. We do find that children expect older children to be better listeners—that is, better able to perform on tasks that require selective attending. Young children also know that certain task factors influence perception. This knowledge is less likely to be found if children are tested with highly verbal procedures. Thus, what we know about children's metaperceptual abilities is influenced by where we test for this knowledge, what kinds of knowledge we test for, and how we test. It should also be mentioned that there is little correlation between children's knowledge of task or factors affecting performance and actual performance. On a selective attention task, for example, Miller and Jordan (1982) found no relationship between children's metaperceptual knowledge and their ability to attend selectively. Under naturalistic conditions young children seem to have some basic knowledge about what must be done to make them better receivers and senders of information. With age they become more aware of the variety of factors influencing their performance and more sensitive to the adequacy of information they sent and received. How this metaperceptual knowledge becomes integrated with performance, or whether such knowledge is necessary for perceptual development is as yet unknown.

METAMEMORY

Metamemory refers to one's awareness of his or her particular memory state (that is, what one knows); as well as his or her awareness of strategies useful for storing, retaining, or retrieving information from memory; and those factors conducive or detrimental to memorization.

One observation made by those who work with young children is that they often give unreliable accounts of their memory ability. Children may report that they know something when in fact they don't. This overgenerous estimation of memory should not be misinterpreted as an act of deception; it often reflects children's insensitivity to their own memory state. Indeed, children show an insensitivity to memory functioning at a number of levels.

An important, though somewhat obvious, aspect of any memory task is to recognize it as a memory task. That is, if we are to use our memory, we need to distinguish between it and other types of mental activity. Children distinguish between memory and some mental states, but not others.

Early research in this area suggested that young children might not distinguish between perceiving and remembering. Appel, Cooper, McCarrel, Sims-Knight, Yussen, and Flavell (1972), for example, presented 4-, 7-, and 11-year-old children with sets of pictures. Half of the children were told to "look at" the pictures, and half were told to "remember" them. Although there was a significant improvement in recall with age, only at the older age level was recall better under "remember" compared to "look at" instructions. The implication seemed to be that younger children didn't distinguish between a memory task (remember) and one that was perceptual (look at).

Actually, the results of this study are ambiguous. It is unclear, for example, whether children didn't know the difference between remembering something and looking at something (metamemory) or whether young children simply didn't remember well (memory performance). In another study that clarified this confusion, Yussen (1975) replicated the findings reported by the Appel et al. study, but found that even young children spent more time attending to pictures when told to remember them. Whereas young children responded differently to instructions to "remember" and "look at" something, they failed to use strategies that would allow them to remember better. Young children, it would seem, do distinguish between memory and perception. These data are also instructive in cautioning us to guard against inferring what children know about cognitive states from their memory performance alone.

Whereas young children clearly distinguish the act of looking at something from the act of trying to remember it, they nonetheless are somewhat confused about what memory is. Wellman and Johnson (1979) found that preschool children believe that something is remembered if it is found, and forgotten if it is not (in spite of any previous knowledge about the location of a hidden item). That is, to the young child, remembering and forgetting do not require that one have had some previous knowledge of an object's location (also see Johnson & Wellman, 1980; Miscione, Marvin, O'Brien, & Greenberg, 1978).

Assuming that children perceive the task at hand as one involving memory, what do they know about preparing for and executing a memory task? It would appear that younger children don't know a lot (cf., Brown, 1978; Flavell & Wellman, 1977). If children are given a list of items to learn and told to notify the experimenter when the list has been committed to memory, young children (kindergarteners and preschoolers) will spend most of their study time in unproductive, nonstrategic activities. Furthermore, they have a poor understanding of when something has been committed to memory. Having studied a list to their satisfaction, and telling the experimenter the list has been memorized, young children actually recall lists within their span of comprehension very poorly (Appel et al., 1972; Flavell et al., 1970; Markman, 1973).

The poor performance of young children on memory tasks is probably related to a number of gaps in their metamemory knowledge. Good mnemonists realize that they must anticipate the nature of the task if they are to use various strategies for retaining and retrieving information from memory. Those who use memory efficiently find out what the task is like, perhaps discovering how much is to be remembered, what is to be remembered, and how information is to be remembered (for example, whether it is to be recalled or recognized) (Brown, 1978).

But young children seem relatively unconcerned about these matters. Kreutzer, Leonard, and Flavell (1975) and Brown (1978) report that kindergarteners, compared to third-graders, are less aware of (a) the ease with which a series of words can be remembered in a narrative, compared to a nonnarrative, list-learning format; (b) the greater ease of learning lists of high associates rather than low associates; and (c) the greater ease of paraphrasing versus verbatim recall. There is also some reason to believe that young children are less aware of the fact that recognition is easier than recall. Levin, Yussen, DeRose, and Pressley (1977) had first-grade, fifth-grade, and college students predict how many words they would be able to recall or recognize on a list-learning task. A significant developmental improvement was found in children's ability to estimate recall performance but less so for recognition (differences in recognition accuracy existed between college students and fifth graders, but not between fifth- and first-grade children). It was also found that the two older age groups predicted better recognition performance compared to recall, but no such differences were predicted by the younger age group (also see Yussen & Berman, 1981).

As with many metamemory skills, what one knows is a complex interaction between knowledge of one's own state and knowledge about specific tasks or situations. For example, in some situations very young children realize that recognition is less difficult than recall. Speer and Flavell (1979) provided kindergarten and first-grade children with stories about two children who had to perform either a recall or a recognition task. Children had to decide which child would remember more and explain their answer. It was found that even kindergarten and first-grade children believed that the recognition task would be easier and voiced strong opinions supporting their answers.

When confronted with a memory task, older children and adults approach the task systematically, applying a variety of strategies to improve memory functioning. With age, children also develop an awareness that certain strategies are particularly important to memory functioning. For example, older children are more aware that organized material is easier to recall than unorganized material (Brown, 1978), that categorized lists are easier to remember than uncategorized lists (Brown, 1978; Moynahan, 1973; Salatas & Flavell, 1976), and that specific types of organization (for example, semantic versus perceptual) facilitate retention more than others (Yussen, Levin, Berman, & Palm, 1979).

Additional research has shown that young children don't recognize the value of either rehearsing or labeling (Brown, 1978; Kreutzer et al., 1975). Brown, for example, showed children videotapes of other children using different study activities, including rehearsing, labeling items, or simply looking at pictures to be remembered. After viewing all of the tapes, children were asked to make bets on which children would have better recall. Four-year-old children believed that no strategy would be any better than another. By the third grade, however, children generally believed that active strategies (rehearsing and labeling) would lead to better performance.

As with knowledge about strategies for retaining information, knowledge about how to facilitate information retrieval also improves with age. Early work examining children's knowledge of the use of retrieval cues suggested that young children were unaware that such cues could be used to facilitate recall. In one study (Corsini, Pick, & Flavell, 1968), younger (4- and 5-year-old) and older (7-year-old) children were given a set of geometric forms presented in a serial order. Children were told to study them for recall some time later. Children were also given the option of using cardboard copies of the to-be-remembered items that could be used to remember where items went. Older children used these cues more spontaneously than younger children (also see Ritter, 1978). But again, children's ability to generate and use retrieval cues is task-dependent. For some tasks we find that young children are very capable of devising logical plans for retrieving information. It has been observed that on relatively simple memory tasks even 3-year-olds use simple mnemonic cues (pointing and body orientation) for remembering where things go (Wellman, Ritter, & Flavell, 1975). Children can even generate a systematic plan for recovering a lost article ("How might you go about finding where you lost your coat?"), but have greater difficulty generating a plan for recovering an abstract idea ("How could you remember when your mother's birthday was?") (Drozdal & Flavell, 1975; Wellman et al., 1975).

As seen in this review, a number of developmental trends emerge in the acquisition of children's knowledge about memory functioning. Performance, however, is a complex interaction between subject knowledge and task variables. We find there is a general improvement in knowing when something is known or how much one knows; yet, on some tasks even young children make accurate predictions of their performance, as in estimating how far they can jump. Children may simply have more practice in estimating how far they can jump than in estimating how many words they can remember.

We find that children also become more aware of what is an easy memory task compared to a difficult one and are more knowledgeable of strategies that facilitate the retention of information and conditions that facilitate its retrieval. Of those children who have good metamemory, it would seem logical to presume that they would also be good memory users, but this isn't necessarily the case. At best there appears to be only a low-to-moderate correspondence between metamemory knowledge and memory performance. Brown (1979), for example, calculated an index of relationship between the percentage of children who predict that active strategies (rehearsal and organization) lead to better recall and the percentage of children who use such strategies spontaneously (predicted/actual). She found that this proportion rose from .22 at the preschool level to .77 by the third grade, and that performance was not totally consistent with prediction even by the end of grade school. Other indices have revealed similar relationships (Cavanaugh & Borkowski, 1980; Levin et al., 1977; Yussen & Berman, 1981).

METAPROCESSING KNOWLEDGE

In referring to *metaprocessing* knowledge, we'll consider what individuals know about problem-solving situations. Problem solving would seem to be affected by what one knows about how to approach a problem and how knowledge about the problem-solving task leads to the adoption of one set of cognitive activities rather than others.

It should be noted before proceeding further that the bulk of metacognitive research has focused on metamemory; thus, little is actually known about this area of knowledge. Nonetheless, effective problem solving presumes an awareness that specific steps need to be taken as problems are solved (DeCecco, 1968; Hayes, 1981; Wood, Bruner, & Ross, 1976). At a minimum these steps include (a) understanding the solution-based criteria of a problem, or that problems have solutions; (b) perceiving possible solutions to a problem; (c) allocating study time effectively; (d) being sensitive to feedback; (e) altering strategies to fit the task; and (f) evaluating information to arrive at a solution to a problem.

An inspection of available research shows that young children are lacking in knowledge about the importance of each of these steps. For example, it is not apparent that young children are aware that some problems have solutions. In fact, much of the problem-solving research reviewed in this text reveals that preschool children tend to adopt nonsolution strategies (position responding) or persevere on one particular hypothesis when solving problems (Bruner et al., 1956; Gholson et al., 1973; Olson, 1966). In this work there is the obvious problem of inferring whether children know that there are such things as solutions to the problems they are solving. A few studies have found that children may be aware that problems have solutions, but only after extensively training in the nature of the task (Cantor & Spiker, 1978).

Another aspect of effective problem solving is knowing how to allocate study time. If one is to profit from the time one is allowed to learn information or to solve a problem, one must approach the problem strategically. Furthermore, there must be a form of self-monitoring so the problem-solver is aware of when a problem is solved or when something has been learned. Several studies have found that in attempting to learn a set of information to perfection, children younger than 8 years of age don't use strategies that incorporate new information into their study set; previously learned material is simply restudied (Brown & Campione, 1977; Masur, McIntyre, & Flavell, 1973). Flavell et al. (1970) have also reported that preschoolers use study time very inappropriately during list-learning tasks. Unlike their younger counterparts, older elementary school-aged children plan systematically to discover what is to be learned, use active strategies to retain information, and use self-testing and anticipational strategies for assessing the extent of their learning.

Another aspect of metaprocessing knowledge is sensitivity to task demands and the ability to alter processing strategies to conform to these demands. Two questions seem relevant here: first are children sensitive to the information that is gained through a particular strategy? Second, are children sensitive to task characteristics and able to alter their strategies accordingly?

With respect to the first question, there is some evidence that young children are not as sensitive to the information content that is gained through particular search strategies. Olson (1966) examined the development of strategies in the solution of pattern identification problems. On these tasks, children had to discover which of two patterns of lights had been designated as "correct" by the experimenter. One could solve this problem by depressing light bulbs on another board. If a light bulb was depressed and it corresponded to part of the pattern that was designated as correct, then that bulb would light (Figure 11-1).

In presenting this problem to children, Olson used two conditions. In one condition (free condition), children were allowed to choose bulbs at will, with only the stipulation that they try to discover which pattern was correct with as few choices as possible. In another condition (constrained condition), children were asked to report if they had acquired enough information to solve the problem after each choice.

This research showed that there were, as might be anticipated, developmental shifts in the spontaneous use of strategies. Older children tended to make more informative selections than younger children. That is, older children tended to select more bulbs that provided critical information about which pattern was correct. Older children also seemed to be more aware of the amount of information gained from particular selection strategies. For

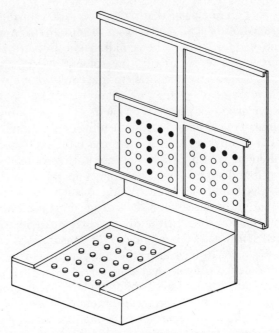

Figure 11-1. Apparatus used in the experiment. *(Olson, 1966)*

example, 3-year-old children didn't differ appreciably in their performance on either the free or constrained conditions. However, older children (5, 7, and 9 years old) made significantly more informative choices in the constrained condition. Significant developmental trends were also noted in the ability of children to solve problems following the acquisition of the minimum amount of information needed for solution. Again, in the constrained condition, compared to the free-choice condition, older children were more likely to solve problems after a minimal amount of information had been attained (Figure 11-2).

These data indicate that elementary school-age children are able to alter their solution strategies in situations that require them to evaluate the information gained from choices. Very young children (3 years of age) would appear to be less sensitive to the information gained from choices and are less apt to vary strategies to gain more information on each choice—although sensitivity to information may vary as a function of the task (cf. Steinberg, 1980). These data are interesting in one other way. In the constrained condition the number of informative choices increased markedly after the 3-year-old level. However, there was relatively little spontaneous use of such a strategy even by 9-year-old children. In spite of children's metacognitive knowledge, they did not use that knowledge unless prompted to do so.

In addition to an increasing sensitivity to the value of information gained during a problem-solving task, there is also evidence that children are increasingly able to alter strategic behavior in response to task characteristics. Children's response to probability learning tasks provides insight into this facet of

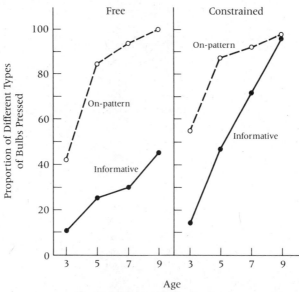

Figure 11-2. Proportion of different types of bulbs pressed on single problems (free and constrained). *(Olson, 1966)*

metaprocessing knowledge. On these tasks, one of several items is partially reinforced at a rate above chance. The task of the subject is to predict on each trial which item will be reinforced. Subjects can't receive reinforcement 100% of the time, but they can maximize reinforcement by choosing the item that is being reinforced most frequently (see Goulet & Goodwin, 1970, for a review of this literature).

A curious, yet reliable, finding in these experiments is that there is a higher percentage of correct responses in both preschool and college populations with performance being poorer during the elementary school years (Figure 11-3). One explanation of these data is that the performance of the youngest and the oldest groups reflects two different approaches to the problem. Preschool children appear to respond to the problem in a nonstrategic fashion; therefore, they respond to reinforcement probabilities only. Older children appear to believe that some strategy can be found that will allow them to obtain reinforcement 100% of the time. They search for a strategy that will lead to perfect performance. College-age subjects, while initially searching for some optimal strategy, eventually alter their approach such that they, like the preschool children, optimize reinforcement by choosing the most frequently rewarded item. Young elementary school-age children, also searching for some perfect strategy, fail to switch to a reward-optimizing strategy. Evidence for this intepretation comes from studies in which subjects have been told prior to the task that they will be unable to be correct all of the time. On these tasks, adults appear to increase the use of maximizing responses, choosing the more frequent event (Goodnow, 1955); however, children don't always alter their behavior in response to such knowledge (Gruen & Wier, 1964).

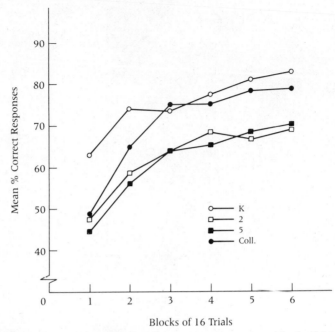

Figure 11-3. Mean percentage of correct responses per block of 16 trials for kindergarten (K), second-grade (2), fifth-grade (5), and college (Coll.) subjects (as shown in *Goulet & Goodwin, 1970*).

In sum, the scant research that has been conducted on metaprocessing knowledge has revealed that, as with other areas of metacognitive knowledge, there are reliable age-related changes in knowledge about what problems are, how to apportion study time, how to use information, and how to alter one's approach to conform to task demands. Like other kinds of metacognitive knowledge, this too is likely influenced by a number of task factors. By simplifying the task, instructing children thoroughly in the nature of the task, or providing tasks familiar and relevant to children, it is likely that more advanced forms of metaprocessing knowledge will be found (Cantor & Spiker, 1978, Steinberg, 1980).

METACOGNITION: A CRITIQUE

In spite of a developing interest in metacognition, research in this area has been open to a variety of criticisms not unrelated to those typically leveled at urban sprawl. In fact, some reviewers (Cavanaugh & Perlmuter, 1982) have gone so far as to suggest that in its present state, what is known about metamemory (and by extension to metacognition as a whole) has little value to the scientific community.

One of the more salient problems in this research has been its show-and-tell quality—it has been primarily atheoretical (Brown, 1978; Cavanaugh & Perlmuter, 1982). The absence of a theoretical framework within which to advance an understanding of metacognition has had several untoward consequences. First, much of the metacognitive research has been single-study, one-shot demonstrations. Thus, research has simply shown that children of a particular age do or don't know something (Brown, 1978). Although this research provides a necessary data base, proliferation of demonstration studies provides little in the way of a coordinated understanding of how metacognitive knowledge develops or how this knowledge relates to the operation of the cognitive system as a whole.

Second, the absence of a firm theoretical orientation has had the effect of allowing particular areas of research, such as metaprocessing knowledge, to be neglected, while allowing other areas (often of questionable importance) too much attention. Brown (1978) notes the many studies of children's knowledge about rehearsal and wonders how frequently this knowledge is used in daily life—is it really an important question? Whereas this knowledge may be appropriate for rote-memorization of word lists in experimental settings, we infrequently experience these kinds of tasks. If we must remember a list exactly (a shopping list, telephone numbers, or names), we write it down on a piece of paper!

A third problem in this research is that by focusing on a particular content area and specific age levels (primarily preschool and early elementary school-aged children), we get a distorted picture of what is likely true of metacognitive development. An examination of research to date gives the impression that by the third grade, children have relatively stable and well-established metacognitive knowledge. But several authors (Brown, 1979; Cavanaugh & Perlmuter, 1982; Flavell, 1979) have cautioned against such a conclusion. Indeed, it is speculated that on a variety of more complex tasks involving real-life situations, even adults are insensitive to their own cognitive states.

Another problem with metacognitive research is that there is an absence of clear descriptions of the concepts with which we're working. Cavanaugh and Perlmuter (1982), for example, note that there has been a persistent lack of distinction between memory knowledge (what one knows about their memory) and executive processes (how one uses their memory). The failure to define clearly and precisely the constructs under study leads to serious difficulties in examining relationships between metamemory and other conceptual processes (cf. Flavell & Wellman, 1977). Clearly defining the components of an information-processing system can only facilitate their systematic examination. Such an attention to definition might ultimately provide some insight into one of the more vexing phenomena in metacognitive research—the low relationship between children's awareness of cognitive processes and their incorporation of that knowledge in performance.

In addition to these theoretical issues, there are a host of methodological ones. Cavanaugh and Perlmuter (1982) cite many of the complaints peculiar to the introspective procedure, abandoned during the 1930s, as equally valid criticisms of the methodology of metamemory (and metacognitive) research. It is observed that these procedures are often unvalidated and of questionable reliability. The introspective character of this research may also alter the experience being reported, and the procedure (usually involving a verbal report) may be a better measure of the child's verbal fluency than the child's actual knowledge state. Consequently, several researchers have called for the examination of metacognitive phenomena using a variety of measures rather than single ones as is common practice (Brown, 1978; Cavanaugh & Perlmuter, 1982). Furthermore, it would be helpful to examine more closely the validity and reliability of some of the measures currently used in metacognitive research.

SUMMARY

Metacognitive research has demonstrated the progressive development of children's knowledge of their cognitive state and variables affecting that state. Older children, on the whole, have much better metacognitive knowledge than younger ones. This rather unremarkable finding must be tempered, however, with the knowledge that what children know is often affected by a variety of task and situational variables. Provided with difficult and unfamiliar tasks, we should expect that young children will perform poorly. Given tasks that are simple and easily understood, even young children will show some metacognitive knowledge.

These findings underscore a persistent problem in developmental research—distinguishing between what children know about something (competence) and their demonstration of knowledge or ability (performance). It may be, for example, that young children know that messages are inadequate or that a memory or problem-solving strategy would be useful, but fail to demonstrate their knowledge because they haven't learned how to apply it to a particular situation. It is increasingly apparent that what children know about their world is intimately related to how and where they are asked about that knowledge.

12

Language and Cognition

As we work our way up the scale of species intelligence, we find that those species at the top of this hierarchy have more elaborate communication systems. Only one of those species has a true language and that species is us. Some writers (Dale, 1976) believe language is the uniquely human quality that distinguishes us from other animal life. Language pervades our everyday lives. It is a subtle, yet ever present, force in our existence. Perhaps while lost in thought you've been surprised and perhaps a bit embarrassed to find yourself talking out loud. It's alright to talk to ourselves, as long as we confine these conversations to that not so silent space between our ears. But it is just such activity that intuitively leads us to accept the notion that language and thought are intimately linked. As we read, write, and reason, we're consciously aware of words and sentences coming to mind. As you study, a form of mental discourse transpires; language seems to permeate thought.

In this chapter we'll consider some ways that psychologists and psycholinguists have viewed the relationship between language and thought. This relationship, as I will characterize it, represents a continuum of sorts. On one extreme is the position that language is a necessary prerequisite for thought. In this position's most radical form, its theorists believe that language limits or structures thought. At the opposite extreme is the view that language is but a manifestation of some underlying intellectual system—both thought and language reflect the development of representational ability. You will notice that this is the Piagetian position, although there are some information-processing theorists who also believe that language is based in the development of some symbolic abilities (Bloom, Lightbrown, & Hood, 1975; Nelson, 1973). Between these extremes are those who regard language as having a special, but not necessarily all-inclusive, role in thought. One of these positions views verbal language as a tool that facilitates certain types of thinking; another posits that language serves as a kind of executive (controller or regulator) that directs thought, calling up particular strategies, inhibiting others, and in general directing what is responded to, how it is processed and what kinds of actions are taken in response to information.

LANGUAGE AS A PREREQUISITE OF THOUGHT

It occasionally has been proposed that language is not simply a correlative, but a necessary, condition for thought. The idea is actually quite old. Aristotle believed that language was essential to instruction. Observing that the deaf were incapable of verbal language, he concluded that they couldn't be educated and, therefore, were unworthy of higher status within the social order. The ancient Romans were no more enlightened. By their law the deaf were classified with the mentally deficient and consequently denied a number of legal and social privileges. The relationship between language and thought is clearly revealed in the differentiation between the rights of Romans who were congenitally deaf and those who had lost their hearing after learning speech and writing; for the latter, there were no sanctions or loss of social position.

In the more recent past, the idea that language structures thought gained great popularity through the writing of Sapir and Whorf (Sapir, 1949; Whorf, 1956). In their theorizing they advocated both linguistic determinism (that higher levels of thinking were dependent upon language) and linguistic relativism (that different languages led to a different structuring of what one knew about their world). Languages do differ with respect to how words can be classified along two dimensions. One dimension is lexical—that is, how words relate to some general class of objects (schnauzers, collies, and poodles all belong to a class of things called dogs). Another dimension is grammatical: certain words are used reliably in certain ways, or certain linguistic structures exist to convey specific kinds of meaning. For example, in English, speakers modify the tense of their verbs to imply past, present, and future events; other languages don't.

These linguistic characteristics were believed to mold thought. "What people think and feel and how they report what they think and feel are determined, to be sure, by their personal history, and by what actually happens in the

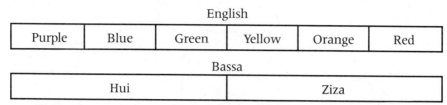

Figure 12-1. Division of hues by speakers of English and Bassa. *(Dale, 1976)*

outside world. But they are also determined by a factor which is often overlooked; namely, the pattern of lingusitic habits which people acquire as members of a particular society" (Kluckhohn, 1963, p. 143). Early research (Brown & Lenneberg, 1954) seemed to support this notion. Speakers of different languages, it was reported, categorized the color spectrum differently—some having a more varied set of terms for colors (as in English), others a less varied set (as in Bassa) (Figure 12-1).

Likewise, language was believed to affect how one conveys an idea. To express the idea of going somewhere in English, we simply say, for example, "I'm going to the store." In Navaho, speakers are compelled to include references to how they went or will be going, if they are going in something, and the manner in which the conveyance is propelled; if they have come from somewhere, they must choose a verb tense that indicates the speed at which they traveled. Kluckhohn notes, "In general, the difference between Navaho thought and English thought—both as manifested in the language and as forced by the very nature of the linguistic forms into such patterns—is that Navaho thought is ordinarily much more specific" (1963, p. 142).

Although popular for a time, the Sapir-Whorf hypothesis became an embattled victim of critical empirical and philosophical review. Recent commentaries on the theory have noted the basic ambiguities in many key concepts:

> Both Sapir and Whorf, as well as some of their critics and supporters, tried to specify which linguistic elements they thought pertinent to the correlation (between language and thought): lexication or grammar, phonetic or semantic components, even surface or deep structure; but they are more careless when they speak of thought and of reality, and when they indulge in a vacuous vocabulary in which world view and presupposition become synonymous with metaphysics and philosophy. [Stam, 1980, p. 257]

Indeed, even if we accept the theory for what it apparently asserts, we encounter a paradox. How can we objectively evaluate a theory that specifies that we can't evaluate it objectively? If language structures thought, then we all wear blinders. How can we reason about a theory of language if we are unable to see beyond the limits of our own language-structured view of reality? As the theoretical and philosophical base to the hypothesis began to unravel, then so did the empirical as instances of cultural universals in perception and thought came to light. Cross-cultural research on color labeling, quite contrary to what had been found earlier, revealed that universal perceptual and cognitive factors actually produced similar patterns of color labels, at least with respect to primary or basic colors (Heider, 1972).

Language, as promoted by the Sapir-Whorf hypothesis, acted to limit thought; but others, quite the contrary, have emphasized the liberating effect of language in thinking. In attending to the developmental process, Bruner (1973a,b), emphasized the key role that representation had on the formation of thought and, consequently, the flexibility of children's thinking. The need to represent one's world is prerequisite to survival. Like any other instrument available to man, representational ability is a tool, a summary way of dealing with our experiences. And as all tools may vary in usefulness, the way in which information is represented varies the effectiveness with which we can manipulate the contents of experience.

Bruner proposed three kinds of representation: enactive, iconic, and symbolic. Things are represented *enactively* by some sequence of activity, a non-reversible habitual act affected on something. To use Bruner's (1973b) example, a knot is represented by the act of tying. A second type of representation is *iconic*—that is, represented in some imaginal code. The image can serve as a scheme around which to organize action. My own image of this concept is represented by something akin to those pictures printed in Boy Scout manuals showing how to tie knots. Arrows run through the knot, indicating the direction (action) of the various segments of the rope as they wrap around each other. The third level of representation is *symbolic*. It involves a linguistic description of the event or object represented. For example, I can hear my father instructing my brothers and me in the art of knotting a tie: "under, over, around and through." These levels of representation, while successive, do not imply stages. That is, there is a reliable sequence in which representation evolves. Neonates rely upon enactive-motoric representation, whereas older infants eventually represent experience iconically. By about 7 years of age, children generally begin to represent experience symbolically. These forms of representation coexist throughout life, although lower levels come to be supplanted by higher ones.

The transition from the iconic to the symbolic form of representation captured Bruner's early interest. He believed that with the adoption of the linguistic-symbolic system the child is freed from the immediacy of the situation at hand. With language, the child can reason into the future, considering possibilities rather than immediacies. In Bruner's words, with language the child can go "beyond the information given."

It is important to emphasize a major point made by Bruner. His position advocated that it is not some intellectual structure that promotes the development of language *per se*, but rather language development that frees the intellect. Work by Bruner and his colleagues (Bruner, Goodnow, & Austin, 1956; Bruner, Olver, & Greenfield, 1966) focused on the various influences exerted by perceptual features of problem-solving situations and children's growing mastery of language. And indeed, a number of suggestive relationships were observed. Presented with a two-dimensional matrix, for example, children between the ages of 5 and 7 years of age could easily reconstruct it from memory. But, if children were asked to transpose the reconstruction (reproduce the matrix in a reversed order), 5- and 6-year-old children invariably failed. Older children, on the other hand, had no difficulty with the task. Younger children were fixed on a literal and figural reconstruction, while older children had abstracted a relationship that allowed them to transpose. Examining the language of children as they described the array, Bruner found that children who could describe in an unconfounded fashion the dimensions along which items varied were those who succeeded on the transposition task. These results suggested to Bruner, as similar data did to Piaget, that young children were confused by misleading perceptual information. But unlike Piaget, Bruner believed that improvement in performance doesn't await the attainment of some particular stage with its concomitant rule structure; language itself provides the structure for advanced forms of thought.

LANGUAGE AND THOUGHT: MANIFESTATIONS OF A COMMON CORE

The Piagetian approach to language and thought has been to regard language and thought consistently as reflections of some common underlying intellectual structure. Piaget states, "Language is a product of intelligence rather than intelligence being a product of language" (1980, p. 167). He proposed the idea that the intellectual structures that develop during the sensorimotor period culminate in the capacity for semiotic or symbolic representation. This semiotic function provides the basis from which children represent objects, events, and people in their absence.

The development of semiotic function derives from the growth of children's imitative abilities during the later stages of the sensorimotor period. Piaget (1963), for example, describes his daughter attempting to extract a chain from a matchbox. The child (16 months of age) has solved the problem on two successive occasions with the matchbox lid open to the extent that it allowed the child easy access to the chain inside. On the occasion described, the lid to the box has been closed so that the aperture is open slightly. Piaget notes,

> Lucienne is not aware of the functioning of the opening and closing of the matchbox and has not seen me [Piaget] prepare the experiment. She only possesses the two preceding schemata: turning the box over in order to empty it of its contents, and sliding her finger into the slit to make the chain come out. It is, of course, this last procedure that she tries first. She puts her finger inside and gropes to reach the chain, but fails completely. A pause follows during which Lucienne manifests a very curious reaction bearing witness not only to the fact that she tries to think out the situation and to represent herself through mental combination of operations to be performed, but also the role played by imitation in the genesis of representations. Lucienne mimics the widening of the slit.
>
> She looks at the slit with great attention; then, several times in succession, she opens and shuts her mouth, at first slightly, then wider and wider! Apparently Lucienne understands the existence of a cavity subjacent to the slit and wishes to enlarge the cavity. [1963, pp. 337–338]

Acting as if to internalize the object and acting upon that representation reflect the emergence of semiotic function. They also represent the basis upon which language, as well as other manifestations of this semiotic function (imagery, delayed imitation, symbolic play), will develop.

The Piagetians believe that synchrony between language and cognitive development is found in both semantic and syntactic development. Inhelder (1980) has observed the rather late acquisition of the passive voice in children's language and the confusion that children have in attaining meaning from the order in which sentences are formed. Young children seem unaware, for example, of the difference between statements such as "The man took the boy to the store" and "The man was taken to the store by the boy." It is not by chance, Inhelder notes, that these differences are appreciated around the age of 7 years, or that period when concrete operations are internalized. The ability to appreciate sentence order presumably stems from the child's ability to appreciate serial relationships in general.

When considering the position advocated by the Piagetians, we must make a distinction between the necessity of language for intelligent behavior (which was defined by Piaget, 1963, as means-end behavior) and more advanced forms of thinking. On the latter, Piaget believed that language is necessary. Piaget (cited in Inhelder, 1980) states,

> Without the system of symbolic expression which constitutes language, the operations would remain at the stage of successive actions without ever being integrated into simultaneous systems or simultaneously encompassing a set of interdependent transformations. Without language, the operations would remain personal and would consequently not be regulated by interpersonal exchange and cooperation. It is in this dual sense of symbolic condensation and social regulation that language is indispensable to the elaboration of thought. [p. 134]

Thus, in a general sense, language serves to facilitate the interaction of the child with others, bringing egocentric perceptions into conflict with the perceptions of others and thus facilitating equilibration. In the development of formal operational thought in particular, Piaget believed language is probably necessary for thought (Beilin, 1980).

RELEVANT RESEARCH

The research in support of either of these two positions has relied upon three types of evidence: correlational studies that have examined the correspondence between intellectual and language development; performance between children with and without language disorders on logical reasoning tasks; and training studies. We'll consider each in turn.

Correlation Studies

Under this category of "evidence" is a variety of studies that have attempted to demonstrate some synchrony in the development of intellectual and linguistic competence. Both of these positions predict a reliable relationship between language and thought, although they differ in the order in which abilities are predicted to emerge. The first view would emphasize the primacy of language in structuring thought, the latter the primacy of intellectual development.

As might be anticipated, there is a clear relationship between the development of language and thought. Zachary (1978) reported that the development of representational thought is directly related to children's ability to speak in sentences. Corrigan (1978) studied three children over an 18-month period and found a reliable relationship between the onset of search for an invisible-displaced object and the use of single-word utterances. Toward the end of stage six of the sensorimotor period Corrigan also observed an increase in vocabulary production and the appearance of specific words allowing children to comment on disappearances (allgone) and reappearances (more). There was, however, no reliable relationship between infants' attainment of the concept of object and the length and complexity of utterances. Harding and Golinkoff (1979) also found a reliable relationship between infants' attainment of the concept of causation and intentional prelinguistic vocalization (that is, vocalization used to direct attention or affect someone else's behavior.) Other studies have noted a reliable relationship between the acquisition of higher-level, semantic structures and the transition from preoperational to concrete operational thought and from concrete to formal operational thought (Beilin, 1975; Rosenthal, 1979; Sinclair-de Zwart, 1973).

The apparent synchrony between language and thought should come as little surprise. It should also be observed that the simultaneous development of these two systems doesn't provide evidence for the necessity of one system in the development of the other. Chomsky (1980) observed that the synchrony between language and thought is, in fact, relatively uninteresting as it merely states the obvious—as children grow older their language and cognitive skills improve. A more compelling line of evidence for a relationship between language and thought is the order in which these skills develop. Do specific conceptual understandings precede the development of certain linguistic structures?

In general there is reason to believe that some linguistic skills are antedated by particular levels of cognitive development. Zachary (1978) demonstrated that the ability of children to communicate in sentences is preceded by representational thought. Cometa and Eson (1978) found that children's understanding of metaphors is apparently dependent upon their understanding of class inclusion. Other linguistic skills have been linked to basic information-processing limitations. Short-term memory limitations or familiarity of specific grammatical structures, for example, may affect children's sensitivity to certain linguistic features (Daneman & Case, 1981; Kuczaj, 1979).

There is also some reason to believe that even prelinguistic infants may develop an awareness of specific concepts and relationships that facilitate language acquisition. Prelinguistic infants apparently develop a notion that (a) vocalizations can be used to affect someone else's behavior or to achieve a goal (Harding & Golinkoff, 1979) and that (b) there are things like agents that affect actions on recipients (Bruner, 1978; Golinkoff & Kerr, 1978). Golinkoff and

Kerr (1978), for example, presented 15- and 18-month-old infants with film clips of an agent (*A*—a man) pushing an object (*B*—the recipient, either a man or a chair). Children's heart rate was monitored and, as would be expected, after successive presentations of the film-clip, the infants' interest waned (heart rate habituated). With the change of the agent–recipient relationship (*B* now pushed *A*), children showed a renewed interest in the films, suggesting to Golinkoff that infants "understood" the agent–recipient relationship.

Some caution should be exercised in inferring a one-way relationship between cognitive development and language. Cognitive development cannot by itself explain how children come to categorize as they do—that is, to set the boundaries of a concept. Schlesinger (1977) notes the need to distinguish between interpreting and categorizing one's surroundings. We know a concept if we know what belongs to it and what doesn't. What, for example, constitutes an agent? In Golinkoff and Kerr's study, would we be likely to attribute agency to a chair—that a chair is something that affects some action upon a recipient? Probably not. As English speakers, we don't normally attribute agency roles to chairs; children learn this early in the second year of life (Golinkoff & Harding, 1980). Schlesinger comments that the way in which concepts such as agent and recipient are learned depends upon the language that is learned; different languages dissect the world differently. Thus, the two processes—the development of a conceptual appreciation for regularities in one's environment and learning how to classify those regularities—are reciprocal and likely inseparable processes.

Just such a reciprocal process is described by Bruner (1978) in his depiction of the mother–infant interaction that he believes establishes a foundation for language learning. Bruner believes the development of the agent–recipient concept inherent in language occurs through a coordinated interplay between the infant's behavior, the mother's interpretation of the infant's behavior, and the reaction of the infant to the mother's intervention. Bruner observes that early in the infant's life, mothers work to interest their children in objects, provoking from them a reaching response. As children begin to reach for things, mothers begin to interpret this reaching as a request. Operating under such expectancies, children gradually refine the reach to pointing—a more specific request. As mothers retrieve objects for their infants in response to their requests, infants are encouraged to enter into this exchange of giving and receiving things. In this interaction Bruner sees a conceptual framework that serves as a model for all communication—a model in which there is role shifting, turn taking, and a coordination of signals with actions. The caretaker's role in this process is critical, for he or she interprets the child's response, instructing the child in the rules of communication exchange, and eventually tightening the criterion of what is an acceptable communication.

In summary, an examination of the covariation of language and cognition has found the two to be reliably related. It has also been observed that in some instances specific conceptual ability appears to precede specific linguistic competence, although it would be wrong to conclude that conceptual development alone can explain language development, or vice versa. Some structuring of the cognitive system is likely to occur through the acquisition of culturally relevant concepts imposed by language. Indeed, the interaction and complexity of this phenomena is likely much greater than heretofore anticipated. Adults and children learn variant language rule systems (partly as a consequence of the unique social context in which each of us is raised and also as a result of individual differences) (cf. Hardy-Brown, 1983; Nelson, 1981). Whereas our linguistic system may assist us in organizing our world, each of us may organize it a bit differently.

Comparisons of Children with Typical and Atypical Language

Another type of evidence mustered in the debate over the relationship between thought and language has involved comparisons of children with normal and atypical language. All things being equal, the argument goes, children with atypical language development should show normal levels of development if language and cognition are independent.

Research with deaf populations (usually believed to have poorer language skills compared to same aged hearing peers) has demonstrated that they are delayed in concept attainment and problem-solving skills. Furth (1964, 1971) reports that on Piagetian tasks, deaf children are moderately delayed (six months to a year behind same-aged hearing counterparts) in their attainment of knowledge of conservation (conservation of mass and continuous quantity) associated with concrete operational development. Delays are particularly noticeable (sometimes as much as three years behind same-aged hearing peers) in the acquisition of concepts associated with the level of formal operational thought. Rather than interpreting this evidence as a deficit specifically related to language, most researchers (Furth, 1971; Liben, 1978a,b) believe that the delays (especially those involving concrete operational knowledge) are due to the limited experiences of the deaf. Research supports this view. When tasks are presented to deaf children and the requirements and characteristics of the problem are clearly communicated, performance on conservation tasks (liquid and mass) and tasks involving metaphorical reasoning is unrelated to deafness *per se* (Rittenhouse, Morreau, & Iran-Nejad, 1981).

With respect to another cognitive system, memory, deaf and hearing children differ in some ways, but in other respects they are much the same. As might be expected, a number of studies have demonstrated that the deaf do not code or represent information in the same modality as do the hearing. It would appear that young deaf children (7–12 years of age) rely upon some nonverbal (Allen, 1970, 1971; Chovan, 1970; Conrad & Rush, 1965) and perhaps visual modes of representation (Hermelin & O'Connor, 1973; MacDougal, 1979). Older deaf children and adults, like their hearing counterparts, may rely upon some symbolic means of representing information in short-term memory, perhaps in some articulatory code (Dodd & Hermelin, 1977; MacDougal, 1979) or a dactylic code mediated by American Sign Language (Belugi, Klima, & Sipple, 1976; Hung, Tzeng, & Warren, 1981; MacDougal, 1979). In other areas of memory function, the deaf display remarkably similar strategies for coping with memory tasks. Liben (Liben & Drury; 1977; Liben,

1979), for example, demonstrated that when asked to remember lists of words, deaf children use both rehearsal and subjective organization at about the same age as hearing children.

As with deaf children, language-impaired children show delays in the cognitive development. These children are generally believed to have normal motor, sensory, and intellectual development; however, for some unknown reason (presumed to be cortical damage), language development is impaired. In a review of literature on the language and cognitive development of these children, Leonard (1979) finds them to be delayed in all aspects of language development (lexical, syntactic, and semantic) as well as delayed in the development of skills requiring representational thought. It should be observed, however, that there have been few comparative studies with these children.

The argument that cognition is dependent on language is not well supported by research with the deaf and is only suggestive with language-impaired children. Any conclusions drawn from comparisons of typical and atypical populations can be misleading, however, since to draw them, we must accept two assumptions. One is that the deaf do not have some symbolic language, and the other is that the populations being compared with normal-hearing children are alike in all other ways save for the absence of normal language. Any exposure to deaf populations will convince you that the first of these assumptions is patently wrong (Bornstein & Roy, 1973; Liben, 1978b). Although the deaf aren't likely to have linguistic skills comparable to same-aged hearing counterparts, their linguistic competence is likely sufficient for logical reasoning (specifically for tasks assessing concrete operational knowledge). If this is so, it would be unwise to conclude that language (whatever form it may take) has no role in cognitive activity. Indeed, the delayed acquisition of formal operational skills by deaf children does suggest that at least at this level linguistic competence is a factor in logical reasoning ability.

There is an additional methodological problem in drawing conclusions about the relationship between language and thought from these data. As observed, these studies assume that typical and atypical populations are alike in all other ways except the presence or absence of normal language. It should be noted that such an assumption is unfounded (cf. Belugi, Klima, Sipple, 1976; Gross & Jackson, 1981; Liben, 1978b). Congenital deafness, for instance, can occur for a variety of reasons with concomitant effects on other aspects of child development. Indeed, the specific reason for deafness, parental reaction to deafness, individual self-concept, exposure to educational environments, and many other factors likely mediate the influence of deafness on cognition. Whereas comparisons of typical and atypical children provide interesting normative data, the methodological problems inherent in these comparisons are great.

Verbal Training and Cognitive Development

Over the past decade a number of authors have attempted to induce higher levels of cognitive performance through verbal training. In these procedures, it is reasoned that if cognitive development can be advanced through verbal rule instruction alone, then it is demonstrated that language can train the intellect.

With great consistency we find that verbal rule instruction does promote cognitive development—a phenomenon that is not entirely consistent with Piagetian views on rule acquisition. Piagetians, for example, propose that real learning is promoted through self-discovery activities in situations that resemble real-world problems (Inhelder, Sinclair, & Bovet, 1974). Active manipulation and exploration in an ecologically meaningful context is believed to produce learning that generalizes across problem-solving situations. Presumably, passive learning through verbal rule instruction should be a relatively ineffective way of producing cognitive development. But studies using verbal rule instruction have successfully taught conservation by training children to use rules for inversion (a transformation can be negated by an equal but opposite transformation), compensation (that which is lost in one dimension is made up for by gains in another dimension), and identity (nothing added or taken away leaves the quantity unchanged) (cf. Anderson & Clark, 1978; Beilin, 1976, 1980; Brainerd, 1978a; Field, 1977). It is of some interest that, whereas verbal rule instruction is relatively effective in promoting conservation, lexical training is not.

Holland and Palermo (1975), for example, examined whether or not children's failure to conserve may stem from a failure to understand the terms *more* and *less*. Five-year-old children who treated *less* as synonymous with *more* were identified and half of these children were trained to differentiate *more* from *less*. Holland and Palermo noted the relative ease with which children learned the discrimination; however, despite their newfound linguistic competence, none of them showed an improvement over the untrained group in knowledge of conservation. A problem with this type of research is in identifying what lexical confusions are made by children. Subsequent investigation of children's understanding of the comparatives *more* and *less* has indicated that 4- and 5-year-old children do not treat *less* as synonymous with *more*, although they understand the concept of *more* sooner than *less* (Wannemacher & Ryan, 1978). The training conducted by Holland and Palermo may have simply reinforced what children knew already (but apparently didn't demonstrate as a consequence of procedural artifacts). A more effective manipulation might involve training children to specifically use the concept of *less*.

If we attempt to draw a conclusion to the general question considered thus far, we must be satisfied with the rather bland judgment, that language and thought are interactive. Questions of whether one (language or intellectual structure) is more important or which comes first are probably unanswerable. We do find some striking relationships between the development of language and thought. We've seen, for instance, that prelinguistic infants may develop some notion of agent–recipient relationships and an idea about the format of communicative exchange prior to acquiring language. But, as Schlesinger (1977) observes, the language environment must have some role in instructing the child about what are more acceptable ways of conceptualizing one's world (e.g., what things are more typically considered agents, recipients, or both).

VERBAL LANGUAGE AS A SPECIALIZED TOOL FOR THOUGHT

One salient characteristic of verbal language is its temporal-sequential quality. If we are to communicate with someone else, we must arrange words and other linguistic markers in some sequential order. Likewise, if we are to understand another's communications, we must decode some sequential string of information. Recognizing this sequential quality of verbal language, some researchers have suggested that the verbal code may be ideally suited for cognitive tasks that require sequential information processing (Blank, 1974; Paivio, 1970). Unlike a picture code, which is basically static, the verbal code is fluid, inherently conveying information about order. To demonstrate the value of verbal coding on sequential information-processing tasks, Paivio, Phillipchalk, and Rowe (1975) presented adults with 12-item lists of either line drawings, sounds of items (which subjects were told to label), or verbal labels of familiar objects. (For example, the subject might see a picture of a horse, hear a horse neighing, or hear the word *horse*.) Items were presented for about four seconds each, and after a list had been presented, subjects were given either a serial or a free-recall test. On free-recall tests, verbal and nonverbal stimuli were recalled equally well; on serial-recall tests, however, verbally presented items were recalled significantly better than pictures. (This effect is particularly salient as pictures are presented at presentation rates that prevent the subject from labeling items spontaneously.)

Additional research promoting the idea that verbal language facilitates sequential information processing has compared the performance of deaf and hearing children on tasks that can be solved via spatial or sequential-processing strategies. O'Connor and Hermelin presented deaf and hearing children with a series of items in a windowed apparatus with the windows spatially arranged in a left-to-right order (O'Connor & Hermelin, 1978, 1973a, b; Hermelin & O'Connor, 1973). Items were presented sequentially in each of the windows but in a manner that the temporal presentation didn't correspond to the left-to-right spatial ordering of the windows. O'Connor and Hermelin find that on tasks of this kind, deaf children tend to recall digits by the spatial order in which they occur (left-to-right), whereas hearing children tend to recall them in a temporal order (first-to-last).

It should not be inferred from this research that verbal language is prerequisite for seriation or coding temporal information (deaf children will process information in a first-to-last order if prompted to do so (O'Connor & Hermelin, 1973a; Jarman, 1979). A tendency to represent information in different sensory modalities, however, may predispose one to use specific types of conceptual strategies. For example, the focusing problem-solving strategy (discussed in Chapter 9) would seem to have a strong sequencing component to it—for example, constructing some hypothesis statement and sequentially testing the relevance of information in that statement. Focusing, as well as other conceptual processes that require sequential information processing, may be abetted by the presence of a verbal language (Gross, 1977a; Lipsitt & Eimas, 1972).

LANGUAGE AS AN EXECUTIVE SYSTEM

A final role that occasionally has been attributed to language is that of an executive or controller. Language has been regarded by some theorists as a system that, as it develops, provides us with a means of communicating with others as well as ourselves. That is, through the internalization of language, we can inhibit certain responses (White, 1965), while organizing other conceptual and behavioral sequences.

Two Soviet psychologists have strongly endorsed this position (Luria, 1982; Vygotsky, 1962). Luria, for example, proposes that the regulatory role of language progresses from one that is external and overt, to one that is internal and overt, to one that is internal and covert. As we develop, our behavior is first regulated by others' language. Our parents tell us what to do, when to do, and how to do. With time, however, our behavior becomes directed by our own verbalizations. At first these verbalizations are overt, as with the child who stares at the street and reminds herself aloud, "Don't play in the street. If you play in the street you'll get spanked." As we grow older though, these verbalizations are believed to be abbreviated and interiorized, serving at some unconscious level to regulate behavior (cf. Tinsley & Waters, 1982).

The use of Luria's ideas about the controlling aspects of language have been incorporated into training programs for the modification of impulsive children's behavior. Meichenbaum (1977) has argued that children who are impulsive (respond quickly and are prone to error in responding) don't use language appropriately to regulate their behavior. Whereas impulsive and reflective preschool children don't vary with respect to the quantity of their spontaneous verbalizations as they solve problems, they do vary in the quality of those verbalizations. Meichenbaum (1977), for example, observed that the private speech of impulsive children in a natural (nursery school) setting is often unrelated to the task at hand. Reflective children, on the other hand, tend to have more verbalizations that are directly related to the situation, and the frequency of these verbalizations increases in problem-solving situations. Additional work has demonstrated that requiring impulsive children to use task-appropriate, self-instructing verbalizations significantly facilitates their problem solving and that this improvement is directly related to their generation of self-guiding statements. Simply listening to someone else remind them to act a certain way has little effect on behavior; having children remind themselves does (Cohen, Schleser, & Meyers, 1981; Meichenbaum & Goodman, 1969, 1971).

SUMMARY

The relationship between language and thought is a complex one. We've seen that in some instances it would appear as though particular types of conceptual knowledge precede linguistic competence; however, we must also attend to the likelihood that our language environment has a powerful influence on how we conceptualize experience. There is widespread agreement among students of cognition that some language is important, if not necessary, for abstract reasoning—as for example on tasks that are believed to underlie formal operational ability.

The question "Is language dependent upon intellectual structure, or is the intellect shaped by language?" is complex and probably unanswerable. There is a belief among some psychologists, however, that language plays a specific role in cognitive activity. One line of research shows that particular types of language codes, either verbal or visual, may provide media for thought that are particularly adapted for special kinds of information processing (sequential or static). Another role attributed to language is that of behavior management. It is presumed that through the internalization of a language system we can organize and regulate behavior.

13

Applications

Today we place ever-increasing demands on the Earth's resources. And technology develops at a staggeringly rapid rate to assist us in discovering, conserving, and using these limited resources more efficiently. In the biological and physical sciences, advances in technology and resulting discoveries have been truly remarkable. Consequently, we have developed the optimism that we can accomplish whatever we can imagine.

Despite the exhilaration that accompanies advances in the hard sciences, it is soberingly clear that these sciences offer only incomplete solutions to the problems confronting humankind. In fact, advances in these sciences often complicate and confuse our understanding of ourselves. For example, artificial organs and life support systems have undoubtedly been a godsend for many, but they have also raised very thorny issues regarding life. "What defines life and death?" "How much of a human being can be replaced artificially before the person loses his or her humanness?" If we are to thrive as a species in such a complex world, it behooves us to discover not only the nature and

227

operation of ourselves as physical beings, but also the nature and operation of ourselves as thinking, conscious, and reflective psychosocial beings.

As we learn to conserve our planet's physical resources, we should also concern ourselves with the judicious use of human resources. We need to discover the uniquely human abilities and qualities we possess, and to apply them to our human experiences. Cognitive research has, in fact, contributed substantially to many facets of human experience (for example, information management and communications). However, three areas in particular profit from recent advances in cognitive development: psychometrics, education, and therapy.

PSYCHOMETRIC APPLICATIONS

In recent years there has been a controversy surrounding the use of standardized testing of mental abilities. Although this concern is laudable, much of it, unfortunately, is based upon popular misconceptions about testing and test scores. Nonetheless, with a growing activism against the use of standardized tests, psychometricians have begun to look toward the cognitive sciences for ideas about what is important to measure and how to measure it. Although we see the beginnings of an application of cognitive theory and research to psychometrics, the real potential to be gained from such an application is yet to be realized.

The Attitude toward Mental Testing

The history of mental testing in the United States is a curious one. Our society has for some time had a unique love–hate relationship with assessment. We have a peculiar enchantment with numbers, statistics, and technological gadgetry (cf. Hanley, 1981). As a society, we've become dependent upon tests for reasons both practical and frivolous. We're tested in school, we're tested on our jobs, and we amuse ourselves by completing tests for "this-and-that" featured in popular magazines, newspapers, radio, and television.

Because we deal with such large numbers of individuals in education, business, and industry, we use tests as a convenient means for screening, evaluating, placing, and selecting personnel. In their most benign form, tests provide a means for identifying those who might profit from particular kinds of help (educational and remedial), for ascertaining eligibility for particular benefits (social security and insurance claims), and for monitoring developmental progress. Until lately, we filled the needs of industry and education with standardized abilities tests that were reliable, moderately valid (at least in a predictive sense), and referenced to the performance of a population of individuals.

With the proliferation of standardized mental tests in America, the public has grown increasingly skeptical of their use (Hanley, 1981). These tests are seen as threats to individual rights and as a source of data for discriminatory public policy (cf. Gould, 1981). Controversy is not new to the testing movement, even though the issues change. Several issues are at the core of the current controversy and center around a concern for what tests measure (construct validity) and how test scores should be interpreted.

Issues of construct validity and score interpretation took on major importance as mental abilities tests were more frequently administered to minority groups. Test critics have argued that standardized mental abilities tests are culturally biased and, hence, prejudicial to the minority group evaluated. In one historic piece of litigation (*Larry P. v. Riles,* 1980), the Federal District Court in California enjoined the California Department of Education from using, permitting the use, or approving the use of any standardized intelligence test to identify black, educationally mentally retarded children for placement into special education classrooms. The court's decision was based on the judgment that standardized tests, in general, are culturally biased and therefore unfairly select a larger number of black children for placement into special education classrooms (see Bersoff, 1981).

The legal restrictions placed upon state departments of education put them in a predicament. By Public Law 94-142 these same departments are required to identify children who would profit from special educational experiences. Thus, the need to identify special groups of children conflicts with restraints imposed on the use of standardized tests (the tools of the psychometrician's trade). To resolve this dilemma, psychometricians have begun to look to the cognitive sciences for help. Specifically, an interest has developed in criterion-referenced testing (Anastasi, 1976, p. 280), or what is also known as "non-biased" testing and classification (Reschly, 1981).

An Integration of Cognitive Theory and Psychometrics

Both Piagetian and information-processing theories provide frameworks for criterion-referenced assessment. Rather than comparing an individual's performance to a group of peers, criterion-referenced testing compares an individual's performance to some nonbiased criterion, such as knowledge of a concept (e.g., conservation) or use of a strategy (e.g., rehearsal).

Piagetian tasks provide us with one set of criteria for evaluating children's knowledge. The use of Piagetian techniques allows us to exercise flexibility in both test administration and interpretation. Implicit in the use of these tasks is the belief that development follows a reliable and orderly course across cultures—although some variability exists between cultures regarding the ages at which children attain specific knowledge (Figurelli & Keller, 1972). It is this developmental sequence to which children's performance is referenced and their knowledge state inferred.

Although it is correct to characterize Piagetian assessment as unstandardized (especially in light of the rigid instructions that must be followed when administering a standardized mental abilities test), as interest in Piagetian assessment has increased, there has also been a trend toward formalizing test administration, scoring, and interpretation. Several available test kits purport to tap operative knowledge. These kits provide a standard set of test items, equipment, guidelines for administration (Goldschmid & Bentler, 1968; Uzgiris &

Hunt, 1975), and in some cases, even norms to which performance can be compared (Goldschmid & Bentler, 1968).

Information-processing theory also holds a promise for new directions in psychometrics (Sternberg, 1981). An application of information-processing theory to an assessment of individual differences leads us to examine what cognitive skills are tapped by tests and how individuals use various components of the information-processing system (perception, memory, and conceptual processes) in their performance. This tack yields more useful information than a reporting of test scores alone. Rather than asking if a child scored higher or lower than other children, we are required to consider why the child performed as he or she did. And, with attention focused on the information-processing system, the psychometrician's attention is directed to what many believe to be the most important criteria of a test—construct validity, or how well a test measures some hypothetical construct (Chronbach & Meehl, 1955).

Although information-processing theory holds great promise for the future of psychological assessment, it is not likely to be the short-term panacea that some might like. There is a host of factors that limit the direct extension of information-processing research to the assessment of individual differences. For one, the relationship between standardized tests of intelligence and components of the information-processing system are often quite low. Skills that are tapped by information-processing tasks are often simplistic and unrelated to the more complex kinds of information-processing that characterize the complex activities typically associated with intelligence. Furthermore, we aren't certain how the intellectual system should be characterized. Just recently, for example, theorists have included into their description of the information-processing system such constructs as executive schemes or systems and meta-cognitive components.

We are also a long way from adapting the methods of information-processing research to the assessment of individual differences. Current research methodology requires repeated and lengthy testing to obtain reliable estimates of ability level and often the use of expensive and unwieldy equipment (computers and tachistoscopes). There is also little information about the validity and reliability of the methods used in research (cf. Banks & Salapatek, 1981). For example, there is a persistent controversy over whether or not primacy effects in young children's serial recall reflect the use of a rehearsal strategy (Brown, Brown, & Caci, 1981) or merely artifacts of the test procedure (Siegel, Allik, & Herman, 1976).

Rather than offering the solution to the problem created by a test-hungry society, psychometricians seem to believe that the inclusion of information gained from both Piagetian and information-processing theory can supplement but not necessarily replace traditional assessment practices. If we are looking toward cognitive science for unbiased and culture-free tests of mental ability, our search will be in vain. There aren't, nor can there be, tests that are culturally unbiased (Scarr, 1978). Any attempt to construct such a test would be unreasonable on two accounts. First, we are all influenced by our culture from birth. Any learning therefore reflects the cultural context in which learning occurs. Second, to propose that it would be possible to assess intellectual ability independently of one's culture is to propose that test scores represent some innate or fixed intellectual capacity—a position abandoned by most psychologists many years ago (Anastasi, 1976, p. 61; Garcia, 1981; Reschly, 1981).

At best, cognitive psychology can suggest a new way of looking at test performance—a method that focuses on how individuals use and control the use of an information-processing system in order to gain an understanding of their surroundings. Neither Piagetian nor information-processing theories are ready-made substitutes for other assessment techniques. Like carpenters' tools, tests are only as good as the individuals who use them. We'd hardly trust an unskilled carpenter to build a house, and yet we have often placed tests and test scores in the hands of those least trained to use them. Good test-users must be aware of the multiplicity of factors that influence test performance and be sensitive to those factors in their interpretation of test performance. Supplementing standardized test information with information from criterion-related tests (such as those derived from Piagetian or information-processing theory) can provide a richer, more constructive, and more useful set of information to the evaluator and the individual evaluated.

EDUCATIONAL APPLICATIONS

As might have been deduced from previous chapters, the educational philosophies that follow from Piagetian and information-processing theory are quite different. On the one hand, Piagetian theory focuses upon the creation of a learning environment that is appropriate to a child's level of intellectual development. Information-processing theory emphasizes the importance of training programs that build sequentially skills that are prerequisite to the use of information.

Assumptions Underlying an Extension of Cognitive Theory to Education

In spite of the very different educational philosophies that derive from these two approaches, there are several similarities. Both theories presume that a motivation to learn is inherent to all individuals. Cognitive theory operates on the assumption that discrepancies between what one understands and what one perceives to be real produces tension, which, in turn, motivates the individual either to accommodate his or her intellectual structure (as in Piagetian theory) or to acquire strategies and rules, or make discriminations (as in information-procesing theory).

The role of the educator in both theories is one of a sensitive monitor of the child's way of understanding the world or manner of processing information. Since both theories emphasize the internal structuring of the intellect, the educator must be sensitive to the child's cognitions. Having ascertained the child's cognitive status, the educator must provide educational experiences that foster cognitive tension (using a more common phrase, they must "challenge children") and thus promote cognitive growth.

A Piagetian Approach to Education

The manner in which the educator creates tension differs depending upon one's theoretical orientation. Piaget (1970) believed that there are essentially two types of learning. One of these can be considered associative learning—learning about the physical (figurative) properties of things in the environment. This is a static type of learning (knowing that water is wet and the sky is blue). Another type of learning involves the discovery of relationships that exist within one's world. Acquisition of associative knowledge can be done by a passive organism, but knowledge about how things are related or how they can be transformed (operative knowledge) must be acquired through active manipulation. As Piaget observed,

> The essential function of intelligence consists in understanding and inventing, in other words, in building up structures by structuring reality. It increasingly appears, in fact, that these two functions are inseparable, since, in order to understand a phenomenon or an event, we must reconstitute the transformations of which they are resultant, and since, also, in order to reconstitute them, we must have worked out a structure of transformations, which presupposes an element of invention or reinvention. [1970, pp. 27–28]

Piaget's view of what constitutes learning and education has profound implications for pedagogy. Specifically, education in traditional classrooms where students take notes and teachers lecture (receptive approaches) were anathema to Piaget. By his definition, they are inappropriate to the acquisition of operative knowledge. In order to learn, a student must be actively involved with elements in the world; only in this way can relationships and transformations implied in the structuring of those experiences be learned. One does not come to appreciate the additivity of units by observing a teacher write "2 + 2 = 4" on a blackboard. Children presumably learn about the combinatorial properties of units by manipulating them—measuring liquids with measuring cups, measuring lengths with rulers, or counting squares of tiles on a floor.

Activity alone doesn't guarantee the acquisition of knowledge. As is typical of Piaget's view of development, education is also qualified by developmental level. Piaget states, "The development of intelligence . . . is dependent upon a natural, or spontaneous, process, in the sense that it may be utilized and accelerated by education at home or in school but that it is not derived from that education and, on the contrary, constitutes the preliminary and necessary condition of efficacy in any form of instruction." It is also noted that emphasis should be placed upon the conditions preliminary and necessary. As Piaget reasons, experience is not a sufficient condition, "because maturation of the nervous system is not complete until about the fifteenth or sixteenth year, it therefore seems evident that it does play a necessary role in the formation of mental structures, even though very little is known about that role" (1970, p.36).

Learning in the Piagetian sense is a complex interaction between maturation and experience. Obviously, in order to be effective educators, we must take into account the maturational level of children. Not only must we discern what children are communicating about their understanding of the world, we must communicate with them in such a manner that knowledge can be assimilated. For example, until children can grasp the concept of a series, it is pointless to provide them with numerical lessons that require the manipulation or transformation of the ordinal, sequential properties of numbers.

Good education involves sequencing. In fact, both Piagetian and information-processing theories emphasize the importance of sequencing instruction—although the nature of the sequence varies between approaches. Within the Piagetian approach, learning sequences must conserve the basic developmental order. For example, consider the number of activities necessary for reading. First, one must develop a concept of a letter. From the Piagetian perspective, the internalization of letter concepts (the construction of letter schemes) is facilitated by active learning. Activity may involve eye movement, tracking letters with fingers, or tracing letter patterns with the body or by writing (Elkind, 1981a). In this manner, it is presumed that children abstract some common schema that can be applied to the recognition of letters that are constructed differently, but schematically share common properties. The ability to perform these activities is dependent upon semiotic function and the coordination of sensorimotor schemes involved in pattern recognition. It is believed that not until 3 or 4 years of age do children have the intellectual maturity to perform these tasks.

Following the internalization of letter schemes, children must learn to associate phonemic with graphic symbols. Children must perceive the letter as a transformation having functional significance—that is, that the letter represents something else, for instance a sound. (Elkind [1981c] refers to this as "identity decoding.") But preschool children perceive an object as having but one function. A letter has one sound or a word one verbal equivalent. Such a perception is problematic for children learning English, since English letters don't have individual correspondences to sounds. For example, the o sound is different in box ($\breve{a}$) and go ($\bar{o}$). Children who learn to read in languages that have greater individual correspondences between letters and sounds (Spanish and Japanese) learn to read the alphabet faster and at an earlier age (Elkind, 1981).

When teaching letter sound equivalents, Piagetians would advocate the use of the Initial Teaching Alphabet (an alphabet of 44 characters representing each of the different English phonemes) (Downing, 1963, 1965). Because children tend to have a one-to-one correspondence between object and function, learning the standard English alphabet (with its multiple object-function relationships) would be a task mismatched to young children's way of thinking. With the advent of concrete operational thought, children are capable of coordinating several dimensions simultaneously, and, therefore, we would anticipate that the standard English alphabet would begin to make sense to these children. The ability to use the standard English alphabet derives from the acquisition of two operations: logical addition and logical multiplication. By using logical addition, children realize that elements can be combined to form some larger class of objects. Thus, the short sound of ($\breve{a}$) and the long sound of ($\bar{a}$) combine to create a class of sounds that characterize the letter a. By using logical multiplication, the child is able to coordinate two classes to arrive at a third defined by their intersect. Thus, children can appreciate that the hard sound of k (k) can be produced by c (as in *can*) or by k (as in *kangaroo*) or by both c and k (as in *check*). Advocates of a Piagetian perspective would propose that introducing equivalence training into a reading curriculum prior to the stage of concrete operational thought would be counterproductive; children prior to this stage aren't believed to have the intellectual structure necessary to profit from this training.

There are a variety of approaches to teaching reading; however, one that seems to conserve much of what is advocated by the Piagetian position is what Singer (1981a) refers to as the language-experience approach (Lee & Van Allen, 1963). In keeping with the emphasis that Piaget places upon active involvement in the learning process, this approach presumes that learning to read is facilitated by having the learner construct meaningful and useful contexts in which the skills necessary for reading become self-evident. Students learning to read within this approach are encouraged to construct stories about their experiences. These stories are written out by the teacher (ultimately to be performed by the child), and children are encouraged to "read" the stories they have written. The reading process evolves as children are encouraged to read by using language expectancies and experiences to recognize and anticipate sentences, then words, then letter-sound correspondences. Thus, learning procedes in a top-down fashion.

An Information-Processing Approach to Education

The information-processing approach to education also emphasizes the importance of sequencing, but with a different emphasis on what needs to be sequenced. This position advocates the notion that skills can be arranged in some hierarchical fashion with lower-level skills being prerequisite for higher-level ones (cf. Fischer, 1980). Gibson (1965; Gibson & Levin, 1975) has characterized how reading skills might be taught by hierarchically sequencing skills. First she proposes the need to discriminate written symbols, next to decode letter sounds, then to learn variable and constant properties of letters, and finally to combine letters into higher order units of information.

In Gibson's analysis, children can be taught to make discriminant responses to letter characters. Once letters are discriminated by children, they are ready to associate sounds with words. Unlike Elkind (1981a), Gibson doesn't view the overlap between English letters and sounds as problematic to a child's acquisition of letter-sound correspondence. Although she acknowledges that the initial acquisition of letter-sound equivalence is slowed by learning an alphabet such as English, she also believes that such variability may actually facilitate later learning once the child has acquired a set for diversity.

A final step in reading, according to Gibson, is the acquisition of higher-order units (the perception of spelling patterns), or "clusters of graphemes in a given environment which [have] an invariant pronunciation according to the rules of English" (1965, p. 1071). Whereas in the initial stage of reading ability, spelling patterns and regularities in the organization of specific graphemes may be responded to by young children (first-graders), they are typically "read" in shorter units. As children become older, they develop the faculty for perceiving larger sequences of letters as meaningful units, making better use of both syntactic and semantic rules in organizing letter and word sequences.

In contrast to the approach advocated by the Piagetians, information-processing theory typically advocates a bottom-to-top approach to learning. As will be recalled from Chapter 3, performance deficiencies in children are thought to stem from skill deficiencies. Hence, the preferred pedagogy is one that emphasizes skill development, or, the skill-based approach (Singer, 1981b). The development of lower-order skills is linked in a logical sequence to higher-order ones. Piaget has been particularly critical of these types of approaches, observing that they are typically receptive and often devoid of meaningful contexts.

A Comparison of Piagetian- and Information-Processing-Based Instructional Programs

Although Piagetian and alternate educational philosophies suggest differing pedagogy, systematic attempts to evaluate their effectiveness have been few in number and often methodologically flawed (cf. Lawton & Hooper, 1978). Comparisons of various teaching methodologies have found little evidence that one approach is better than the other. Indeed, factors that seem important to an effective teaching program—such as the commitment of the teachers to the program, the consistency of daily routine, daily planning, and evaluation—appear unrelated to the theory or philosophy from which the program is developed (Lawton & Hooper, 1978; Singer, 1981b).

In an examination of four educational programs developed from interpretations of Piaget's theory, Lawton and Hooper (1978) found that none clearly demonstrated significant changes in performance that could be attributed to the training program. Other studies of teaching methodology, evaluating a wide range of curriculum approaches from experience-based to skill-based approaches, have also failed to demonstrate the effectiveness of any one approach (Bond & Dykstra, 1967).

Defenders of Piagetian-based programs have argued that they have not been given ample time to demonstrate their program's effectiveness. They argue that pressure is placed upon demonstration programs to produce short-term results, while Piagetian programs emphasize a type of learning that is more gradual and apparent only after long periods of time (Lawton & Hooper, 1978; Singer, 1981b). Furthermore, the criteria that are used to evaluate programs may often be incompatible with the type of knowledge that Piagetian programs teach (associative versus operative knowledge). Indeed, it is possible that fundamental differences in theory and educational philosophy may create a condition in which it may be virtually impossible to evaluate one pedagogy relative to another. A more fundamental question, which may be an example of begging the question, is what kind of pedagogy do we as a society find desirable and important?

Although strong empirical support has not yet been shown for the Piagetian approach to education, neither can much be said for the skill-based approaches. Skill-based approaches (for example, traditional phonics programs emphasizing letter-sound correspondence, which move toward combinations of sounds to form words), have been found, however, to promote better short-term gains in word recognition when compared to other approaches (Bond & Dykstra, 1967). One characteristic of the information-processing approaches to education is the idea that there be a development of subskills in a systematic manner (cf. Singer, 1981a). Despite this most fundamental assumption of the information-processing view, however, there is little evidence to support the idea that any one particular sequence of skill development is necessary for particular types of learning (Samuels, 1976).

An Application of Cognitive Theory to Education Programs for the Mentally Handicapped

In addition to suggesting how cognitive theory might be translated into mainstream educational practice, cognitive research has also begun to provide a useful source of information on the specific processing and skill deficits of mentally handicapped children. This information is a potential windfall to educators because it breaks away from the traditional practice of identification and classification to descriptions of what specific limitations produce performance deficits. Obviously this approach not only identifies children who have learning handicaps, but also provides a guide to remediation. As we've seen before, both Piagetian and information-processing theories differ with respect to how they characterize intelligence and, consequently, how the mentally retarded can be helped.

Piagetians view mental retardation as a fixation of mental development at lower stages of development. Inhelder (1968) saw the severely retarded fixated at the sensorimotor stage, the trainable mentally retarded fixated at the preoperational stage, and the educable mentally retarded stuck at the period of concrete operations. Knowing about the structure of the intellect at each of these stages provides the educator with information about how children interpret reality and should suggest to the educator stage-appropriate lessons. In fact, several training studies have demonstrated the value of active learning experiences coupled with specific instruction in operative rules for facilitating the mental development of educable mental retardates (Sternlicht, 1981).

Information-processing research focuses on specific skills that are absent or not used by mentally handicapped children. Although retarded children perform equivalently to nonretarded children on some tasks (for example, recognition memory tasks), they perform much more poorly on tasks requiring active processing of information.

Current thinking on the nature of mental retardation (from an information-processing perspective) points to the inefficiency with which retardates use strategies and their failure to generalize or transfer strategies to new situations (Campione, Brown, & Ferrara, 1982). Although mentally retarded children are believed to have the capacity to learn strategies and rules that will elevate their performance to levels comparable to nonretarded children, they don't spontaneously extrapolate knowledge about strategy use from training programs. In order for training to be effective with retarded populations, a greater degree of specificity in training is required, and specific attention needs to be given to developing training programs that foster the generalization of rules and strategies to new and unfamiliar contexts.

Problems in the Extension of Cognitive Theory to Educational Practice

In reconsidering the contributions of cognitive theory to education, we're left with the impression that both Piagetian and information-processing theory have generated some interesting ideas about how education might proceed. We've yet to demonstrate, however, that either theory can provide a useful guide to curriculum construction. Problems exist within both theories that have limited their usefulness in educational settings. For example, within both theories, concepts and relationships are vaguely defined and, in fact, are empirically undemonstrated. Piaget, for example, has argued that the coordination of operations within stages leads to the ability to generalize knowledge to new situations. However, such an assumption has never been demonstated to be unequivocably true (Lawton & Hooper, 1978). With respect to information-processing theory, important components of the information-processing system and the relationships between these components, as yet, are not well specified. Brown (1979) and Campione et al. (1982) have noted the importance of metacognitive knowledge in reading and other activities; yet, the metacognitive component has been typically ignored in many traditional skill-based approaches to education and has only recently captured the attention of developmental psychologists.

The problems inherent in theories can create havoc when the theory is used to guide curriculum development. Unvalidated theoretical assumptions may be taken as empirical fact when placed in a pedagogical framework. The Piagetian notion of developmental sequencing and the use of stage as an index of educational readiness has been more apparent than real, and such an assumption needs greater study before it is accepted as fact (Lawton & Hooper, 1978). Ambiguity in theory also leads to a variety of curricular interpretation. Preschool programs developed about a "Piagetian" framework have been considerably varied in materials, structure of the learning environment, concepts taught, and outcomes anticipated and measured.

To presume that most educational programs are founded upon some well-established, well-researched cognitive–behavioral theory is naive. The bridge between psychology and education that John Dewey envisioned over 100 years ago is yet under construction. Many observers of the educational scene

(Elkind, 1981b; Piaget, 1970) have noted the artistic manner in which educators have created curriculum, and indeed, Singer (1981b) observes the institutionalized attitude that it is the teacher rather than the method that makes a difference in education. For those who decry the failure of these methods to prove their worth, it is only fair to regard the evidence with some reserve. The few programs that have attempted to compare instructional approaches have been small-scale demonstration projects (with the possible exception of the Piagetian-influenced British primary educational system) (Elkind, Hetzel, & Coe, 1981). One is, in fact, struck by the limited extent to which cognitive research and theory have been applied to the American educational scene.

THERAPEUTIC APPLICATIONS

Over the past several years a considerable amount of research has developed around the application of cognitive self-regulation or self-monitoring techniques in the treatment of a variety of behavioral disorders. This form of treatment has been found to be effective with both children and adults. The therapy itself, referred to as cognitive behavior modification, involves the induction of verbal, self-instruction coupled with a fading technique, which presumably promotes the internalization of self-guiding principles (Meichenbaum, 1977). This work is heavily influenced by the work of Luria (1982) and others, who advocate the systematic internalization of a verbal, self-regulatory system. The procedure itself is modeled directly after the steps believed to accompany the internalization of the self-regulatory system discussed by Luria (see Chapter 12).

In cognitive behavior modification, children are first exposed to an adult model who demonstrates a task. While accomplishing the task, the model talks aloud, verbalizing important steps within the task, focusing attention on the task, self-evaluating, and reinforcing one's self for performance. Following adult modeling, children are required to perform the same task while the adult verbalizes the steps to be taken, evaluates performance, and instructs the child. Next, the child is required to perform the task, but verbalizing aloud to him- or herself. And, finally children are required to perform the task while "talking" to themselves silently.

One early study that examined this type of intervention was conducted by Meichenbaum and Goodman (1971). In this study impulsive children's performance improved significantly on tasks that required reflective and controlled responding (for example, the Porteus Maze test and the Matching Familiar Figures test; see Figure 13-1) following cognitive behavioral modification. Other work reviewed by Meichenbaum (1977) supports the *promise* of this approach for working with individuals across a wide range of mental ability levels (also see Gow & Ward, 1980). The word *promise* is used purposefully; as acknowledged by both Meichenbaum (1977) and others (Hobbs, Moguin, Tyroler, & Lahey, 1980), systematic studies of the effectiveness of this partic-

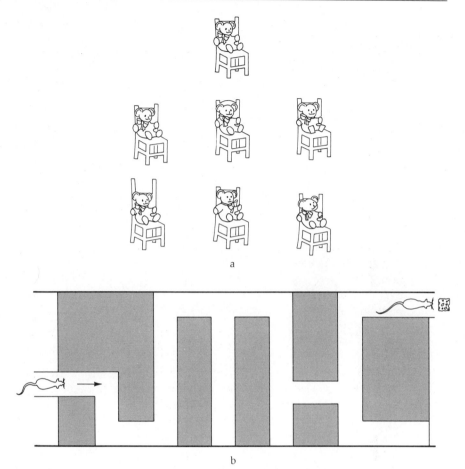

a

b

Figure 13-1. Sample items from (a) the Matching Familiar Figures Test (in which children must match the standard on top with one of the items below, *Kagan, 1966*) and (b) the Porteus Maze Test (in which children must trace a line through the maze without touching the sides, *Porteus, 1950*).

ular therapeutic technique have not been entirely consistent. No single outcome measure has been shown to be reliably affected by cognitive behavior modification. In fact, it is unclear just exactly why this particular form of behavior modification works when it does.

Meichenbaum (1977) obviously believes that the strength of the method lies with the internalization of some verbal, regulatory system. Showing children a cognitive, self-verbalizing model alone shouldn't produce effective behavioral change; change occurs when children internalize this process and hence assume control of their own behavior. Another possibility is that these self-modification programs induce children to adopt alternate information-processing strategies—strategies that facilitate performance on tasks specific to those that require part (rather than whole) processing such as the Matching Familiar Figures Test (Zelniker et al., 1977).

Despite disagreement about how this process works, there is a general optimism about the value of cognitive instructional techniques in therapy. The reason for this optimism is found when one considers the range of behaviors that therapists have attempted to modify with the technique. For example, the list includes such behaviors as social introversion (Jakibchuk & Smergilio, 1976; Oden & Asher, 1977), resistance to temptation (Kanfer & Zich, 1974), and hyperactivity and aggression (Goodwin & Mahoney, 1975). As with any new technique, it should be an optimism tempered with some caution for its shortcomings. Hobbs et al. (1980) have cited a number of problems with studies that have used this technique. Very few studies, for example, have actually been conducted on clinical populations. Rather, much of this research has involved normal school children who have been conveniently classified into research populations (impulsive and reflective subjects). Thus, little is known about how this technique actually works with clinical populations. As mentioned earlier, research that has been conducted has failed to demonstrate that any one behavior is consistently modified as a consequence of intervention. The general opinion regarding cognitive behavior modification is that the technique warrants further study; its value is not so much in what it is now, but in a hope for what it might become.

SUMMARY

With all three applications of cognitive developmental research, it has been suggested that there is a great promise for the integration of theory and research findings into the solution of many of the practical problems confronting society. This optimism is not founded in the state of the art, but rather the potential that the cognitive sciences hold. Cognitive psychology is the study of how individuals perceive, acquire, store, evaluate, use, and manage information. These processes are fundamentally important to virtually all kinds of human endeavor. As you have seen in this text, we have begun to gain some understanding of how we, as information users, develop. We would be shortsighted, if not foolish, to believe that we are even close to understanding how this system as a whole operates. We do have some insights, and it would profit us to explore more thoroughly how these insights might be integrated into the ever-evolving solutions that we contrive to address to the more practical and mundane aspects of our existence.

References

Ackerman, B. P. Children's recall of contextually integrable and nonintegrable episodic events. *Journal of Experimental Child Psychology,* 1982, *33,* 429–438.

Acredolo, C., & Acredolo, L. P. Identity, compensation, and conservation. *Child Development,* 1979, *50,* 524–535.

Acredolo, L. P. The development of spatial orientation in infancy. *Developmental Psychology,* 1978, *14,* 224–234.

Acredolo, L. P., & Evans, D. Developmental changes in the effects of landmarks on infant's spatial behavior. *Developmental Psychology,* 1980, *16,* 312–318.

Adams, M. J. Logical competence and transitive inference in young children. *Journal of Experimental Child Psychology,* 1978, *25,* 477–489.

Alexander, R. Pattern rate and inter-pattern intervals in development of matching simple auditory-visual patterns. *Developmental Psychology,* 1977, *13,* 332–336.

Allen, D. V. Acoustic interference in paired-associate learning as a function of hearing abilities. *Psychonomic Science,* 1970, *18,* 231–233.

Allen, D. V. Color-word interference in deaf and hearing children. *Psychonomic Science,* 1971, *1971,* 295–296.

Allik, J., & Valsiner, J. Visual development in ontogenesis: Some reevaluations. In H. W. Reese & L. P. Lipsitt (Eds.), *Advances in child development and behavior* (Vol. 15). New York: Academic Press, 1980.

Altemeyer, R., Fulton, D., & Berney, K. Long-term memory improvement: Confirmation of a finding by Piaget. *Child Development,* 1969, *40,* 845–857.

Anastasi, A. *Psychological testing* (4th ed.). New York: Macmillan, 1976.

Anderson, D. R., & Clark, A. T. Comparison of conservation training procedures. *Psychological Reports,* 1978, *43,* 495–499.

Anderson, D. R., & Levin, S. R. Young children's attention to "Sesame Street." *Child Development,* 1976, *47,* 806–811.

241

Anderson, J. R., & Bower, G. H. *Human associative memory.* Washington, D.C.: Winston, 1973.

Anderson, R. C. Can first graders learn an advanced problem solving skill. *Journal of Educational Psychology,* 1965, *56,* 283–294.

Anderson, R. C. Part versus whole task procedures for teaching. *Journal of Educational Psychology,* 1968, *59,* 207–214.

Annoshian, L. J., Hartman, S. R., & Scharf, J. S. Determinants of young children's search strategies in large scale environments. *Developmental Psychology.* 1982, *18,* 608–616.

Annoshian, L. J., & McCulloch, R. A. Developmental changes in dichotic listening with categorized word lists. *Developmental Psychology,* 1979, *15,* 280–287.

Antell, S. E., & Keating, D. P. Perception of numerical invariance in neonates. *Child Development,* 1983, *54,* 695–701.

Appel, L. F., Cooper, R. B., McCarrel, N., Sims-Knight, J., Yussen, S., & Flavell, J. H. The development of the distinction between perceiving and memorizing. *Child Development,* 1972, *43,* 1365–1381.

Aronson, E., & Rosenbloom, S. Space perception in early infancy: Perception within a common auditory-visual space. *Science,* 1971, *172,* 1161.

Asarnow, J. R., & Meichenbaum, D. Verbal rehearsal and serial recall: The mediational training of kindergarten children. *Child Development,* 1979, *50,* 1173–1177.

Aslin, R. N., Pisoni, D. B., Hennessy, B. L., & Perey, A. J. Discrimination of voice onset time by human infants: New findings and implications for the effects of early experience. *Child Development,* 1981, *52,* 1135–1145.

Atkinson, R. C., Hansen, D. N., & Bernbach, H. A. Short-term memory with young children. *Psychonomic Science,* 1964, *1,* 255–256.

Atkinson, R. C., & Shiffrin, R. M. Human memory: A proposed system and its control processes. In K. W. Spence & J. T. Spence (Eds.), *The psychology of learning and motivation* (Vol. 2). New York: Academic Press, 1968.

Baddeley, A. D. Short-term memory or word sequences as a function of acoustic, semantic and formal similarity. *Quarterly Journal of Experimental Psychology,* 1966, *18,* 362–368.

Baddeley, A. D. The trouble with levels: A reexamination of Craik and Lockhart's framework for memory research. *Psychological Review,* 1978, *85,* 139–152.

Baddeley, A. D., & Warrington, E. K. Amnesia and the distinction between long- and short-term memory. *Journal of Verbal Learning and Verbal Behavior,* 1970, *9,* 176–189.

Baldwin, J. M. James Mark Baldwin. In C. Murchinson (Ed.), *A history of psychology in autobiography* (Vol. 1). Worcester, Mass.: Clark University Press, 1930.

Banks, M. S., & Salapatek, P. Infant pattern vision: A new approach based on the contrast sensitivity function. *Journal of Experimental Child Psychology,* 1981, *31,* 1–45.

Barrera, M. E., & Maurer, D. Discrimination of strangers by the three-month-old. *Child Development,* 1981, *52,* 558–563. (a)

Barrera, M. E., & Maurer, D. Recognition of mother's photographed face by the three-month-old. *Child Development,* 1981, *52,* 714–716. (b)

Barstsis, S. W., & Ford, L. H., Jr. Reflexion-impulsivity, conservation, and the development of the ability to control cognitive tempo. *Child Development,* 1977, *48,* 953–959.

Bartlett, F. C. *Remembering: A study in experimental and social psychology.* New York: Macmillan, 1932.

Bartoshuk, A. K. Human neonatal cardiac acceleration to sound: Habituation and dishabituation. *Perceptual Motor Skills,* 1962, *15,* 15–17.

Baumeister, A. A., & Smith, S. Thematic elaboration and proximity in children's recall, organization, and long-term retention of pictorial materials. *Journal of Experimental Child Psychology,* 1979, *28,* 132–148.

Beagles-Roos, J., & Gat, I. Specific impact of radio and television on children's story comprehension. *Journal of Educational Psychology,* 1983, *75,* 128–137.

Beilin, H. *Studies in the cognitive basis of language development.* New York: Academic Press, 1975.

Beilin, H. Constructing cognitive operations linguistically. In H. W. Reese (Ed.), *Advances in child development and behavior* (Vol. 11). New York: Academic Press, 1976.

Beilin, H. Piaget's theory: Refinement, revision or rejection? In R. H. Kluwe & H. Spada (Eds.), *Developmental models of thinking.* New York: Academic Press, 1980.

Beilin, H., & Franklin, I. C. Logical operations in area and length measurement: Age and training effects. *Child Development,* 1962, *33,* 607–618.

Bell, S. The development of the concept of object and its relationship to infant–mother attachment. *Child Development,* 1970, *41,* 291–312.

Bellotti v. *Baird (II);* 99 S. Ct. 3035 (1979).

Belugi, V., Klima, E. S., & Sipple, P. Remembering in signs. *Cognition,* 1976, *3,* 93–124.

Belmont, J. M. Relations of age and intelligence to short-term color memory. *Child Development,* 1972, *43,* 19–29.

Bersoff, D. N. Testing and the law. *American Psychologist,* 1981, *36,* 1047–1056.

Bertenthal, B. I., Campos, J. J., & Haith, M. M. Development of visual organization: The perception of subjective contours. *Child Development,* 1980, *51,* 1072–1080.

Blackburne-Stover, G., Belenky, M. F., & Gilligan, C. Moral development and reconstructive memory: Recalling a decision to terminate an unplanned pregnancy. *Developmental Psychology,* 1982, *18,* 862–870.

Blanks, M. Cognitive functions of language in preschool years. *Developmental Psychology,* 1974, *10,* 229–245.

Bloom, L., Lightbrown, P., & Hood, L. Structure and variation as child language. *Monographs and the Society for Research in Child Development,* 1975, *40,* (2, serial no. 160).

Bond, G. L., & Dykstra, R. The cooperative research program in first grade reading instruction. *Reading Research Quarterly,* 1967, *2,* 5–142.

Bornstein, H., & Roy, H. L. Comment on "Linguistic deficiency and thinking: Research with deaf subjects 1964–1969." *Psychological Bulletin,* 1973, *79,* 211–214.

Bornstein, M. H. Chromatic vision in infancy. In H. W. Reese & L. D. Lipsitt (Eds.), *Advances in child development and behavior* (Vol. 12). New York: Academic Press, 1978.

Bornstein, M. H., Ferdinandsen, K., & Gross, C. G. Perception of symmetry in infancy. *Developmental Psychology,* 1981, *17,* 82–86.

Boswell, D. A., & Green, H. F. The abstraction and recognition of prototypes by children and adults. *Child Development,* 1982, *53,* 1028–1037.

Bourne, L. E., Jr. *Human conceptual behavior.* Boston: Allyn & Bacon, 1966.

Bousfield, W. A. The occurrence of clustering and the recall of randomly arranged associates. *Journal of General Psychology,* 1953, *49,* 229–240.

Bower, G. H., & Trabasso, T. Reversals prior to solution in concept identification. *Journal of Experimental Psychology,* 1963, *66,* 409–418.

Bower, T. G. R. Slant perception and shape constancy in infants. *Science,* 1966, *151,* 832–834. (a)

Bower, T. G. R. The visual world of infants. *Scientific American,* 1966, *215,* 80–92. (b)

Bower, T. G. R. *Development in infancy.* San Francisco, Calif.: W. H. Freeman, 1974.

Bower, T. G. R. *A primer of infant development.* San Francisco, Calif.: W. H. Freeman, 1977.

Braine, M. D. S. The ontogeny of certain logical operations: Piaget's formulation examined by nonverbal methods. *Psychological Monograhs,* 1959, *73,* No. 5.

Braine, M. D. S., & Shanks, B. C. The conservation of shape property and a proposal about the origin of conservations. *Canadian Journal of Psychology,* 1965, *19,* 197–207.

Brainerd, C. J. *The stage problem in behavioral development.* Unpublished manuscript, University of Alberta, 1973.

Brainerd, C. J. Learning research and Piagetian theory. In L. S. Siegel & C. J. Brainerd (Eds.), *Alternatives to Piaget: Critical essays on the theory.* New York: Academic Press, 1978. (a)

Brainerd, C. J. The stage question in cognitive-developmental theory. *The Behavioral and Brain Sciences,* 1978, *2,* 173–213. (b)

Brainerd, C. J. Commentary. In L. Hood & L. Bloom, What, when and how about why: A longitudinal study of early expression and causality. *Monographs of the Society for Research in Child Development,* 1979, *44* (Serial No. 181).

Bremner, J. G. Spatial errors made by infants: Inadequate spatial cues or evidence of egocentrism? *British Journal of Psychology,* 1978, *69,* 77–84.

Bremner, J. G., & Bryant, P. E. Place versus response as the basis of spatial errors made by infants. *Journal of Experimental Child Psychology,* 1977, *23,* 163–171.

Breslow, L. Reevaluation of the literature on the development of transitive inferences. *Psychological Bulletin,* 1981, *89,* 325–351.

Broadbent, D. E. *Perception and communication.* New York: Pergamon Press, 1958.

Brodzinsky, D. M. Relationship between cognitive style and cognitive development: A 2-year longitudinal study. *Developmental Psychology,* 1982, *18,* 617–626.

Broerse, J., Peltola, C., & Crassini, B. Infants' reaction to perceptual paradox during mother-infant interaction. *Developmental Psychology,* 1983, *19,* 310–316.

Brosseau, R., & Andrist, R. K. *Looking forward: Life in the twentieth century as predicted in the pages of American magazines from 1895 to 1905.* New York: American Heritage Press, 1970.

Brown, A. L. Judgments of recency for long sequences of pictures: The absence of a developmental trend. *Journal of Experimental Child Psychology,* 1973, *15,* 473–480.

Brown, A. L. The development of memory: Knowing about knowing, and knowing how to know. In H. W. Reese (Ed.), *Advances in child development and behavior* (Vol. 10). New York: Academic Press, 1975. (a)

Brown, A. L. Recognition, reconstruction, and recall of narrative sequences by preoperational children. *Child Development,* 1975, *46,* 156–166. (b)

Brown, A. L. Knowing when, where, and how to remember: A problem of metacognition. In R. Glaser (Ed.), *Advances in instructional psychology* (Vol. 1). Hillsdale, N.J.: Erlbaum, 1978.

Brown, A. L. *Metacognitive development and reading.* Unpublished manuscript, Center for the Study of Reading, University of Illinois, Urbana, Illinois, 1979.

Brown, A. L., & Campione, J. C. Training strategic study time apportionment in educable retarded children. *Intelligence,* 1977, *1,* 94–107.

Brown, A. L., & Murphy, M. D. Reconstruction of arbitrary versus logical sequences by preschool children. *Journal of Experimental Child Psychology,* 1975, *20,* 307–326.

Brown, R., & Bellugi, U. Three processes in the child's acquisition of syntax. *Harvard Educational Review,* 1964, *34,* 133–151.

Brown, R., & McNeil, D. The "tip of the tongue" phenomenon. *Journal of Verbal Learning and Verbal Behavior,* 1966, *5,* 377–382.

Brown, R. M. An examination of visual and verbal coding processes in preschool children. *Child Development,* 1977, *48,* 38–45.

Brown, R. M., Brown, N., & Caci, M. Serial position effects in young children: Temporal or spatial? *Child Development,* 1981, *52,* 1191–1201.

Brown, R. W., & Lenneberg, E. H. A study in language and cognition. *Journal of Abnormal and Social Psychology,* 1954, *49,* 454–462.

Bruner, J. S. On the course of cognitive growth. *American Psychologist,* 1964, *19,* 1–15.

Bruner, J. S. Culture and cognitive growth. In J. M. Anglin (Ed.), *Beyond the information given.* New York: Norton, 1973. (a)

Bruner, J. S. The growth of representational processes in childhood. In J. M. Anglin (Ed.), *Beyond the information given.* New York: Norton, 1973. (b)

Bruner, J. S. Learning how to do things with words. In J. S. Bruner & A. Garton (Eds.), *Human growth and development.* Oxford: Clarendon Press, 1978.

Bruner, J. S., Goodnow, J. J., & Austin, G. A. *A study of thinking.* New York: Wiley, 1956.

Bruner, J. S., Olver, R. R., & Greenfield, P. M. *Studies in cognitive growth.* New York: Wiley, 1966.

Bruner, J. S., & Porter, M. C. Interference in visual recognition. *Science,* 1964, *144,* 242–245.

Bryant, P. E., & Trabasso, T. Transitive inferences and memory in young children. *Nature,* 1971, *232,* 456–458.

Bugelski, B. R. Words and things and images. *American Psychologist,* 1970, *25,* 1002–1012.

Burns, S. M., & Brainerd, C. J. Effects of constructive and dramatic play on perspective taking in very young children. *Developmental Psychology,* 1979, *15,* 512–521.

Buss, R. R., Yussen, S. R., Mathews II, S. R., Miller, G. E., & Rembold, K. L. Development of children's use of story schema to retrieve information. *Developmental Psychology,* 1983, *19,* 22–28.

Butterworth, G. Object disappearance and error in Piaget's stage IV task. *Journal of Experimental Child Psychology,* 1977, *23,* 391–401.

Butterworth, G., Jarret, N., & Hicks, L. Spatiotemporal identity in infancy: Perceptual competence or conceptual deficit? *Developmental Psychology,* 1982, *18,* 435–449.

Caldwell, E. C., & Hall, V. C. Concept learning in discrimination tasks. *Development Psychology,* 1970, *2,* 41–48.

Calvert, S. L., Huston, A. C., Watkins, B. A., & Wright, J. C. The relation between selective attention to television forms and children's comprehension of content. *Child Development,* 1982, *53,* 601–610.

Campione, J. C., Brown, A. L., & Ferrara, R. A. Mental retardation and intelligence. In R. J. Sternberg (Ed.), *Handbook of human intelligence.* Cambridge, England: Cambridge University Press, 1982.

Campos, J. J., Hiatt, S., Ramsey, D., Henderson, C., & Svejda, M. The emergence of fear on the visual cliff. In M. Lewis & L. A. Rosenblum (Eds.), *The development of affect* (Vol. 1). New York: Plenum Press, 1978.

Campos, J. J., Langer, A., & Krowitz, A. Cardiac responses on the visual cliff in prelocomotor infants. *Science,* 1970, *170,* 196–197.

Cantor, G. N. The effects of three types of pretraining on discrimination in preschool children. *Journal of Experimental Psychology,* 1955, *49,* 339–342.

Cantor, J. S., & Spiker, C. C. The problem-solving strategies of kindergarten and first-grade children during discrimination learning. *Journal of Experimental Child Psychology,* 1978, *26,* 341–358.

Carlson, J. S., & Ryan, F. L. Levels of cognitive functioning as related to anxiety. *Journal of Experimental Education,* 1969, *37,* 17–20.

Caron, A., Caron, R., Caldwell, R., & Weiss, S. Infant perception of the structural properties of the face. *Developmental Psychology,* 1973, *9,* 385–399.

Caron, A. J., Caron, R. F., & Carlson, V. R. Infant perception of the invariant shape of objects varying in slant. *Child Development,* 1979, *50,* 716–721.

Carpenter, D. L. Development of depth perception mediated by motion parallax in unidimensional projections of rotation in depth. *Journal of Experimental Child Psychology,* 1979, *28,* 280–299.

Carter, P., & Strauss, M. S. Habituation is not enough, but it's not a bad start: A reply to Sophian. *Merrill-Palmer Quarterly,* 1981, *27,* 333–337.

Case, R. Responsiveness to conservation training as a function of induced subjective uncertainty, M-space, and cognitive style. *Canadian Journal of Behavioral Science,* 1977, *9,* 12–25.

Case, R. Structures and strictures: Some functional limitations on the course of cognitive growth. *Cognitive Psychology,* 1974, *6,* 544–573.

Case, R., Kurland, M., & Goldberg, J. Operational efficiency and the growth of short-term memory span. *Journal of Experimental Child Psychology,* 1982, *33,* 386–404.

Cavanaugh, J. C., & Borkowski, J. G. Searching for metamemory-memory connections: A developmental study. *Developmental Psychology,* 1980, *16,* 441–453.

Cavanaugh, J. C., & Perlmuter, C. J. Metamemory: A critical examination. *Child Development,* 1982, *53,* 11–28.

Ceci, S. J., & Howe, M. J. A. Semantic knowledge as a determinant of developmental differences in recall. *Journal of Experimental Child Psychology,* 1978, *26,* 230–245.

Ceci, S. J., Lea, S. E. G., & Howe, M. J. A. Structural analysis of memory traces in children from 4 to 10 years of age. *Developmental Psychology,* 1980, *16,* 203–212.

Chang, H., & Trehub, S. E. Infant's perception of temporal grouping in auditory patterns. *Child Development,* 1977, *48,* 1666–1670.

Chase, W. G., & Simon, H. A. Perception in chess. *Cognitive Psychology,* 1973, *4,* 55–81.

Chazan, S. E. Development of object permanence as a correlate of dimensions of maternal care. *Developmental Psychology,* 1981, *17,* 79–81.

Chi, M. T. H., & Koeske, R. D. Network representation of a child's dinosaur knowledge. *Developmental Psychology,* 1983, *19,* 29–39.

Chomsky, N. *Language and mind.* New York: Harcourt Brace Jovanovich, 1968.

Chomsky, N. Discussion of "Language within cognition." In M. Piatelli-Palmarini (Ed.), *Language and learning: The debate between Jean Piaget and Noam Chomsky.* Cambridge, Mass.: Harvard University Press, 1980.

Chovan, W. L. Vocal mediative responses in short-term memory of severely and profoundly deaf children. *Perceptual and Motor Skills,* 1970, *31,* 539–544.

Chronbach, I. J., & Meehl, P. E. Construct validity in psychology tests. *Psychological Bulletin,* 1955, *52,* 281–302.

Clifton, R. K., Morrongielo, B. A., Kullig, J. W., & Dowd, J. M. Newborns' orientation toward sound: Possible implications for cortical development. *Child Development,* 1981, *52,* 833–838.

Cohen, L. B., DeLoache, J. S., & Strauss, M. S. Infant visual perception. In J. Osofsky (Ed.), *Handbook of infancy.* New York: Wiley, 1978.

Cohen, R., Schleser, R., & Meyers, A. Self-instructions: Effects of cognitive level and active rehearsal. *Journal of Experimental Child Psychology,* 1981, *32,* 65–76.

Cohn, J. F., & Tronick, E. Z. Three-month-old infants' reaction to simulated maternal depression. *Child Development,* 1983, *54,* 185–193.

Colby, K. M. Simulations of belief systems. In R. C. Schank & E. M. Colby (Eds.), *Computer models of thought and language.* San Francisco: W. H. Freeman, 1973.

Cole, M., Frankle, F., & Sharp, D. Development of free recall in children. *Developmental Psychology,* 1971, *4,* 109–123.

Colehart, M. Iconic memory: A reply to Professor Holding. *Memory and Cognition,* 1975, *104,* 268–294.

Collins, A. M., & Quillian, M. R. Retrieval time from semantic memory. *Journal of Verbal Learning and Verbal Behavior,* 1969, *8,* 240–247.

Cometa, M. S., & Eson, M. E. Logical operations and metaphor interpretation: A Piagetian model. *Child Development,* 1978, *49,* 649–659.

Condon, W. S., & Sander, L. W. Neonate movement is synchronized with adult speech: Interactional participation and language acquisition. *Science,* 1974, *183,* 99–101.

Condry, S. M., Halton, M., Jr., Neisser, U. Infant sensitivity to audio-visual discrepancy: A failure to replicate. *Bulletin of the Psychonomic Society,* 1977, *9,* 431–432.

Conrad, R. The chronology of the development of covert speech in children. *Developmental Psychology,* 1971, *5,* 398–405.

Conrad, R., & Rush, M. L. On the nature of short-term memory encoding by the deaf. *Journal of Speech and Hearing Disorders,* 1965, *30,* 336–346.

Cook, M., Fields, J., & Griffith, K. The perception of solid form in early infancy. *Child Development,* 1978, *49,* 866–869.

Cornell, E. H. Learning to find things: A reinterpretation of object permanence studies. In L. S. Siegel & C. J. Brainerd (Eds.), *Alternatives to Piaget: Critical essays on the theory.* New York: Academic Press, 1978.

Corrigan, R. Language development as related to stage 6 object permanence. *Journal of Child Language,* 1978, *5,* 173–189.

Corsini, D. A., Pick, A. D., & Flavell, J. H. Production of nonverbal mediators in young children. *Child Development,* 1968, *39,* 53–58.

Cosgrove, J. M., & Patterson, C. J. Plans and the development of listener skills. *Developmental Psychology,* 1977, *13,* 557–564.

Cowan, N., Suomi, K., & Morse, P. A. Echoic storage in infant perception. *Child Development,* 1982, *53,* 984–990.

Craik, F. I. M., Gardiner, J. M., & Watkins, M. J. Further evidence for a negative recency effect in free recall. *Journal of Verbal Learning and Verbal Behavior,* 1970, *9,* 554–560.

Craik, F. I. M., & Lockhart, R. S. Levels of processing: A framework for memory research. *Journal of Verbal Learning and Verbal Behavior,* 1972, *11,* 671–684.

Craik, F. I. M., & Tulving, E. Depth of processing and the retention of words in episodic memory. *Journal of Experimental Psychology: General,* 1975, *104,* 268–294.

Craik, F. I. M., & Watkins, M. J. The role of rehearsal in short-term memory. *Journal of Verbal Learning and Verbal Behavior,* 1973, *12,* 599–607.

Cramer, P. Changes from visual memory organization as a function of age. *Journal of Experimental Child Psychology,* 1976, *22,* 50–57.

Crovitz, H. F. *Galton's walk: Method for the analysis of thinking, intelligence and creativity.* New York: Harper & Row, 1970.

Dahlem, N. W. Reconstitutive memory in kindergarten children. *Psychonomic Science,* 1968, *13,* 331–332.

Dahlem, N. W. Reconstitutive memory in kindergarten children revisited. *Psychonomic Science,* 1969, *17,* 101–103.

Dale, P. S. *Language development* (2nd ed.). New York: Holt, Rinehart & Winston, 1976.

Damon, W., & Hart, D. The development of self-understanding from infancy through adolescence. *Child Development,* 1982, *53,* 841–864.

Daneman, M., & Case, R. Syntactic form, semantic complexity, and short-term memory: Influences on children's acquisition of new linguistic structures. *Developmental Psychology,* 1981, *17,* 367–378.

Danner, F. W., & Day, M. C. Eliciting formal operations. *Child Development*, 1977, *48*, 1600–1606.

Dark, V. J., & Loftus, G. R. The role of rehearsal in long-term memory performance. *Journal of Verbal Learning and Verbal Behavior*, 1976, *15*, 479–490.

Davis, J. M., & Rovee-Collier, C. K. Alleviated forgetting of a learned contingency in 8-week-old infants. *Developmental Psychology*, 1983, *19*, 353–365.

Davis, S. M., & McCroskey, R. L. Auditory fusion in children. *Child Development*, 1980, *51*, 75–80.

Day, R. H., & McKenzie, B. E. Perceptual shape constancy in early infancy. *Perception*, 1973, *2*, 315–320.

Day, R. H., & McKenzie, B. E. Infant perception of invariant size of approaching and receding objects. *Developmental Psychology*, 1981, *17*, 670–677.

DeCecco, J. P. *The psychology of learning and instruction: Educational psychology.* Englewood Cliffs, N.J.: Prentice-Hall, 1968.

Degelman, D., & Rosinski, R. Motion parallax and children's distance perception. *Developmental Psychology*, 1979, *15*, 147–152.

Denney, D. R. Modification of children's information processing behaviors through learning: A review of the literature. *Child Study Journal*, 1973, [Monographs 1–3] 1–22.

Denney, D. R. The effects of exemplary and cognitive models and self-rehearsal on children's interrogative strategies. *Journal of Experimental Child Psychology*, 1975, *19*, 476–488.

Denney, D. R., Denney, N. W., & Ziobrowski, M. J. Alterations in the information processing strategies of young children following observation of adult models. *Developmental Psychology*, 1973, *8*, 202–208.

Denney, N. W. Free classification in preschool children. *Child Development*, 1972, *43*, 1161–1170.

Denney, N. W., & Turner, M. C. Facilitating cognitive performance in children: A comparison of strategy modeling and strategy modeling with overt-self-verbalization. *Journal of Experimental Child Psychology*, 1979, *28*, 119–131.

Dodd, B., & Hermelin, B. Phonological coding by the prelinguistically deaf. *Perception and Psychophysics*, 1977, *21*, 413–417.

Dodwell, P. C. Children's understanding of number and related concepts. *Canadian Journal of Psychology*, 1960, *14*, 191–205.

Downing, J. A. *The initial teaching alphabet: Reading experiment.* Chicago: Scott, Foresman, 1965.

Downing, J. A. The augmented Roman alphabet for learning to read. *The Reading Teacher*, 1963, *16*, 325–336.

Doyle, A. Listening to distraction: A developmental study of selective attention. *Journal of Experimental Child Psychology*, 1973, *15*, 100–115.

Drozdal, J. G., & Flavell, J. H. A developmental study of logical search behavior. *Child Development*, 1975, *46*, 389–393.

Duncan, E. M., Whitney, P., & Kunen, S. Integration of visual and verbal information in children's memories. *Child Development*, 1982, *53*, 1215–1223.

Dunst, C. J., Brooks, P. J., & Doxsey, P. A. Characteristics of hiding places and the transition to stage IV performance in object permanence tasks. *Developmental Psychology*, 1982, *18*, 671–681.

Eimas, P. D. A developmental study of hypothesis behavior and focusing. *Journal of Experimental Child Psychology*, 1969, *8*, 160–172.

Eimas, P. D. Effects of memory aids on hypothesis behavior and focusing in young children and adults. *Journal of Experimental Child Psychology*, 1970, *10*, 319–336. (a)

Eimas, P. D. Information processing in problem solving as a function of developmental level and stimulus saliency. *Developmental Psychology,* 1970, *2,* 224–229. (b)

Eimas, P. D., & Miller, J. L. Discrimination of information for manner of articulation. *Infant Behavior and Development,* 1980, *3,* 367–385.

Eimas, P., Siqueland, E. R., Jusczyk, P., & Vigorito, J. Speech perception in infants. *Science,* 1971, *171,* 303–306.

Elkind, D. Children's discovery of the conservation of mass, weight, and volume. *Journal of Genetic Psychology,* 1961, *98,* 219–227. (a)

Elkind, D. The development of quantitative thinking. *Journal of Genetic Psychology,* 1961, *98,* 37–46. (b)

Elkind, D. Quantity conceptions in college students. *Journal of Social Psychology,* 1962, *57,* 459–465.

Elkind, D. Discrimination, seriation and numeration of size difference in young children. *Journal of Genetic Psychology,* 1964, *104,* 275–296.

Elkind, D. Piaget's conservation problems. *Child Development,* 1967, *38,* 15–27.

Elkind, D. Beginning reading: A stage-structure analysis. In D. Elkind (Ed.), *Children and adolescents: Interpretive essays on Jean Piaget* (3rd ed.). New York: Oxford University Press, 1981. (a)

Elkind, D. Piaget and education. In D. Elkind (Ed.), *Children and adolescents: Interpretive essays on Jean Piaget* (3rd ed.). New York: Oxford University Press, 1981. (b)

Elkind, D. Reading, logic, and perception. In D. Elkind (Ed.), *Children and adolescents: Interpretive essays on Jean Piaget* (3rd ed.). New York: Oxford University Press, 1981. (c)

Elkind, D., Barocas, R., & Rosenthal, B. Combinatorial thinking in adolescents from graded and ungraded classrooms. *Perceptual and Motor Skills,* 1968, *27,* 1015–1018.

Elkind, D., Hetzel, D., & Coe, J. Piaget and the British primary education. In D. Elkind (Ed.), *Children and adolescents: Interpretive essays on Jean Piaget* (3rd ed.). New York: Oxford University Press, 1981.

Elkind, D., & Weiss, J. Studies in perceptual development: III Perceptual exploration. *Child Development,* 1967, *38,* 553–562.

Emmerick, H. J., & Ackerman, B. P. The effects of pictorial detail and elaboration on children's retention. *Journal of Experimental Child Psychology,* 1976, *21,* 241–248.

Engen, T., & Lipsitt, L. P. Decrement and recovery of responses to olfactory stimuli in human neonates. *Journal of Comparative and Physiological Psychology,* 1965, *59,* 312–316.

Engen, T., Lipsitt, L. P., & Peck, M. B. Ability of newborn infants to discriminate sapid substances. *Developmental Psychology,* 1974, *10,* 741–744.

Erdelyi, M. H., & Kleinbard, J. Has Ebbinghaus decayed with time?: The growth of recall (hyperamnesia) over days. *Journal of Experimental Psychology: Human Learning and Memory,* 1978, *4,* 275–289.

Erikson, E. H. *Childhood and society* (2nd ed.). New York: Norton, 1963.

Erikson, E. H. *Identity: Youth and crisis.* New York: Norton, 1968.

Evans, W. F., & Gratch, G. The stage IV error in Piaget's theory of object concept development: Difficulties in object conceptualization or spatial location. *Child Development,* 1972, *43,* 682–688.

Eysenck, M. W. Levels of processing: A critique. *British Journal of Psychology,* 1978, *69,* 157–169.

Eysenck, M. W., & Eysenck, M. C. Processing depth, elaboration of encoding memory stores, and expanded processing capacity. *Journal of Experimental Psychology: Human Learning and Memory,* 1979, *5,* 472–481.

Fagen, J. W., Yengo, L. A., Rovee-Collier, C. K., & Enright, M. K. Reactivation of a visual discrimination in early infancy. *Developmental Psychology,* 1981, *17,* 266–274.

Fantz, R. Pattern vision in newborn infants. *Science,* 1963, *140,* 296–297.

Farnham-Diggory, S. *Information processing in children.* New York: Academic Press, 1972.

Feldman, A., & Acredolo, L. The effect of active versus passive exploration on memory for spatial location in children. *Child Development,* 1979, *50,* 698–704.

Field, D. The importance of the verbal content in the training of Piagetian conservation skills. *Child Development,* 1977, *48,* 1583–1592.

Figurelli, J. C. & Keller, H. R. The effects of training and socio–economic class upon the acquisition of conservation concepts. *Child Development,* 1972, *43,* 293–298.

Finkle, D. L. A developmental comparison of the processing of two types of visual information. *Journal of Experimental Child Psychology,* 1973, *16,* 250–266.

Finkle, D. L., & Smythe, L. Short-term storage of spatial information. *Developmental Psychology,* 1973, *9,* 424–428.

Fischer, K. W. A theory of cognitive development: The control and construction of hierarchies of skills. *Psychological Review,* 1980, *87,* 477–533.

Fisher, L. B., Ferdinandsen, K., & Bornstein, M. H. The role of symmetry in infant form discrimination. *Child Development,* 1981, *52,* 457–462.

Fisher, R. P., & Craik, F. I. M. Interaction between encoding and retrieval operations in cued recall. *Journal of Experimental Psychology: Human Learning and Memory,* 1977, *3,* 701–711.

Flavell, J. H. *The developmental psychology of Jean Piaget.* Princeton, N.J.: Van Nostrand, 1963.

Flavell, J. H. An analysis of cognitive-developmental sequences. *Genetic Psychological Monographs,* 1972, *86,* 279–350.

Flavell, J. H. *Cognitive development.* Englewood Cliffs, N.J.: Prentice-Hall, 1977.

Flavell, J. H. Metacognition and metacognitive monitoring: A new area of cognitive developmental inquiry. *American Psychologist,* 1979, *34,* 906–911.

Flavell, J. H. On cognitive development. *Child Development,* 1982, *53,* 1–10.

Flavell, J. H., Beach, D. R., & Chinsky, J. M. Spontaneous verbal rehearsal in memory tasks as a function of age. *Child Development,* 1966, *37,* 283–289.

Flavell, J. H., Friedrichs, A. G., & Hoyt, J. D. Developmental changes in memorization processes. *Cognitive Psychology,* 1970, *1,* 324–340.

Flavell, J. H., Speers, J. R., Green, F. L., & August, D. L. The development of comprehension monitoring and knowledge about communication. *Monographs of the Society for Research in Child Development,* 1981, *46* (Serial No. 192).

Flavell, J. H., & Wellman, H. M. Metamemory. In R. V. Kail & J. W. Hagen (Eds.), *Perspectives on the development of memory and cognition.* Hillsdale, N.J.: Erlbaum, 1977.

Flavell, J. H., & Wohlwill, J. F. Formal and functional aspects of cognitive development. In D. Elkind & J. H. Flavell (Eds.), *Studies in cognitive development.* New York: Oxford University Press, 1969.

Fodor, J. On the impossibility of acquiring "more powerful" structures. In M. Piatelli-Palmarini (Ed.), *Language and learning: The debate between Jean Piaget and Noam Chomsky.* Cambridge, Mass.: Harvard University Press, 1980.

Fox, R., & McDaniels, C. The perception of biological motion by human infants. *Science,* 1982, *218,* 486–487.

Freedman, D. G. Behavioral assessment in infancy. In G. B. A. Stoelinga & J. J. Van Der Werff Ten Bosch (Eds.), *Normal and abnormal development of brain and behavior.* Baltimore, Md.: William and Wilkins, 1971.

Friedman, W. J. Development of time concepts in children. In H. W. Reese & L. P. Lipsitt (Eds.), *Advances in child development and behavior* (Vol. 12). New York: Academic Press, 1978.

Furth, H. G. Linguistic deficiency and thinking: Research with deaf subjects 1964–1969. *Psychological Bulletin*, 1971, *76*, 58–72.

Furth, H. G. Research with the deaf: Implications for language and cognition. *Psychological Bulletin*, 1964, *62*, 145–164.

Furth, H. G., Ross, B., & Youniss, J. Operative understanding in children's immediate and long-term reproductions of drawings. *Child Development*, 1974, *45*, 63–70.

Galbraith, R. C., & Day, R. D. Developmental changes in clustering criteria? A closer look at Denney and Ziobrowski. *Child Development*, 1978, *49*, 889–891.

Garcia, J. The logic and limits of mental aptitude testing. *American Psychologist*, 1981, *36*, 1172–1180.

Gardner, G. E. Aggression and violence: The enemies of precision learning. *American Journal of Psychiatry*, 1971, *128*, 445–450.

Garner, W. R. Letter discrimination and identification. In A. D. Pick (Ed.), *Perception and its development: A tribute to Eleanor J. Gibson*. Hillsdale, N.J.: Erlbaum, 1979.

Garner, W. R., & Haun, F. Letter identification as a function of perceptual limitation and type attribute. *Journal of Experimental Psychology: Human Perception and Performance*, 1978, *4*, 199–209.

Geffen, G., & Sexton, M. A. The development of auditory strategies of attention. *Development Psychology*, 1978, *14*, 11–17.

Geis, M. F., & Hall, D. M. Encoding and incidental memory in children. *Journal of Experimental Child Psychology*, 1976, *22*, 58–66.

Geis, M. F., & Hall, D. M. Encoding and congruity in children's incidental memory. *Child Development*, 1978, *49*, 857–861.

Gelman, R. The nature and development of early number concepts. In H. W. Reese (Ed.), *Advances in child development and behavior* (Vol. 7). New York: Academic Press, 1972.

Gelman, R. Cognitive development. In M. R. Rosenzweig & L. W. Porter (Eds.), *Annual review on psychology* (Vol. 29). Palo Alto, Calif.: Annual Reviews, 1978.

Gelman, R., & Gallistel, C. R. *The young child's understanding of number: A window on early cognitive development*. Cambridge, Mass.: Harvard University Press, 1978.

Gelman, R., & Spelke, E. The development of thoughts about animate and inanimate objects: Implications for research on social cognition. In J. H. Flavell & L. Ross (Eds.), *Social cognitive development*. Cambridge, England: Cambridge University Press, 1981.

Ghatala, E. S., Carbonari, J. P., & Bobele, L. Z. Developmental changes in incidental memory as a function of processing level, congruity, and repetition. *Journal of Experimental Child Psychology*, 1980, *29*, 74–87.

Gholson, B. *The cognitive-developmental basis of human learning: Studies in hypothesis testing*. New York: Academic Press, 1980.

Gholson, B., & Beilin, H. A developmental model of human learning. In H. W. Reese & L. P. Lipsitt (Eds.), *Advances in child development and behavior* (Vol. 13). New York: Academic Press, 1979.

Gholson, B., & Cohen, R. Operativity and strategic hypothesis testing. *The Genetic Epistemologist*, 1980, *9*, 1–5.

Gholson, B., & Danziger, S. Effect of two levels of stimulus complexity upon hypothesis sampling systems among second and sixth grade children. *Journal of Experimental Child Psychology*, 1975, *20*, 105–118.

Gholson, B., Levine, M., & Phillips, S. Hypotheses, strategies, and stereotypes in discrimination learning. *Journal of Experimental Child Psychology*, 1972, *13*, 423–446.

Gholson, B., & McConville, K. Effects of stimulus differentiation training upon hypotheses, strategies, and stereotypes in discrimination learning among kindergarten children. *Journal of Experimental Child Psychology,* 1974, *18,* 81–97.

Gholson, B., Phillips, S., & Levine, M. Effects of temporal relationship of feedback and stimulus information upon discrimination learning strategies. *Journal of Experimental Child Psychology,* 1973, *15,* 425–441.

Gholson, B., O'Connor, J., & Stern, I. Hypothesis sampling systems among preoperational and concrete operational kindergarten children. *Journal of Experimental Child Psychology,* 1976, *21,* 61–76.

Gibson, E. J. Learning to read. *Science,* 1965, *148,* 1066–1072.

Gibson, E. J. *Principles of perceptual learning and development.* New York: Appleton-Century-Crofts, 1969.

Gibson, E. J., Gibson, J. J., Pick, A. D., & Osser, H. A. A developmental study of the discrimination of letter-like forms. *Journal of Comparative and Physiological Psychology,* 1962, *55,* 897–906.

Gibson, E. J., & Levin, H. *The psychology of reading.* Cambridge, Mass.: The MIT Press, 1975.

Gibson, E. J., & Levin, H. Afterword in A. D. Pick (Ed.), *Perception and its development: A tribute to Elanor J. Gibson.* Hillsdale, N.J.: Erlbaum, 1979.

Gibson, E. J., Owsley, C. J., & Johnston, J. Perception of invariants by five-month-old infants: Differentiation of two types of motion. *Developmental Psychology,* 1978, *14,* 407–415.

Ginsburg, H., & Opper, S. *Piaget's theory of intellectual development: An introduction.* Englewood Cliffs, N.J.: Prentice-Hall, 1969.

Gladstone, R. Conservation and compensation. *Journal of Genetic Psychology,* 1981, *138,* 193–205.

Glanzer, M., & Clark, W. H. The verbal loop hypothesis: Binary numbers. *Journal of Verbal Learning and Verbal Behavior,* 1963, *2,* 301–309.

Glass, A. L., Holyoak, K. J., & Santa, J. L. *Cognition.* Reading, Mass.: Addison-Wesley, 1979.

Glenn, S. M., Cunningham, C. C., & Joyce, P. F. A study of auditory preferences in non-handicapped infants and infants with Down's Syndrome. *Child Development,* 1981, *52,* 1303–1307.

Goldfield, E., & Dickerson, D. J. Keeping track of locations during movement in 8- and 10-month-old infants. *Journal of Experimental Child Psychology,* 1981, *32,* 48–64.

Goldschmid, M. L., & Bentler, P. M. *Manual: Concept assessment kit—conservation.* San Diego, Calif.: Educational and Industrial Testing Service, 1968.

Golinkoff, R. M., & Harding, C. G. *The development of causality: The distinction between animates and inanimates.* Paper presented at the International Conference on Infant Studies, New Haven, Conn., April 1980.

Golinkoff, R. M., & Kerr, J. L. Infants' perception of semantically defined action role changes in filmed events. *Merrill-Palmer Quarterly,* 1978, *24,* 53–61.

Gollin, E. S. Further studies of visual recognition of incomplete objects. *Perceptual Motor Skills,* 1961, *13,* 307–314.

Gollin, E. S. A developmental approach to learning and cognition. In L. P. Lipsitt & H. W. Reese (Eds.), *Advances in child development and behavior,* (Vol. 2). New York: Academic Press, 1965.

Goodnow, J. J. Determinants of choice-distribution in two-choice situations. *American Journal of Psychology,* 1955, *68,* 106–116.

Goodwin, S. E., & Mahoney, M. J. Modification of aggression through modeling: An experimental probe. *Journal of Behavioral Therapy and Experimental Psychiatry,* 1975, *6,* 200–202.

Gorman, R. M. *Discovering Piaget: A guide for teachers.* Columbus, Ohio: Charles E. Merrill, 1972.

Gottfried, A. W., Rose, S. A., & Bridger, W. H. Effects of visual, haptic, and manipulatory experiences on infants' visual recognition memory of objects. *Developmental Psychology,* 1978, *14,* 305–312.

Gould, S. J. *The mismeasurement of man.* New York: Norton Company, 1981.

Goulet, L. R., & Goodwin, K. S. Development and choice behavior in probabilistic and problem-solving tasks. In H. W. Reese & L. P. Lipsitt (Eds.), *Advances in child development and behavior* (Vol. 5). New York: Academic Press, 1970.

Gow, L., & Ward, J. Effects of modification of conceptual tempo on acquisition of work skills. *Perceptual Motor Skills,* 1980, *50,* 107–116.

Gratch, G. Recent studies based on Piaget's view of object concept development. In L. B. Cohen & P. Salapatek (Eds.), *Infant perception: From sensation to cognition* (Vol. 4). New York: Academic Press, 1975.

Gratch, G. Responses to hidden persons or things by 5-, 9-, and 16-month-old infants in a visual tracking situation. *Developmental Psychology,* 1982, *18,* 232–237.

Gratch, G., & Landers, W. F. Stage IV of Piaget's theory of infant's object concepts: A longitudinal study. *Child Development,* 1971, *42,* 359–372.

Green, M. G. Structure and sequence in children's concepts of chance and probability: A replication of Piaget and Inhelder. *Child Development,* 1978, *49,* 1045–1053.

Greeno, J. G. Psychology of learning, 1960–1980: One participant's observations. *American Psychologist,* 1980, *35,* 713–728.

Gross, T. F. The effect of mode of encoding on children's problem-solving efficiency. *Developmental Psychology,* 1977, *13,* 521–522. (a)

Gross, T. F. *Hypothesis testing in preschool children following coding and rehearsal pretraining.* Unpublished doctoral dissertation, University of Maine, Orono, Me., 1977. (b)

Gross, T. F., & Jackson, C. A. *Short-term memory coding strategies in deaf children and adults.* Paper presented to the Annual Convention of the American Speech and Hearing Association, Los Angeles, Calif., 1981.

Gross, T. F., & Mastenbrook, M. Examination of the effects of state anxiety on problem-solving efficiency under high and low memory conditions. *Journal of Educational Psychology,* 1980, *72,* 605–609.

Gross, T. F., & Montes, G. *Intentional and incidental memory following three levels of orienting activity.* Paper presented to the 61st Annual Convention of the Western Psychological Association, Los Angeles, Calif., 1981.

Gruen, G. E., & Wier, M. N. Effects of instructions, penalty, and age on probability learning. *Child Development,* 1964, *35,* 265–273.

Haaf, R. A. Complexity and facial resemblance as determinants of response to facelike stimuli by 5- and 10-week-old infants. *Journal of Experimental Child Psychology,* 1974, *18,* 480–487.

Haaf, R. A. Visual response to complex faceline patterns by 15- and 20-week-old infants. *Developmental Psychology,* 1977, *13,* 77–78.

Haaf, R. A., & Bell, R. Q. A facial dimension in visual discrimination by human infants. *Child Development,* 1967, *38,* 893–899.

Haaf, R. A., & Brown, C. Infants' response to facelike patterns: Developmental changes between 10 and 15 weeks of age. *Journal of Experimental Child Psychology,* 1976, *22,* 155–160.

Haaf, R. A., Smith, P. H., & Smitley, S. Infant response to facelike patterns under fixed-trial and infant-control procedure. *Child Development,* 1983, *54,* 172–177.

Hagen, J., & Hail, G. The development of attention in children. In A. O. Pick (Ed.), *Minnesota symposia on child development* (Vol. 7). Minneapolis: University of Minnesota Press, 1973.

Hagen, J. W., Jongeward, R. H., & Kail, R. V. Cognitive perspectives on the development of memory. In H. W. Reese (Ed.), *Advances in child development and behavior* (Vol. 10). New York: Academic Press, 1975.

Hagen, J. W., & Kail, R. V. Facilitation and distraction in short-term memory. *Child Development*, 1973, *44*, 831–836.

Hagen, J. W., & Kingsley, P. R. Labeling effects in short-term memory. *Child Development*, 1968, *39*, 113–121.

Haith, M. M. Development changes in visual information processing and short-term visual memory. *Human Development*, 1971, *14*, 249–261.

Haith, M. M. *Rules that babies look by: The organization of newborn visual activity.* Hillsdale, N.J.: Erlbaum, 1980.

Haith, M. M., Bergman, T., & Moore, W. Eye contact and face scanning in early infancy. *Science*, 1977, *198*, 883–855.

Haith, M. M., & Goodman, G. S. Eye movement control in newborns in darkness and in unstructured light. *Child Development*, 1982, *53*, 974–977.

Haith, M. M., Morrison, F. J., Sheingold, K., & Mindes, P. Short-term memory for visual information in children and adults. *Journal of Experimental Child Psychology*, 1970, *9*, 454–469.

Hall, G. S. *Youth: Its education, regimen, and hygiene.* New York: Appleton and Co., 1912.

Hall, V. C., & Kingsley, R. Conservation and equilibration theory. *Journal of Genetic Psychology*, 1968, *113*, 195–213.

Hanley, W. Validity, vaudeville, and values: A short history of social concerns over standardized testing. *American Psychologist*, 1981, *36*, 1021–1034.

Harding, C. G., & Golinkoff, R. M. The origins of intentional vocalizations in prelinguistic infants. *Child Development*, 1979, *50*, 33–40.

Hardy-Brown, K. Universals and individual differences: Disentangling two approaches to the study of language acquisition. *Developmental Psychology*, 1983, *19*, 610–624.

Harris, P. L. Examination and search in infants. *British Journal of Psychology*, 1971, *62*, 469–473.

Harris, G. J., & Fleer, R. W. High speed memory scanning in mental retardates: Evidence for a central processing deficit. *Journal of Experimental Child Psychology*, 1974, *17*, 452–459.

Hayes, D. S., & Birnbaum, D. W. Preschoolers' retention of televised events: Is a picture worth a thousand words? *Developmental Psychology*, 1980, *16*, 410–416.

Hayes, D. S., Chemelski, B. E., & Birnbaum, D. W. Young children's incidental and intentional retention of televised events. *Developmental Psychology*, 1981, *17*, 230–232.

Hayes, D. S., & Rosner, S. R. The phonetic effect: The influence of overt rehearsal and verbal instructions. *Journal of Experimental Child Psychology*, 1975, *20*, 391–399.

Hayes, D. S., & Shultze, S. A. Visual encoding in preschoolers' serial retention. *Child Development*, 1977, *48*, 1066–1070.

Hayes, J. R. *The complete problem solver.* Pennsylvania, Pa.: The Franklin Institute Press, 1981.

Hebb, D. O. *The organization of behavior.* New York: Wiley, 1949.

Heider, E. R. Universals in color naming and memory. *Journal of Experimental Psychology*, 1972, *93*, 10–20.

Heil, J. Does cognitive psychology rest on a mistake? *Mind*, 1981, *90*, 321–342.

Held, R., & Hein, A. Movement-produced stimulation in the development of visually guided behavior. *Journal of Comparative and Physiological Psychology*, 1963, *56*, 872–876.

Hermelin, B., & O'Connor, N. Ordering in recognition memory after ambiguous initial or recognition displays. *Canadian Journal of Psychology*, 1973, *27*, 191–199.

Hill, D. Relation of field independence to development of conservation. *Perceptual and Motor Skills*, 1980, *50*, 1247–1250.

Hill, K. T., & Sarason, S. B. The relationship between test anxiety and defensiveness to test and school performance over the elementary-school years: A further longitudinal study. *Monographs of the Society for Research in Child Development*, 1961, *31* (Serial No. 2).

Hiscock, M., & Kinsbourne, M. Asymmetries of selective listening and attention switching in children. *Developmental Psychology*, 1980, *16*, 70–82.

Hobbs, S. A., Moguin, L. E., Tyroler, M., & Lahey, B. B. Cognitive behavior therapy with children: Has clinical utility been demonstrated? *Psychological Bulletin*, 1980, *87*, 147–165.

Hodkins, B. Language effects in assessment of class inclusion ability. *Child Development*, 1981, *52*, 470–478.

Holding, D. H. Sensory storage reconsidered. *Memory and Cognition*, 1975, *3*, 21–41.

Holland, K. J., & Palermo, D. S. On learning "less": Language and cognitive development. *Child Development*, 1975, *46*, 437–445.

Hood, L., & Bloom, L. What, when, and how about why: A longitudinal study of early expressions of causality. *Monographs of the Society for Research in Child Development*, 1979, *44* (Serial No. 181).

Hooper, F. H., Toniolo, T. A., & Sipple, T. S. A longitudinal analysis of logical reasoning relationships: Conservation and transitive inference. *Developmental Psychology*, 1978, *14*, 674–682.

Hoving, K. L., Konick, D. S., & Wallace, J. Memory storage and retrieval within and across modalities in children. *Journal of Experimental Child Psychology*, 1975, *19*, 440–447.

Hoving, K. L., Morin, R. E., & Konick, D. S. Recognition reaction time and size of the memory set: A developmental study. *Psychonomic Science*, 1970, *21*, 247–248.

Hoving, K. L., Spencer, T., Robb, K. Y., & Schulte, D. Developmental changes in visual information processing. In P. A. Ornstein (Ed.), *Memory development in children*. Hillsdale, N.J.: Erlbaum, 1978.

Hung, D. L., Tzeng, O. J. L., & Warren, D. H. A chronometric study of sentence processing in deaf children. *Cognitive Psychology*, 1981, *13*, 583–610.

Hunt, R. R., Elliot, J. M., & Spence, M. J. Independent effects of process and structure on encoding. *Journal of Experimental Psychology: Human Learning and Memory*, 1979, *5*, 339–347.

Hutt, S. J., Hutt, C., Lenard, H. G., Bernuth, H. V., & Muntjewerff, W. J. Auditory responsivity in the human neonate. *Nature*, 1968, *218*, 888–890.

Huttenlocker, J., & Burke, D. Why does memory span increase with age? *Cognitive Psychology*, 1976, *8*, 1–31.

Huttenlocker, J., & Presson, C. C. The coding and transformation of spatial information. *Cognitive Psychology*, 1979, *11*, 375–394.

Hyde, T. S., & Jenkins, J. J. Recall for words as a function of semantic, graphic, and syntactic orienting tasks. *Journal of Verbal Learning and Verbal Behavior*, 1973, *12*, 471–480.

Ingals, R. P., & Dickerson, D. J. Development of hypothesis behavior in human concept identification. *Developmental Psychology*, 1969, *1*, 707–716.

Ingison, R. I., & Levin, J. R. The effect of children's spontaneous cognitive sets on discrimination learning. *Journal of Experimental Child Psychology*, 1975, *20*, 59–65.

Inhelder, B. *The diagnosis of reasoning in the mentally retarded*. New York: Chandler Publishing Co., 1968.

Inhelder, B. Memory and intelligence in the child. In D. Elkind & J. H. Flavell (Eds.), *Studies in cognitive development: Essays in honor of Jean Piaget.* New York: Oxford University Press, 1969.

Inhelder, B. Cognitive schemes and their possible relations to language acquisition. In M. Piatelli-Palmarini (Eds.), *Language and learnings: The debate between Jean Piaget and Noam Chomsky.* Cambridge, Mass.: Harvard University Press, 1980.

Inhelder, B., & Piaget, J. *The growth of logical thinking from childhood to adolescence.* New York: Basic Books, 1958.

Inhelder, B., & Piaget, J. *The early growth of logic in the child, classification and seriation.* New York: Harper & Row, 1964.

Inhelder, B., Sinclair, H., & Bovet, M. *Learning and the development of cognition.* New York: Harvard University Press, 1974.

Ironsmith, M., & Whitehurst, G. J. The development of listener abilities in communication: How children deal with ambiguous information. *Child Development,* 1978, *49,* 348−352.

Jackson, E., Campos, J. J., & Fisher, K. W. The question of décalage between object permanence and person permanence. *Developmental Psychology,* 1978, *14,* 1−10.

Jakibchuk, Z., & Smergilio, V. L. The influence of symbolic modeling on the social behavior of preschool children with low levels of social responsiveness. *Child Development,* 1976, *47,* 838−841.

Jarman, R. F. Matching of auditory-visual and temporal-spatial information by seven- and nine-year-old children. *Child Development,* 1979, *50,* 575-577.

Jirari, C., Sarty, M., & Wu, P. Y. K. Visual following and pattern discrimination of face-like stimuli by human neonates. *Clinical Research,* 1973, *21,* 320.

Johnson, C. N., & Wellman, H. M. Children's developing understanding of mental verbs: Remember, know, and guess. *Child Development,* 1980, *51,* 1095−1102.

Jones, B. F., & Hall, J. W. School applications of the mnemonic keyword method as a study strategy by eighth graders. *Journal of Educational Psychology,* 1982, *74,* 230−237.

Kagan, J., & Lewis, M. Studies of attention in the human infant. *Merrill-Palmer Quarterly,* 1965, *11,* 95−127.

Kail, R., & Bisanz, J. Information processing and cognitive development. In H. W. Reese (Ed.), *Advances in child development and behavior* (Vol. 17). New York: Academic Press, 1982.

Kagan, J. Reflection-impulsivity: The generality and dynamics of conceptual tempo. *Journal of Abnormal Psychology,* 1966, *71,* 17-24.

Kanfer, F. H., & Zich, J. Self-control training: The effects of external control on children's resistance to temptation. *Developmental Psychology,* 1974, *10,* 108−115.

Katchadourian, H. *The biology of adolescence.* San Francisco, Calif.: W. H. Freeman, 1977.

Kellas, G., McCauley, C., & McFarland, C. E. Developmental aspects of storage and retrieval. *Journal of Experimental Child Psychology,* 1975, *19,* 51−62.

Kelly, G., *The Psychology of Personal Constructs* (Vols. 1 & 2). New York: Norton, 1955.

Kendler, T. S., & Kendler, H. H. An ontogeny of optional shift behavior. *Child Development,* 1970, *41,* 1−17.

Kenniston, A. H., & Flavell, J. H. A developmental study of intelligent retrieval. *Child Development,* 1979, *50,* 1144−1152.

Kessen, W., Levine, J., & Wendrich, K. A. The imitation of pitch in infants. *Infant Behavior and Development,* 1979, *2,* 93−99.

Kingsley, P. R., & Hagen, J. W. Induced versus spontaneous rehearsal in short-term memory in nursery school children. *Developmental Psychology,* 1969, *1,* 40−46.

Kintsch, W. *Learning, memory, and conceptual processes.* New York: Wiley, 1970.

Klahr, D. Information-processing models of intellectual development. In R. H. Kluwe & H. Spada (Eds.), *Developmental models of thinking.* New York: Academic Press, 1980.

Klahr, D., & Siegler, R. S. The representation of children's knowledge. In H. Reese & L. P. Lipsitt, *Advances in child development and behavior.* New York: Academic Press, 1978.

Klahr, D., & Wallace, J. G. *Cognitive development: An information processing view.* Hillsdale, N.J.: Erlbaum, 1976.

Kluckhohn, C. *Mirror for man.* New York: Premier Book, 1963.

Knight, R. G., & Wooles, I. M. Experimental investigation of chronic organic amnesia: A review. *Psychological Bulletin,* 1980, *88,* 753–771.

Kobasigawa, A., & Middleton, D. B. Free recall of categorized items by children at three grade levels. *Child Development,* 1972, *43,* 1067–1072.

Kopp, C. B. Antecedents of self-regulation: A developmental perspective. *Developmental Psychology,* 1982, *18,* 199–214.

Koslowski, B. Quantitative and qualitative changes in the development of seriation. *Merrill-Palmer Quarterly,* 1980, *26,* 391–405.

Kosslyn, S. M., & Pomerantz, J. R. Imagery, propositions, and the form of internal representations. *Cognitive Psychology,* 1977, *9,* 52–76.

Kreutzer, M. A., Leonard, C., & Flavell, J. H. An interview study of children's knowledge about memory. *Monographs of the Society for Research in Child Development,* 1975, *40* (Serial No. 159).

Kuczaj, S. A. Evidence for a language learning strategy: On the relative ease of acquisition of prefixes and suffixes. *Child Development,* 1979, *50,* 1–13.

Kunen, S., Green, D., & Waterman, D. Spread of encoding within the nonverbal visual domain. *Journal of Experimental Psychology: Human Learning and Memory,* 1979, *5,* 574–584.

Lamb, M. E. The effects of maternal deprivation on the development of the concept of object and person. *Journal of Behavioral Science,* 1973, *1,* 355–364.

Lane, D. M., & Presson, D. A. The development of selective attention. *Merrill-Palmer Quarterly,* 1982, *28,* 317–337.

Lange, G. The development of conceptual and rote recall skills among school age children. *Journal of Experimental Child Psychology,* 1973, *15,* 394–407.

Langsdorf, P., Izard, C. E., Rayias, M., & Hembree, E. A. Interest expression, visual fixation, and heart rate changes in 2- to 8-month-old infants. *Developmental Psychology,* 1983, *19,* 375–386.

Larry, P. v. *Riles,* 495F. Supp. 926 (N.D. Cal. 1979) appeal docketed, No. 80-4027 (9th Cir., Jan. 17, 1980).

Lasky, R. E., Romano, N., & Wenters, J. Spatial localization in children after changes in position. *Journal of Experimental Child Psychology,* 1980, *29,* 225–248.

Lasky, R. E., & Spiro, D. The processing of tachistoscopically presented visual stimuli by five-month-old infants. *Child Development,* 1980, *51,* 1292–1294.

Laughlin, P. R. Selection strategies in concept attainment as a function of relevant problem attributes. *Journal of Experimental Psychology,* 1966, *71,* 773–776.

Laughlin, P. R., Moss, I. L., & Miller, S. M. Information processing in children as a function of adult model, stimulus display, school grade, and sex. *Journal of Educational Psychology,* 1969, *60,* 188–193.

Laurendeau, M., & Pinard, A. *Causal thinking in the child.* New York: International Universities Press, 1962.

Laurendeau, M., & Pinard, A. *The development of the concept of space in the child.* New York: International Universities Press, 1970.

Laurence, M. W. Age differences in performance and subjective organization in the free-recall learning of pictorial material. *Canadian Journal of Psychology,* 1966, *30,* 388–399.

Lawrence, V. W., Kee, D. W., & Hellige, J. B. Developmental differences in visual backward masking. *Child Development,* 1980, *51,* 1081–1089.

Lawton, J. T., & Hooper, F. H. Piagetian theory and early childhood education: A critical analysis. In L. S. Siegel & C. J. Brainerd (Eds.), *Alternatives to Piaget: Critical essays on the theory.* New York: Academic Press, 1978.

Lee, D. M., & Van Allen, R. V. *Learning to read through experience* (2nd Ed.). New York: Appleton-Century-Crofts, 1963.

Leherissey, B. L., O'Neil, H. F., & Hansen, D. N. Effects of memory support on state anxiety and performance in computer-assisted learning. *Journal of Educational Psychology,* 1971, *62,* 413–420.

Lenneberg, E. H. *Biological foundations of language.* New York: Wiley, 1967.

Leonard, L. B. Language impairment in children. *Merrill-Palmer Quarterly,* 1979, *25,* 205–232.

Levin, I. The development of time concepts in young children: Reasoning about duration. *Child Development,* 1977, *48,* 435–444.

Levin, I. Interference of time-related and unrelated cues with duration comparisons of young children: Analysis of Piaget's formulation of the relation of time and speed. *Child Development,* 1979, *50,* 469–477.

Levin, I., Gilat, I., & Zelniker, T. The role of cue salience in the development of time concepts: Duration comparisons in young children. *Developmental Psychology,* 1980, *16,* 661–671.

Levin, I., Israeli, E., Darom, E. The development of time concepts in young children: The relations between duration and succession. *Child Development,* 1978, *49,* 755–764.

Levin, J. R., Yussen, S. R., DeRose, T. M., & Pressley, G. M. Developmental changes in assessing recall and recognition memory capacity. *Developmental Psychology,* 1977, *13,* 608–615.

Levine, M. Hypothesis behavior by humans during discrimination learning. *Journal of Experimental Psychology,* 1966, *71,* 331–338.

Lewis, C. C. How adolescents approach decisions: Changes over grades seven to twelve and policy implications. *Child Development,* 1981, *52,* 538–544.

Lewis, M., & Brooks-Gunn, D. B. *Social cognition and the acquisition of self.* New York: Plenum Press, 1979.

Liben, L. S. Operative understanding of horizontality and its relation to long-term memory. *Child Development,* 1974. *45,* 416–424.

Liben, L. S. Evidence for developmental differences in spontaneous seriation and its implication for past research on long-term memory improvement. *Developmental Psychology,* 1975, *11,* 121–125. (a)

Liben, L. S. Long-term memory for pictures related to seriation, horizontality, and verticality concepts. *Developmental Psychology,* 1975, *11,* 795–806. (b)

Liben, L. S. Memory in the context of cognitive development: The Piagetian approach. In R. V. Kail, Jr. & J. W. Hagen (Eds.), *Perspectives on development of memory and cognition.* Hillsdale, N.J.: Erlbaum, 1976.

Liben, L. S. Memory from a cognitive-developmental perspective: A theoretical and empirical review. In W. Overton & J. Gallagher (Eds.), *Knowledge and development: Advances in research and theory* (Vol. 1). New York: Plenum Press, 1977.

Liben, L. S. Developmental perspectives on the experiential deficiencies of deaf children. In L. S. Liben (Ed.), *Deaf children: Developmental perspective.* New York: Academic Press, 1978. (a)

Liben, L. S. The development of deaf children: An overview of issues. In L. S. Liben (Ed.), *Deaf children: Developmental perspectives*. New York: Academic Press, 1978. (b)

Liben, L. S. Free recall by deaf and hearing children: Semantic clustering and recall in trained and untrained persons. *Journal of Experimental Child Psychology*, 1979, *27*, 105–119.

Liben, L. S. Copying and reproducing pictures in relation to subjects' operative levels. *Developmental Psychology*, 1981, *17*, 357–365.

Liben, L. S., & Drury, A. M. Short-term memory in deaf and hearing children in relation to stimulus characteristics. *Journal of Experimental Child Psychology*, 1977, *24*, 60–73.

Liben, L. S., Moore, M. L., & Golbeck, S. L. Preschoolers' knowledge of their classroom environment: Evidence from small-scale and life-size spatial tasks. *Child Development*, 1982, *53*, 1275–1284.

Lieberman, D. A. Behaviorism and the mind: A (limited) call for a return to introspection. *American Psychologist*, 1979, *34*, 319–333.

Lingle, K. M., & Lingle, J. H. Effects of selected object characteristics on object-permanence test performance. *Child Development*, 1981, *52*, 367–369.

Linn, S., Reznik, S. J., Kagan, J., & Hans, S. Salience of visual patterns in the human infant. *Developmental Psychology*, 1982, *18*, 651–657.

Lipsitt, L. P., & Eimas, P. D. Developmental psychology. In M. R. Rosenzweig & L. W. Porter (Eds.), *Annual Review of Psychology* (Vol. 23). Palo Alto, Calif.: Annual Reviews, 1972.

Liss, P. H., & Haith, M. M. The speed of visual processing in children and adults: Effects of backward and forward masking. *Perception and Psychophysics*, 1970, *8*, 396–398.

Lloyd, S. E., Sinha, L. G., & Freeman, N. H. Spatial reference system and the canonicality effect in infant search. *Journal of Experimental Child Psychology*, 1981, *32*, 1–10.

Lockhart, R. S., Craik, F. I. M., & Jacoby, L. Depth of processing, recognition and recall. In J. Brown (Ed.), *Recall and recognition*. New York: Wiley, 1976.

Loftus, E. F., & Loftus, G. R. On the permanence of stored information in the human brain. *American Psychologist*, 1980, *35*, 409–420.

Lorayne, H., & Lucas, J. *The memory book.* New York: Ballantine Books, 1974.

Lorenz, K. *Evolution and modification of behavior.* Chicago: University of Chicago Press, 1965.

Lovell, K., & Ogilvie, E. A study of the conservation of weight in the junior school child. *British Journal of Educational Psychology*, 1961, *31*, 138–144. (b)

Lovell, K., & Ogilvie, E. The growth of the concept of volume in junior school children. *Journal of Child Psychology and Psychiatry*, 1961, *2*, 118–126. (a)

Lovell, K., & Ogilvie, E. A study of the conservation of substances in the junior school child. *British Journal of Educational Psychology*, 1960, *30*, 109–118.

Lucas, T. C., & Uzgiris, I. C. Spatial factors in the development of the object concept. *Developmental Psychology*, 1977, *13*, 492–500.

Lunzer, E. A., & Pumfrey, P. D. Understanding proportionality. *Mathematics Teaching*, 1966, *34*, 7–13.

Luria, A. R. *Language and cognition.* New York: Wiley, 1982.

Maccoby, E. E., & Konrad, K. W. Age trends in selective listening. *Journal of Experimental Child Psychology*, 1966, *3*, 113–122.

MacDougal, J. C. The development of visual processing and short-term memory in deaf and hearing children. *American Annals of the Deaf*, 1979, *124*, 16–22.

Mackay-Soroka, S., Trehub, S. E., Bull, D. D., & Corter, C. M. Effects of encoding and retrieval conditions on infants' recognition memory. *Child Development*, 1982, *53*, 815–818.

Maisto, A. A., & Baumeister, A. A. A developmental study of choice reaction time: The effects of two forms of stimulus degradation on encoding. *Journal of Experimental Child Psychology*, 1975, *20*, 456–464.

Maltzman, I. Thinking: From a behavioristic point of view. *Psychological Review,* 1955, *62,* 275–286.

Mandler, G. Organization and memory. In K. W. Spence & J. T. Spence (Eds.), *Psychology of learning and motivation* (Vol. 1). New York: Academic Press, 1967.

Markman, E. M. Empirical vs. logical solutions to part-whole comparison problems concerning classes and collections. *Child Development,* 1978, *49,* 168–177.

Markman, E. M. Classes and collections: Conceptual organization and numerical abilities. *Cognitive Psychology,* 1979, *11,* 395–411. (a)

Markman, E. M. Realizing what you don't understand: Elementary school children's awareness of inconsistencies. *Child Development,* 1979, *50,* 643–655. (b)

Markman, E. M. Factors affecting the young child's ability to monitor his memory. Unpublished doctoral dissertation, University of Pennsylvania, 1973.

Markman, E. M., & Siebert, J. Classes and collections: Internal organization and resulting holistic properties. *Cognitive Psychology,* 1976, *8,* 561–577.

Martorano, S. C. A developmental analysis of performance on Piaget's formal operational tasks. *Developmental Psychology,* 1977, *13,* 666–672.

Martorano, S. H. Zentall, T. R. Children's knowledge of the separation of variables concept. *Journal of Experimental Child Psychology,* 1980, *30,* 513–526.

Maslow, A. H. *Toward a psychology of being.* New York: Van Nostrand Reinhold, 1968.

Massaro, D. W. A comparison of forward versus backward recognition masking. *Journal of Experimental Psychology,* 1973, *100,* 434–436.

Masson, M. E. J., & McDaniel, M. A. The role of organizational processes in long-term retention. *Journal of Experimental Psychology: Human Learning and Memory,* 1981, *7,* 100–110.

Masur, E. F., McIntyre, C. W., & Flavell, J. H. Developmental changes in apportionment of study time among items in a multitrial free recall task. *Journal of Experimental Child Psychology,* 1973, *15,* 237–246.

Maurer, D., & Barrera, M. E. Infants' perception of natural and distorted arrangements of a schematic face. *Child Development,* 1981, *52,* 196–202.

Maurer, D., & Salapatek, P. Developmental changes in the scanning of faces by young infants. *Child Development,* 1976, *47,* 523–527.

Maurer, D., Siegel, L. S., Lewis, T. L., Kristofferson, M. W., Barnes, R. A., & Levy, B. A. Long-term memory improvement? *Child Development,* 1979, *50,* 106–118.

McCarty, D. L. Investigation of a visual imagery mnemonic device for acquiring face-name associations. *Journal of Experimental Psychology: Human Learning and Memory,* 1980, *16,* 145–155.

McDaniel, M. A., & Masson, M. E. Long-term retention: When incidental semantic processing fails. *Journal of Experimental Psychology: Human Learning and Memory,* 1977, *3,* 270–281.

McGurk, H., & Lewis, M. Space perception in early infancy: Perception within a common auditory-visual space? *Science,* 1974, *186,* 649–650.

McKenzie, B. E., & Day, R. H. Infants' attention to stationary and moving objects at different distances. *Australian Journal of Psychology,* 1976, *28,* 45–51.

McKenzie, B. E., Tootle, H. E., & Day, R. H. Development of visual size constancy during the first year of human infancy. *Developmental Psychology,* 1980, *16,* 163–174.

McKinney, J. D. Effects of overt verbalization of information before and after instance selections on concept attainment. *Psychological Reports,* 1973, *32,* 459–464. (a)

McKinney, J. D. Problem solving strategies in impulsive and reflective second-graders. *Developmental Psychology,* 1973, *8,* 145. (b)

McNeil, D. The development of language. In P. H. Mussen (Ed.), *Carmichael's manual of child psychology* (3rd Ed.). New York: Wiley, 1970.

Meichenbaum, D. *Cognitive-behavior modification: An integrative approach.* New York: Plenum Press, 1977.

Meichenbaum, D., & Goodman, J. The developmental control of operant motor responding by verbal operants. *Journal of Experimental Child Psychology,* 1969, *7,* 553–565.

Meichenbaum, D., & Goodman, J. Training impulsive children to talk to themselves: A means of developing self-control. *Journal of Abnormal Psychology,* 1971, *77,* 115–126.

Melson, W. H., & McCall, R. B. Attentional responses of five-month girls to discrepant auditory stimuli. *Child Development,* 1970, *41,* 1159–1171.

Meltzoff, A. N., & Moore, M. K. Imitation of facial and manual gestures by human neonates. *Science,* 1977, *198,* 75–78.

Meltzoff, A. N., & Moore, M. K. Newborn infants imitate adult facial features. *Child Development,* 1983, *54,* 702–709.

Mendelson, M. J., & Ferland, M. B. Auditory-visual transfer in four-month-old infants. *Child Development,* 1982, *53,* 1022–1027.

Meyers, J., & Martin, R. Relationships of state and trait anxiety to concept-learning performance. *Journal of Educational Psychology,* 1974, *66,* 33–39.

Milewski, A. E. Visual discrimination and detection of configural invariance in three-month infants. *Developmental Psychology,* 1979, *15,* 357–363.

Miller, D. T., Weinstein, S. M., & Karniol, R. Effects of age and self-verbalization on children's ability to delay gratification. *Developmental Psychology,* 1978, *14,* 569–570.

Miller, G. A. The magical number seven, plus or minus two: Some limits on our capacity for processing information. *Psychological Review,* 1956, *63,* 81–97.

Miller, G. A., Galanter, E., & Pribram, K. *Plans and the structure of behavior.* New York: Holt, Rinehart & Winston, 1960.

Miller, J. L., & Eimas, P. D. Organization in infant speech perception. *Canadian Journal of Psychology,* 1979, *33,* 353–367.

Miller, L. K., & Barg, M. D. Comparison of exclusive versus inclusive classes by young children. *Child Development,* 1982, *53,* 560–567.

Miller, P. H., & Jordan, R. Attentional strategies, attention, and metacognition in Puerto Rican children. *Developmental Psychology,* 1982, *18,* 133–139.

Miller, P. H., & Weiss, M. G. Children's and adult's knowledge about what variables affect selective attention. *Child Development,* 1982, *53,* 543–549.

Miller, P. H., & Zalenski, R. Preschoolers' knowledge about attention. *Developmental Psychology,* 1982, *18,* 871–875.

Milner, B. Memory and the medial temporal regions of the brain. In K. H. Prilbram & D. E. Broadbent (Eds.), *Biology of memory.* New York: Academic Press, 1970.

Mims, R. M., & Gholson, B. Effects of type and amount of feedback upon hypothesis sampling systems among 7- and 8-year-old children. *Journal of Experimental Child Psychology,* 1977, *24,* 358–371.

Miscione, J. L., Marvin, R. S., O'Brien, R. G., & Greenberg, M. T. A developmental study of preschool children's understanding of the words "know" and "guess." *Child Development,* 1978, *49,* 1107–1113.

Morrison, F. J., Holmes, D. L., & Haith, M. M. A developmental study of the effect of familiarity on short-term memory. *Journal of Experimental Child Psychology,* 1974, *18,* 412–425.

Moscovitch, M., & Craik, F. I. M. Depth of processing, retrieval cues, and uniqueness of encoding factors in recall. *Journal of Verbal Learning and Verbal Behavior,* 1976, *15,* 447–458.

Mosher, F. A., & Hornsby, J. R. On asking questions. In J. S. Bruner (Ed.), *Studies in cognitive growth.* New York: Wiley, 1966.

Moshman, D. Consolidation and stage formation in the emergence of formal operations. *Developmental Psychology,* 1977, *13,* 95–100.

Moynahan, E. D. The development of knowledge concerning the effect of categorization upon free recall. *Child Development,* 1973, *44,* 238–246.

Murray, F. S., & Szymczyk, J. M. Effects of distinctive features on recognition of incomplete pictures. *Developmental Psychology,* 1978, *14,* 356–362.

Mueller, C. G. Some origins of psychology as a science. In M. R. Rosenzweig & L. W. Porter (Eds.), *Annual review of psychology* (Vol. 30). Palo Alto, Calif.: Annual Reviews, 1979.

Mueller, J. H. Anxiety and cue utilization in human learning and memory. In M. Zuckerman & C. D. Spielberger (Eds.), *Emotions and anxiety: New concepts, methods, and application.* Hillsdale, N.J.: Erlbaum, 1975.

Murphy, M. D., & Brown, A. L. Incidental learning in preschool children as a function of cognitive analysis. *Journal of Experimental Child Psychology,* 1975, *19,* 509–523.

Naus, M. J., Ornstein, P. A., & Hoving, K. L. Developmental implications of multistore and depth-of-processing models of memory. In P. A. Ornstein (Ed.), *Memory development in children.* Hillsdale, N.J.: Erlbaum, 1978.

Neimark, E. D. Current status of formal operational research. *Human Development,* 1979, *22,* 60–67.

Neimark, E. D. Intellectual development during adolescence. In F. D. Horowitz (Ed.), *Review of child development research* (Vol. 4). Chicago: University of Chicago Press, 1975.

Neimark, E. D. Natural language concepts: Additional evidence. *Child Development,* 1974, *45,* 508–511.

Neisser, U. *Cognitive psychology.* New York: Appleton-Century-Crofts, 1967.

Nelson, K. J. Variations in children's concepts by age and category. *Child Development,* 1974, *45,* 577–584.

Nelson, D. L., Reed, V. S., & McEvoy, C. L. Learning to order pictures and words: A model of sensory and semantic encoding. *Journal of Experimental Psychology: Human Learning and Memory,* 1977, *3,* 485–497.

Nelson, D. L., Walling, J. R., & McEvoy, C. L. Doubts about depth. *Journal of Experimental Psychology: Human Learning and Memory,* 1979, *5,* 24–44.

Nelson, K. Structure and strategy in learning to talk. *Monograph of the Society for Research in Child Development,* 1973, *38,* (1–2, Serial No. 149).

Nelson, K. Individual differences in language development: Implications for development and language. *Developmental Psychology,* 1981, *17,* 170–187.

Nelson, K., & Kosslyn, S. M. Semantic retrieval in children and adults. *Developmental Psychology,* 1975, *11,* 807–813.

Newell, A. Artificial intelligence and the concept of the mind. In R.C. Schank, & K. M. Colby (Eds.), *Computer models of thought and language.* San Francisco, Calif.: W. H. Freeman, 1973.

Newell, A., Shaw, J. C., & Simon, H. A. Elements of a theory of human problem solving. *Psychological Review,* 1958, *65,* 151–166.

Newell, A., & Simon, H. A. *Human problem solving.* Englewood Cliffs, N.J.: Prentice-Hall,1972.

Niebuhr, V. N., & Molfese, V. J. Two operations in class inclusion: Quantification of inclusion and hierarchical classification. *Child Development,* 1978, *49,* 892–894.

Norman, D. A. (Ed.). *Models of human memory.* New York: Academic Press, 1970.

Northern, J. L., & Downs, M. P. *Hearing in children.* Baltimore, Md.: Williams & Wilkins, 1974.

Nottelmann, E. D., & Hill, K. T. Test anxiety and off-task behavior in evaluative situations. *Child Development,* 1977, *48,* 225–231.

Nunnally, J. C., & Lemond, L. C. Exploratory behavior and human development. In H. W. Reese & L. P. Lipsitt (Eds.), *Advances in child development and behavior* (Vol. 8). New York: Academic Press, 1973.

O'Connor, N., & Hermelin, B. Short-term memory for the order of pictures and syllables by deaf and hearing children. *Neuropsychologica,* 1973, *11,* 437–442. (a)

O'Connor, N., & Hermelin, B. Spatial or temporal organization of short-term memory. *Quarterly Journal of Experimental Psychology,* 1973, *25,* 335–343. (b)

O'Connor, N., & Hermelin, B. *Seeing and hearing and space and time.* New York: Academic Press, 1978.

Oden, G. C. A fuzzy logical model of letter identification. *Journal of Experimental Psychology: Human Perception and Performance,* 1979, *5,* 336–352.

Oden, S., & Asher, S. Coaching children in social skills for friendship making. *Child Development,* 1977, *48,* 495–506.

Olson, D. R. On conceptual strategies. In J. S. Bruner, R. R. Olver, & P. Greenfield (Eds.), *Studies in cognitive growth.* New York: Wiley, 1966.

Olson, G. M. An information processing analysis of visual memory and habituation in infants. In T. S. Tighe & N. Leaton (Eds.), *Habituation: Perspectives from child development, animal behavior, and neurophysiology.* Hillsdale, N.J.: Erlbaum, 1976.

Ornstein, P. A. Memory development in children. In R. Liebert, R. Poulos, & G. Mormor (Eds.), *Developmental Psychology* (2nd ed.). Englewood Cliffs, N.J.: Prentice-Hall, 1977.

Ornstein, P. A., Naus, M. J., & Liberty, C. Rehearsal and organizational processes in children's memory. *Child Development,* 1975, *26,* 818–830.

Ornstein, P. A., Naus, M. J., & Stone, B. P. Rehearsal training and developmental differences in memory. *Developmental Psychology,* 1977, *13,* 15–24.

Owings, R. A., & Baumeister, A. A. Levels of processing, encoding strategies, and memory development. *Journal of Experimental Child Psychology,* 1979, *28,* 100–118.

Paivio, A. On the functional significance of imagery. *Psychological Bulletin,* 1970, *73,* 385–392.

Paivio, A., & Csapo, K. Concrete-image and verbal memory codes. *Journal of Experimental Psychology,* 1969, *80,* 279–285.

Paivio, A., Philipchalk, R., & Rowe, E. J. Free and serial recall of pictures, sounds, and words. *Memory and Cognition,* 1975, *3,* 586–590.

Palermo, D. S. Imagery in children's learning: Discussion. *Psychological Bulletin,* 1970, *73,* 415–421.

Palermo, D. S. Characteristics of word association responses obtained from children grades one through four. *Developmental Psychology,* 1971, *5,* 118–123.

Palermo, D. S., & Jenkins, J. J. *Oral word association norms for children in grades one through four* (Research Bulletin No. 60). Department of Psychology, Pennsylvania State University, 1966.

Parrill-Burnstein, M. Teaching kindergarten children to solve problems: An information-processing approach. *Child Development,* 1978, *49,* 700–706.

Parsons, C. Inhelder and Piaget's, The growth of logical thinking: II. A logician's viewpoint. *British Journal of Psychology,* 1960, *51,* 75–84.

Pascual-Leone, J. A mathematical model for the transition rule in Piaget's developmental stages. *Acta Psychologica,* 1970, *32,* 301–345.

Pascual-Leone, J. Constructive problems for constructive theories: The current relevance of Piaget's work and a critique of information-processing simulation psychology. In R. H. Kluwe and H. Spada (Eds.), *Developmental models of thinking.* New York: Academic Press, 1980.

Patterson, C. J., O'Brien, C., Kister, M. C., Carter, D. B., & Kotsonis, M. E. Development of comprehension monitoring as a function of context. *Developmental Psychology,* 1981, *17,* 379–389.

Peil, E. J. *Invention and discovery of reality.* New York: Wiley, 1975.

Peterson, C. R., & Peterson, M. J. Short-term retention of individual verbal items. *Journal of Experimental Psychology,* 1959, *58,* 193–198.

Pezdek, K., & Hartman, E. F. Children's television viewing: Attention and comprehension of auditory versus visual information. *Child Development,* 1983, *54,* 1015–1023.

Phillips, S., & Levine, M. Probing for hypotheses with adults and children: Blank trials and introtracts. *Journal of Experimental Psychology: General,* 1975, *104,* 327–354.

Piaget, J. *The language and thought of the child.* London: Routledge & Kegan Paul, 1926.

Piaget, J. *The child's conception of the world.* New York: Harcourt, Brace & World, 1929.

Piaget, J. *The child's conception of physical causality.* New York: Harcourt, Brace & World, 1930.

Piaget, J. Jean Piaget. In E. G. Boring, H. S. Langfeld, H. Werner, & R. M. Yerkes (Eds.), *A history of psychology in autobiography* (Vol. 4). Worcester, Mass.: Clark University Press, 1952.

Piaget, J. *The construction of reality in the child.* New York: Basic Books, 1954.

Piaget, J. The general problems of the psychobiological development of the child. In J. M. Tanner & B. Inhelder (Eds.), *Discussions on child development* (Vol. 4). London: Tavistock, 1960.

Piaget, J. *Play, dreams, and imitation in childhood.* New York: Norton, 1962.

Piaget, J. *The origin of intelligence in children.* New York: Norton, 1963.

Piaget, J. Cognitions and conservations: Two views. *Contemporary Psychology,* 1967, *12,* ᶜ32–533.

Piaget, J. *On the development of memory and identity.* Worcester, Mass.: Clark University Press, 1968.

Piaget, J. *The child's conception of time.* London: Routledge & Kegan Paul, 1969. (a)

Piaget, J. *The mechanisms of perception.* New York: Basic Books, 1969. (b)

Piaget, J. *Science of education and the psychology of the child.* New York: Viking Press, 1970.

Piaget, J. Intellectual evolution from adolescence to adulthood. *Human Development,* 1972, *15,* 1–12.

Piaget, J. The role of action in the development of thinking. In W. F. Overton & J. M. Gallagher (Eds.), *Knowledge and development: Advances in research and theory* (Vol. 1). New York: Plenum Press, 1977.

Piaget, J. Language and cognition. In M. Piattelli-Palmarini (Ed.), *Language and learning: The debate between Jean Piaget and Noam Chomsky.* Cambridge, Mass.: Harvard University Press, 1980.

Piaget, J., Grize, J. B., Szeminska, A., & Vinh Bang. *Epistemology and psychology of functions.* Dordrecht, Holland: D. Reidel, 1977.

Piaget, J., & Inhelder, B. *The child's conception of space.* London: Routledge & Kegan Paul, 1956.

Piaget, J., & Inhelder, B. *The psychology of the child.* New York: Basic Books, 1969.

Piaget, J., & Inhelder, B. *Memory and intelligence.* New York: Basic Books, 1973.

Piaget, J., & Inhelder, B. *The origin of the idea of chance in children.* New York: Norton, 1975.

Piaget, J., & Inhelder, B. *Le Développment des quantiés physiques chez l'enfant.* Neuchâtel: Delachaux et Niestlé, 1962.

Piaget, J., Inhelder, B., & Szeminska, A. *The child's conception of geometry.* New York: Basic Books, 1960.

Piaget, J., & Szeminska, A. *The child's conception of number.* New York: Humanities Press, Inc., 1952.

Pick, A. D. Improvement of visual and tactual form discrimination. *Journal of Experimental Psychology,* 1965, *69,* 331–339.

Pinard, A. *The conservation of conservation: The child's acquisition of a fundamental concept.* Chicago: The University of Chicago Press, 1981.

Pinard, A., & Chassé, G. Pseudoconservation of the volume and surface area of a solid object. *Child Development,* 1977, *48,* 1559–1566.

Pinard, A., & Laurendeau, M. "Stage" in Piaget's cognitive developmental theory: Exegesis of a concept. In D. Elkind & J. H. Flavell (Eds.), *Studies in cognitive development.* New York: Oxford University Press, 1969.

Pomerlau-Malcuit, A., & Clifton, R. K. Neonatal heartrate response to tactile, auditory, and vestibular stimulation in different states. *Child Development,* 1973, *44,* 485–496.

Porteus, S. D. *The Porteus maze test and intelligence.* New York: The Psychological Corporation, 1950.

Posner, M. I., & Keele, S. On the genesis of abstract ideas. *Journal of Experimental Psychology,* 1968, *77,* 353–363.

Posner, M. I., & McLeod, P. Information processing models—In search of elementary operations. In M. R. Rosenzweig & L. W. Porter (Eds.), *Annual review of psychology* (Vol. 33). Palo Alto, Calif.: Annual Review, 1982.

Postman, L. Verbal learning and memory. In M. R. Rosenzweig & L. W. Porter (Eds.), *Annual Review of Psychology* (Vol. 26). Palo Alto, Calif.: Annual Reviews, 1975.

Postman, L., & Keppel, G. (Eds.). *Verbal learning and memory.* Baltimore, Md.: Penguin Books, 1969.

Pratt, M. W., & Bates, K. R. Young editors: Preschoolers' evaluation and production of ambiguous messages. *Developmental Psychology,* 1982, *18,* 30–42.

Pressley, M. Elaboration and memory development. *Child Development,* 1982, *53,* 296–309.

Proctor, R. W. Attention and modality-specific interference in visual short-term memory. *Journal of Experimental Psychology: Human Learning and Memory,* 1978, *4,* 239–245.

Pumfrey, P. The growth of the schema of proportionality. *British Journal of Educational Psychology,* 1968, *38,* 202–204.

Puffal, P. B. Egocentrism in spatial thinking: It depends on your point of view. *Developmental Psychology,* 1975, *11,* 297–303.

Rader, N., Spiro, D. J., & Firestone, P. B. Performance on a Stage IV object-permanence task with standard and nonstandard covers. *Child Development,* 1979, *50,* 908–910.

Raugh, M. R., & Atkinson, R. C. A mnemonic method for learning foreign language vocabulary. *Journal of Experimental Child Psychology,* 1975, *67,* 1–16.

Rebelsky, F. G., Starr, R. H. Jr., & Luria, Z. Language development: The first four years. In Y. Brackbill (Ed.), *Infancy and early childhood.* New York: Free Press, 1967.

Reese, H. W. Imagery and contextual meaning. *Psychological Bulletin,* 1970, *73,* 404–414.

Reese, H. W., & Lipsitt, L. P. *Experimental child psychology.* New York: Academic Press, 1970.

Reiser, J. Spatial orientation of six-month-old infants. *Child Development,* 1979, *50,* 1078–1087.

Reschly, D. J. Psychological testing in educational classification and placement. *American Psychologist,* 1981, *36,* 1094–1102.

Restle, F. The selection of strategies in cue learning. *Psychological Review*, 1962, *69*, 329–343.

Richmond, S., & Gholson, B. Strategy modeling, age, and information processing efficiency. *Journal of Experimental Child Psychology*, 1978, *26*, 58–70.

Ricoeur, P. The question of proof in Freud's psychoanalytic writings. *Journal of the American Psychoanalytic Association*, 1977, *25*, 835–871.

Riley, C. A., & Trabasso, T. Comparatives, logical structures and encoding in a transitive inference task. *Journal of Experimental Child Psychology*, 1974, *17*, 187–203.

Rittenhouse, R. K., Morreau, L. E., & Iran-Nejad, A. Metaphor and conservation in deaf and hard-of-hearing children. *American Annals of the Deaf*, 1981, *26*, 450–453.

Ritter, D. J. The development of knowledge of an external retrieval cue strategy. *Child Development*, 1978, *49*, 1227–1230.

Roediger, H. L., III, & Payne, D. G. Hypermnesia: The role of repeated testing. *Journal of Experimental Psychology: Learning, memory, and cognition*, 1982, *8*, 66–72.

Rosch, E. H. On the internal structure of perceptual and semantic categories. In T. E. Moore (Ed.), *Cognitive development and the requisition of language*. New York: Academic Press, 1973.

Rohwer, W. D. Jr. Images and pictures in children's learning: Research results and educational implications. *Psychological Bulletin*, 1970, *73*, 393–403.

Rosch, E., Mervis, C. B., Gray, W. D., Johnson, D. M., & Boyes-Braem, P. Basic objects in natural categories. *Cognitive Psychology*, 1976, *8*, 382–439.

Rosenthal, D. A. Language skills and formal operations. *Merrill-Palmer Quarterly*, 1979, *25*, 133–143.

Rosner, S. R. The effect of rehearsal and chunking instructions on children's multi-trial free recall. *Journal of Experimental Child Psychology*, 1971, *11*, 73–82.

Rosner, S. R., & Hayes, D. S. A developmental study of category item production. *Child Development*, 1977, *48*, 1062–1065.

Rosner, S. R., & Lindsay, D. T. The effects of retention interval on preschool children's short-term memory of verbal items. *Journal of Experimental Child Psychology*, 1975, *18*, 72–80.

Ross, B. M., & Kerst, S. M. Developmental memory theories: Baldwin and Piaget. In H. W. Reese & L. P. Lipsitt (Eds.), *Advances in child development and behavior* (Vol. 12). New York: Academic Press, 1978.

Ross, H. S., & Killey, J. C. The effect of questioning on retention. *Child Development*, 1977, *48*, 312–314.

Rossi, S. I., & Wittrock, M. C. Developmental shifts in verbal recall between mental age 2 and 5. *Child Development*, 1971, *42*, 333–338.

Rovee-Collier, C. K., & Sullivan, M. W. Organization of infant memory. *Journal of Experimental Psychology: Human Learning and Memory*, 1980, *6*, 798–807.

Ruff, H. A. The development of perception and recognition of objects. *Child Development*, 1980, *51*, 981–992.

Ruff, H. A. Role of manipulation in infants' responses to invariant properties of objects. *Developmental Psychology*, 1982, *18*, 682–691.

Rumelhart, D. E. Toward an interactive model of reading. In S. Dornic (Ed.), *Attention and performance* (Vol. 6). Hillsdale, N.J.: Erlbaum, 1977.

Rundus, D. Analysis of rehearsal processes in free recall. *Journal of Experimental Psychology*, 1971, *89*, 63–77.

Rundus, D. Maintenance rehearsal and single-level processing. *Journal of Verbal Learning and Verbal Behavior*, 1977, *16*, 665–681.

Russel, J. Children's memory for the premises in a transitive measurement task assessed by elicited and spontaneous justification. *Journal of Experimental Child Psychology*, 1981, *31*, 300–309.

Rychlak, J. F. *The psychology of rigorous humanism.* New York: Wiley, 1979.

Salapatek, P. Pattern perception of early infancy. In L. Cohen & L. Salapatek (Eds.), *Infant perception: From sensation to cognition: Basic visual processes* (Vol. 1). New York: Academic Press, 1975.

Salapatek, P., & Kessen, W. Visual scanning of triangles by the human newborn. *Journal of Experimental Child Psychology,* 1966, *3,* 155–167.

Salapatek, P., & Kessen, W. Prolonged investigation of a plane geometric triangle by the human newborn. *Journal of Experimental Child Psychology,* 1973, *15,* 22–29.

Salatas, H., & Flavell, J. H. Retrieval of recently learned information: Development of strategies and control skills. *Child Development,* 1976, *47,* 941–948.

Saltz, E., Dixon, D., Klein, S., & Becker, G. Studies of natural language concepts. III. Concept overdiscrimination in comprehension between two and four years of age. *Child Development,* 1977, *48,* 1682–1685.

Saltz, E., Soller, E., & Siegel, I. E. The development of natural language concepts. *Child Development,* 1972, *43,* 1191–1202.

Samuels, S. J. Hierarchical subskills in the reading acquisition process. In J. T. Guthrie (Ed.), *Aspects of reading acquisition.* Baltimore, Md.: Johns Hopkins University Press, 1976.

Santa, J. L., & Lawmers, L. L. Encoding specificity: Fact or artifact. *Journal of Verbal Learning and Verbal Behavior,* 1974, *13,* 412–423.

Sapir, E. The status of linguistics as a science. In D. G. Mandelbaum (Ed.), *Selected writings of Edward Sapir in language, culture, and personality.* Berkeley: University of California Press, 1949.

Sarason, I. G. Experimental approaches to test anxiety: Attention and uses of information. In C. D. Spielberger (Eds.), *Anxiety: Current trends in theory and research.* New York: Academic Press, 1972.

Sarason, S. B., Davidson, K. S., Lighthall, F. F., Waite, R. R., & Ruebush, K. *Anxiety in elementary school children.* New York: Wiley, 1960.

Scarr, S. From evolution to Larry P., or what shall we do about IQ tests? *Intelligence,* 1978, *2,* 325–342.

Schlesinger, I. M. The role of cognitive development and linguistic input in language acquisition. *Journal of Child Language,* 1977, *4,* 153–169.

Schofield, F. C., & Uzgiris, I. C. *Infant-mother relationship and object concept.* Paper presented at the meeting of the Society for Research in Child Development, Santa Monica, Calif., 1969.

Schuberth, R. E., Werner, J. S., & Lipsitt, L. P. The stage IV error in Piaget's theory of object concept development: A reconsideration of the spatial localization hypothesis. *Child Development,* 1978, *49,* 744–748.

Schwartz, A. N., Campos, J. J., & Baisel, E. J. The visual cliff: Cardiac and behavioral responses on the deep and shallow side at five and nine months of age. *Journal of Experimental Child Psychology,* 1973, *15,* 86–99.

Schwartz, M., & Day, R. H. Visual shape perception in early infancy. *Monographs of the Society for Research in Child Development,* 1979, *44* (Serial No. 182).

Sexton, M. A., & Geffen, G. Development of three strategies of attention in dichotic monitoring. *Developmental Psychology,* 1979, *15,* 299–310.

Shatz, M., & Gelman, R. The development of communication skills. *Monograph of the Society for Research in Child Development,* 1973, *38* (Serial No. 152).

Sheingold, K. Developmental differences in intake and storage of visual information. *Journal of Experimental Child Psychology,* 1973, *16,* 1–11.

Shriberg, L. K., Levin, J. R., McCormick, C. B., & Pressley, M. Learning about "famous" people via the keyword method. *Journal of Educational Psychology,* 74, 238–247.

Sieber, J. E., Kameya, L. I., & Paulson, F. L. Effect of memory support on the problem-solving ability of test-anxious children. *Journal of Educational Psychology,* 1970, *61,* 159–168.

Siegel, A. W., Allik, J. P., & Herman, J. F. The primacy effect in young children: Verbal fact or spatial artifact. *Child Development,* 1976, *47,* 242–247.

Siegler, R. S. The effects of simple necessity and sufficiency on children's causal inferences. *Child Development,* 1976, *47,* 1058–1063.

Siegler, R. S. Developmental sequences within and between concepts. *Monographs of the Society for Research in Child Development,* 1981, *46* (No. 2).

Siegler, R. S., & Richards, D. D. Development of time, speed, and distance concepts. *Developmental Psychology,* 1979, *15,* 188–198.

Silverman, I. W. Context and number conservation. *Child Study Journal,* 1979, *9,* 205–212.

Silverman, I. W., & Briga, J. By what process do young children solve small number conservation problems? *Journal of Experimental Child Psychology,* 1981, *32,* 115–126.

Silverman, W. P. High speed scanning of non-alphanumeric symbols in cultural-familial retarded and non-retarded children. *American Journal of Mental Deficiency,* 1974, *79,* 44–51.

Simon, H. A. Information processing models of cognition. In M. R. Rosenzweig & L. W. Porter (Eds.), *Annual review of psychology* (Vol. 30). Palo Alto, Calif.: Annual Reviews, 1979.

Sinclair-de Zwart, H. Language acquisition and cognitive development. In T. E. Moore (Ed.), *Cognitive development and the acquisition of language.* New York: Academic Press, 1973.

Sinclair, K. E. The influence of anxiety on several measures of classroom performance. *Australian Journal of Education,* 1969, *13,* 296–307.

Singer, H. Instruction in reading acquisition. In O. J. L. Tzeng & H. Singer (Eds.), *Perception of print: Reading research in experimental psychology.* Hillsdale, N.J.: Erlbaum, 1981. (a)

Singer, H. Teaching the acquisition phase of reading development: An historical perspective. In O. J. L. Tzeng & H. Singer (Eds.), *Perspection of print: Reading research in experimental psychology.* Hillsdale, N.J.: Erlbaum, 1981. (b)

Siqueland, E. R., & Lipsitt, L. P. Conditional headturning in human newborns. *Journal of Experimental Child Psychology,* 1966, *3,* 356–376.

Slobin, D. Cognitive pre-requisites for the acquisition of grammar. In C. A. Ferguson & D. I. Slobin (Eds.), *Studies of child language development.* New York: Holt, Rinehart & Winston, 1973.

Smedslund, J. Development of concrete transitivity of length in children. *Child Development,* 1963, *34,* 389–405.

Smith, L., Kemler, D., & Aronfreed, J. Developmental trends in voluntary selective attention: Differential effects of source distinctness. *Journal of Experimental Child Psychology,* 1975, *20,* 352–362.

Smith, P. K., & Dutton, S. Play and training in direct and innovative problem solving. *Child Development,* 1979, *50,* 830–836.

Snow, C. E., & Ferguson, C. A. (Eds.). *Talking to children.* Cambridge, England: Cambridge University Press, 1977.

Sophian, C. Habituation is not enough: Novelty preferences, search, and memory in infancy. *Merrill-Palmer Quarterly,* 1980, *26,* 239–257.

Spears, W. C., & Hohle, R. H. Sensory and perception processes in infants. In Y. Brackbill (Ed.), *Infancy and early childhood.* New York: Free Press, 1967.

Speer, J. R., & Flavell, J. H. Young children's knowledge of the relative difficulty of recognition and recall memory tasks. *Developmental Psychology,* 1979, *15,* 214–217.

Speilberger, C. D., Gonzales, H. P., & Fletcher, T. Test anxiety reduction learning strategies, and academic performance. In H. F. O'Neil, Jr. & C. D. Spielberger (Eds.), *Cognitive and affective learning strategies*. New York: Academic Press, 1979.

Spiker, C. C. Application of Hull-Spence theory to the discrimination learning of children. In H. W. Reese (Ed.), *Advances in child development and behavior* (Vol. 16). New York: Academic Press, 1971.

Spiker, C. C., & Cantor, J. H. Introtacts as predictors of discrimination performance in kindergarten children. *Journal of Experimental Child Psychology*, 1977, *23*, 520–538.

Stam, J. H. An historical perspective on "linguistic relativity." In R. W. Rieber (Ed.), *Psychology of language and thought*. New York: Plenum Press, 1980.

Steinberg, E. R. Evaluation process in young children's problem solving. *Contemporary Educational Psychology*, 1980, *5*, 276–281.

Sternberg, R. J. Testing and cognitive psychology. *American Psychology*, 1981, *36*, 1181–1189.

Sternberg, S. Memory scanning: Mental processes revealed by reaction time experiments. *American Scientist*, 1969, *57*, 421–457.

Sternlicht, M. The development of cognitive judgment in the mentally retarded: A selective review of Piagetian-inspired research. *Journal of Genetic Psychology*, 1981, *139*, 55–68.

Stevenson, H. W. *Children's learning*. New York: Appleton-Century-Crofts, 1972.

Stone, C. A., & Day, M. C. Levels of availability of a formal operational strategy. *Child Development*, 1978, *49*, 1054–1065.

Stratton, P. M., & Connolly, K. Discrimination by newborns of the intensity, frequency and temporal characteristics of auditory stimuli. *British Journal of Psychology*, 1973, *64*, 219–232.

Strauss, M. S. Abstraction of prototypical information by adults and 10-month-old infants. *Journal of Experimental Psychology: Human Learning and Memory*, 1979, *5*, 618–632.

Sugarman, S. The cognitive basis of classification in very young children: An analysis of object ordering trends. *Child Development*, 1981, *52*, 1172–1178.

Sullivan, M. W., Rovee-Collier, C. K., & Tynes, D. M. A conditioning analysis of infant long-term memory. *Child Development*, 1979, *50*, 152–162.

Talland, G. A. *Deranged memory: A psychonomic study of the amnesic syndrome*. New York: Academic Press, 1965.

Tenney, Y. The child's conception of organization and recall. *Journal of Experimental Child Psychology*, 1975, *19*, 100–114.

Terman, L. M., & Merrill, M. A. *Measuring intelligence*. Boston: Houghton-Mifflin, 1937.

Thomas, H. Unfolding the baby's mind: The infant's selection of visual stimuli. *Psychological Review*, 1973, *80*, 468–488.

Thomson, D. M., & Tulving, E. Associative encoding and retrieval: Weak and strong cues. *Journal of Experimental Psychology*, 1970, *86*, 255–262.

Till, R. E., & Jenkins, J. J. The effects of cue orienting task on free recall of words. *Journal of Verbal Learning and Verbal Behavior*, 1973, *12*, 489–498.

Tinsley, V. S., & Waters, H. S. The development of verbal control over motor behavior: A replication and extension of Luria's findings. *Child Development*, 1982, *53*, 746–753.

Tomlinson-Keasey, C., Eisert, D. C., Kahle, L. R., Hardy-Brown, K., & Keasey, B. The structure of concrete operational thought. *Child Development*, 1979, *50*, 1153–1163.

Trevarthen, C. Descriptive analyses of infant communicative behavior. In H. R. Schaffer (Ed.), *Studies in mother-infant interaction*. London: Academic Press, 1977.

Tschirgi, J. E. Sensible reasoning: A hypothesis about hypotheses. *Child Development*, 1980, *51*, 1–10.

Tulving, E., & Thomson, D. M. Encoding specificity and retrieval processes in episodic memory. *Psychological Review*, 1973, *80*, 352–373.

Tversky, B. Pictorial and verbal encoding in preschool children. *Developmental Psychology,* 1973, *8,* 149–153.

Uzgiris, I. C. Situational generality of conservation. *Child Development,* 1964, *35,* 831–841.

Uzgiris, I. C., & Hunt, J. McV. *Assessment in infancy: Ordinal scales of psychological development.* Urbana, Ill.: University of Illinois Press, 1975.

Van Horn, K. R., & Bartz, W. H. Information seeking strategies in cognitive development. *Psychonomic Science,* 1968, *11,* 341–342.

Vaughan, M. E. Clustering, age, and incidental learning. *Journal of Experimental Child Psychology,* 1968, *6,* 323–325.

Vliestra, A. G. The effect of strategy training and stimulus saliency on attention and recognition in preschoolers. *Journal of Experimental Child Psychology,* 1978, *25,* 17–32.

Vurpilot, E. The development of scanning strategies and their relation to visual differentiation. *Journal of Experimental Child Psychology,* 1968, *6,* 622–650.

Vygotsky, L. S. *Thought and speech.* Cambridge, Mass.: MIT Press, 1962.

Walk, R. D. Monocular compared to binocular depth perception in human infants. *Science,* 1968, *162,* 473–478.

Walk, R. D. Depth perception and experience. In R. D. Walk & H. L. Pick Jr. (Eds.), *Perception and experience* (Vol. 1). New York: Plenum Press, 1978.

Walk, R. D., & Gibson, E. J. A comparative and analytical study of visual depth perception. *Psychological Monographs,* 1961, *75,* (15, Whole No. 519).

Walker, A. S. Intermodal perception of expressive behaviors by human infants. *Journal of Experimental Child Psychology,* 1982, *33,* 514–535.

Walsh, D. A., & Jenkins, J. J. Effects of orienting task on free recall in incidental learning: "Difficulty," "effort," and "process" exploration. *Journal of Verbal Learning and Verbal Behavior,* 1973, *12,* 481–488.

Wannemacher, J. T., & Ryan, M. L. "Less" is not "more": A study of children's comprehension of "less" in various task contexts. *Child Development,* 1978, *49,* 660–668.

Wason, P. C., & Johnson-Laird, P. N. *Psychology of reasoning.* Cambridge, Mass.: Harvard University Press, 1972.

Waters, H. S., & Waters, E. Semantic processing in children's free recall: Evidence for the importance of attentional factors and encoding variability. *Journal of Experimental Psychology: Human Learning and Memory,* 1976, *2,* 370–380.

Watson, J. S., Hayes, L. A., & Vietze, P. Bidimensional sorting in preschoolers with an instrumental learning task. *Child Development,* 1979, *50,* 1178–1183.

Watson, J. B. *Behaviorism.* New York: Norton, 1924.

Waugh, N. C., & Norman, D. A. Primary memory. *Psychological Review,* 1965, *72,* 89–104.

Weiss, S. L., Robinson, G., & Hastie, R. The relationship of depth of processing to free recall in second and fourth graders. *Developmental Psychology,* 1977, *13,* 325–526.

Weithorn, L. A., & Campbell, J. B. The competency of children and adolescents to make informed treatment decisions. *Child Development,* 1982, *53,* 1589–1598.

Wellman, H. M., & Johnson, C. N. Understanding of mental process: A developmental study of "remember" and "forget." *Child Development,* 1979, *50,* 79–98.

Wellman, H. M., & Lempers, J. D. The naturalistic communicative abilities of two-year-olds. *Child Development,* 1977, *48,* 1052–1057.

Wellman, H. M., Ritter, K., & Flavell, J. H. Deliberate memory behavior in the delayed reaction of very young children. *Developmental Psychology,* 1975, *11,* 780–787.

Wellman, H. M., Somerville, S. C., & Haake, R. J. Development of search procedures in real-life spatial environments. *Developmental Psychology,* 1979, *15,* 530–542.

Wellsandt, R. F., & Meyer, P. A. Visual masking, mental age, and retardation. *Journal of Experimental Child Psychology,* 1974, *18,* 512–519.

Wetherick, N. E., & Alexander, J. The role of semantic information in short-term memory in children aged 5 to 9 years. *British Journal of Psychology,* 1977, *68,* 71–75.

White, S. R. Evidence for the hierarchical arrangement of learning processes. In L. P. Lipsitt and C. C. Spiker (eds.), *Advances in Child Development and Behavior.* Vol. 2. New York: Academic Press, 1965.

Whorf, B. L. Languages and logic. In J. B. Carroll (Ed.), *Language, thought and reality: Selected writings of Benjamin Lee Whorf.* Cambridge, Mass.: MIT Press, 1956.

Wickens, D. D. Encoding categories of words: An empirical approach to meaning. *Psychological Review,* 1970, *77,* 1–15.

Wilkinson, A. Counting strategies and semantic analysis as applied to class inclusion. *Cognitive Psychology,* 1976, *8,* 64–85.

Winer, G. A. Class–inclusion reasoning in children: A review of the empirical literature. *Child Development,* 1980, *51,* 309–328.

Wood, J., Bruner, J., & Ross, G. The mode of tutoring in problem solving. *Journal of Child Psychology and Psychiatry,* 1976, *17,* 89–100.

Wright, J. C., & Vliestra, A. G. The development of selective attention: From perception exploration to logical search. In H. W. Reese (Ed.), *Advances in child development and behavior* (Vol. 10). New York: Academic Press, 1975.

Yarrow, L. J. Attachment and dependency. In J. L. Gewirtz (Ed.), *Attachment and dependency.* New York: Winston, 1972.

Yoshimura, E. K., Moely, B. E., & Shapiro, S. I. The influence of age and presentation order upon children's free recall and learning to learn. *Psychonomic Science,* 1971, *23,* 261–263.

Yussen, S. R. Some reflections on strategic remembering in young children. In G. H. Hale (Chair), *Development of selective processes in cognition.* Symposium of the Society for Research in Child Development, Denver, 1975.

Yussen, S. R., & Berman, L. Memory predictions for recall and recognition in first-, third-, and fifth-grade children. *Developmental Psychology,* 1981, *17,* 224–229.

Yussen, S. R., & Bird, J. E. The development of metacognitive awareness in memory, communication, and attention. *Journal of Experimental Child Psychology,* 1979, *28,* 300–313.

Yussen, S. R., Levin, J. R., Berman, L., & Palm, J. Developmental changes in the awareness of memory benefits associated with different types of picture organization. *Developmental Psychology,* 1979, *15,* 447–449.

Yussen, S. R., Levy, V. M. Developmental changes in predicting one's own span of short-term memory. *Journal of Experimental Child Psychology,* 1975, *19,* 502–508.

Zachary, W. Ordinality and interdependence of representation and language development in infancy. *Child Development,* 1978, *49,* 681–687.

Zaprophets, A. V. The development of perception in the preschool child. In P. H. Mussen (Ed.), European research in cognitive development. *Monographs of the Society for Research in Child Development,* 1965, *30* (Serial No. 100).

Zelniker, T., & Jeffrey, W. E. Reflective and impulsive children: Strategies of information processing underlying differences in problem solving. *Monographs of the Society for Research in Child Development,* 1976, *41* (Serial No. 168).

Zelniker, T., Renan, A., Sorer, I., & Shavit, Y. Effect of perceptual processing strategies on problem solving of reflective and impulsive children. *Child Development,* 1977, *48,* 1436–1442.

Zukier, H., & Hagen, J. W. The development of selective attention under distracting conditions. *Child Development,* 1978, *49,* 870–873.

NAME INDEX

273

SUBJECT INDEX